Shugo Chara!

3

PEACH-PIT

Translated by
Satsuki Yamashita

Adapted by
Nunzio DeFilippis and Christina Weir

Lettered by
North Market Street Graphics

BALLANTINE BOOKS · NEW YORK

A Del Rey Manga/Kodansha Trade Paperback Original

Shugo Chara! volume 3 copyright © 2007 by PEACH-PIT
English translation copyright © 2007 by PEACH-PIT

Published in the United States by Del Rey Books, an imprint of The Random House Publishing Group, a division of Random House, Inc., New York.

DEL REY is a registered trademark and the Del Rey colophon is a trademark of Random House, Inc.

Publication rights arranged through Kodansha Ltd.

First published in Japan in 2007 by Kodansha Ltd., Tokyo

ISBN 978-0-345-50146-2

Original cover design by Akiko Omo

Printed in the United States of America

www.delreymanga.com

9 8 7 6 5 4

Translator—Satsuki Yamashita
Adaptors—Nunzio DeFilippis and Christina Weir
Lettering—North Market Street Graphics

Contents

Honorifics Explained

Throughout the Del Rey Manga books, you will find Japanese honorifics left intact in the translations. For those not familiar with how the Japanese use honorifics and, more important, how they differ from American honorifics, we present this brief overview.

Politeness has always been a critical facet of Japanese culture. Ever since the feudal era, when Japan was a highly stratified society, use of honorifics—which can be defined as polite speech that indicates relationship or status—has played an essential role in the Japanese language. When addressing someone in Japanese, an honorific usually takes the form of a suffix attached to one's name (example: "Asuna-san"), is used as a title at the end of one's name, or appears in place of the name itself (example: "Negi-sensei," or simply "Sensei").

Honorifics can be expressions of respect or endearment. In the context of manga and anime, honorifics give insight into the nature of the relationship between characters. Many English translations leave out these important honorifics and therefore distort the feel of the original Japanese. Because Japanese honorifics contain nuances that English honorifics lack, it is our policy at Del Rey not to translate them. Here, instead, is a guide to some of the honorifics you may encounter in Del Rey Manga.

-san: This is the most common honorific, and is equivalent to Mr., Miss, Ms., or Mrs. It is the all-purpose honorific and can be used in any situation where politeness is required.

-sama: This is one level higher than "-san" and is used to confer great respect.

-dono: This comes from the word "tono," which means "lord." It is an even higher level than "-sama" and confers utmost respect.

-kun: This suffix is used at the end of boys' names to express familiarity or endearment. It is also sometimes used by men among friends, or when addressing someone younger or of a lower station.

-chan: This is used to express endearment, mostly
                       toward girls. It is also used for little boys, pets,
                       and even among lovers. It gives a sense of childish
                       cuteness.

Bozu: This is an informal way to refer to a boy, similar to
                       the English terms "kid" and "squirt."

Sempai/
Senpai: This title suggests that the addressee is one's
                       senior in a group or organization. It is most often
                       used in a school setting, where underclassmen
                       refer to their upperclassmen as "sempai." It can
                       also be used in the workplace, such as when a
                       newer employee addresses an employee who has
                       seniority in the company.

Kohai: This is the opposite of "sempai" and is used
                       toward underclassmen in school or newcomers in
                       the workplace. It connotes that the addressee is
                       of a lower station.

Sensei: Literally meaning "one who has come before," this
                       title is used for teachers, doctors, or masters of
                       any profession or art.

-[blank]:   This is usually forgotten in these lists, but it is
                       perhaps the most significant difference between
                       Japanese and English. The lack of honorific means
                       that the speaker has permission to address the
                       person in a very intimate way. Usually, only
                       family, spouses, or very close friends have this
                       kind of permission. Known as *yobisute,* it can
                       be gratifying when someone who has earned the
                       intimacy starts to call one by one's name without
                       an honorific. But when that intimacy hasn't been
                       earned, it can be very insulting.

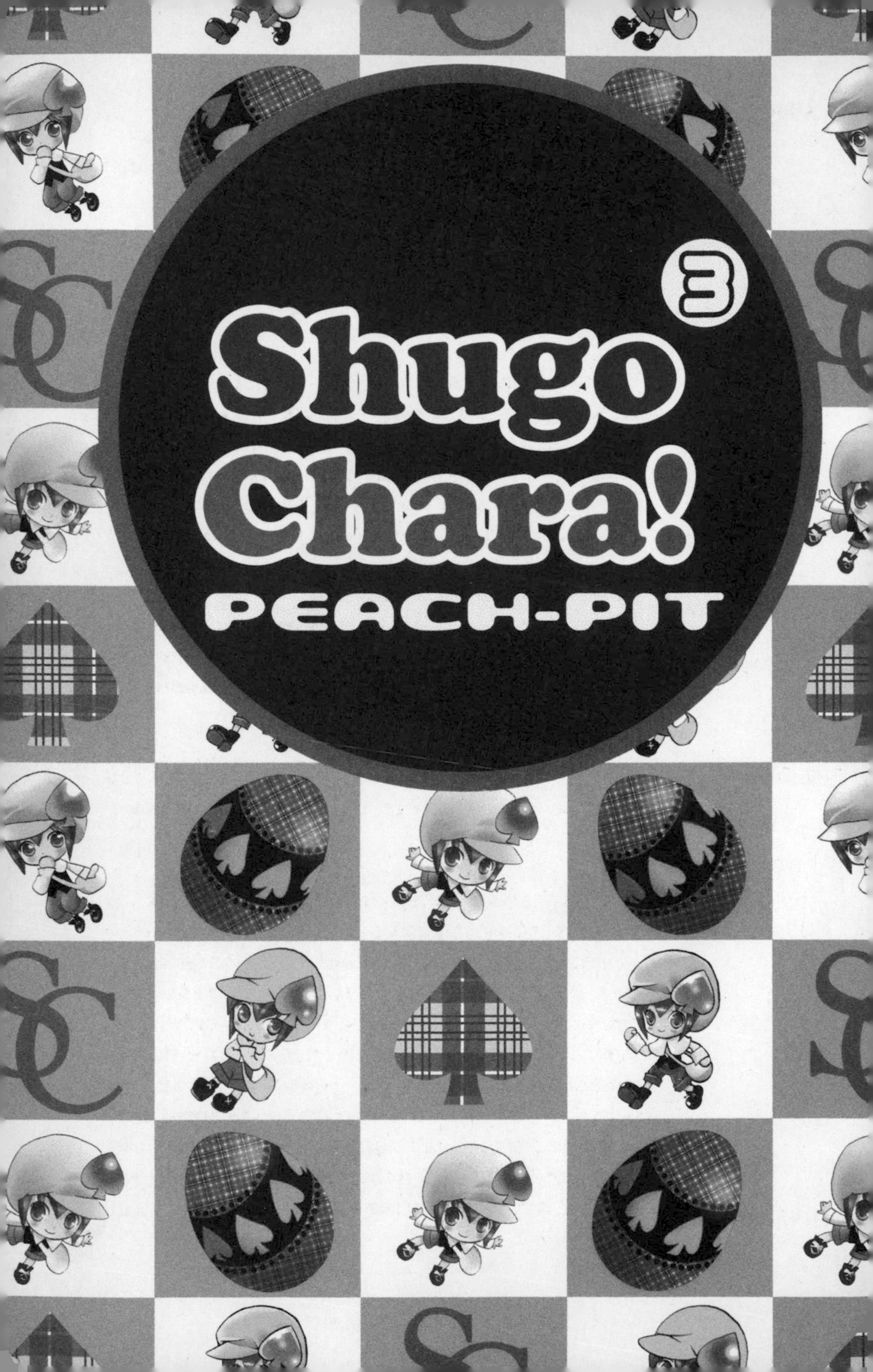
3
Shugo Chara!
PEACH-PIT

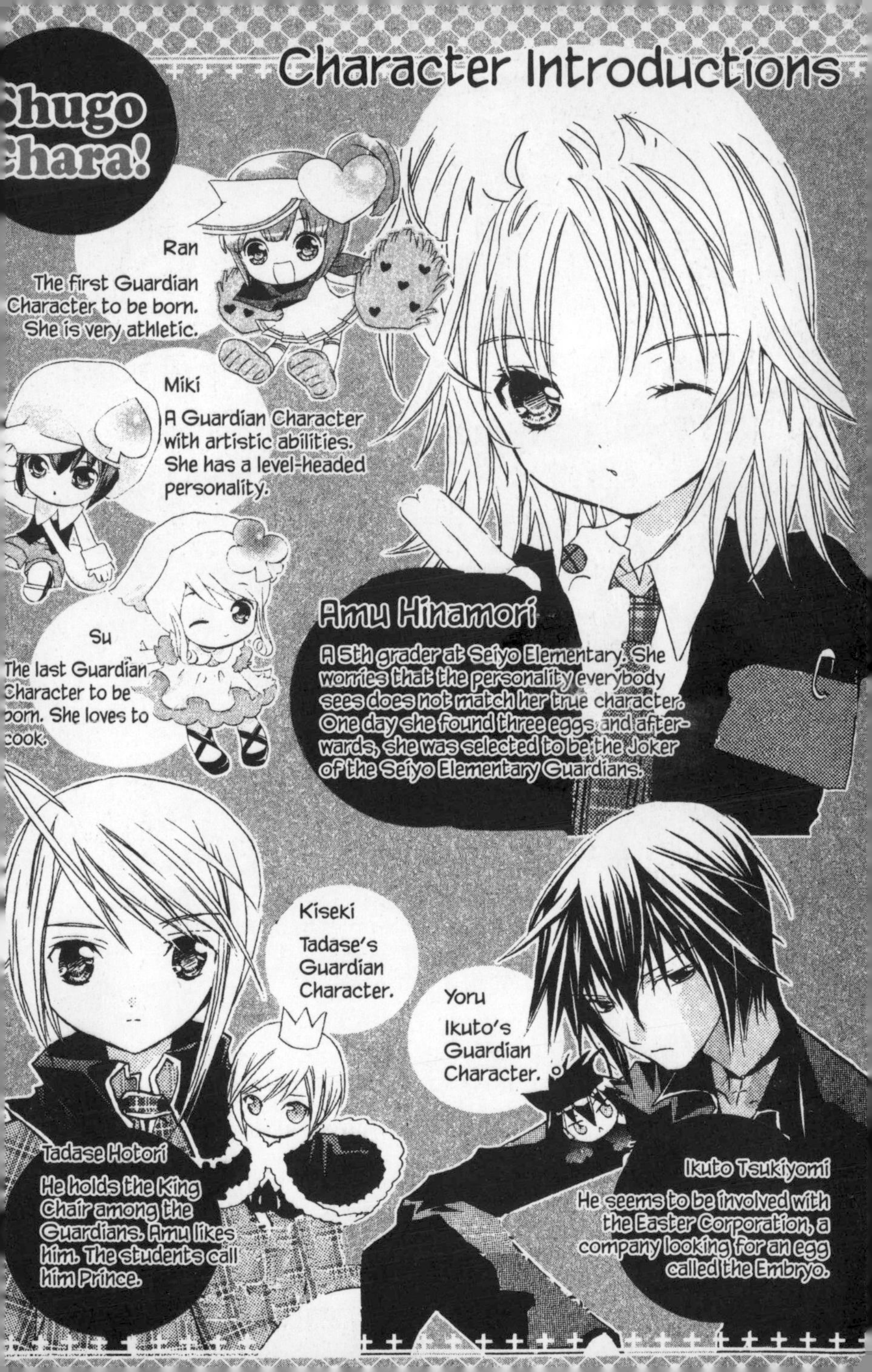
Character Introductions
Shugo Chara!
Amu Hinamori
A 5th grader at Seiyo Elementary. She worries that the personality everybody sees does not match her true character. One day she found three eggs and afterwards, she was selected to be the Joker of the Seiyo Elementary Guardians.
Ran
The first Guardian Character to be born. She is very athletic.
Miki
A Guardian Character with artistic abilities. She has a level-headed personality.
Su
The last Guardian Character to be born. She loves to cook.
Ikuto Tsukiyomi
He seems to be involved with the Easter Corporation, a company looking for an egg called the Embryo.
Yoru
Ikuto's Guardian Character.
Kiseki
Tadase's Guardian Character.
Tadase Hotori
He holds the King Chair among the Guardians. Amu likes him. The students call him Prince.

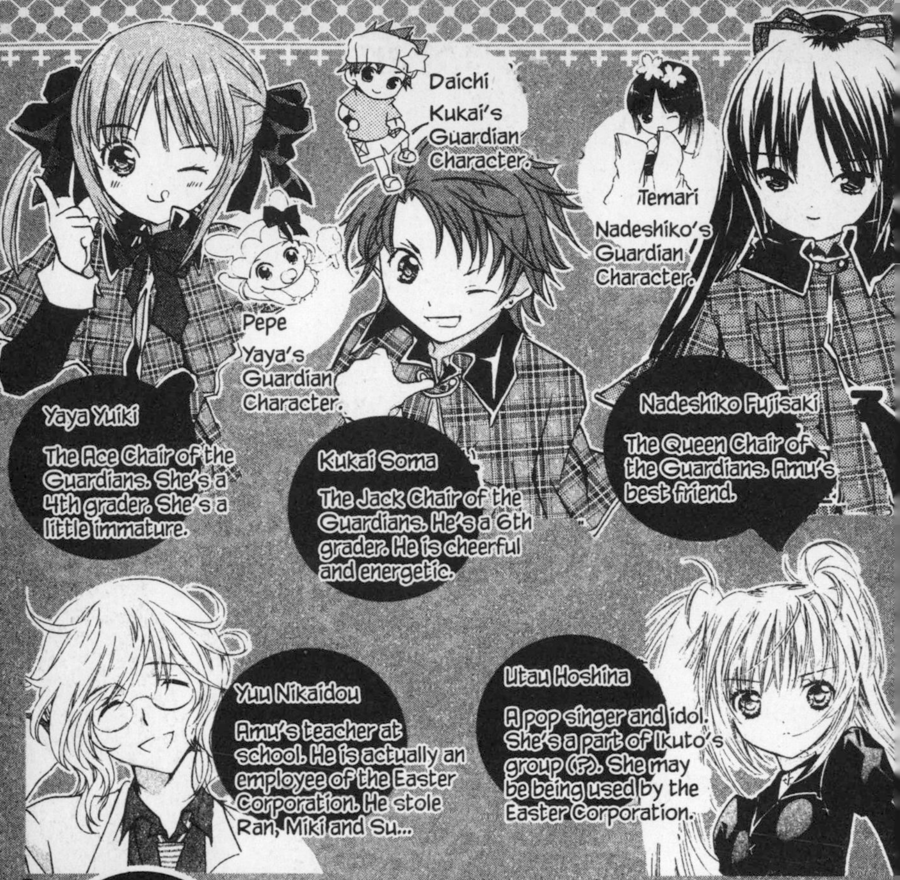
Daichi
Kukai's Guardian Character.
Temari
Nadeshiko's Guardian Character.
Pepe
Yaya's Guardian Character.
Yaya Yuiki
The Ace Chair of the Guardians. She's a 4th grader. She's a little immature.
Kukai Soma
The Jack Chair of the Guardians. He's a 6th grader. He is cheerful and energetic.
Nadeshiko Fujisaki
The Queen Chair of the Guardians. Amu's best friend.
Yuu Nikaidou
Amu's teacher at school. He is actually an employee of the Easter Corporation. He stole Ran, Miki and Su...
Utau Hoshina
A pop singer and idol. She's a part of Ikuto's group (!?). She may be being used by the Easter Corporation.

The Story So Far

● Everybody thinks Amu is so cool. But that isn't who she really is. Deep inside, she is shy and a little cynical. One day she wished she could be more true to herself, and the next day she found three eggs in her bed!

● Ran, Miki, and Su hatched from the eggs. They are Amu's "Guardian Characters." They say that they are Amu's "true selves," and when Amu Character Changes with them, she can become good at sports, art, or cooking! Soon after they hatched, Amu found herself recruited to become one of the Guardians of Seiyo Elementary.

● But Nikaidou-sensei is really an employee of the sinister Easter Corporation. They are searching for the Embryo, an egg known to grant any wish. He took away Ran, Miki, and Su!! What is Nikaidou-sensei really up to? And what is Amu going to do!?

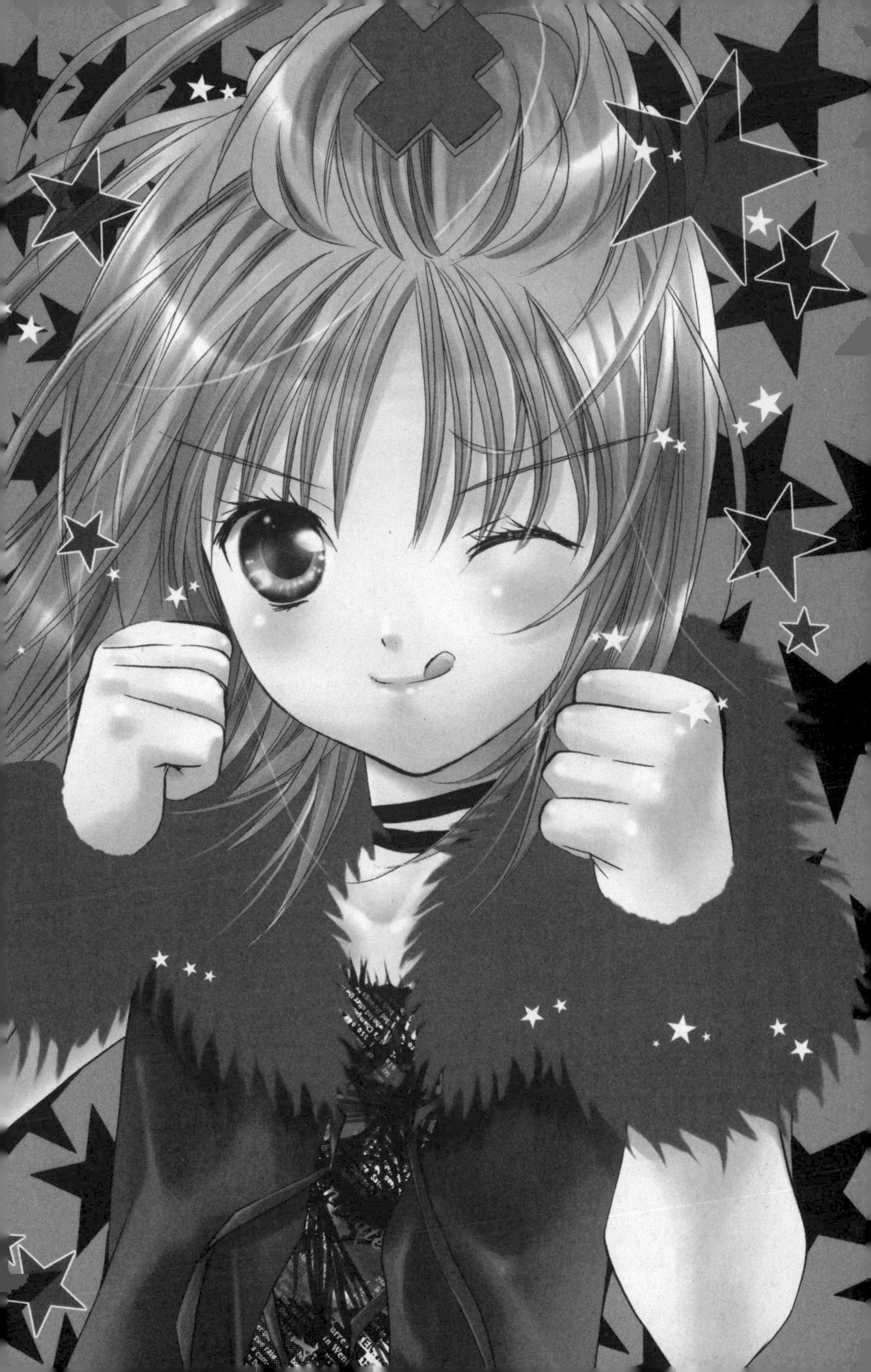

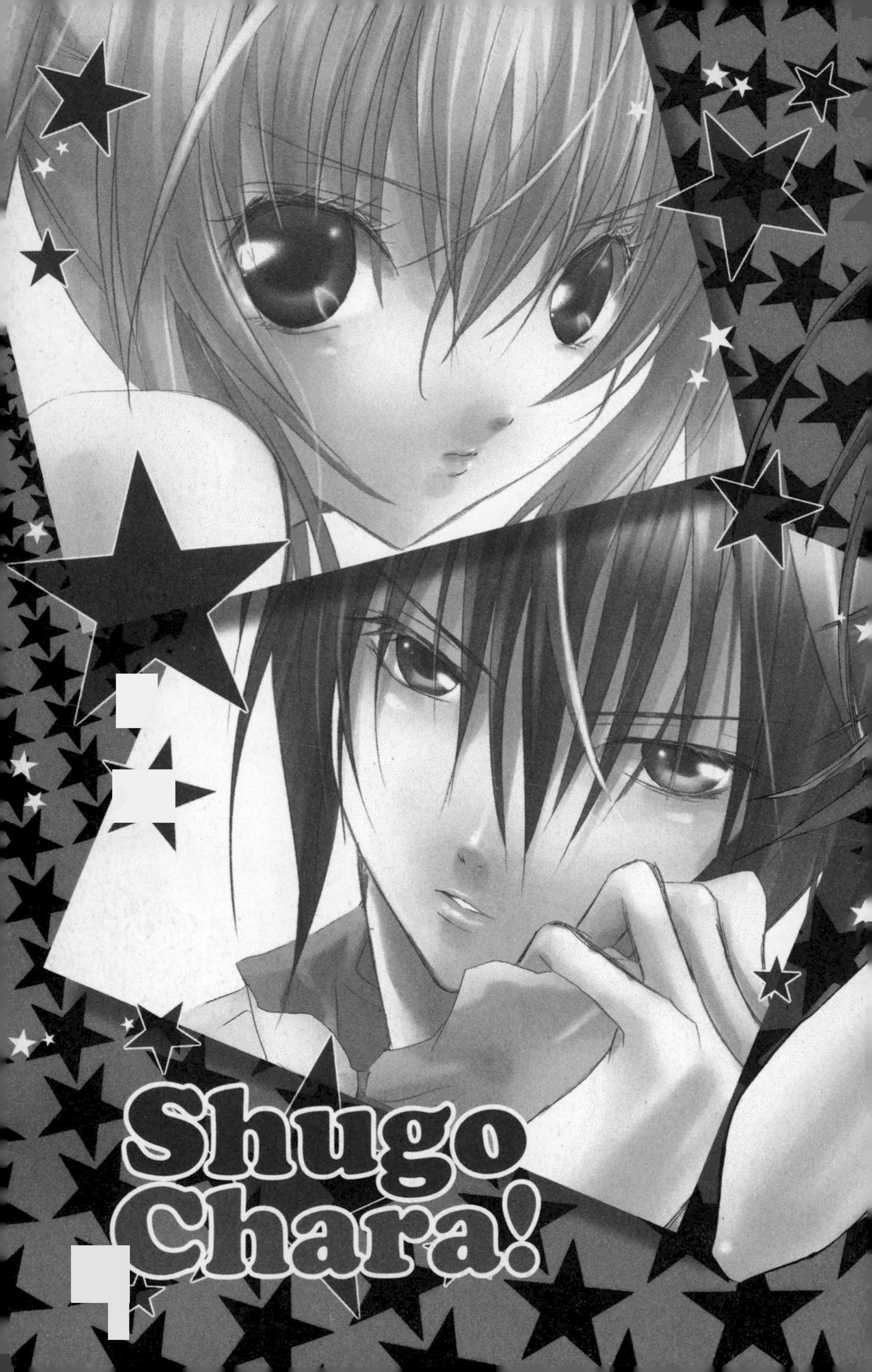
Shugo
Chara!

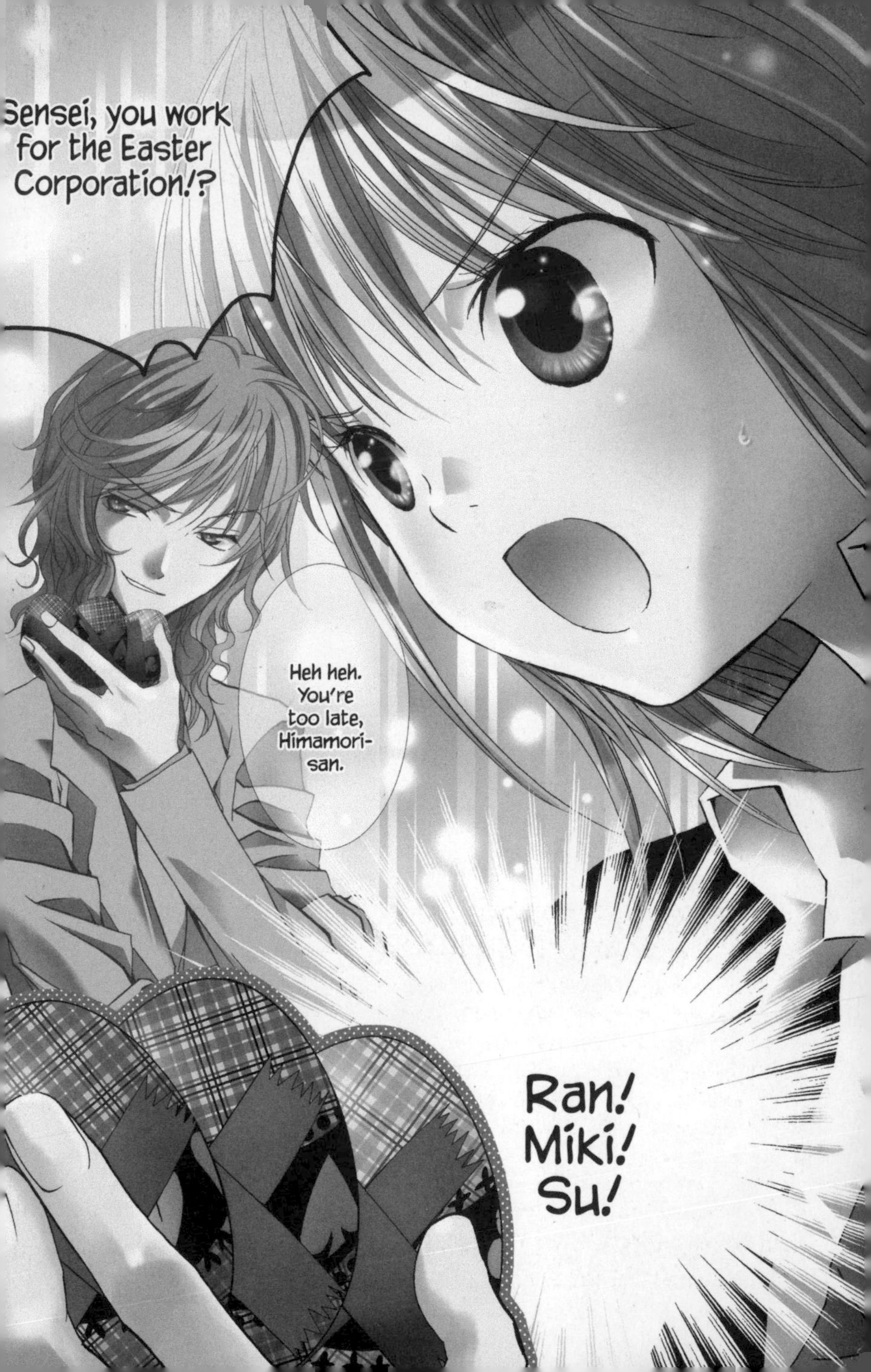
Sensei, you work for the Easter Corporation!?
Heh heh. You're too late, Himamori-san.
Ran! Miki! Su!

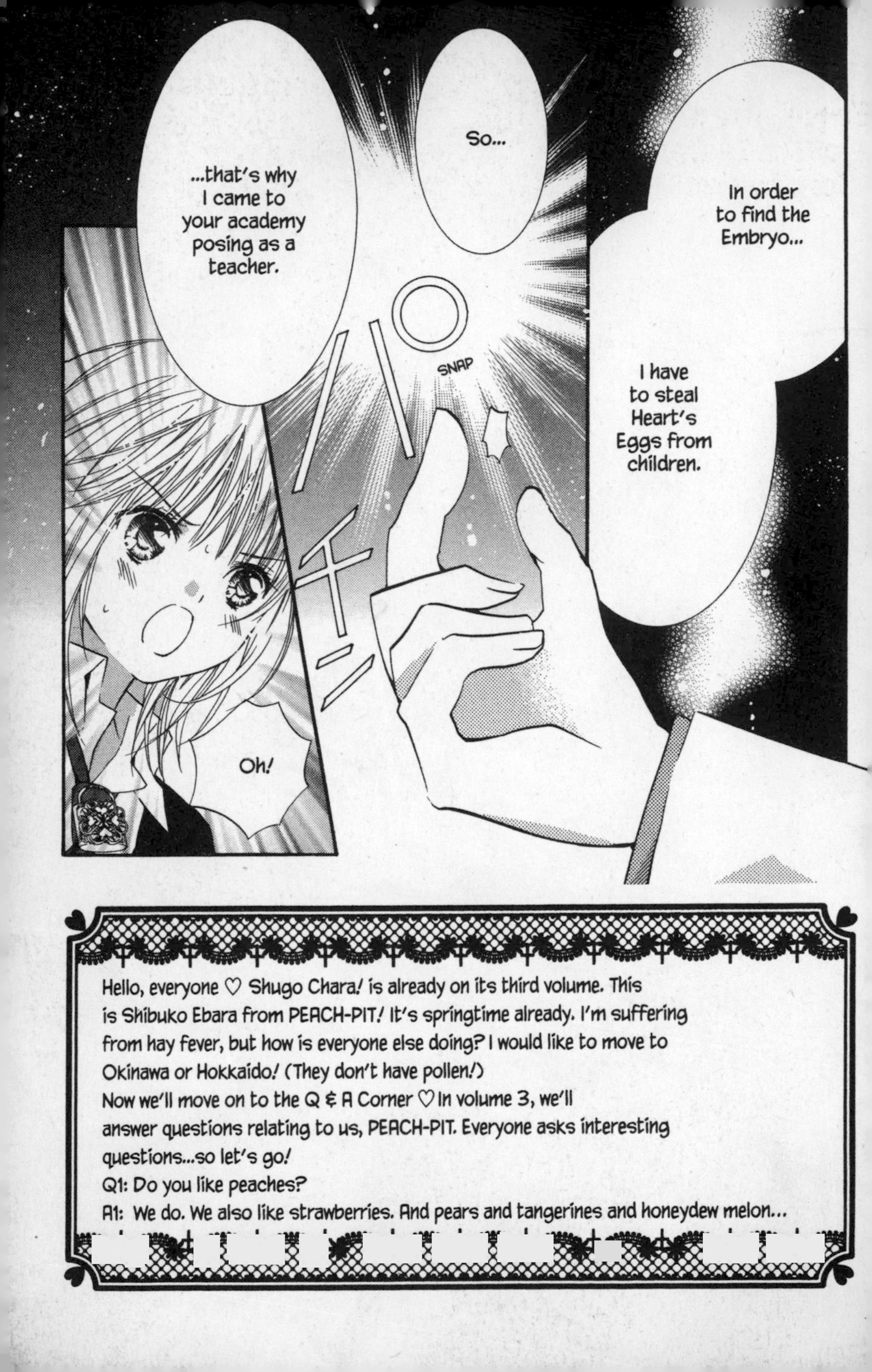
In order to find the Embryo...
I have to steal Heart's Eggs from children.
So...
...that's why I came to your academy posing as a teacher.
SNAP
Oh!

Hello, everyone ♡ Shugo Chara! is already on its third volume. This is Shibuko Ebara from PEACH-PIT! It's springtime already. I'm suffering from hay fever, but how is everyone else doing? I would like to move to Okinawa or Hokkaido! (They don't have pollen!)

Now we'll move on to the Q & A Corner ♡ In volume 3, we'll answer questions relating to us, PEACH-PIT. Everyone asks interesting questions...so let's go!

Q1: Do you like peaches?

A1: We do. We also like strawberries. And pears and tangerines and honeydew melon...

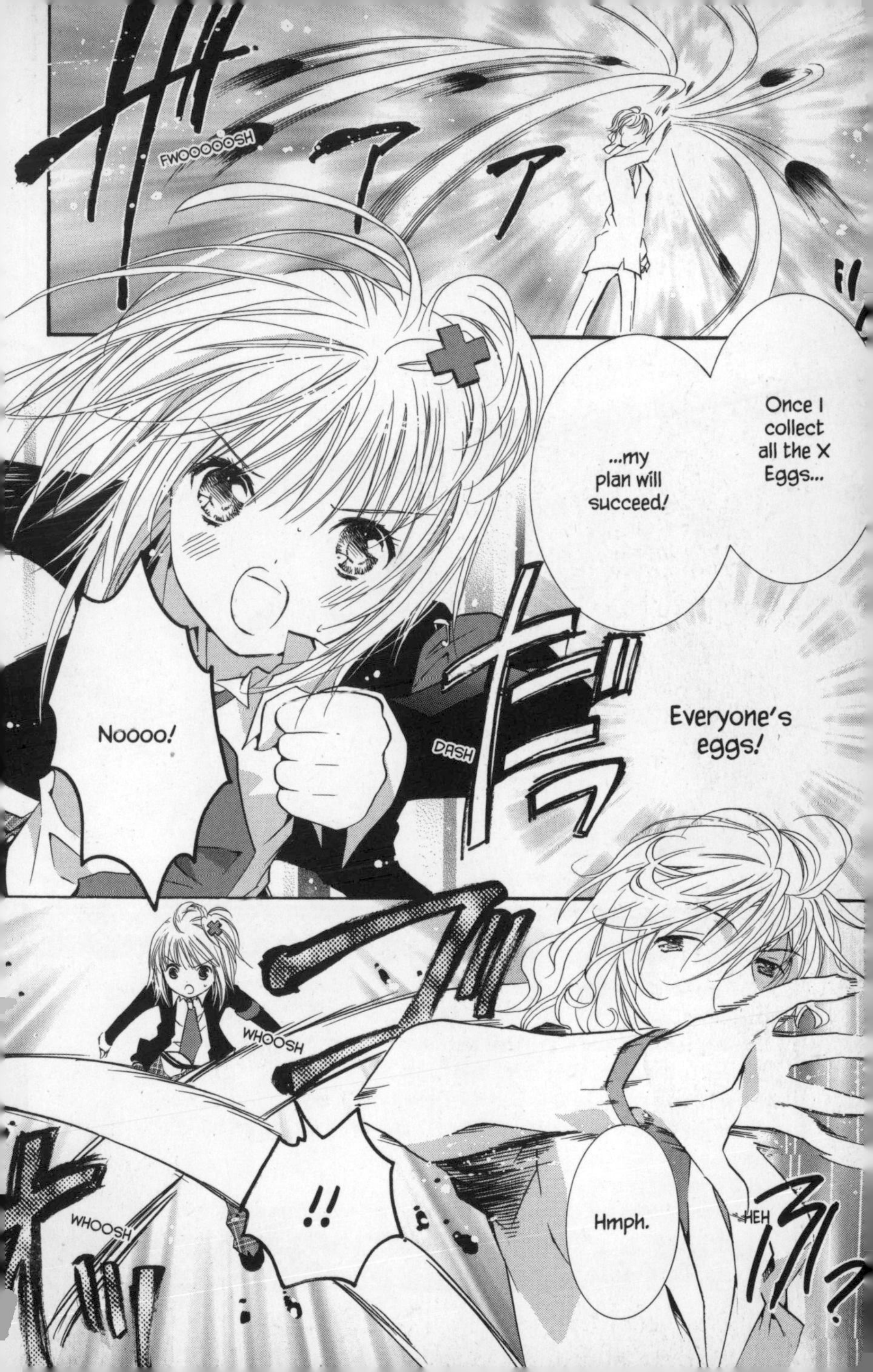
FWOOOOOSH
Once I collect all the X Eggs...
...my plan will succeed!
Everyone's eggs!
DASH
Noooo!
HEH
Hmph.
!!
WHOOSH
WHOOSH

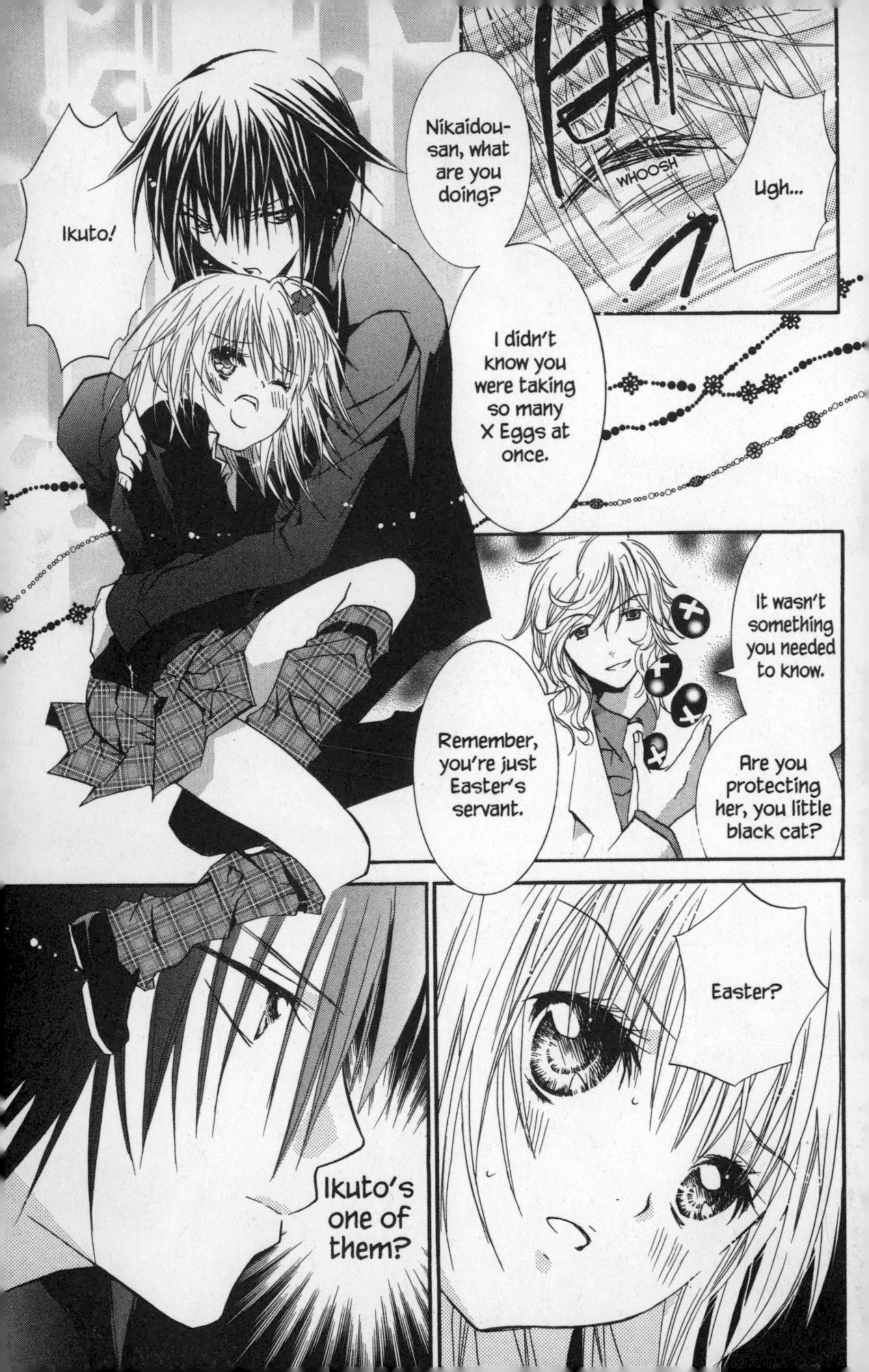

Ugh...
WHOOSH
Ikuto!
Nikaidou-san, what are you doing?
I didn't know you were taking so many X Eggs at once.
It wasn't something you needed to know.
Are you protecting her, you little black cat?
Remember, you're just Easter's servant.
Easter?
Ikuto's one of them?

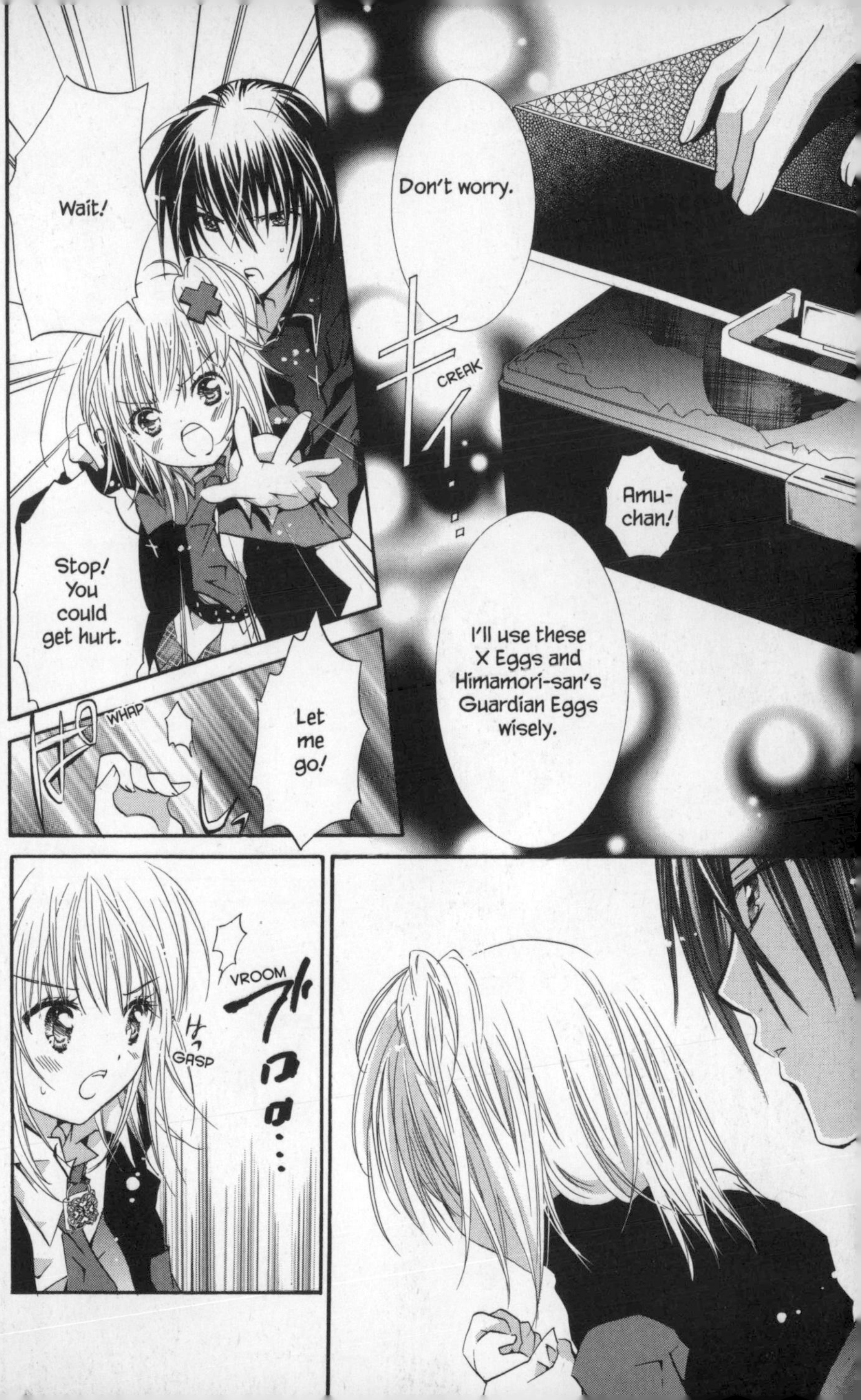
Don't worry.
CREAK
Amu-chan!
I'll use these X Eggs and Himamori-san's Guardian Eggs wisely.
Wait!
Stop! You could get hurt.
WHAP
Let me go!
VROOM
GASP

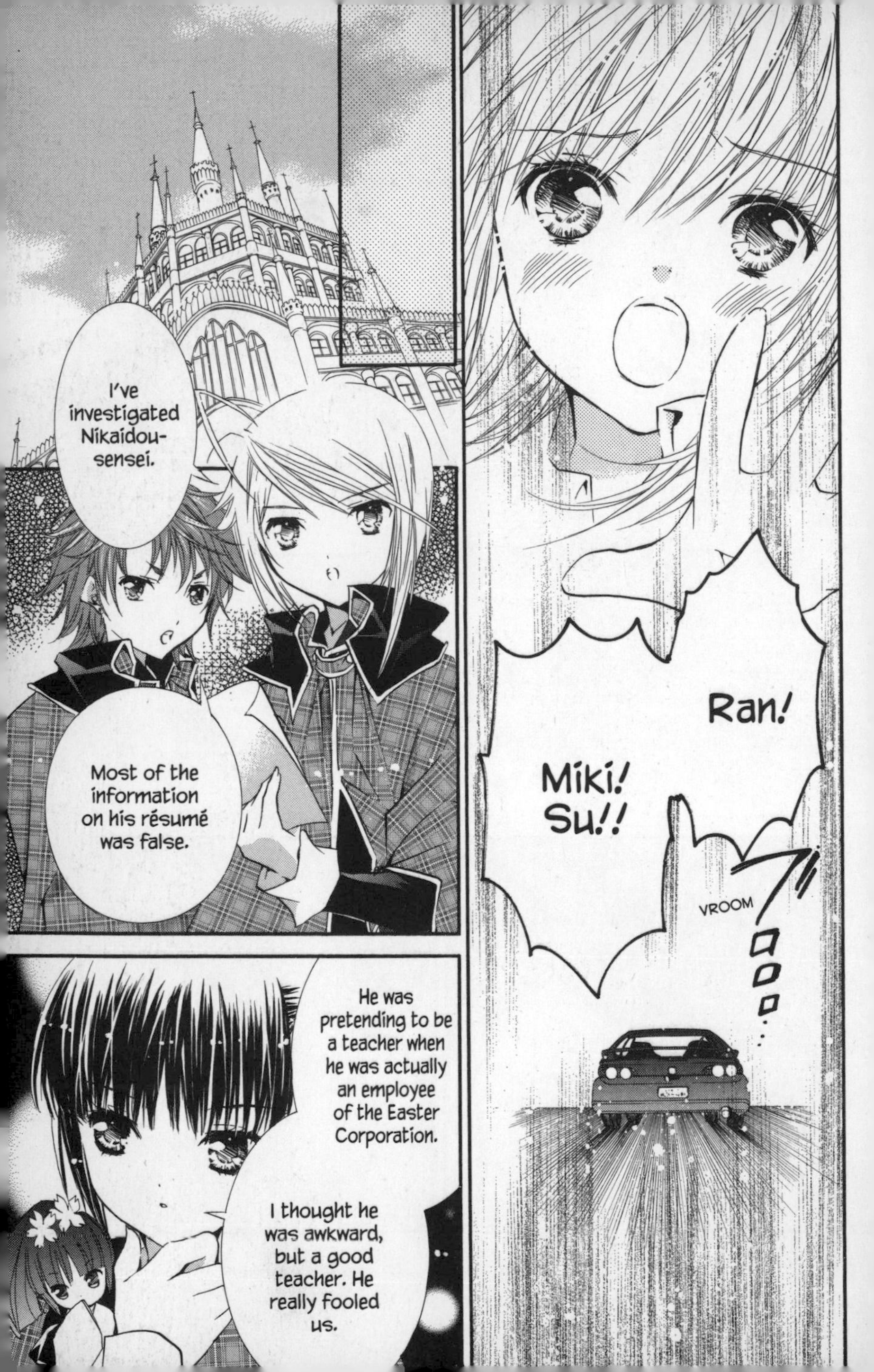
Ran!
Miki! Su!!
VROOM
I've investigated Nikaidou-sensei.
Most of the information on his résumé was false.
He was pretending to be a teacher when he was actually an employee of the Easter Corporation.
I thought he was awkward, but a good teacher. He really fooled us.

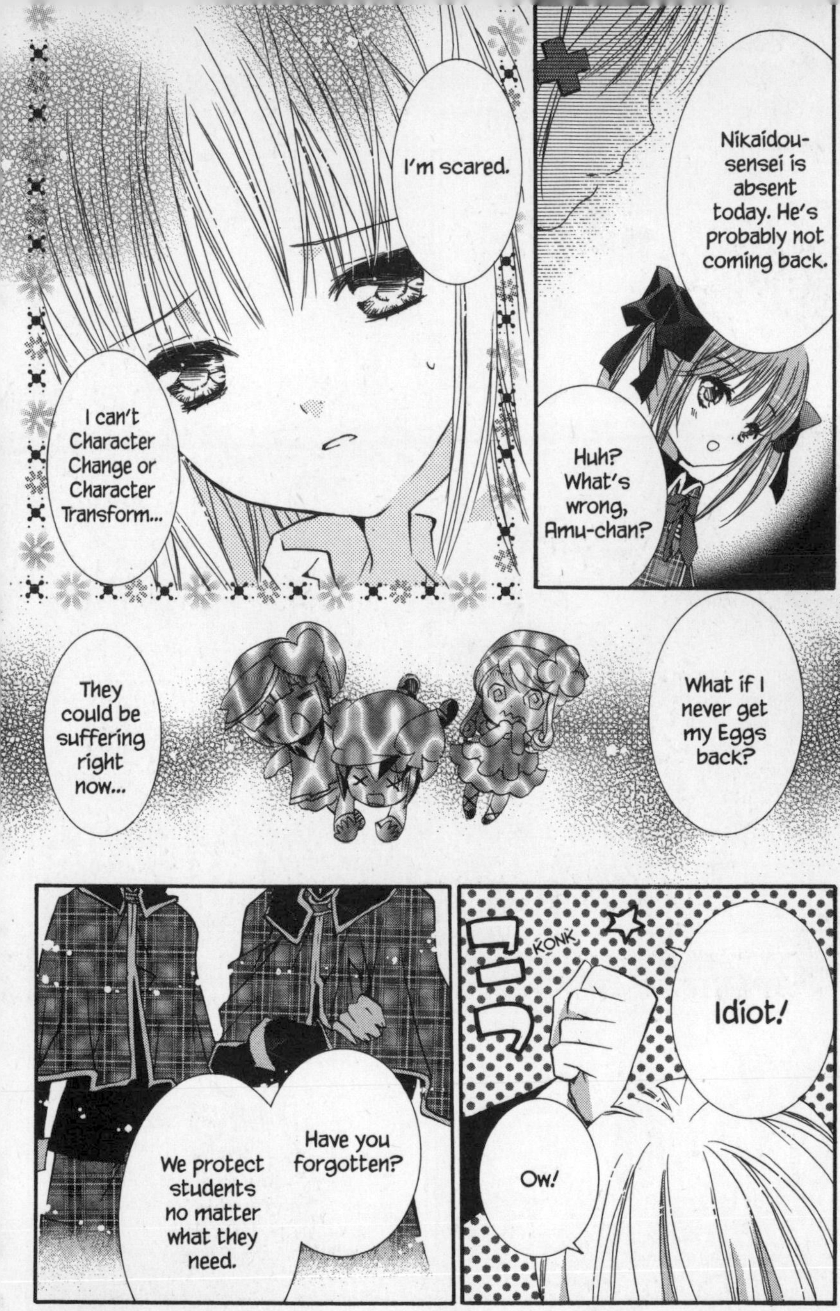
Nikaidou-sensei is absent today. He's probably not coming back.
Huh? What's wrong, Amu-chan?
I'm scared.
I can't Character Change or Character Transform...
What if I never get my Eggs back?
They could be suffering right now...
KONK
Idiot!
Ow!
Have you forgotten?
We protect students no matter what they need.

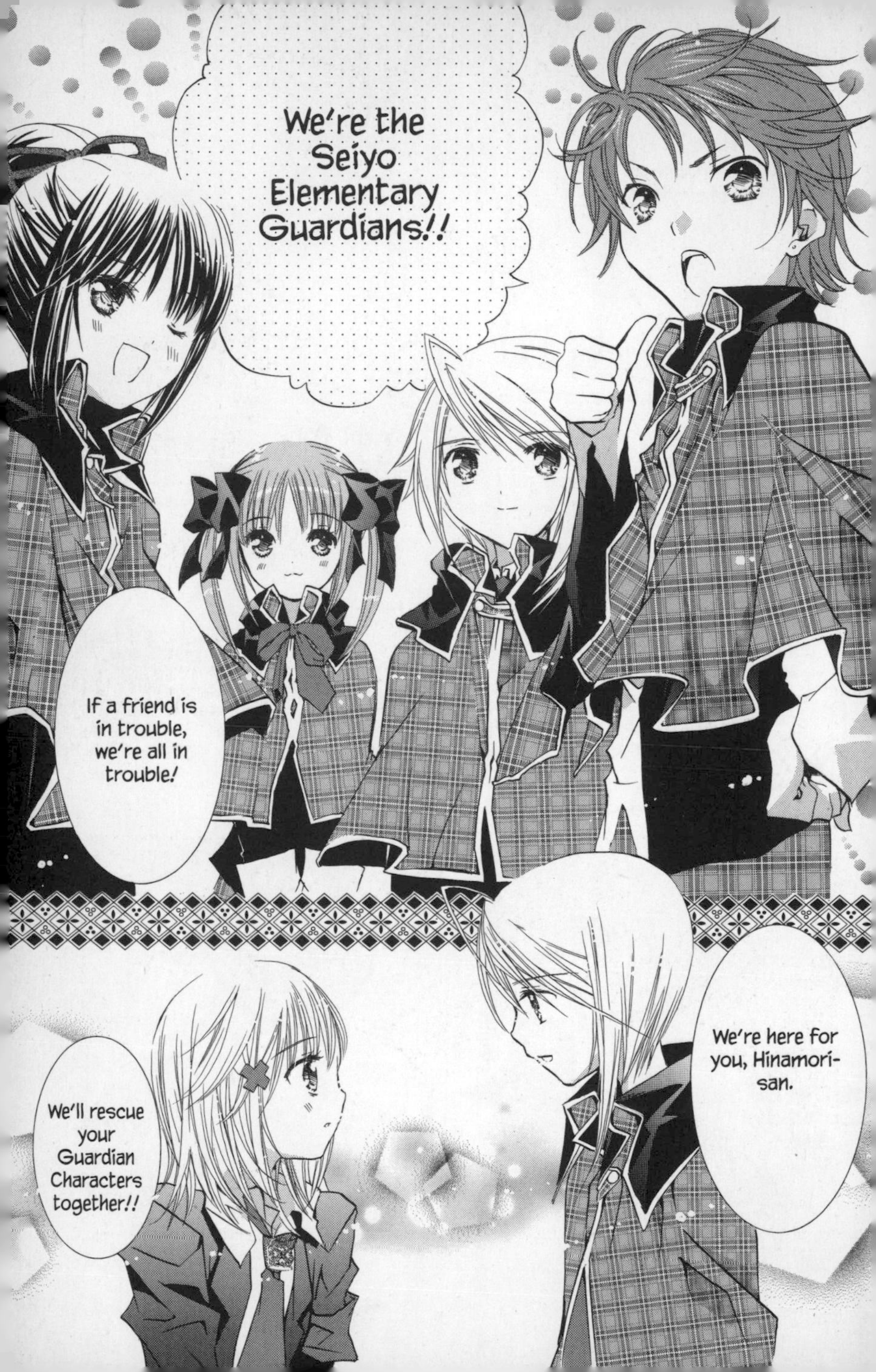
We're the Seiyo Elementary Guardians!!
If a friend is in trouble, we're all in trouble!
We're here for you, Hinamori-san.
We'll rescue your Guardian Characters together!!

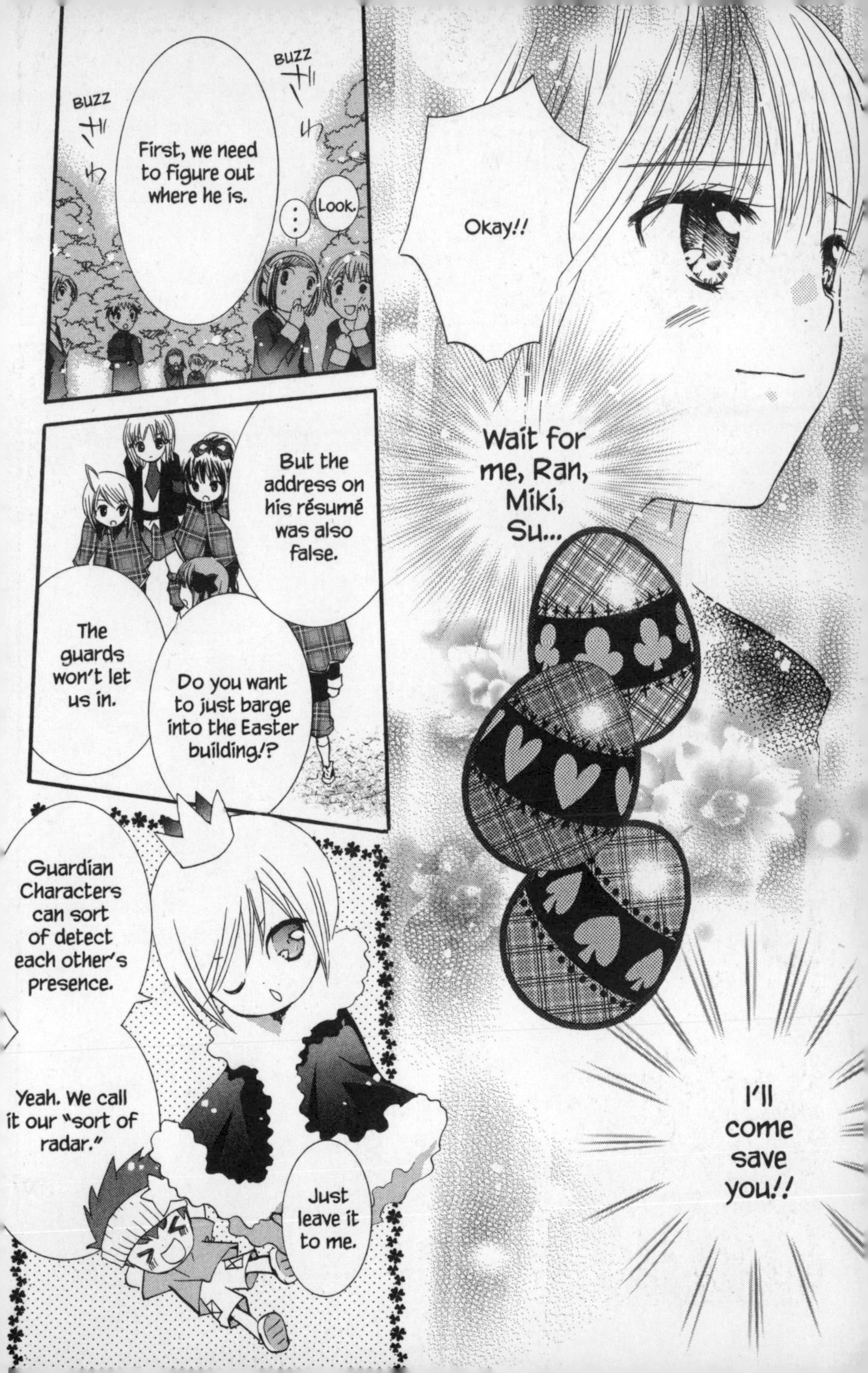
Okay!!
Wait for me, Ran, Miki, Su...
I'll come save you!!
BUZZ
Look.
...
First, we need to figure out where he is.
BUZZ
But the address on his résumé was also false.
Do you want to just barge into the Easter building!?
The guards won't let us in.
Guardian Characters can sort of detect each other's presence.
Yeah. We call it our "sort of radar."
Just leave it to me.

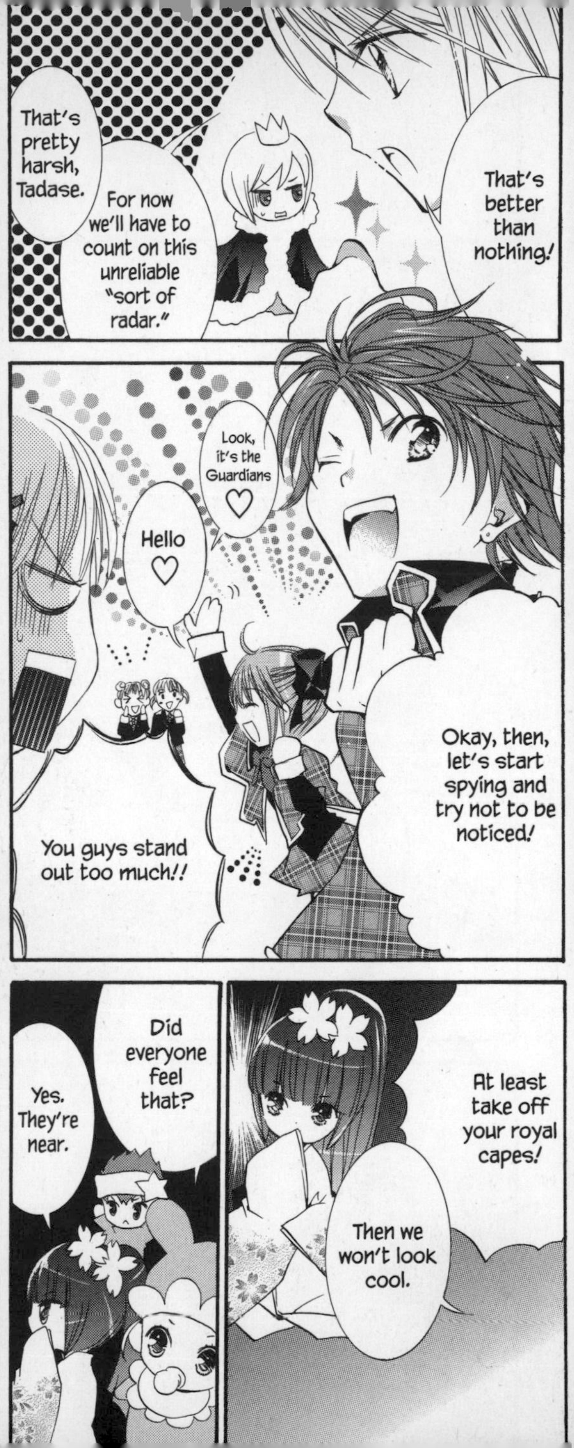
That's better than nothing!
For now we'll have to count on this unreliable "sort of radar."
That's pretty harsh, Tadase.
Okay, then, let's start spying and try not to be noticed!
Look, it's the Guardians ♡
Hello ♡
You guys stand out too much!!
At least take off your royal capes!
Then we won't look cool.
Did everyone feel that?
Yes. They're near.

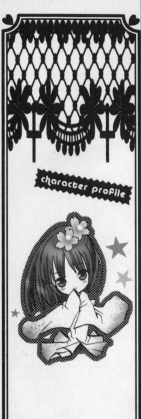

character profile

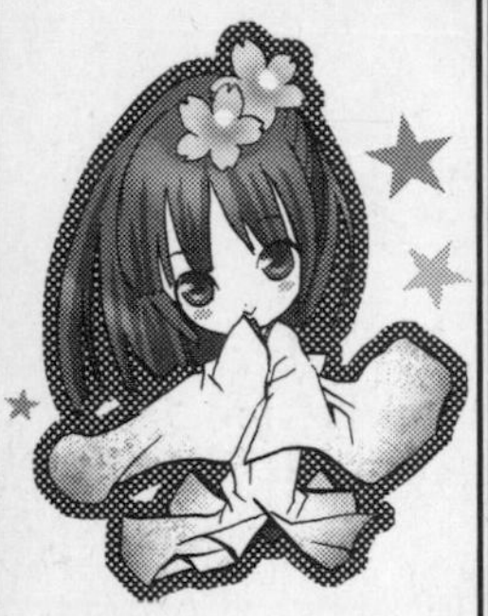

TEMARI

Guardian Character of: Nadeshiko

Special Skill: Naginata

Hates: Mud

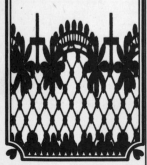

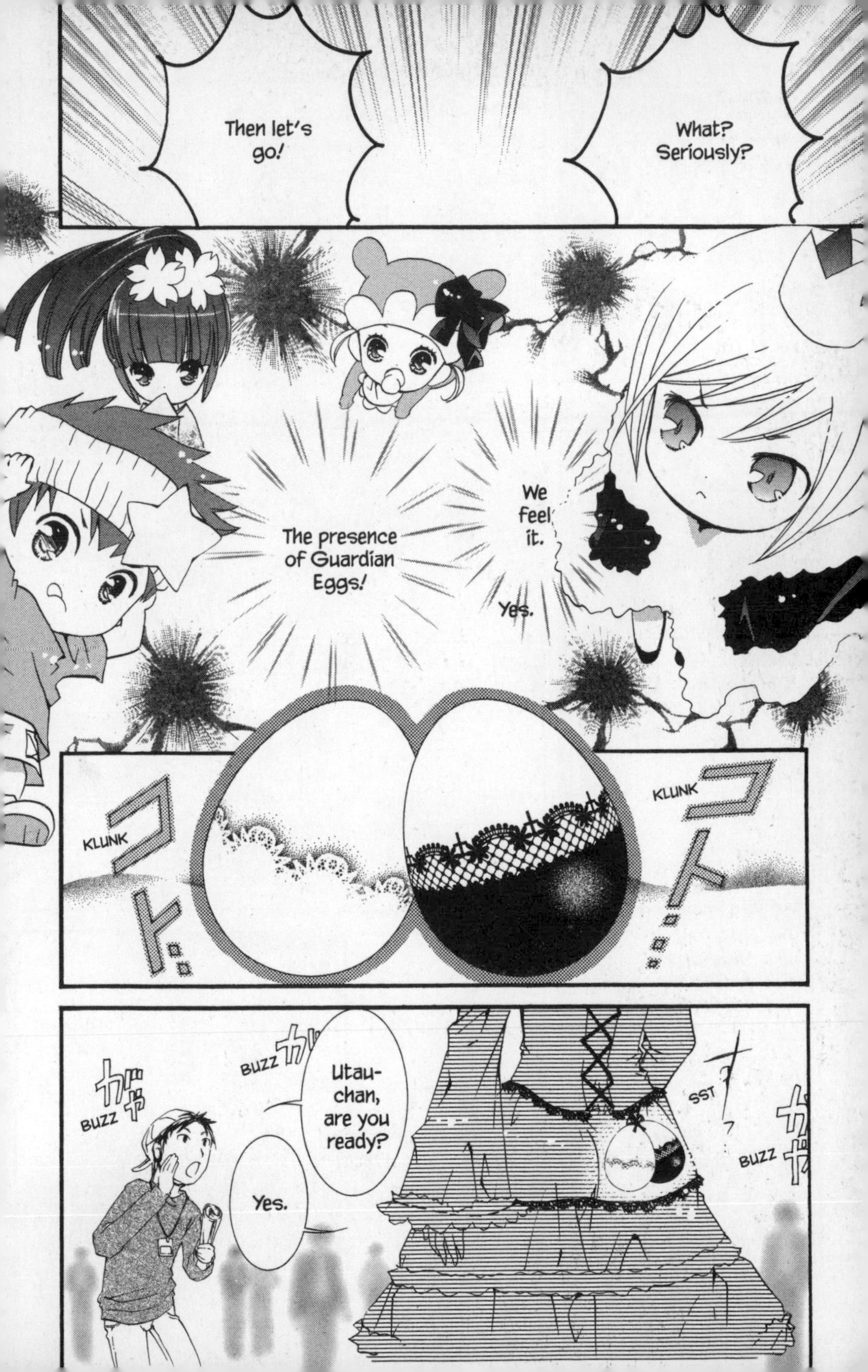
What? Seriously?
Then let's go!
We feel it.
The presence of Guardian Eggs!
Yes.
KLUNK
KLUNK
BUZZ
SST
Utau-chan, are you ready?
BUZZ
BUZZ
Yes.

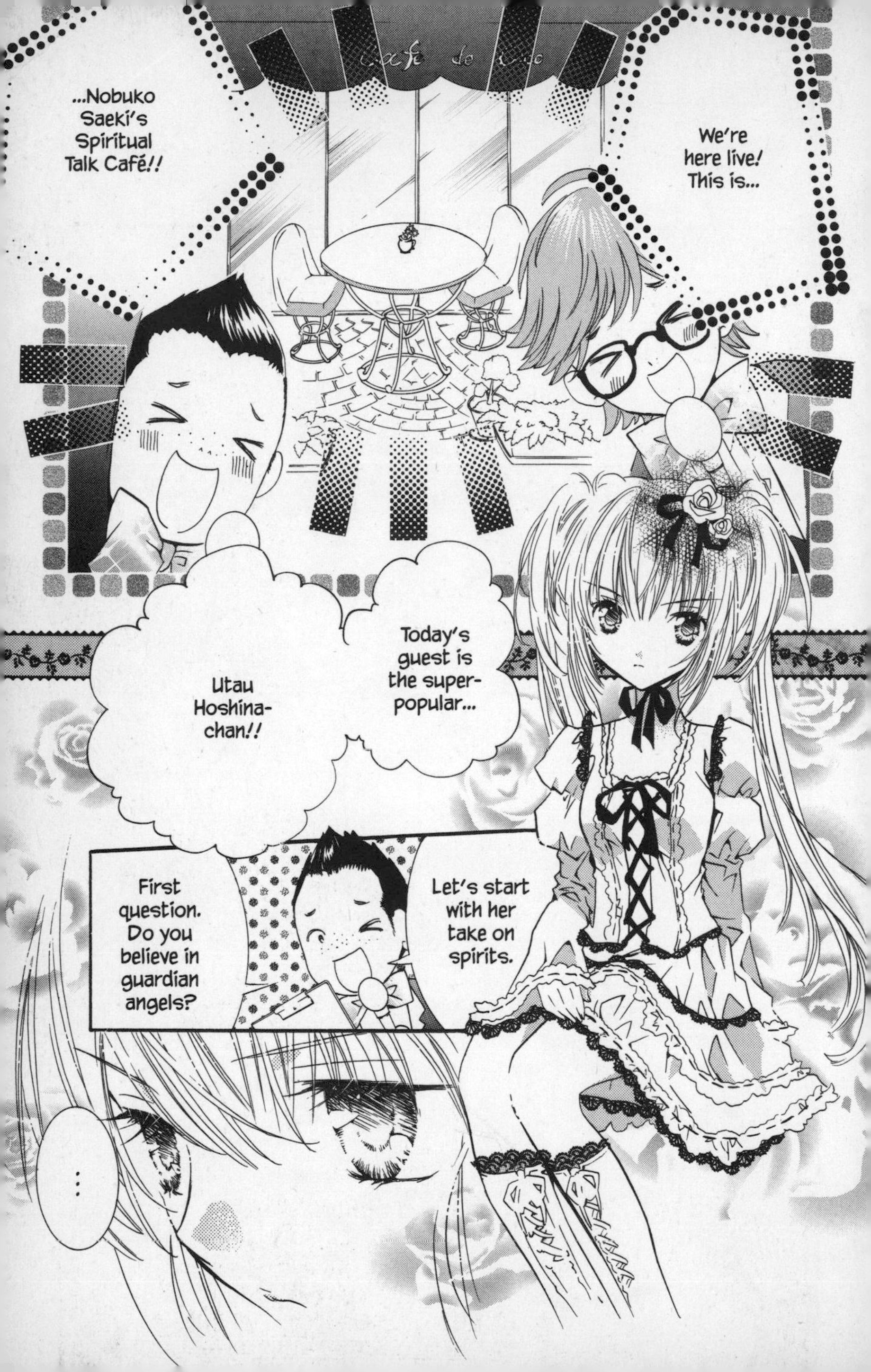
We're here live! This is...
...Nobuko Saeki's Spiritual Talk Café!!
Today's guest is the super-popular...
Utau Hoshina-chan!!
Let's start with her take on spirits.
First question. Do you believe in guardian angels?
...

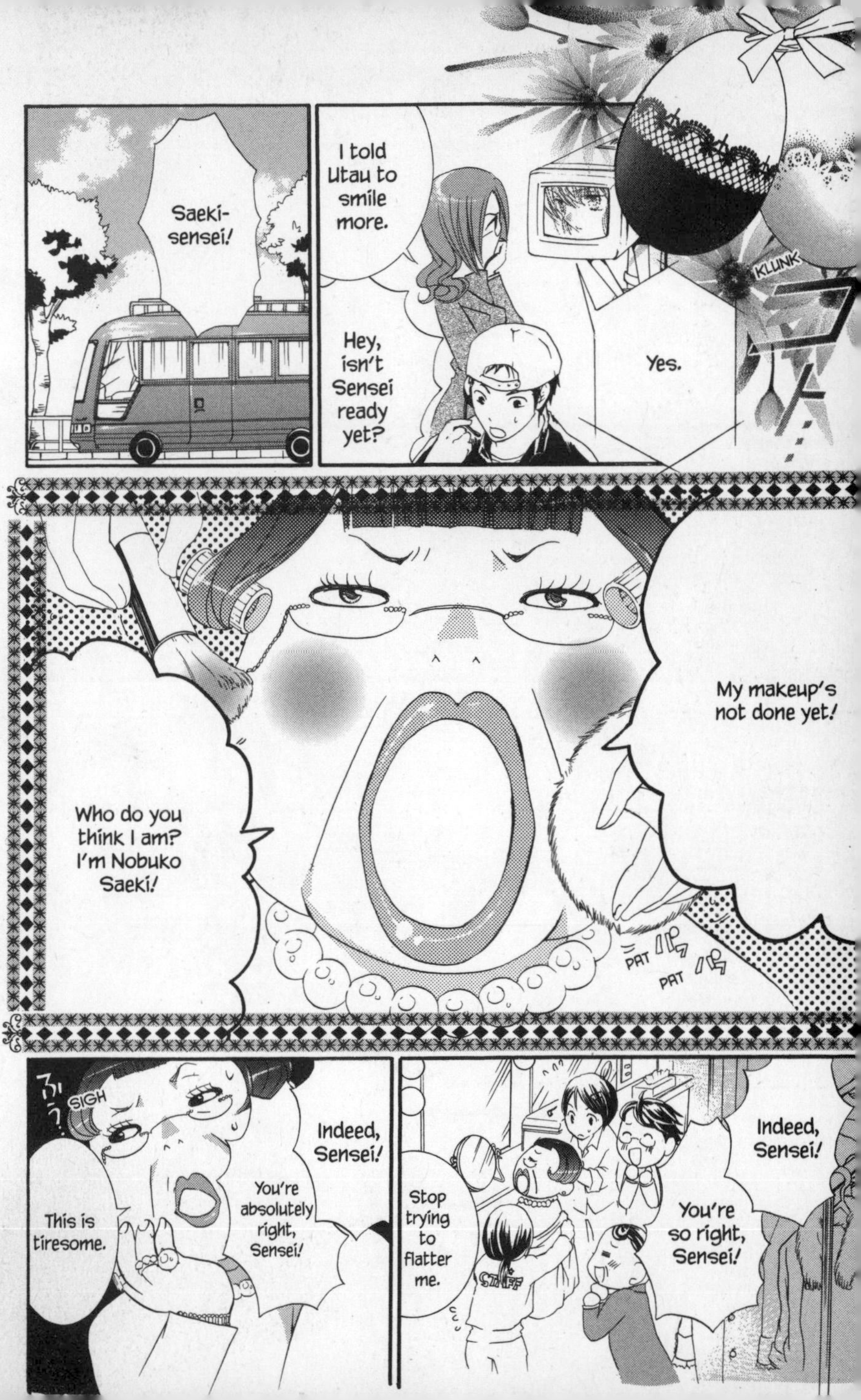
KLUNK
Yes.
I told Utau to smile more.
Hey, isn't Sensei ready yet?
Saeki-sensei!
My makeup's not done yet!
Who do you think I am? I'm Nobuko Saeki!
PAT
PAT
Indeed, Sensei!
You're so right, Sensei!
Stop trying to flatter me.
Indeed, Sensei!
You're absolutely right, Sensei!
SIGH
This is tiresome.

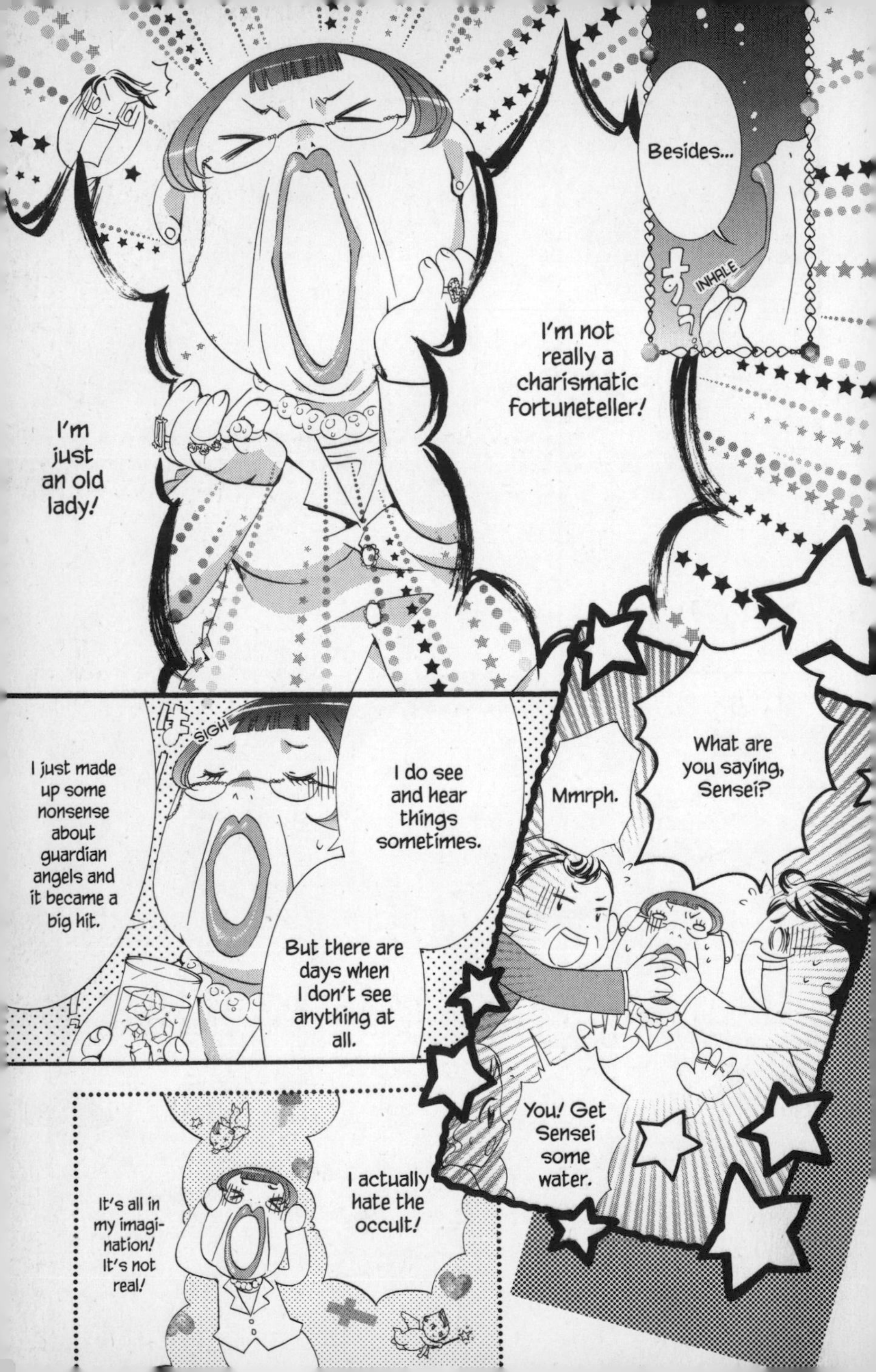
Besides...
INHALE
I'm not really a charismatic fortuneteller!
I'm just an old lady!
What are you saying, Sensei?
Mmrph.
You! Get Sensei some water.
SIGH
I do see and hear things sometimes.
But there are days when I don't see anything at all.
I just made up some nonsense about guardian angels and it became a big hit.
I actually hate the occult!
It's all in my imagination! It's not real!

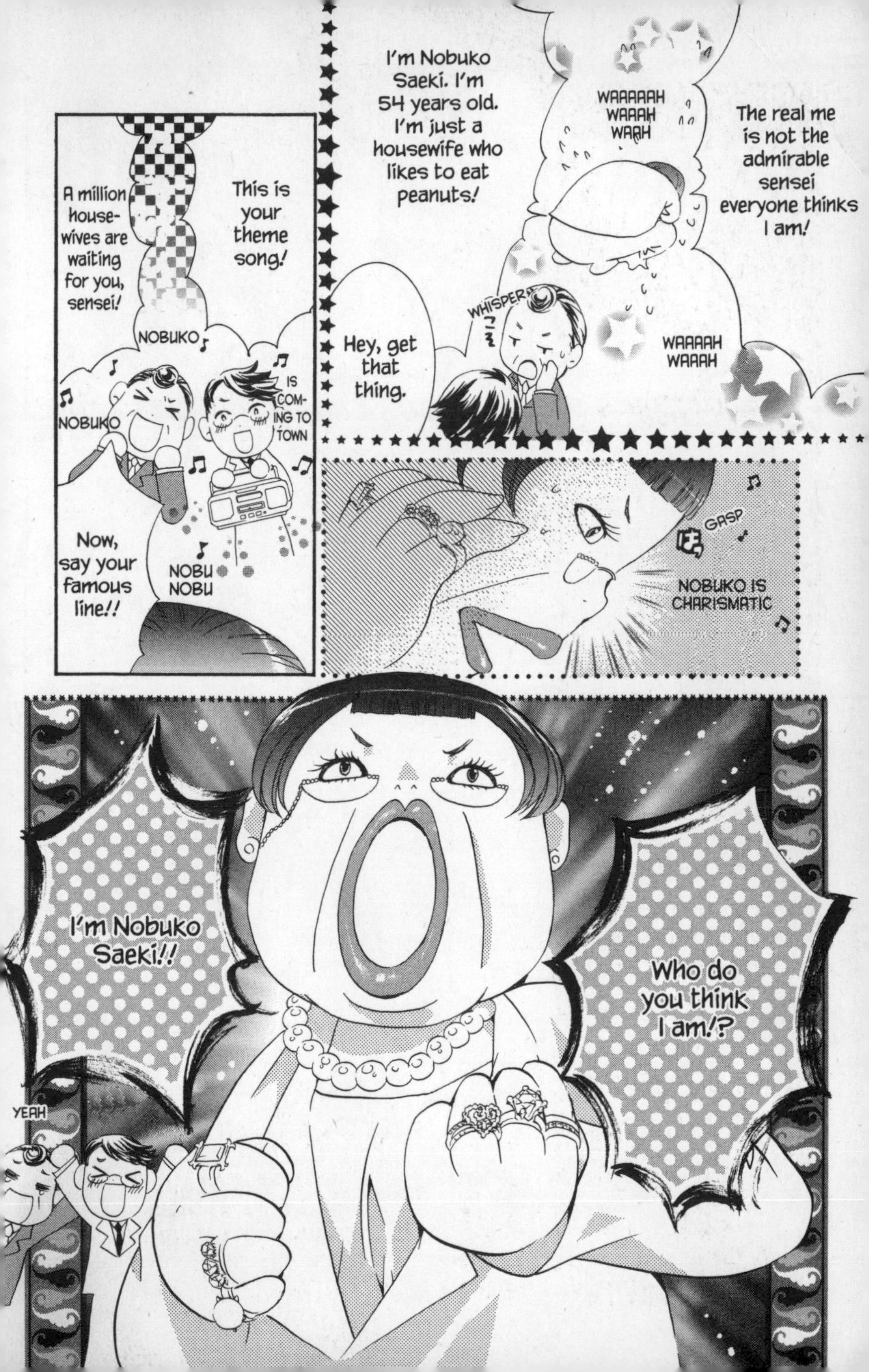
The real me is not the admirable sensei everyone thinks I am!
WAAAAAH WAAAH WAAH
I'm Nobuko Saeki. I'm 54 years old. I'm just a housewife who likes to eat peanuts!
WAAAAH WAAAH
WHISPER
Hey, get that thing.
GASP
NOBUKO IS CHARISMATIC
This is your theme song!
A million housewives are waiting for you, sensei!
NOBUKO
IS COMING TO TOWN
NOBUKO
NOBU NOBU
Now, say your famous line!!
Who do you think I am!?
I'm Nobuko Saeki!!
YEAH

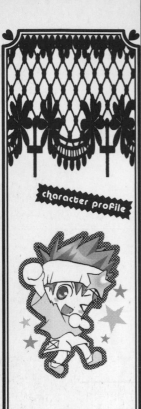

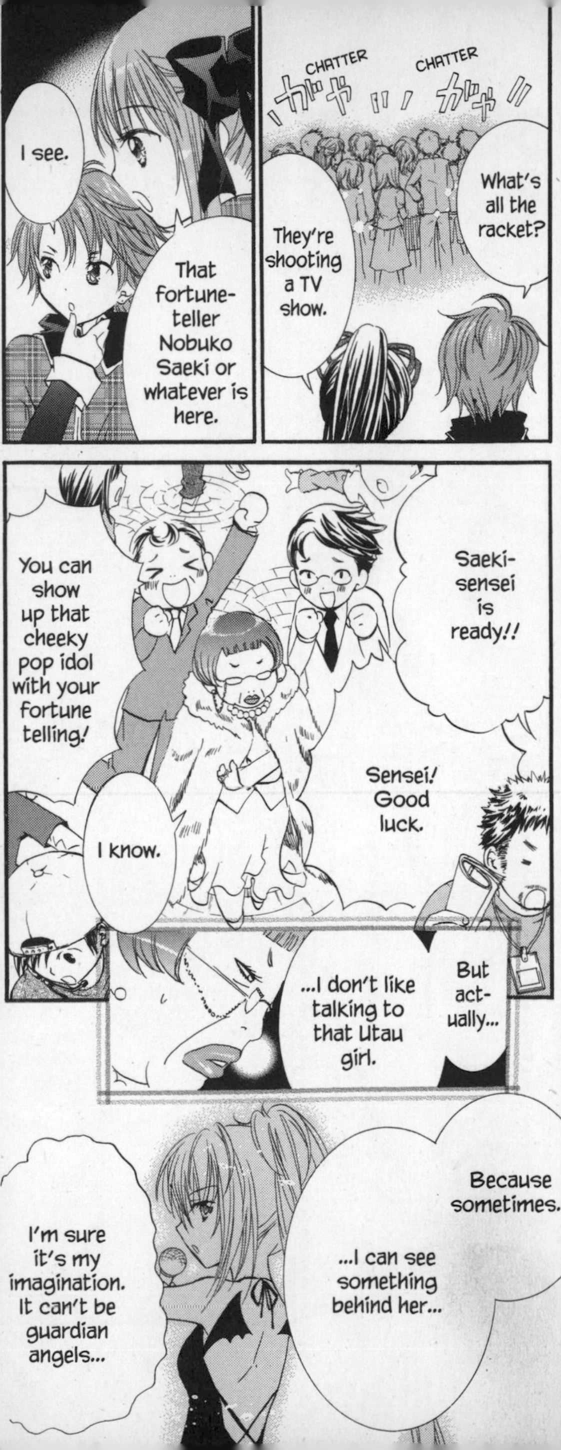
CHATTER
CHATTER
What's all the racket?
They're shooting a TV show.
That fortune-teller Nobuko Saeki or whatever is here.
I see.
Saeki-sensei is ready!!
You can show up that cheeky pop idol with your fortune telling!
Sensei! Good luck.
I know.
But actually...
...I don't like talking to that Utau girl.
Because sometimes...
...I can see something behind her...
I'm sure it's my imagination. It can't be guardian angels...

character profile

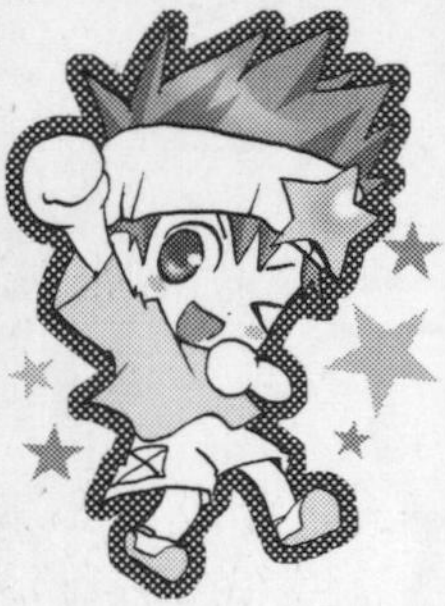

DAICHI

Guardian Character of: Kukai
Special Skill: Skateboarding
Hates: Sitting quietly

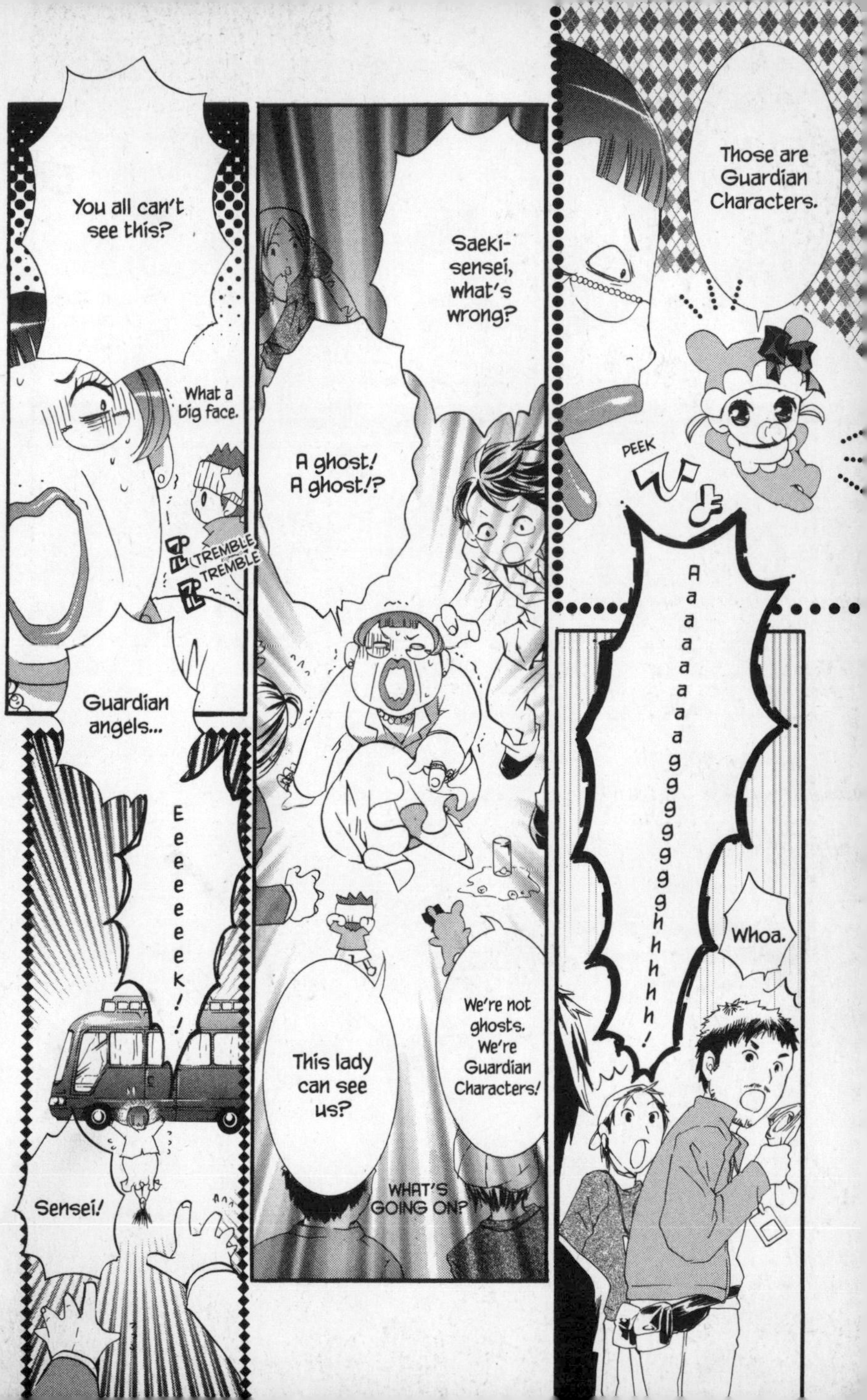
Those are Guardian Characters.
PEEK
Aaaaaaaaggggghhhhh!
Whoa.
Saeki-sensei, what's wrong?
A ghost! A ghost!?
We're not ghosts. We're Guardian Characters!
This lady can see us?
WHAT'S GOING ON?
You all can't see this?
What a big face.
TREMBLE TREMBLE
Guardian angels...
Eeeeeeek!!
Sensei!

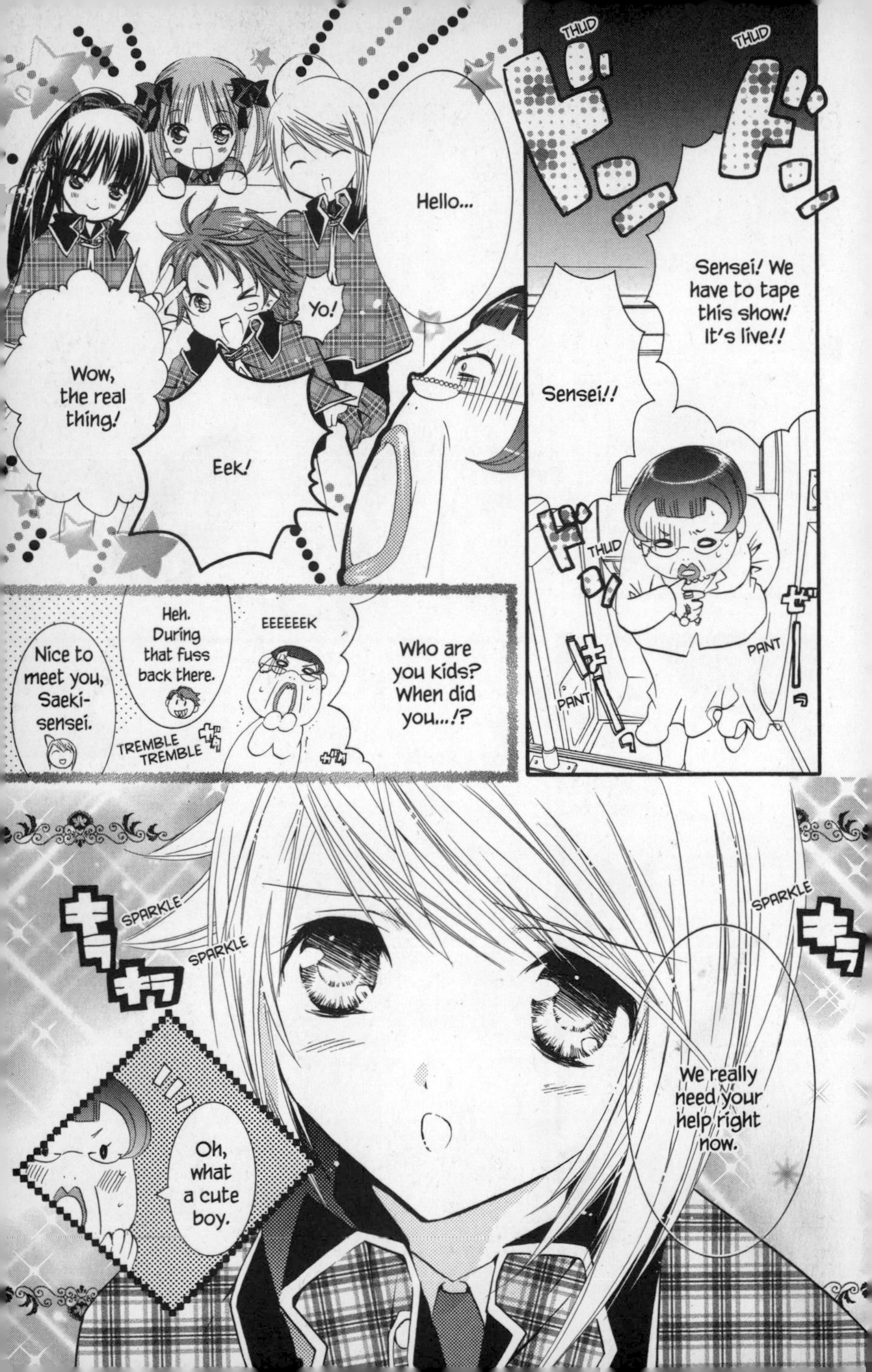
THUD
THUD
Sensei! We have to tape this show! It's live!!
Sensei!!
THUD
PANT
PANT
Hello...
Yo!
Wow, the real thing!
Eek!
Who are you kids? When did you...!?
EEEEEEK
Heh. During that fuss back there.
Nice to meet you, Saeki-sensei.
TREMBLE TREMBLE
SPARKLE
We really need your help right now.
SPARKLE
SPARKLE
Oh, what a cute boy.

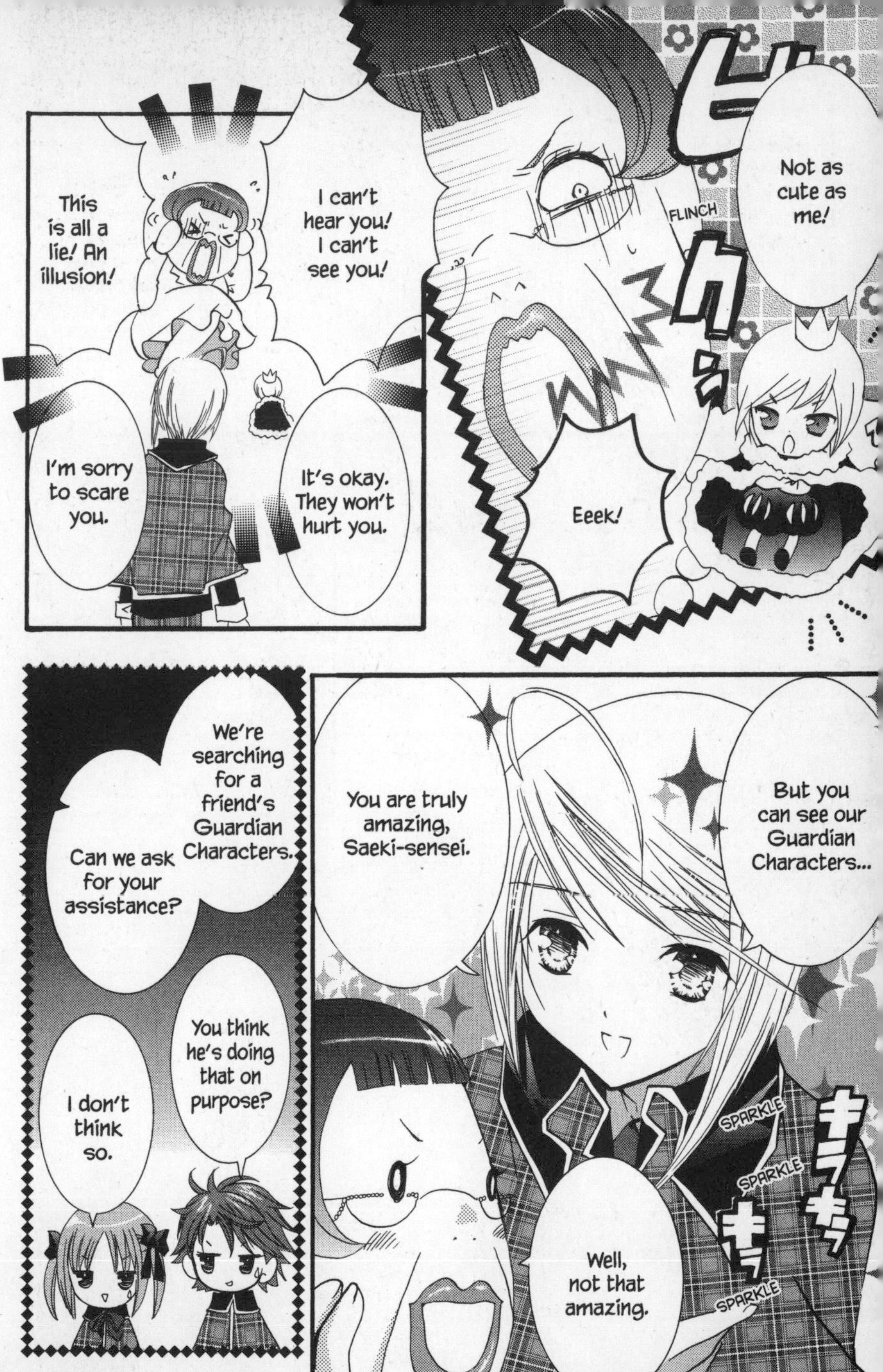
Not as cute as me!
FLINCH
Eeek!
I can't hear you! I can't see you!
This is all a lie! An illusion!
It's okay. They won't hurt you.
I'm sorry to scare you.
But you can see our Guardian Characters...
You are truly amazing, Saeki-sensei.
SPARKLE
SPARKLE
SPARKLE
Well, not that amazing.
We're searching for a friend's Guardian Characters.
Can we ask for your assistance?
You think he's doing that on purpose?
I don't think so.

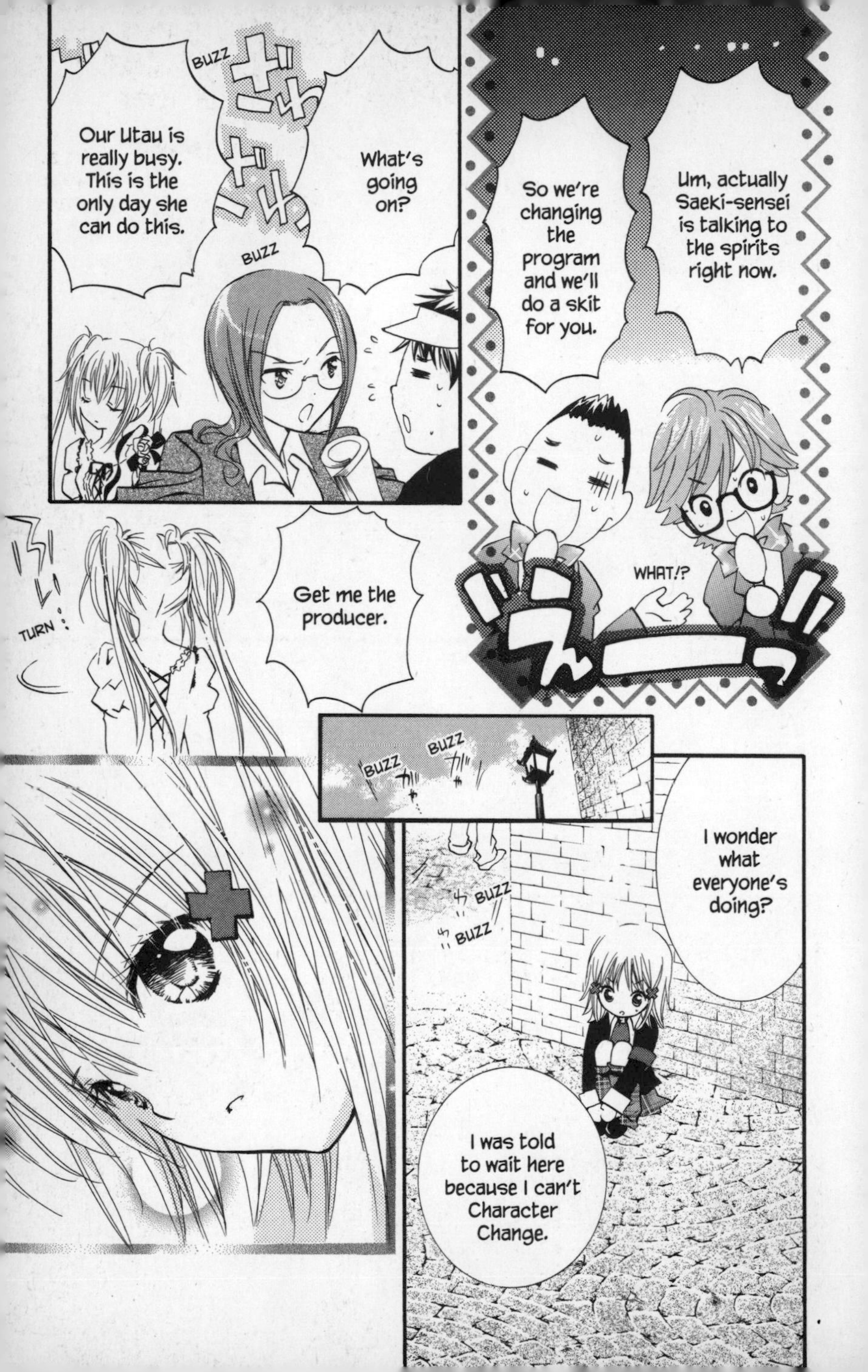
Um, actually Saeki-sensei is talking to the spirits right now.
So we're changing the program and we'll do a skit for you.
WHAT!?
BUZZ
What's going on?
Our Utau is really busy. This is the only day she can do this.
BUZZ
Get me the producer.
TURN
BUZZ
BUZZ
I wonder what everyone's doing?
BUZZ
BUZZ
I was told to wait here because I can't Character Change.

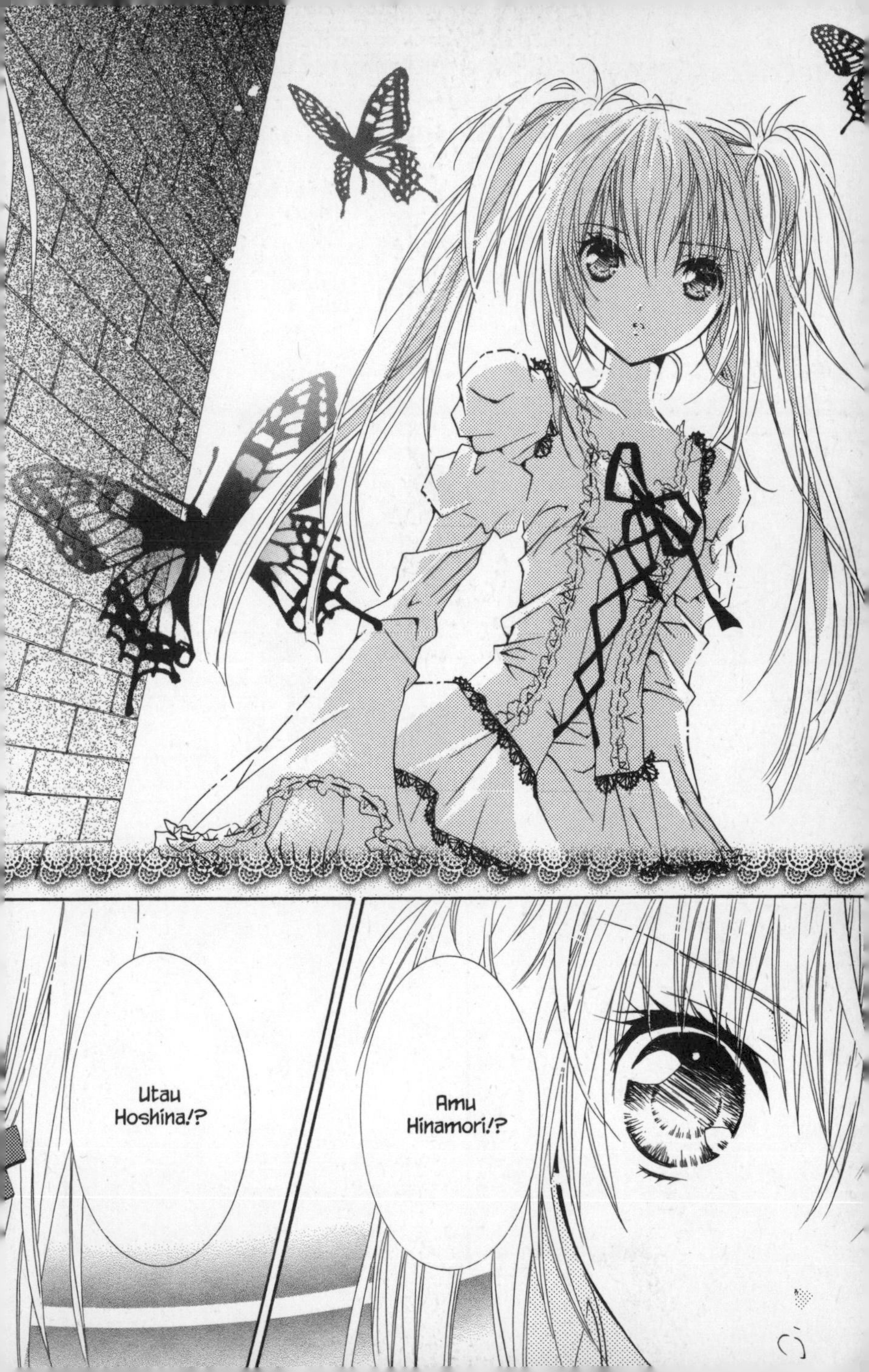
Amu Hinamori!?
Utau Hoshina!?

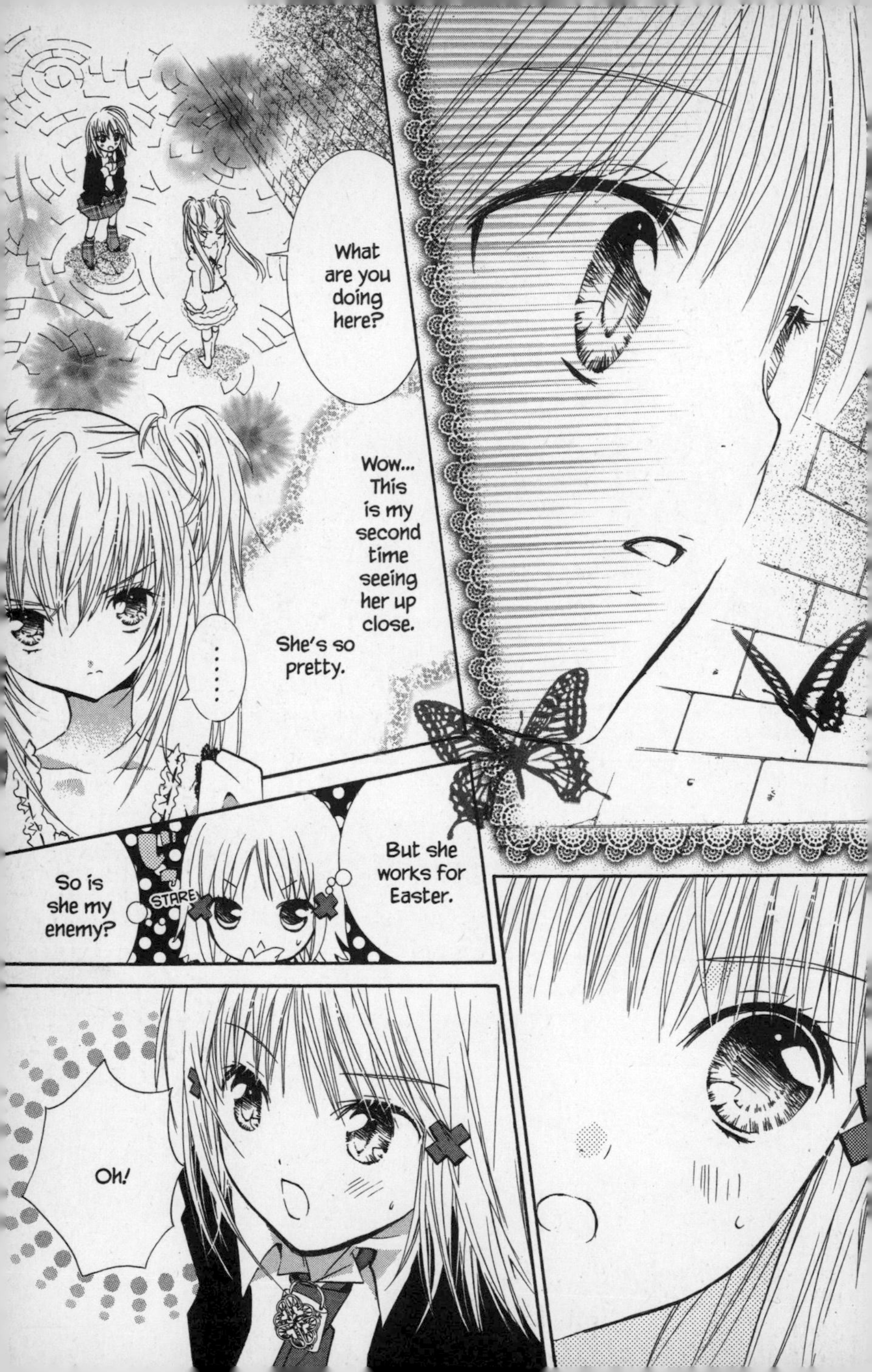

What are you doing here?
Wow... This is my second time seeing her up close.
She's so pretty.
......
But she works for Easter.
STARE
So is she my enemy?
Oh!

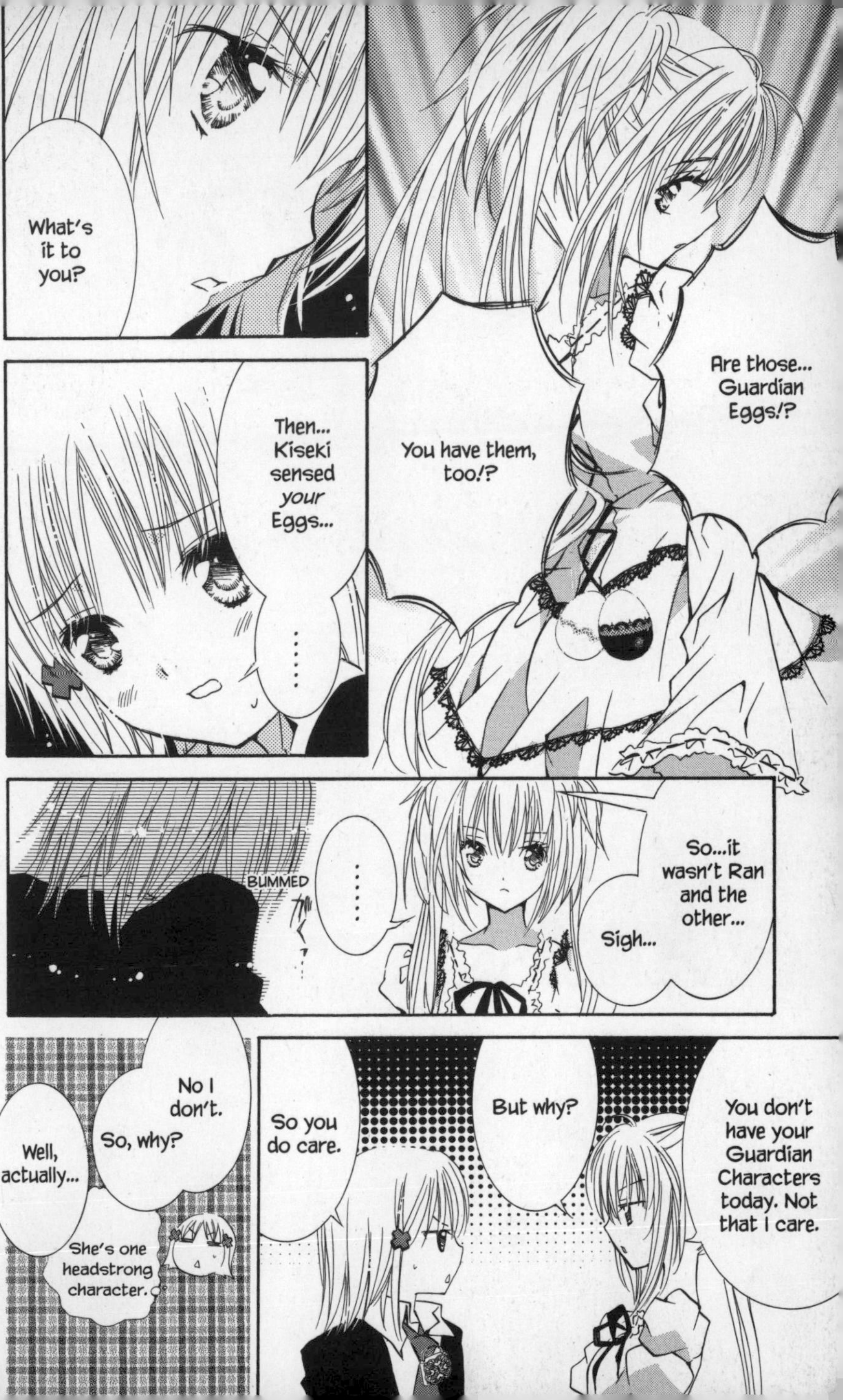
Are those... Guardian Eggs!?
You have them, too!?
What's it to you?
Then... Kiseki sensed *your* Eggs...
......
So...it wasn't Ran and the other...
Sigh...
......
BUMMED
You don't have your Guardian Characters today. Not that I care.
But why?
So you do care.
No I don't.
So, why?
Well, actually...
She's one headstrong character.

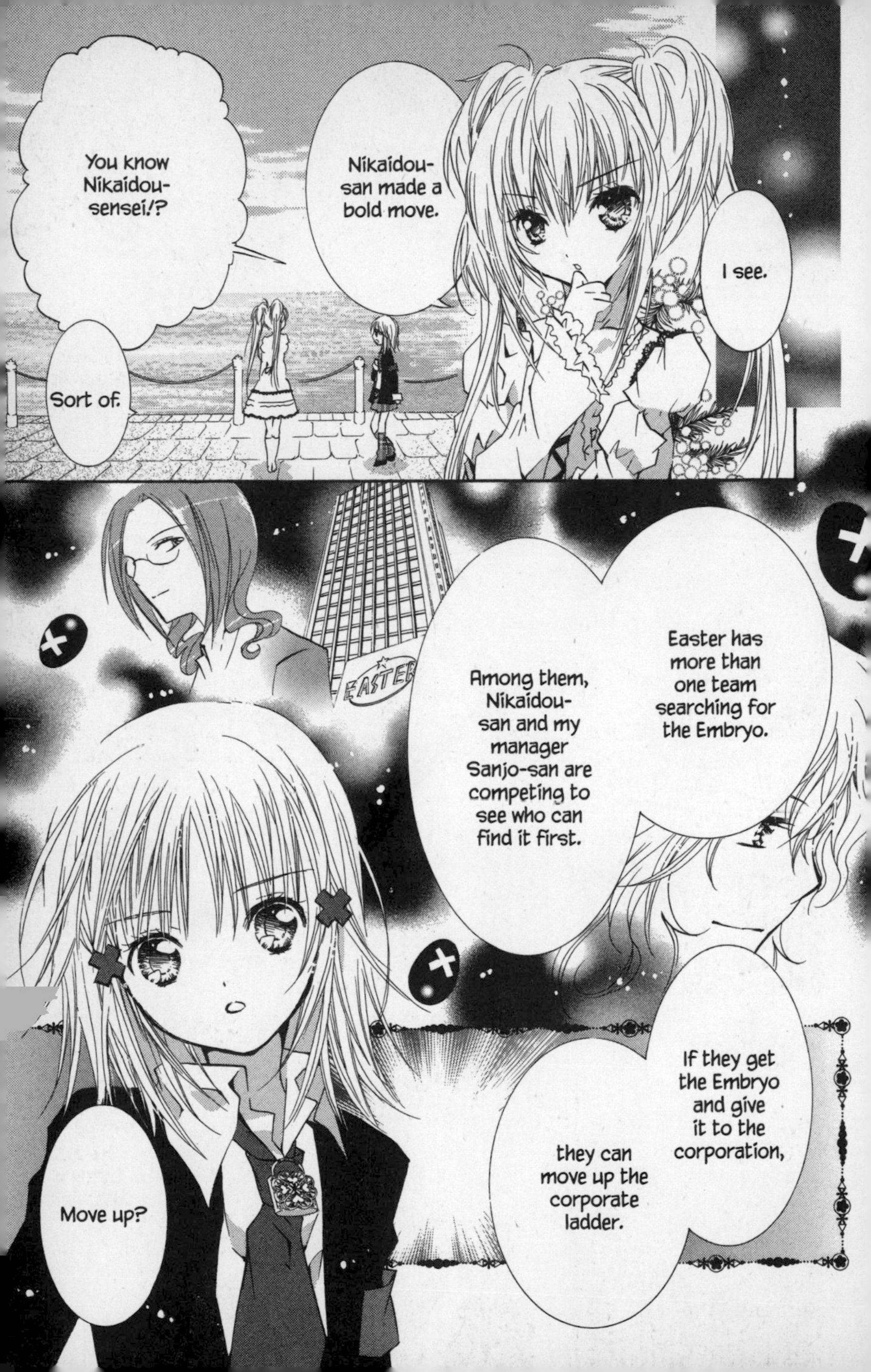
Nikaidou-san made a bold move.
You know Nikaidou-sensei!?
Sort of.
I see.
Easter has more than one team searching for the Embryo.
Among them, Nikaidou-san and my manager Sanjo-san are competing to see who can find it first.
EASTER
If they get the Embryo and give it to the corporation,
they can move up the corporate ladder.
Move up?

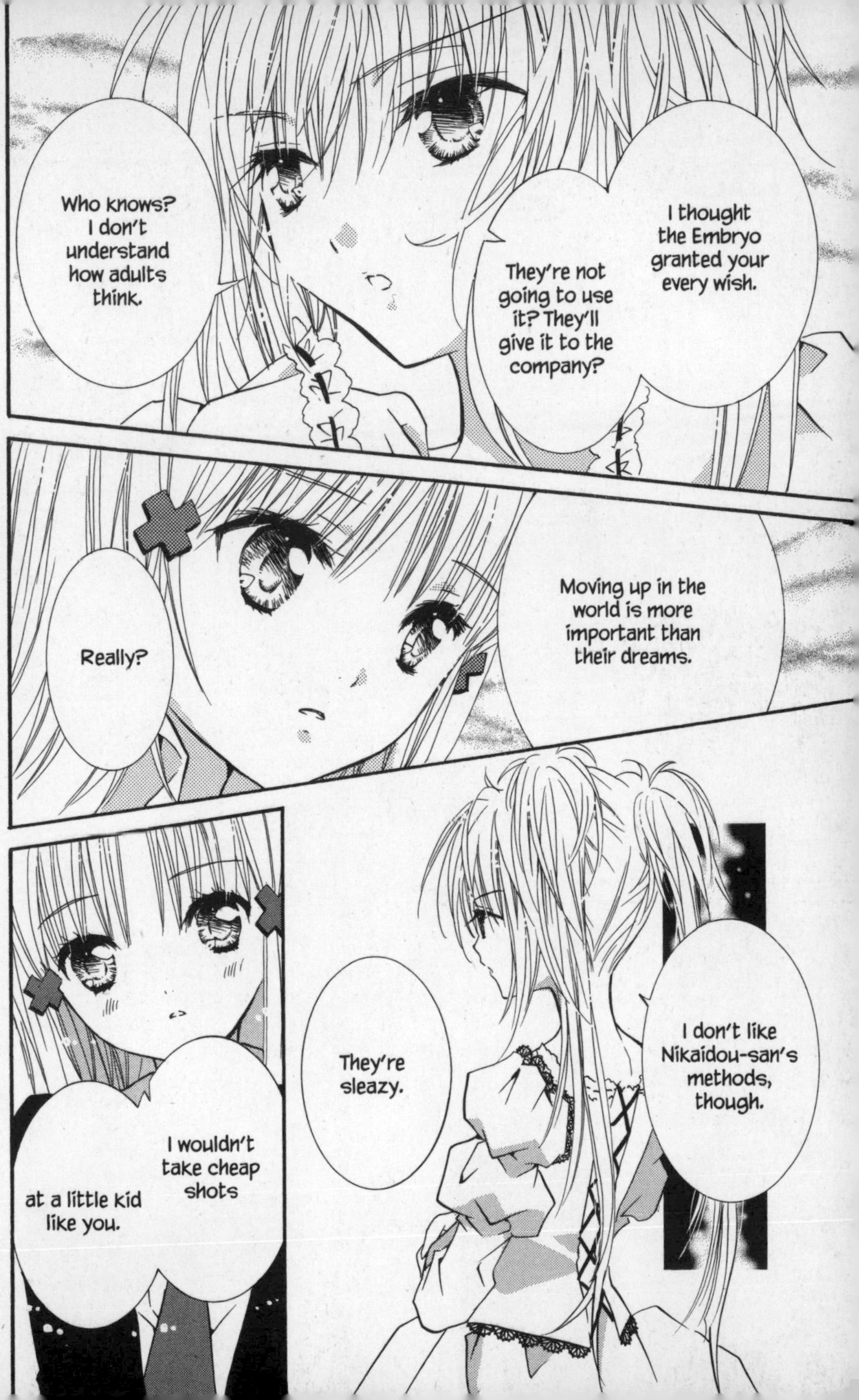
I thought the Embryo granted your every wish.
They're not going to use it? They'll give it to the company?
Who knows? I don't understand how adults think.
Moving up in the world is more important than their dreams.
Really?
I don't like Nikaidou-san's methods, though.
They're sleazy.
I wouldn't take cheap shots
at a little kid like you.

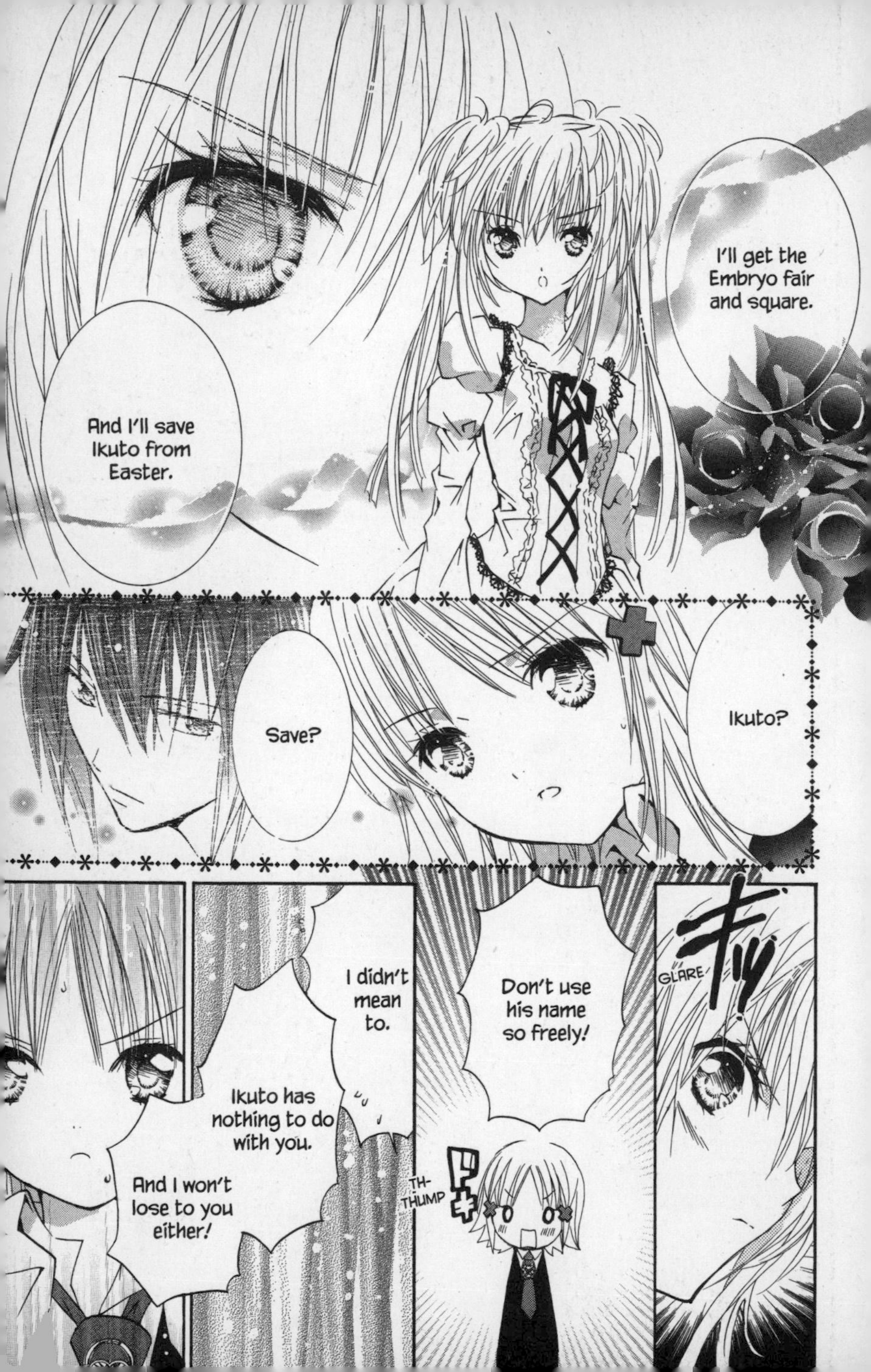
I'll get the Embryo fair and square.
And I'll save Ikuto from Easter.
Ikuto?
Save?
GLARE
Don't use his name so freely!
TH-THUMP
I didn't mean to.
Ikuto has nothing to do with you.
And I won't lose to you either!

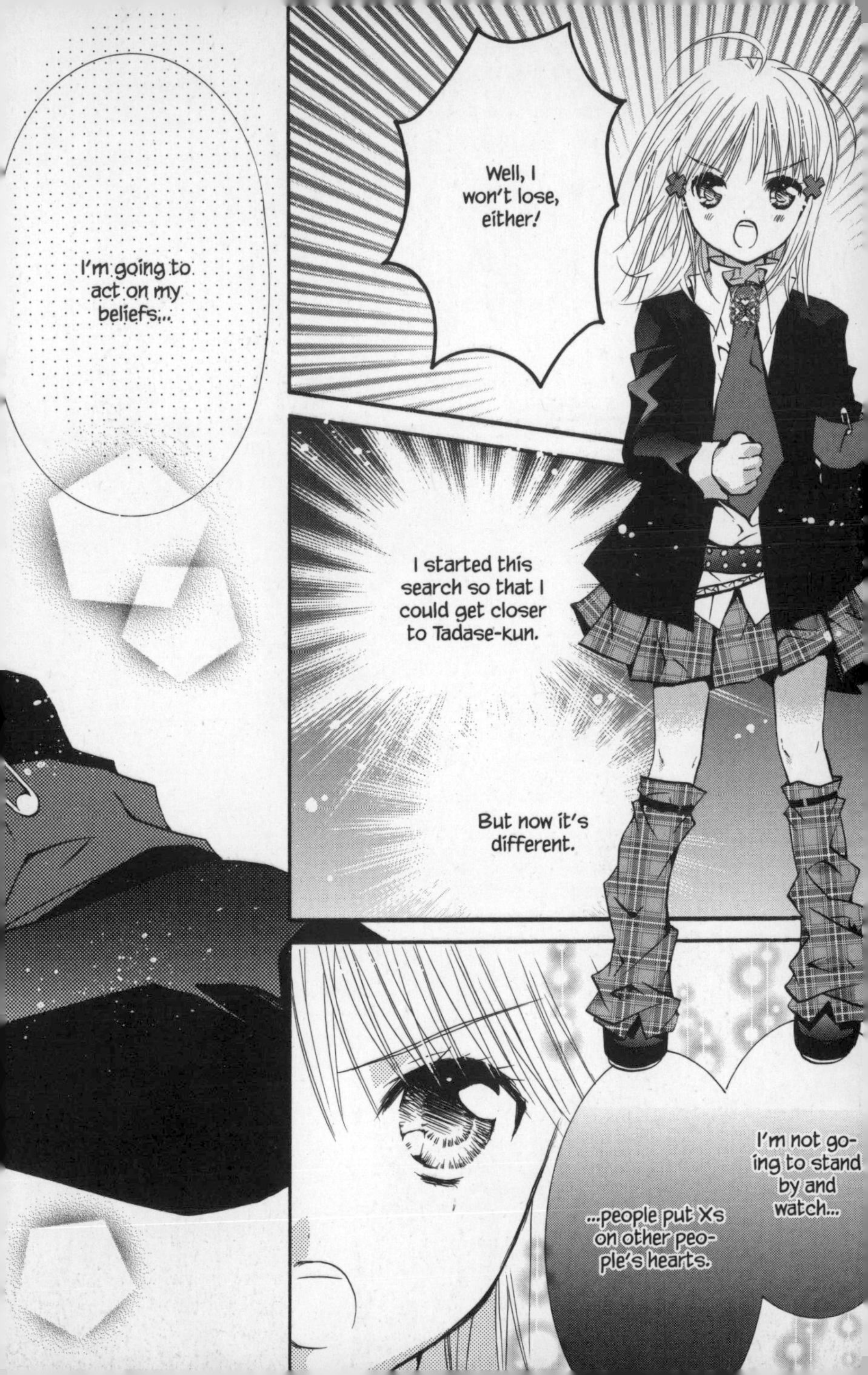
Well, I won't lose, either!
I started this search so that I could get closer to Tadase-kun.
But now it's different.
I'm not going to stand by and watch...
...people put Xs on other people's hearts.
I'm going to act on my beliefs...

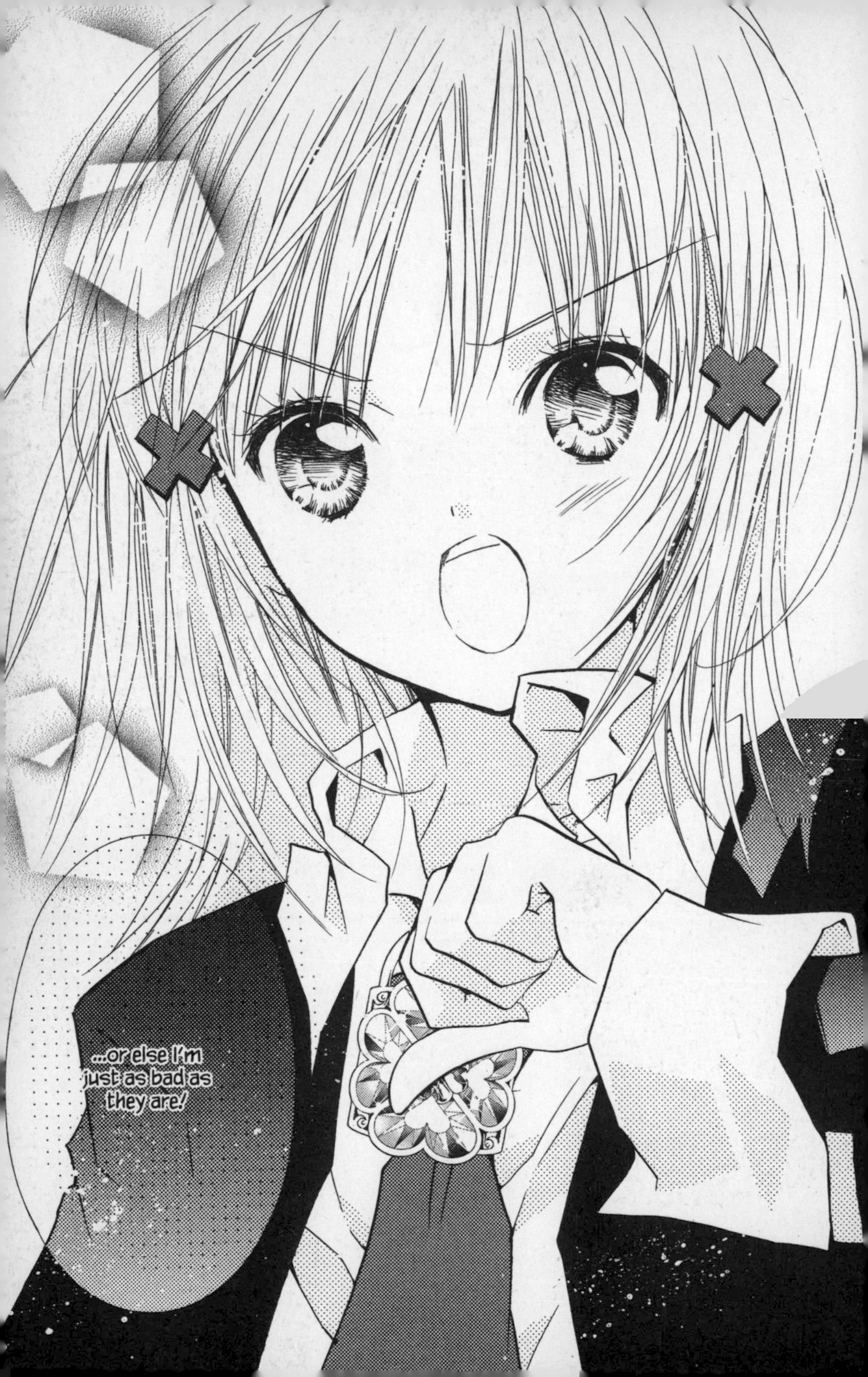
...or else I'm just as bad as they are!

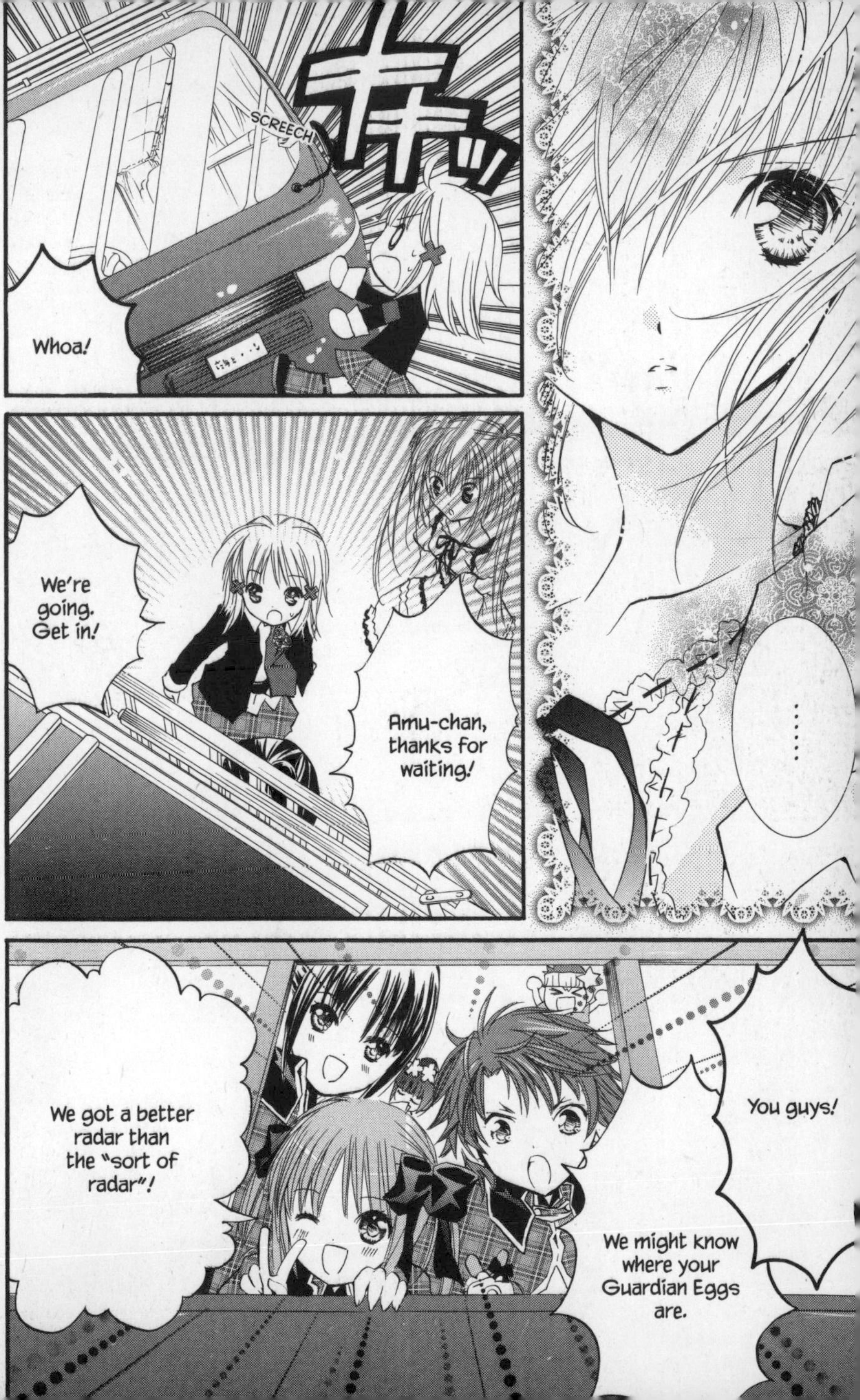
……
キキッ
SCREECH
Whoa!
Amu-chan, thanks for waiting!
We're going. Get in!
You guys!
We might know where your Guardian Eggs are.
We got a better radar than the "sort of radar"!

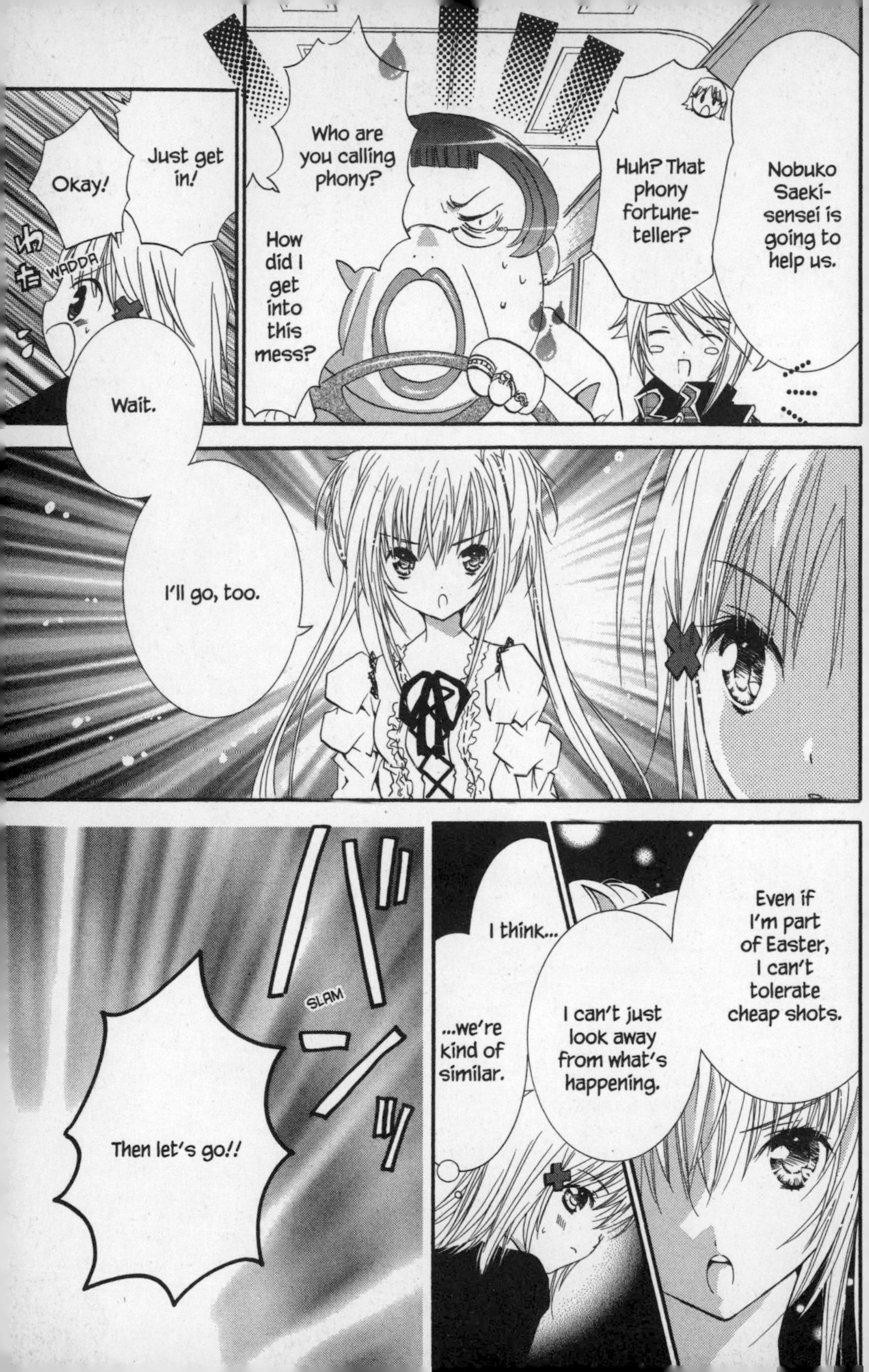
Nobuko Saeki-sensei is going to help us.
Huh? That phony fortune-teller?
Who are you calling phony?
How did I get into this mess?
Just get in!
Okay!
WADDA
Wait.
I'll go, too.
Even if I'm part of Easter, I can't tolerate cheap shots.
I can't just look away from what's happening.
I think...
...we're kind of similar.
SLAM
Then let's go!!

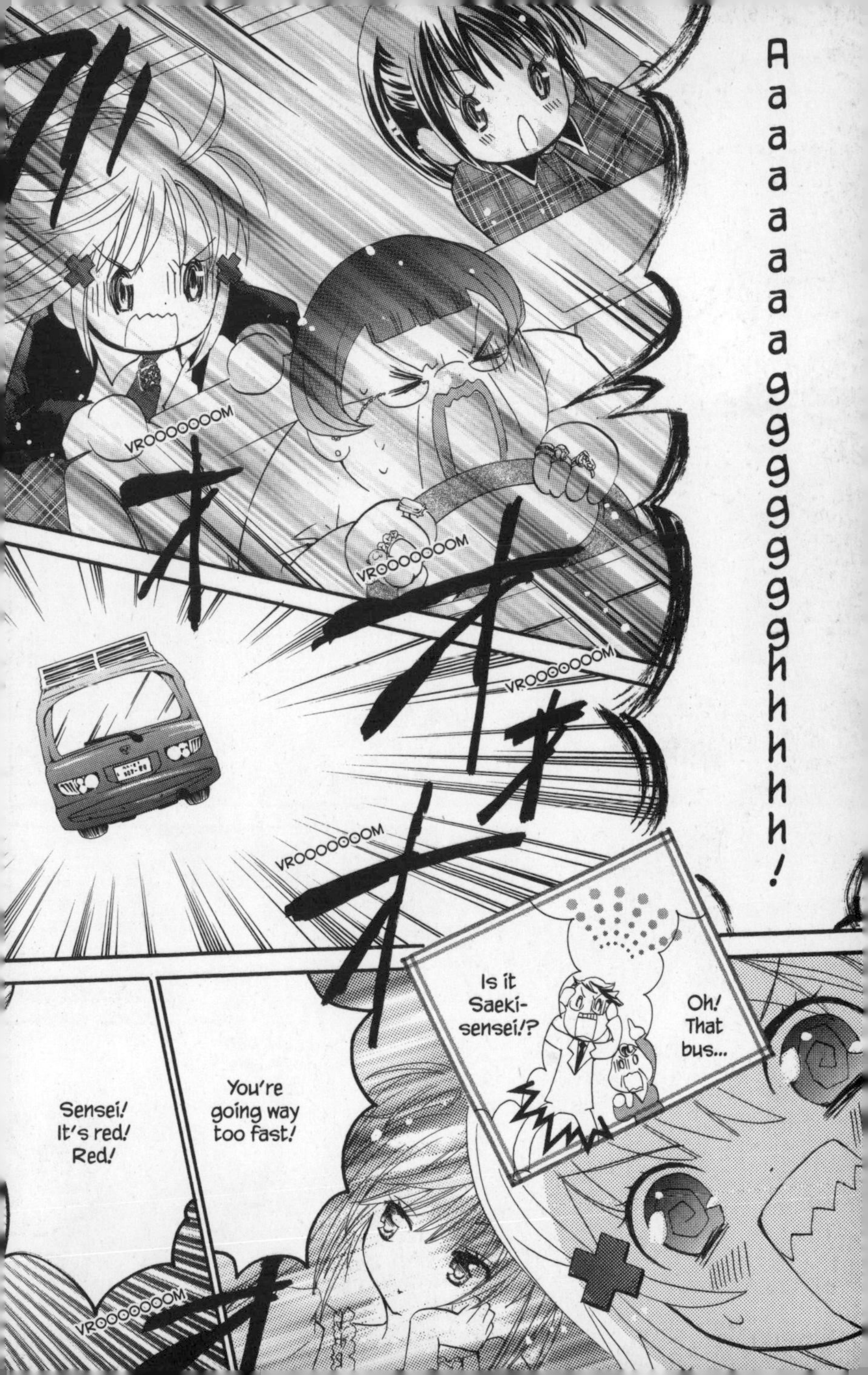
Aaaaaaaggggggghhhhh!
VROOOOOOOM
VROOOOOOOM
VROOOOOOOM
VROOOOOOOM
Oh! That bus...
Is it Saeki-sensei!?
You're going way too fast!
Sensei! It's red! Red!
VROOOOOOOM

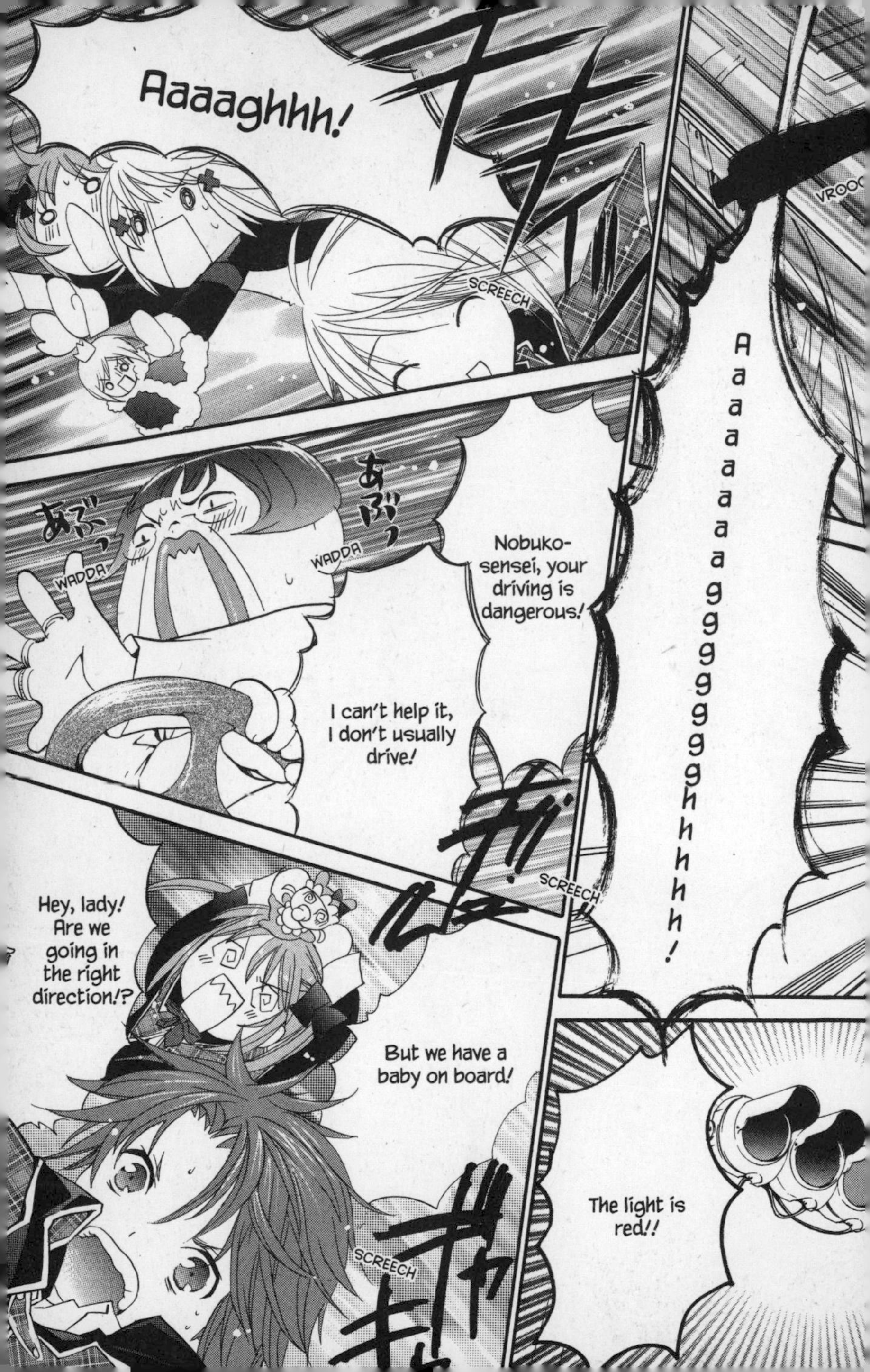
VROOO
Aaaaaaaaggggggghhhhh!
Aaaaghhh!
SCREECH
あぶっ
WADDA
あぶっ
WADDA
Nobuko-sensei, your driving is dangerous!
I can't help it, I don't usually drive!
SCREECH
The light is red!!
Hey, lady! Are we going in the right direction!?
But we have a baby on board!
SCREECH

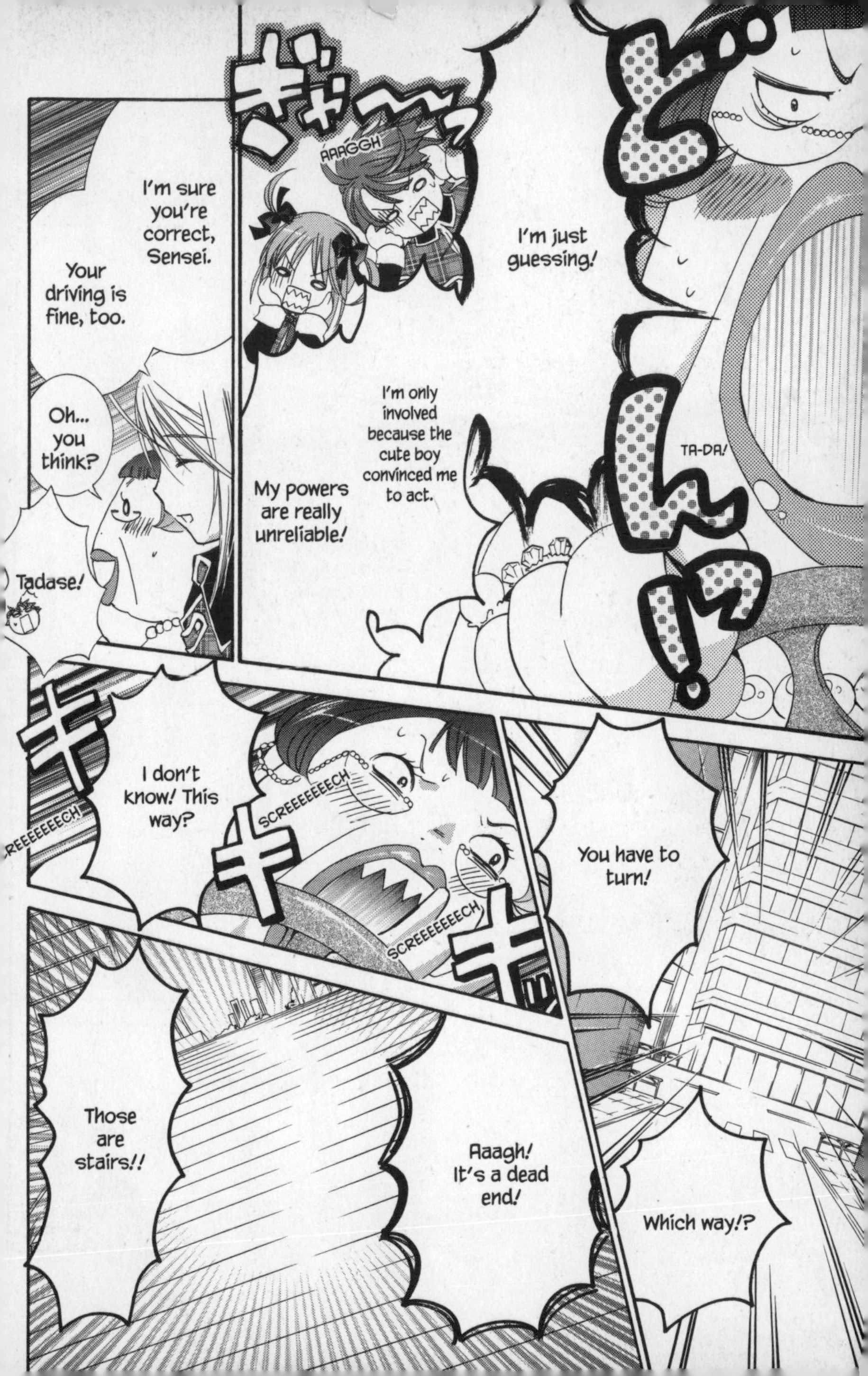
AAAGGH
I'm just guessing!
TA-DA!
I'm only involved because the cute boy convinced me to act.
My powers are really unreliable!
I'm sure you're correct, Sensei.
Your driving is fine, too.
Oh... you think?
Tadase!
You have to turn!
Which way!?
SCREEEEEEECH
SCREEEEEEECH
SCREEEEEEECH
I don't know! This way?
REEEEEEECH
Aaagh! It's a dead end!
Those are stairs!!

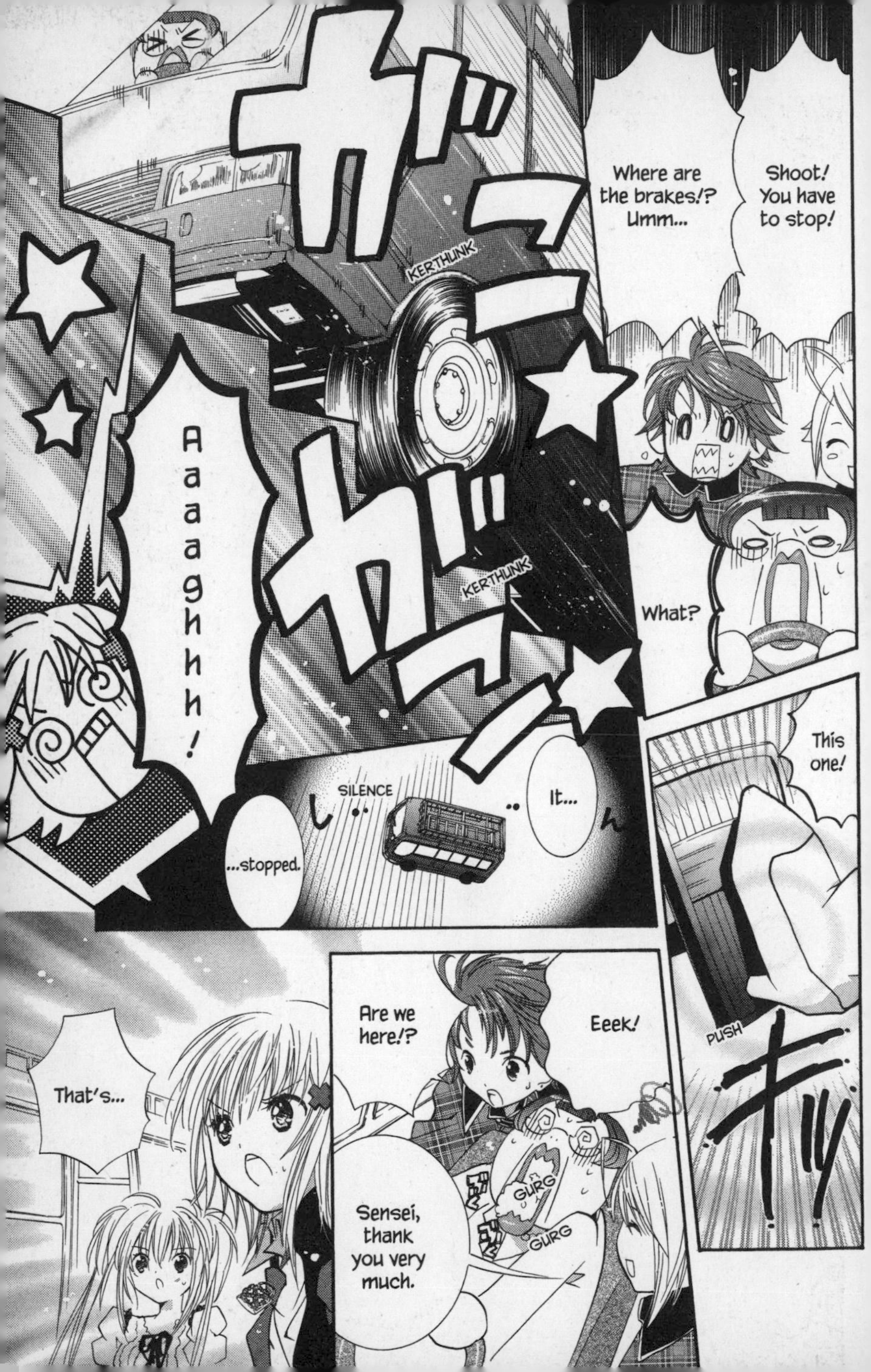
Shoot! You have to stop!
Where are the brakes!? Umm...
What?
This one!
PUSH
KERTHUNK
KERTHUNK
Aaaaghhhh!
SILENCE
It...
...stopped.
Eeek!
Are we here!?
GURG
GURG
Sensei, thank you very much.
That's...

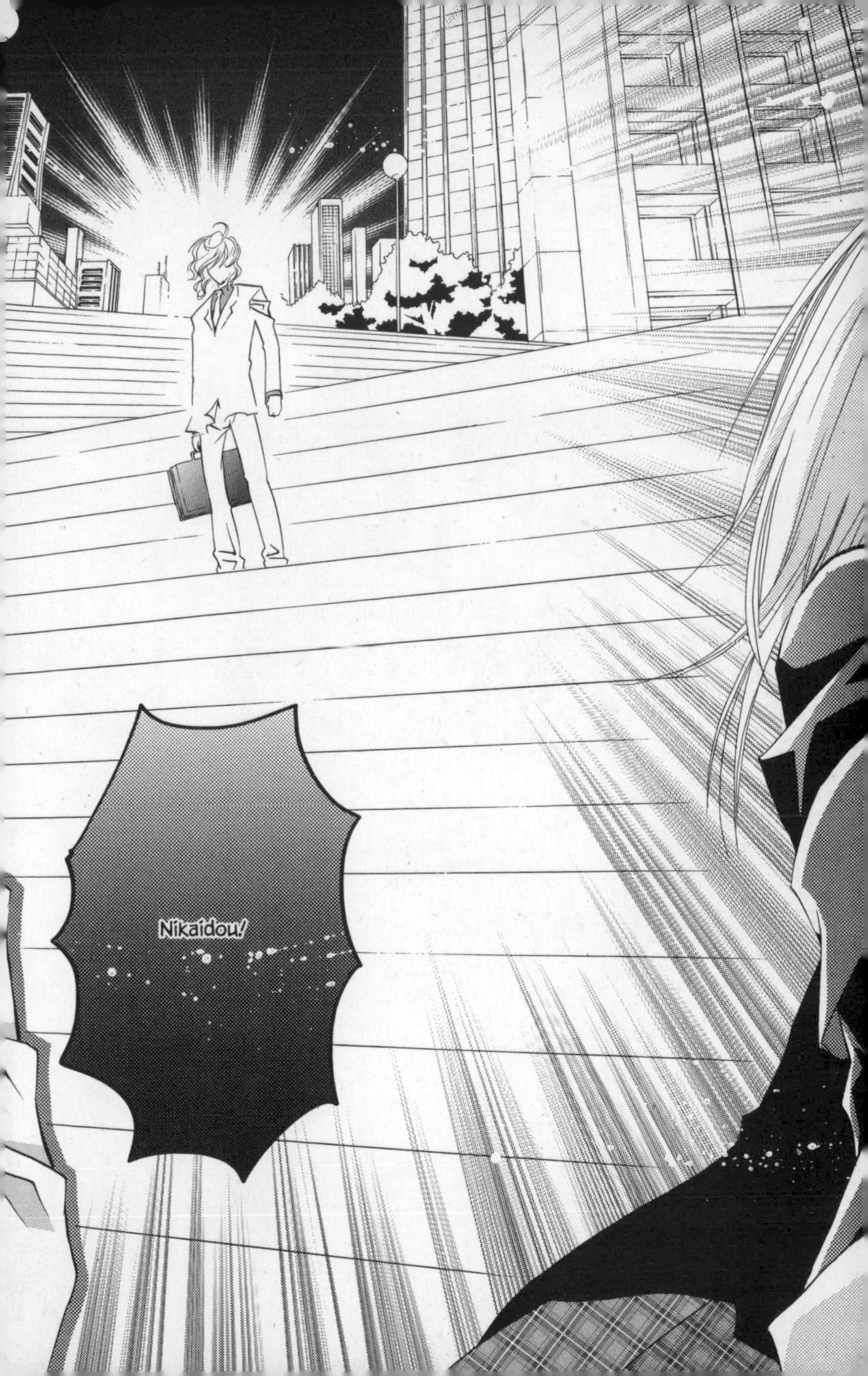
Nikaidou!

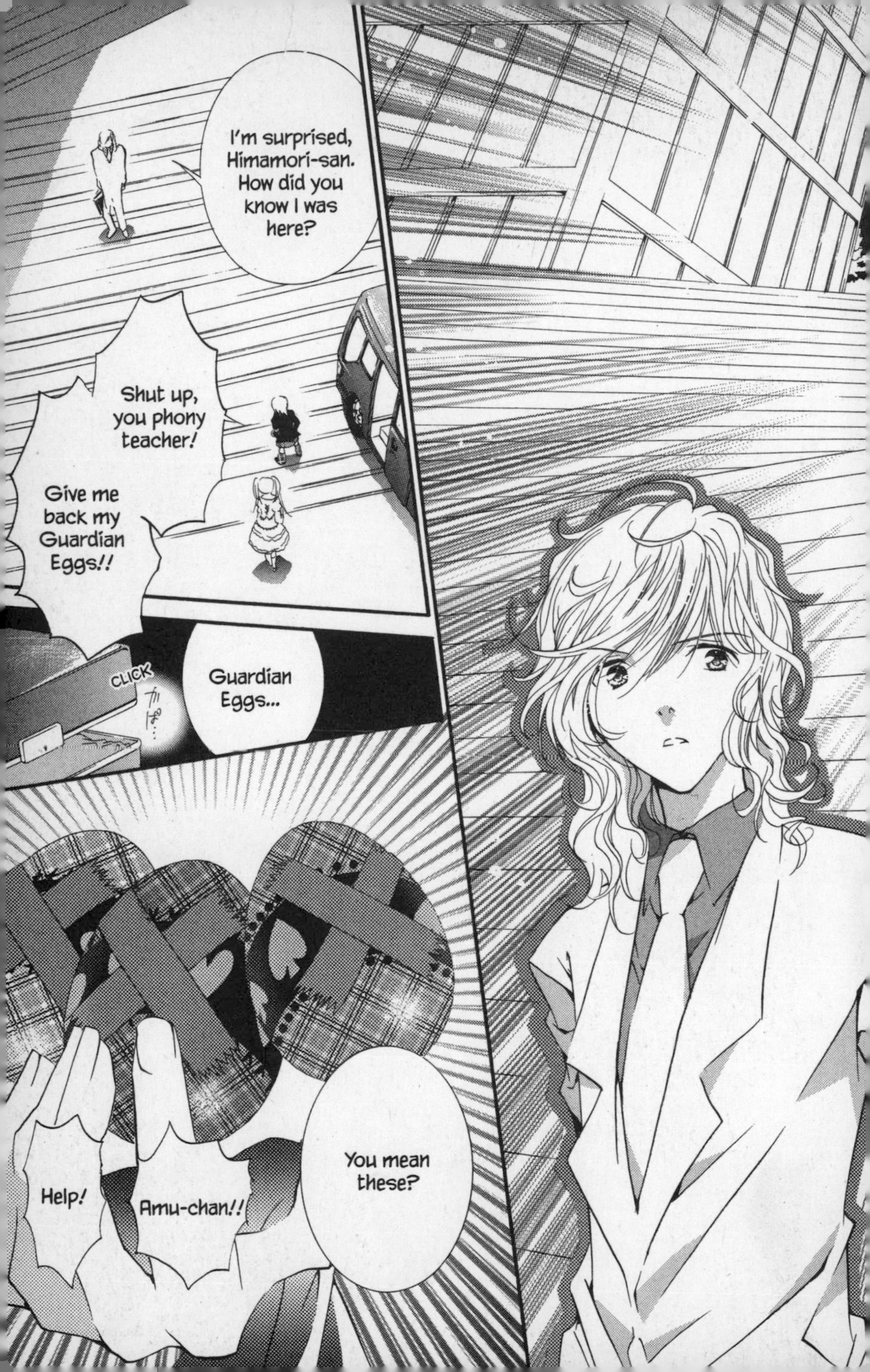
I'm surprised, Himamori-san. How did you know I was here?
Shut up, you phony teacher!
Give me back my Guardian Eggs!!
Guardian Eggs...
CLICK
You mean these?
Amu-chan!!
Help!

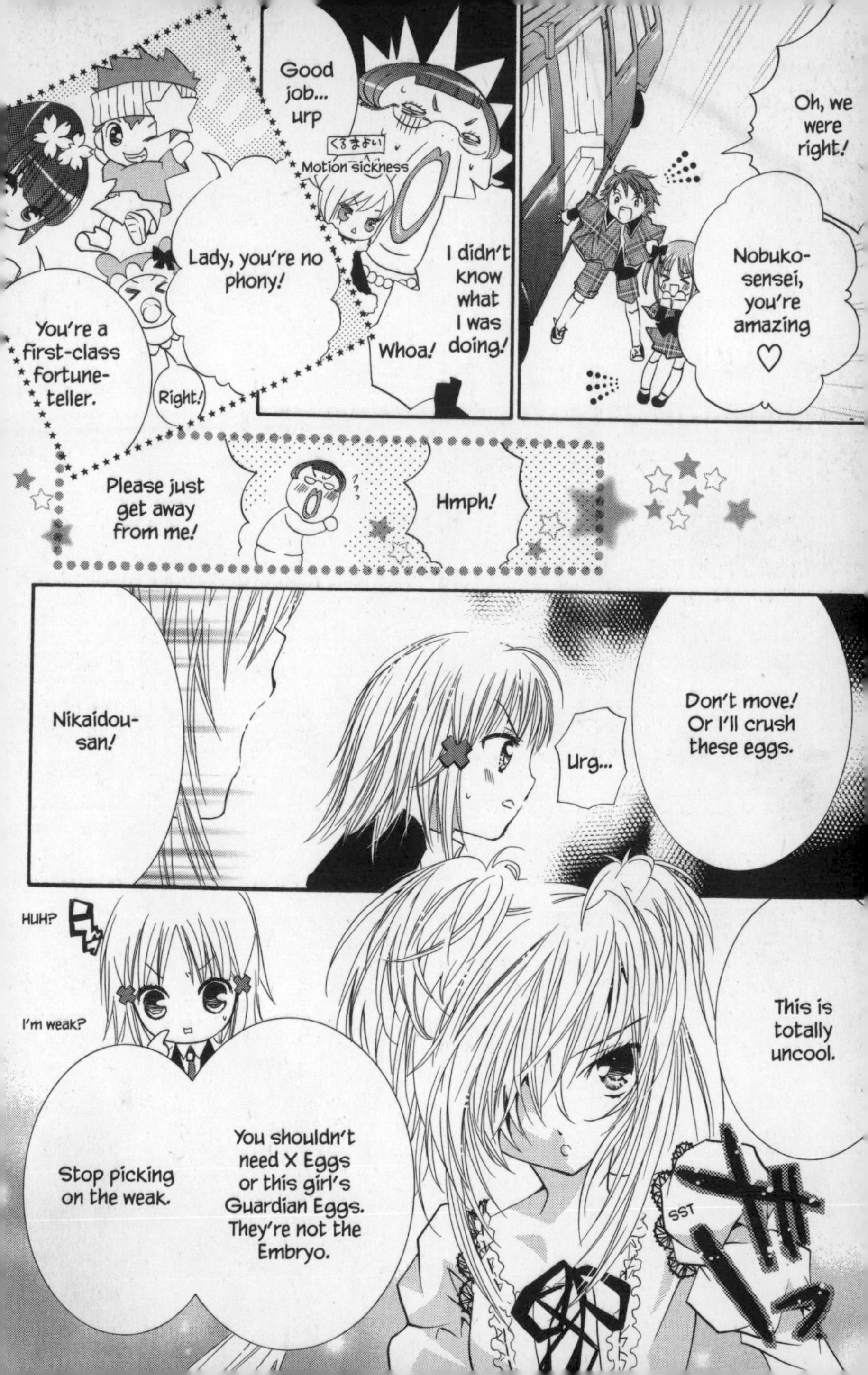

Oh, we were right!
Nobuko-sensei, you're amazing ♡
Good job... urp
くるまよい
Motion sickness
I didn't know what I was doing!
Whoa!
Lady, you're no phony!
You're a first-class fortune-teller.
Right!
Hmph!
Please just get away from me!
Don't move! Or I'll crush these eggs.
Urg...
Nikaidou-san!
This is totally uncool.
SST
You shouldn't need X Eggs or this girl's Guardian Eggs. They're not the Embryo.
Stop picking on the weak.
HUH?
I'm weak?

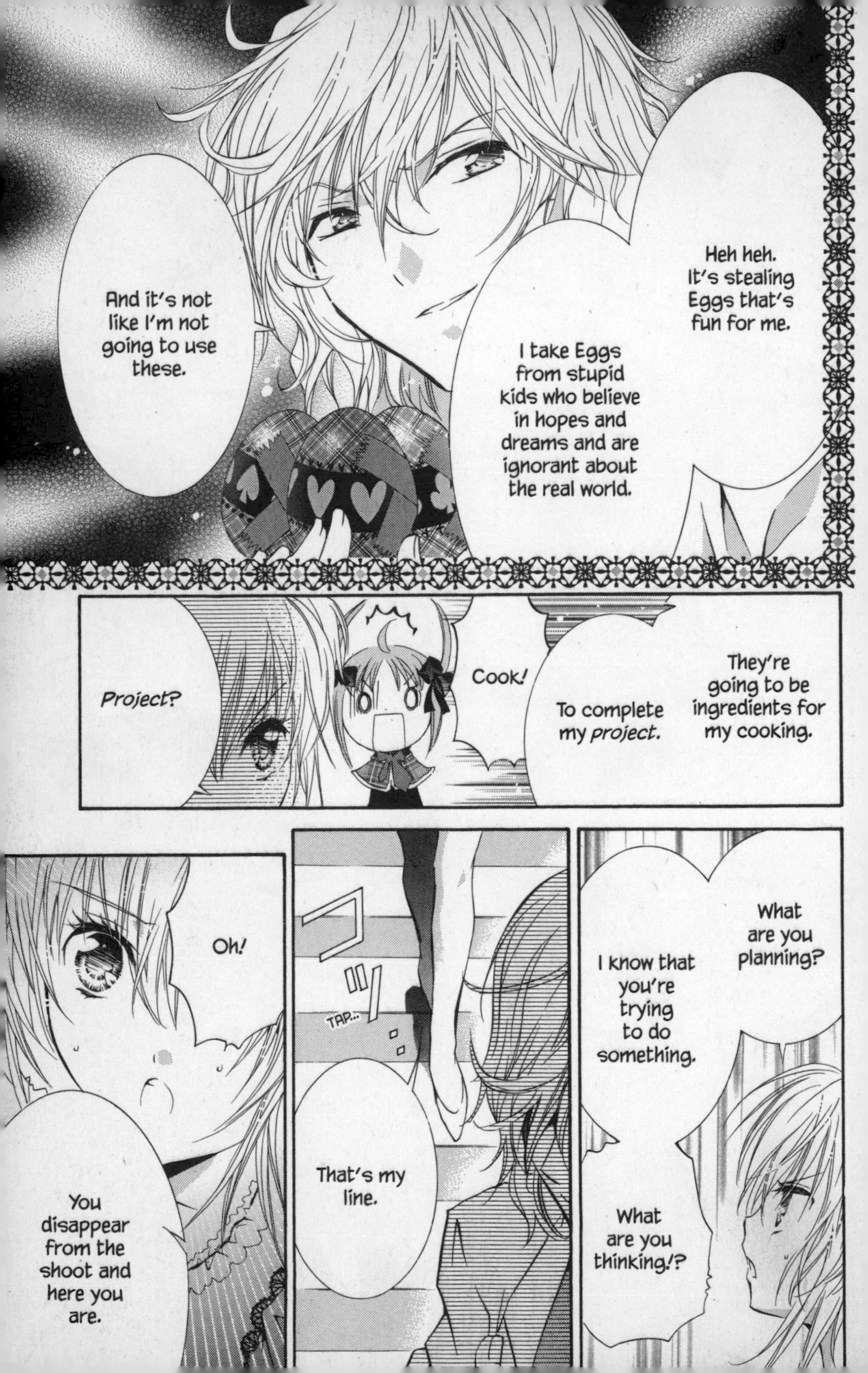
Heh heh. It's stealing Eggs that's fun for me.
I take Eggs from stupid kids who believe in hopes and dreams and are ignorant about the real world.
And it's not like I'm not going to use these.
They're going to be ingredients for my cooking.
To complete my *project*.
Cook!
Project?
What are you planning?
I know that you're trying to do something.
What are you thinking!?
TAP...
That's my line.
Oh!
You disappear from the shoot and here you are.

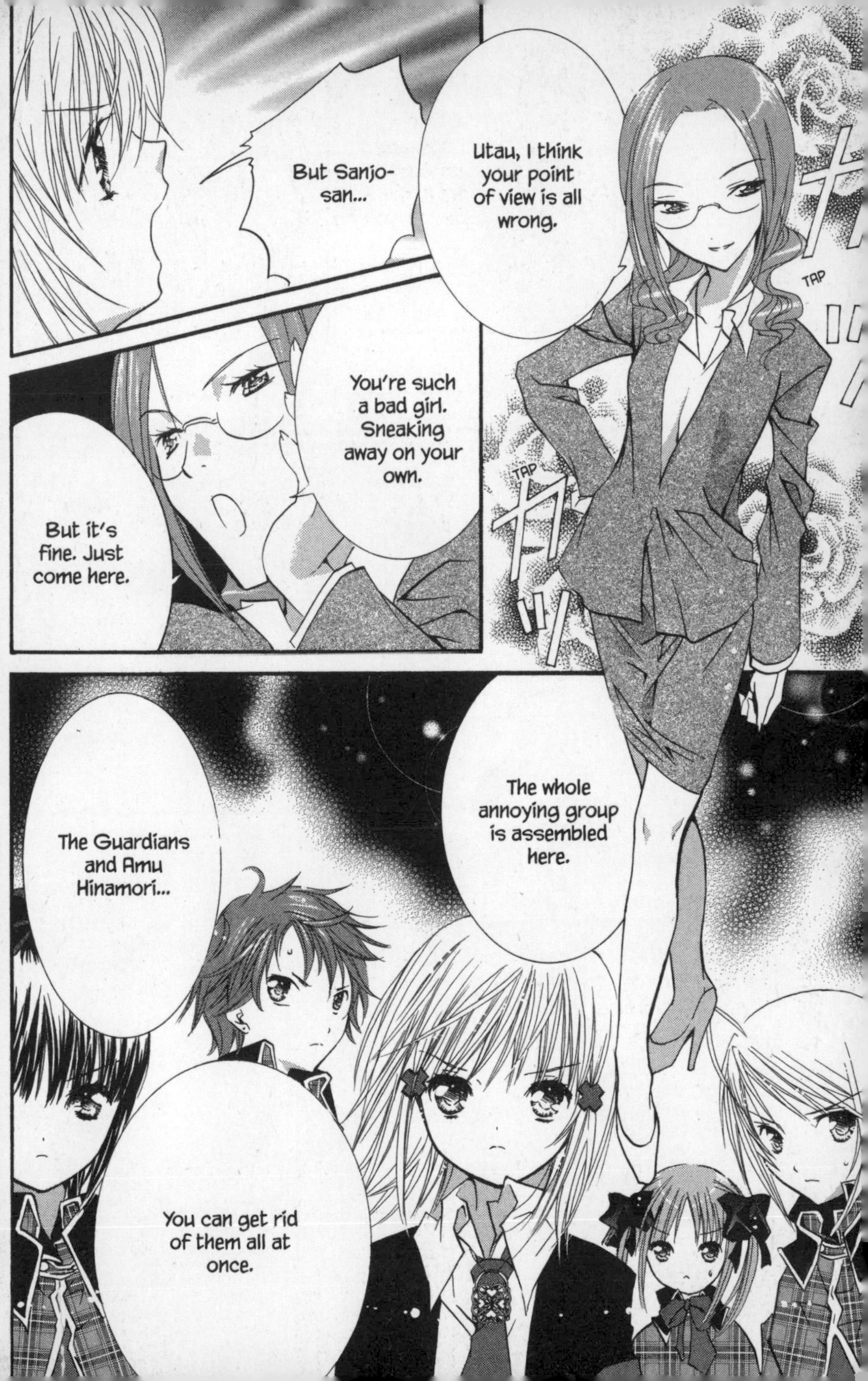
Utau, I think your point of view is all wrong.
TAP
TAP
But Sanjo-san...
You're such a bad girl. Sneaking away on your own.
But it's fine. Just come here.
The whole annoying group is assembled here.
The Guardians and Amu Hinamori...
You can get rid of them all at once.

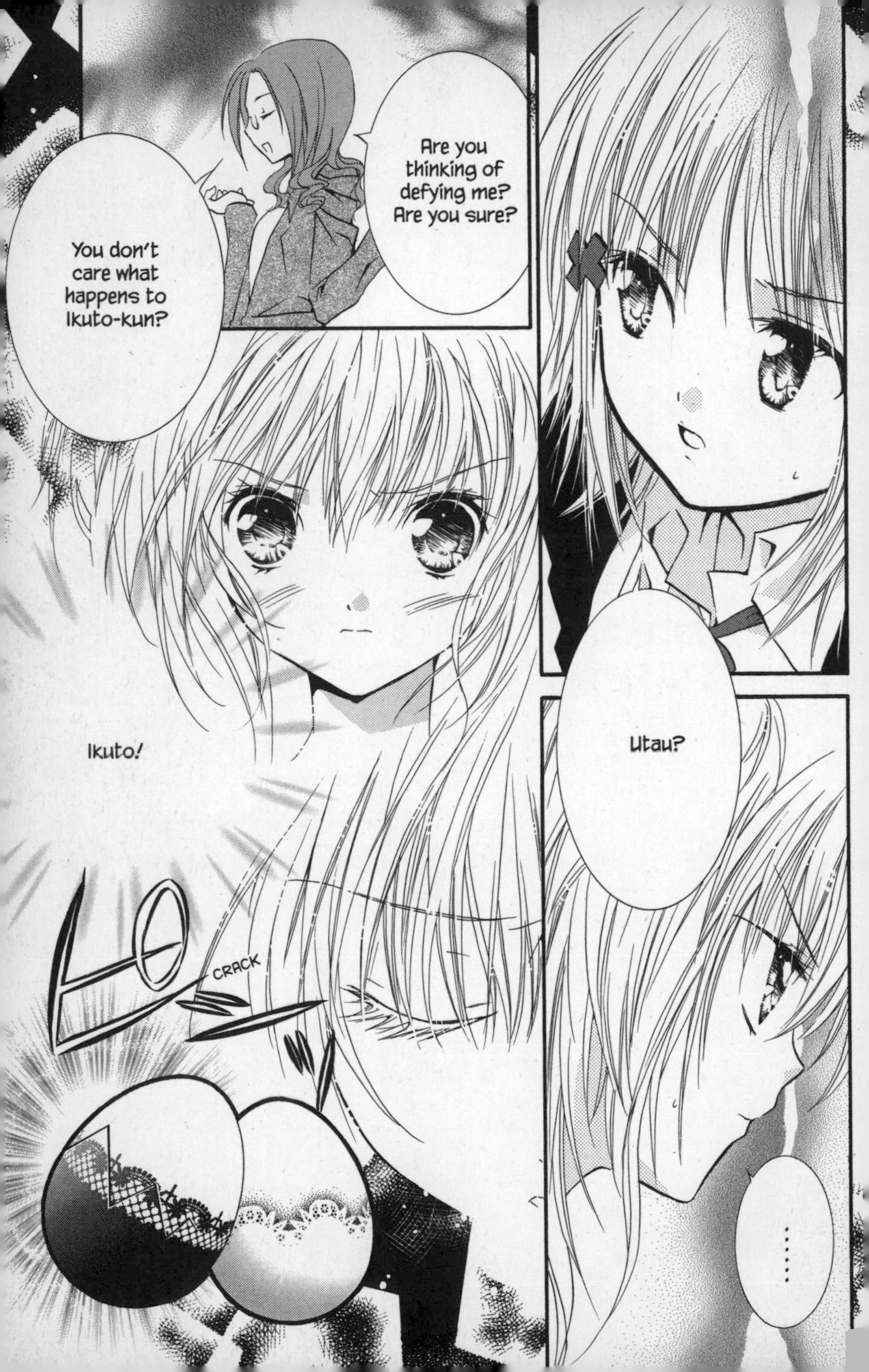
Utau?
......
Are you thinking of defying me? Are you sure?
You don't care what happens to Ikuto-kun?
Ikuto!
CRACK

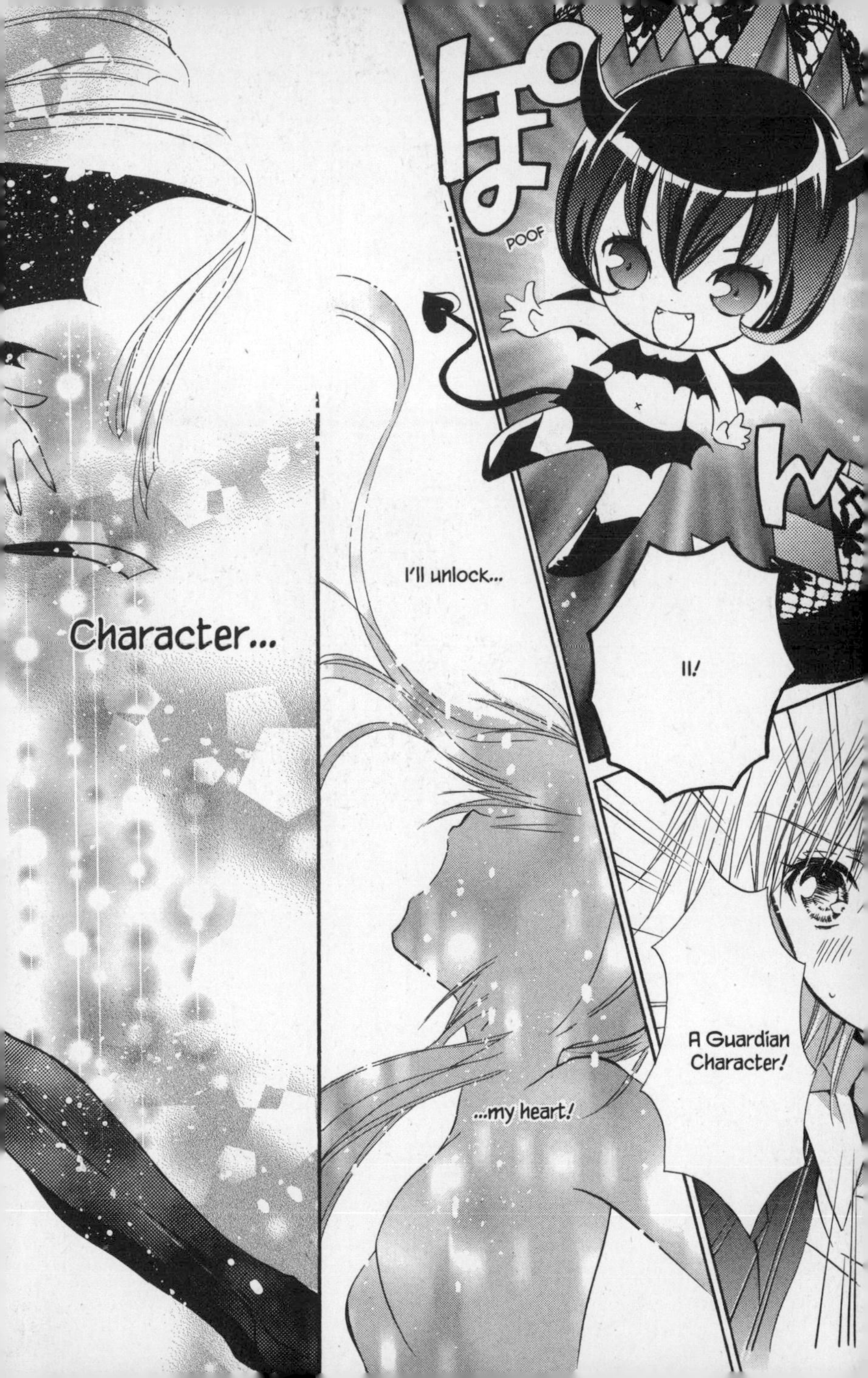
ぽん
POOF
I'll unlock...
!!
A Guardian Character!
...my heart!
Character...

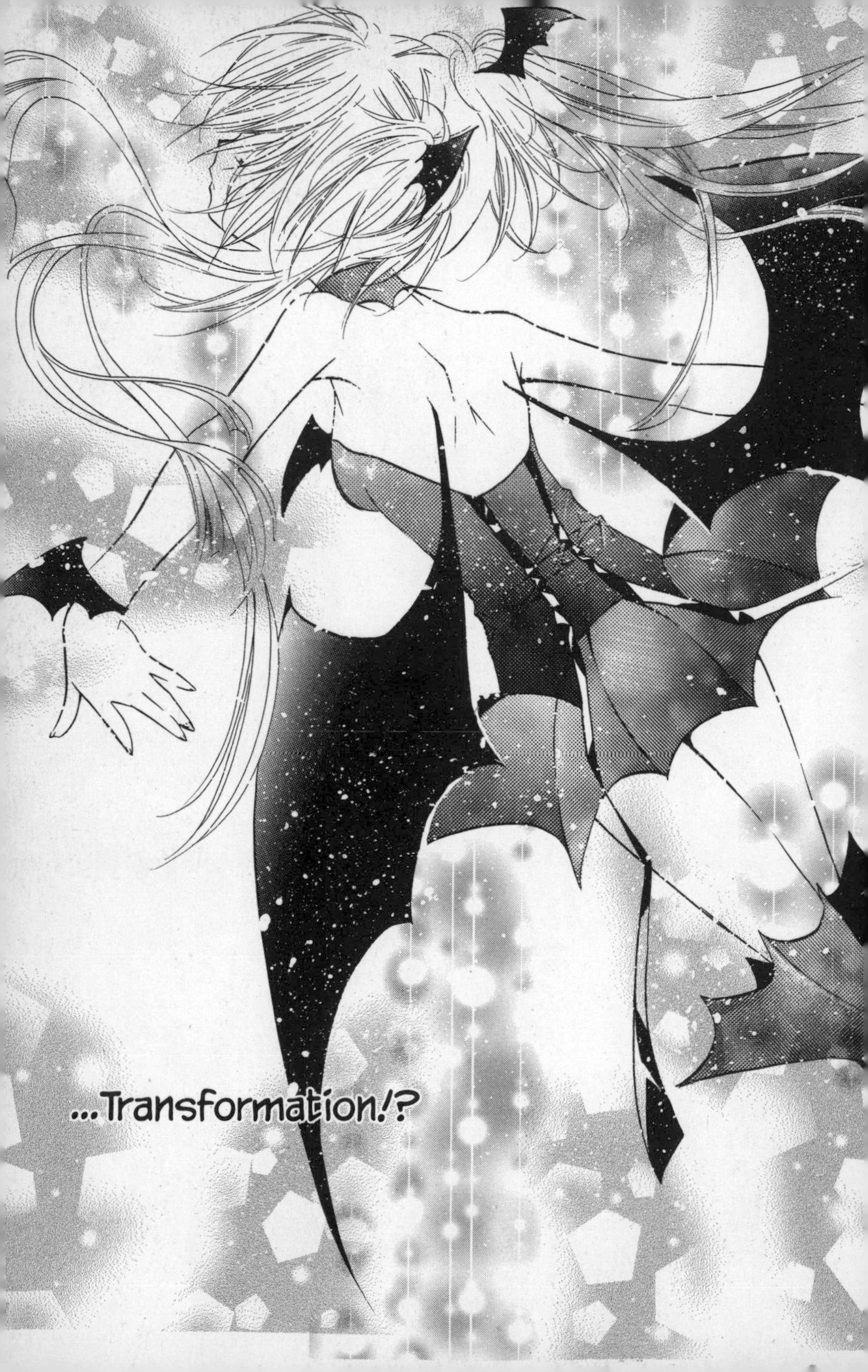
...Transformation!?

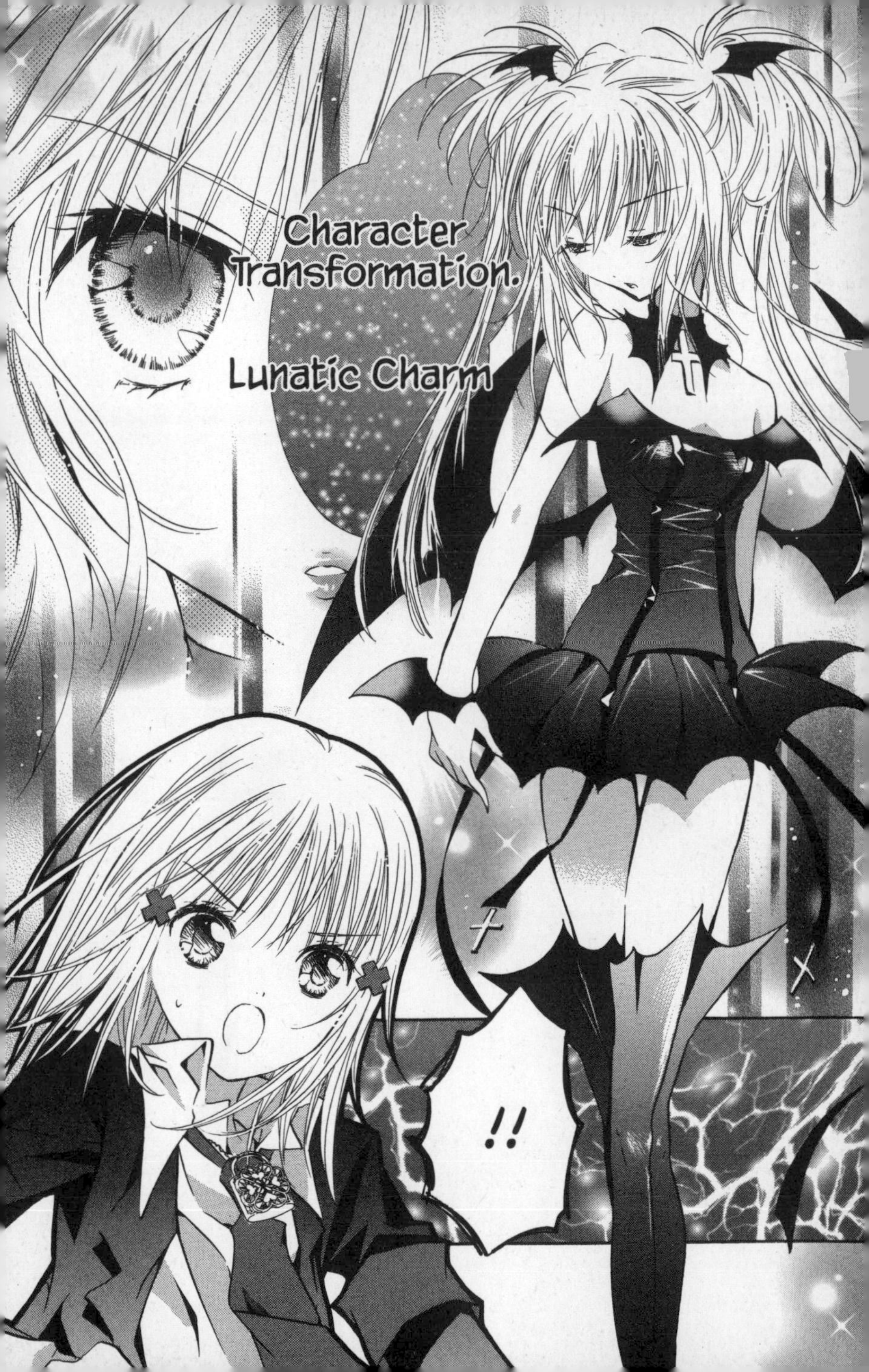
Character Transformation.
Lunatic Charm
!!

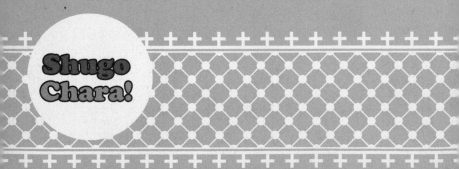

Shugo
Chara!

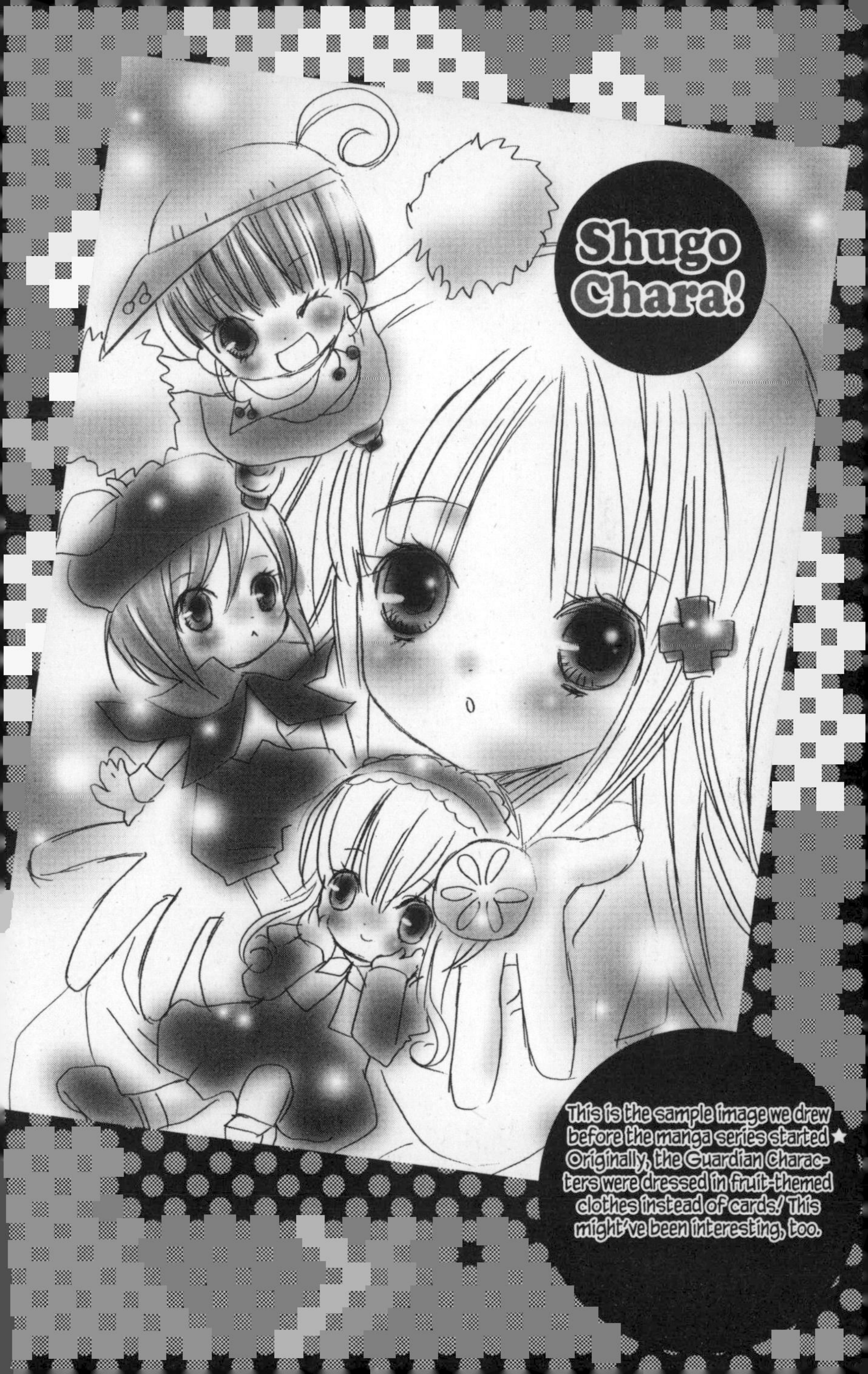
Shugo Chara!
This is the sample image we drew before the manga series started★ Originally, the Guardian Characters were dressed in fruit-themed clothes instead of cards! This might've been interesting, too.

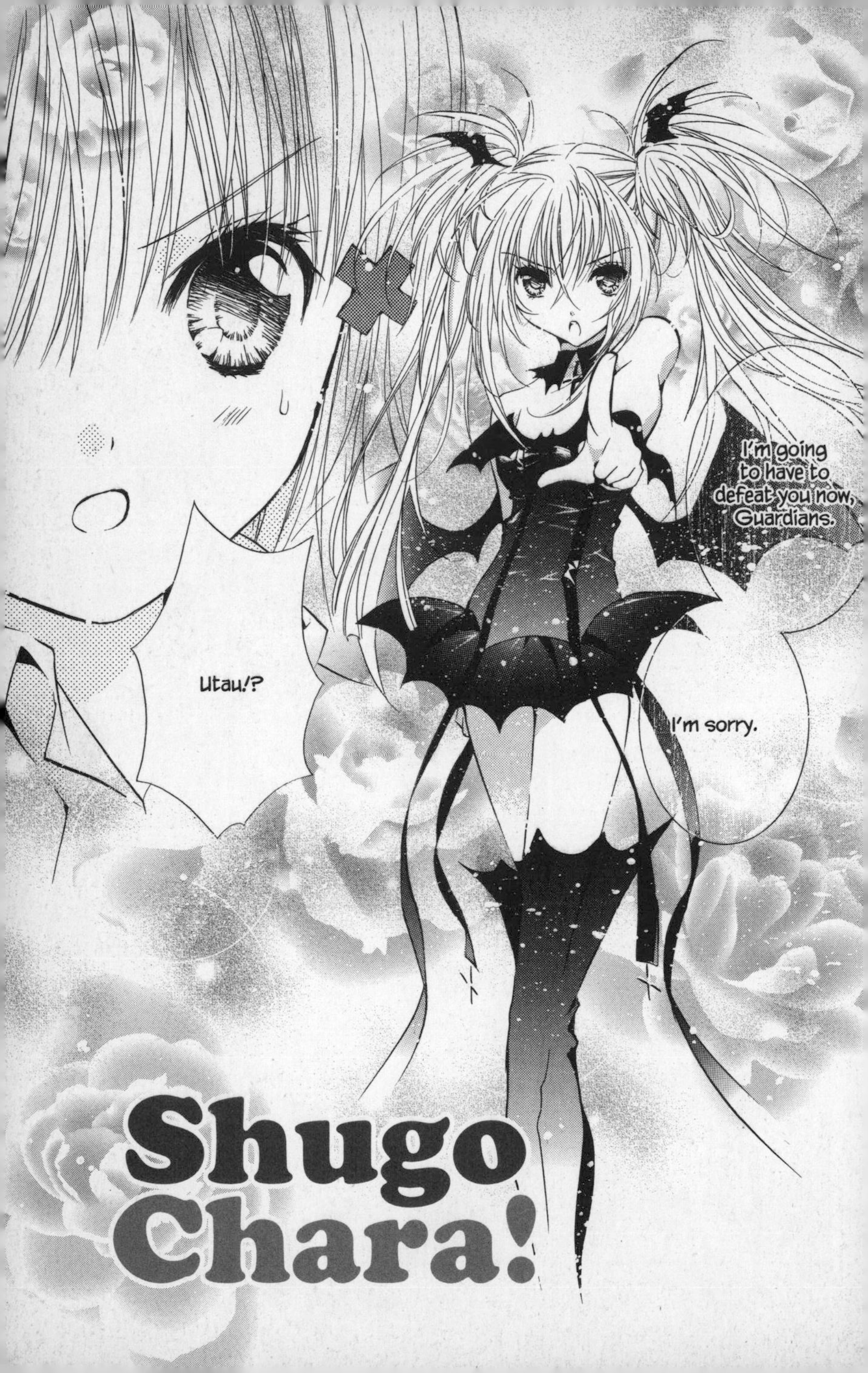
I'm going to have to defeat you now, Guardians.
Utau!?
I'm sorry.
Shugo Chara!

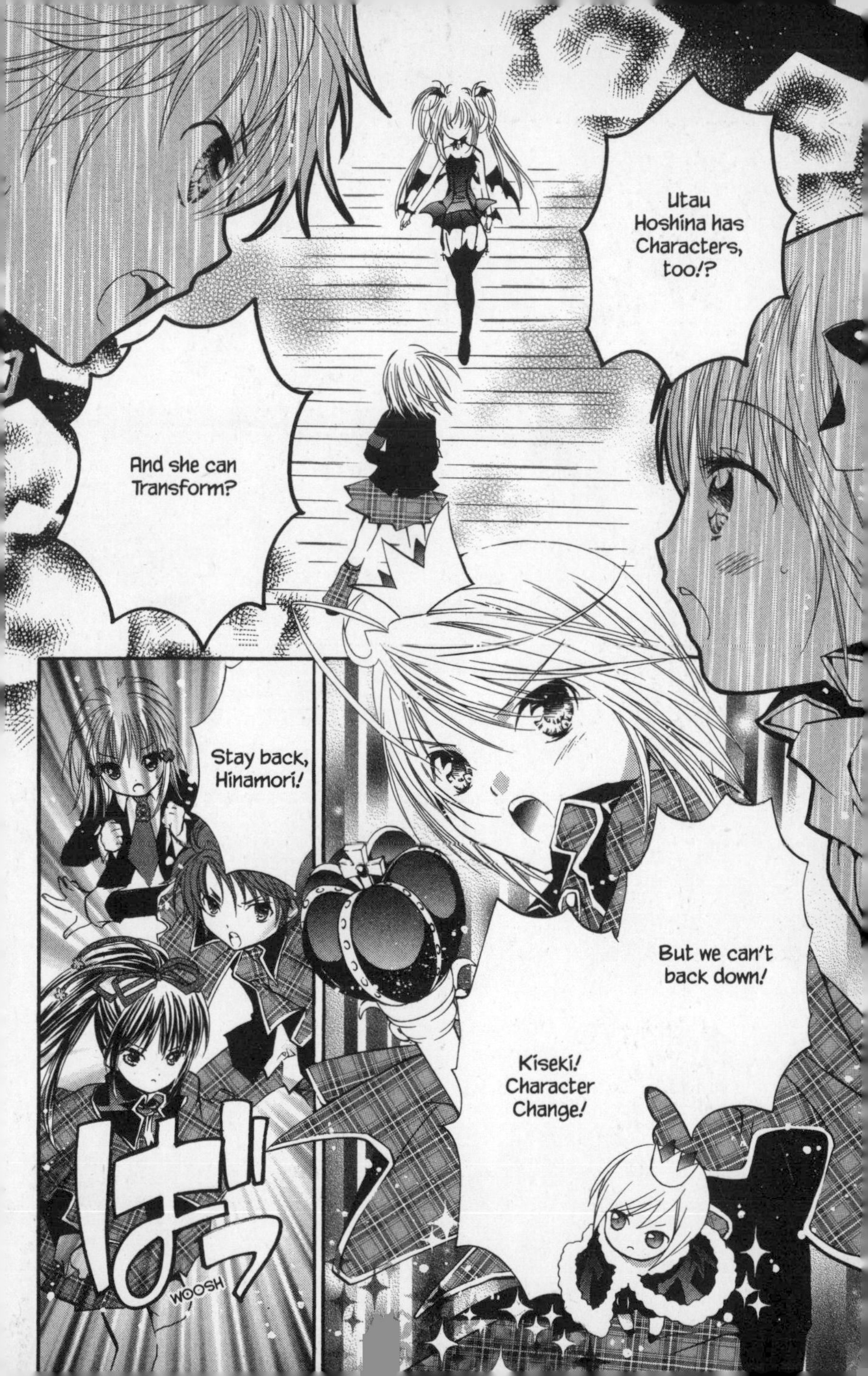
Utau Hoshina has Characters, too!?
And she can Transform?
But we can't back down!
Kiseki! Character Change!
Stay back, Hinamori!
WOOSH

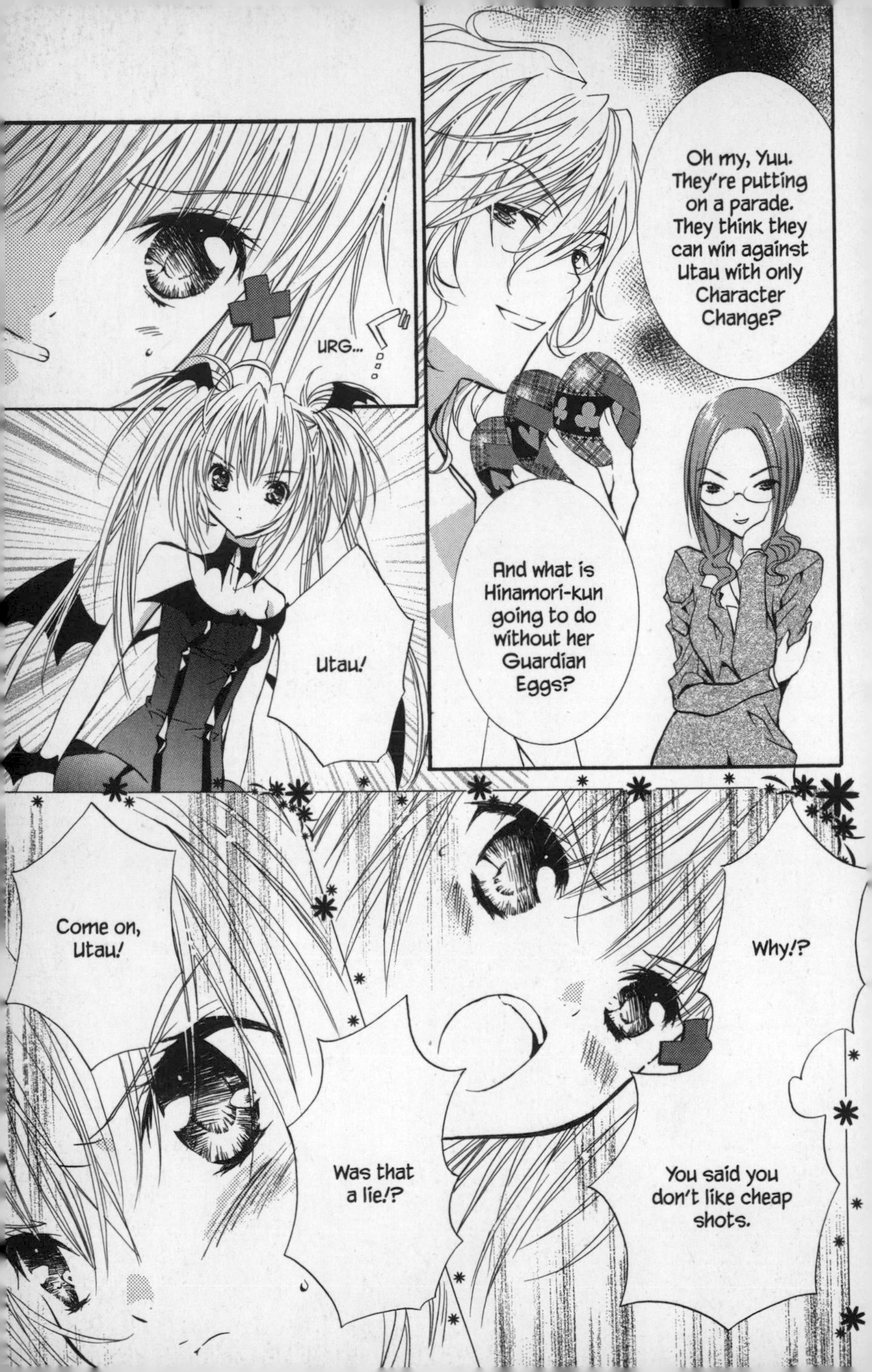
Oh my, Yuu. They're putting on a parade. They think they can win against Utau with only Character Change?
And what is Hinamori-kun going to do without her Guardian Eggs?
URG...
Utau!
Why!?
You said you don't like cheap shots.
Was that a lie!?
Come on, Utau!

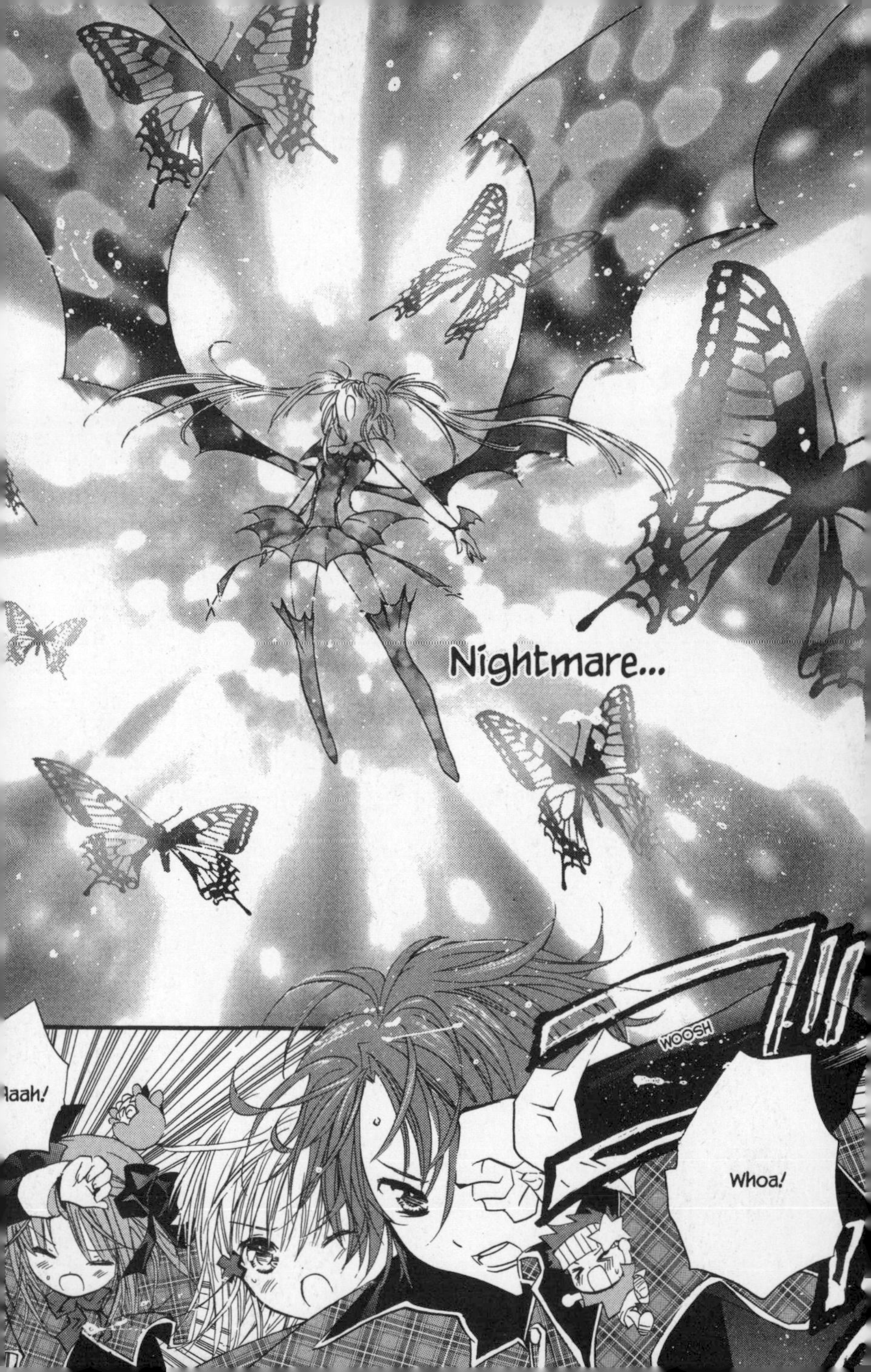
Nightmare...
WOOSH
Whoa!
aah!

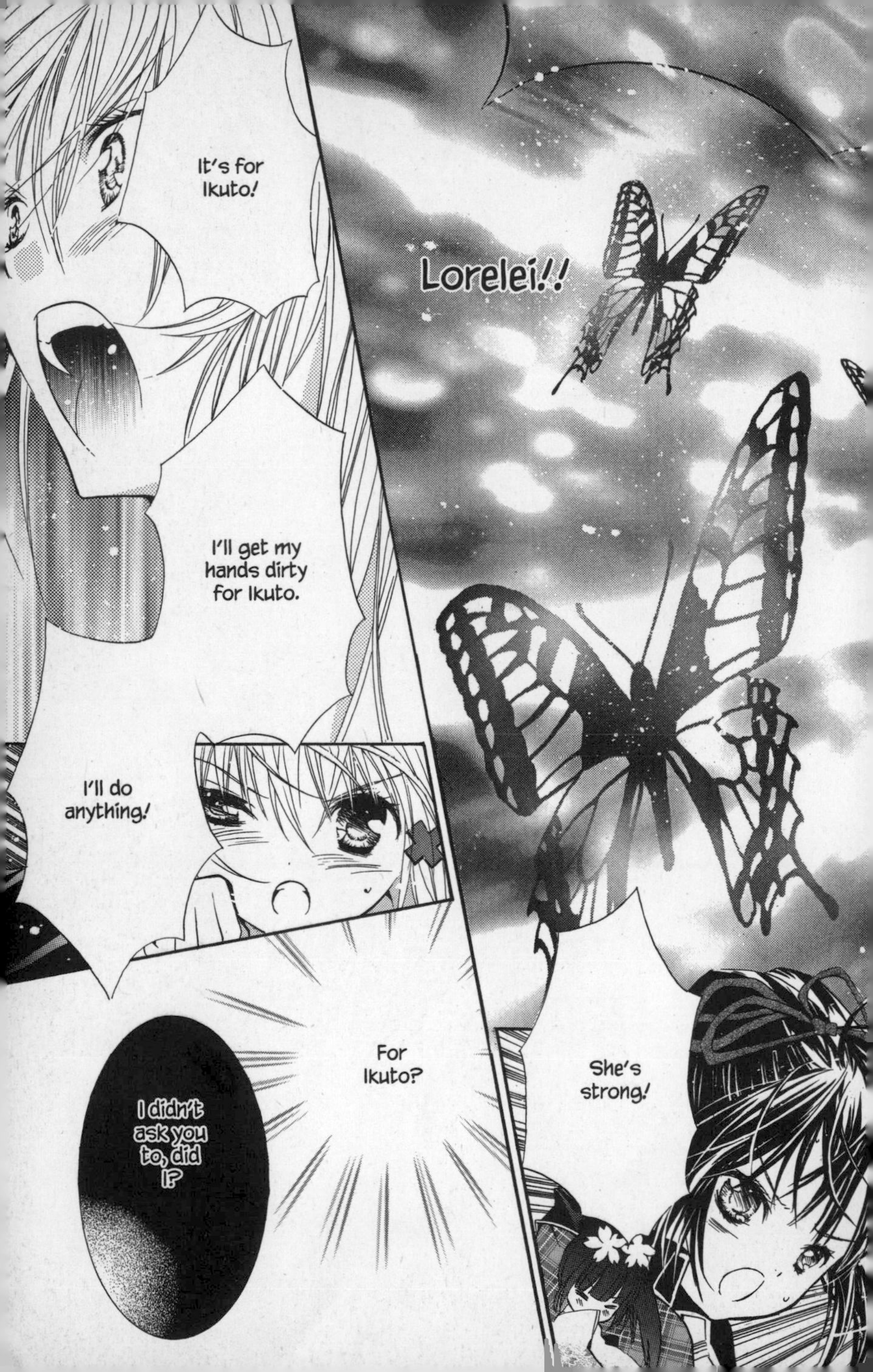
Lorelei!!
It's for Ikuto!
I'll get my hands dirty for Ikuto.
She's strong!
I'll do anything!
For Ikuto?
I didn't ask you to, did I?

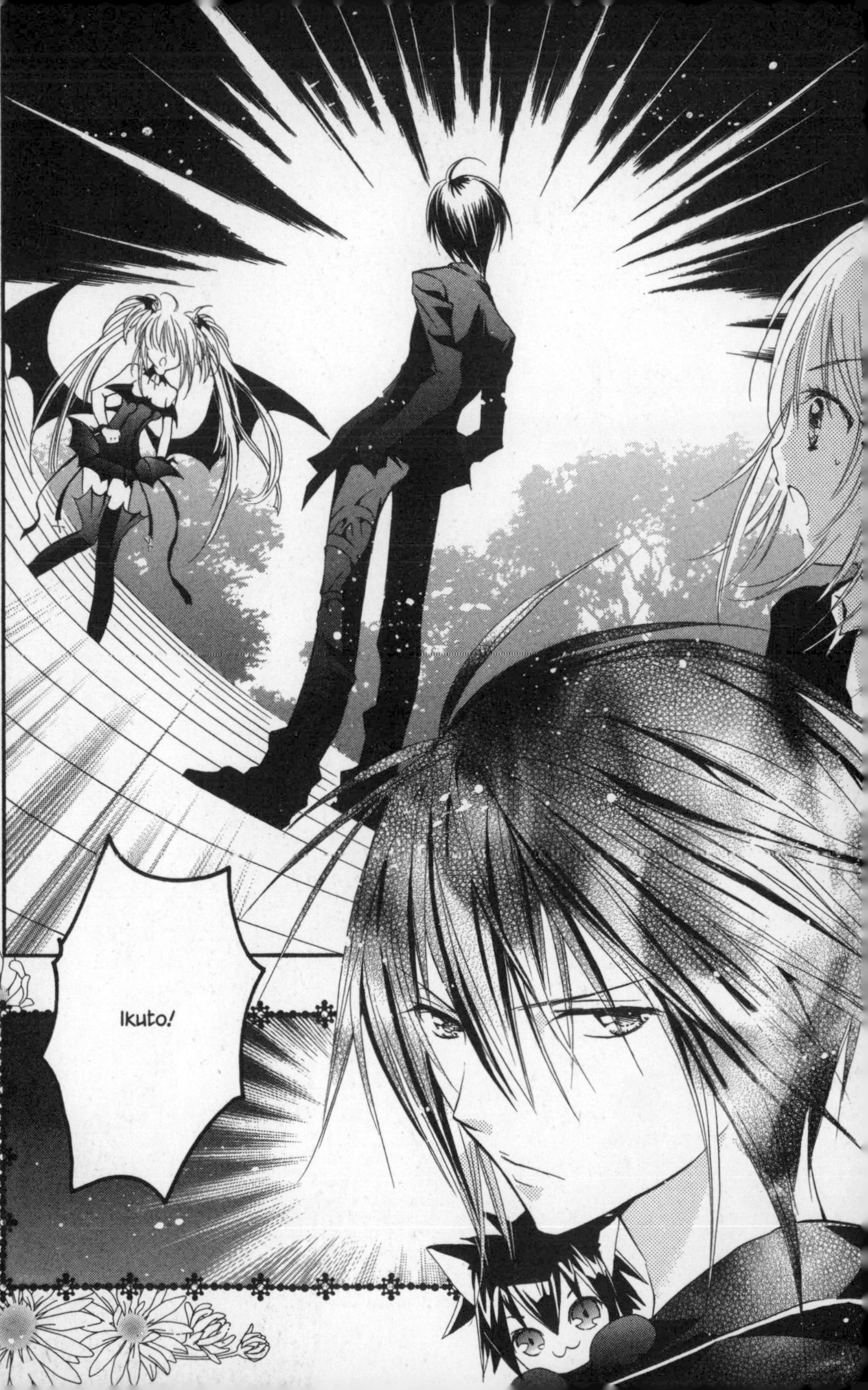
Ikuto!

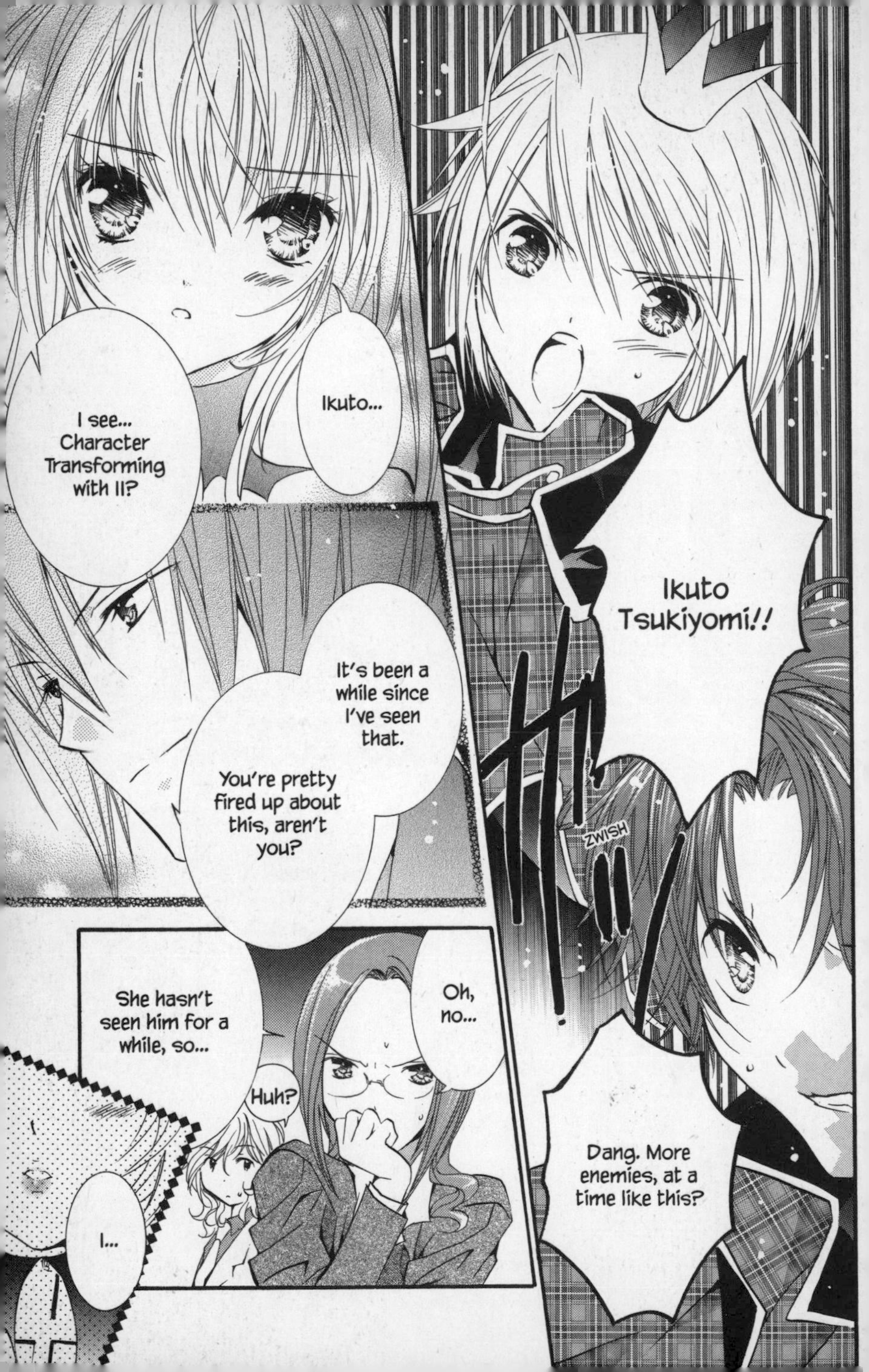
Ikuto Tsukiyomi!!
ZWISH
Ikuto...
I see... Character Transforming with II?
It's been a while since I've seen that.
You're pretty fired up about this, aren't you?
Dang. More enemies, at a time like this?
Oh, no...
She hasn't seen him for a while, so...
Huh?
I...

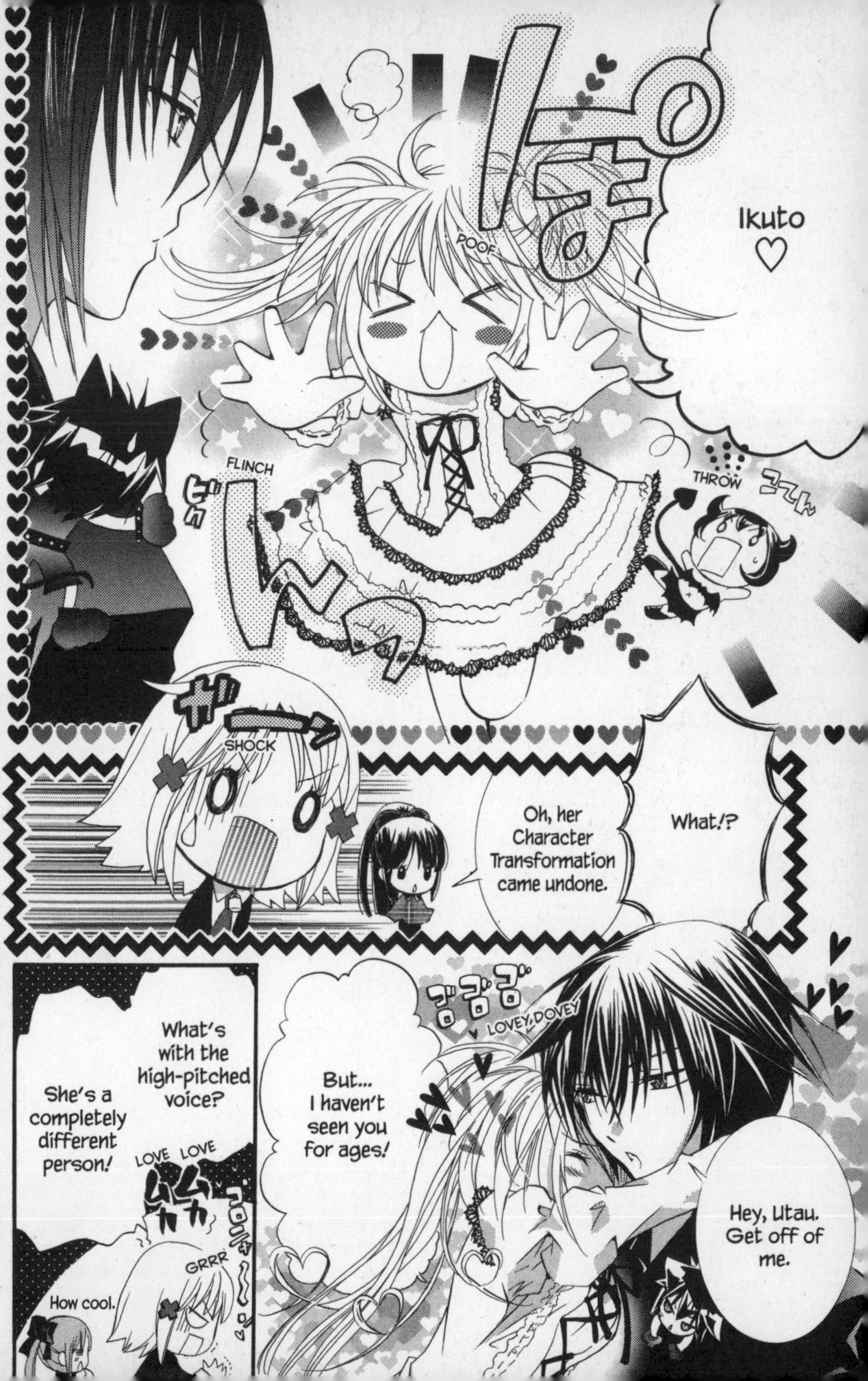
Ikuto ♡
POOF
THROW
FLINCH
What!?
Oh, her Character Transformation came undone.
SHOCK
Hey, Utau. Get off of me.
LOVEY DOVEY
But... I haven't seen you for ages!
What's with the high-pitched voice?
She's a completely different person!
LOVE LOVE
GRRR
How cool.

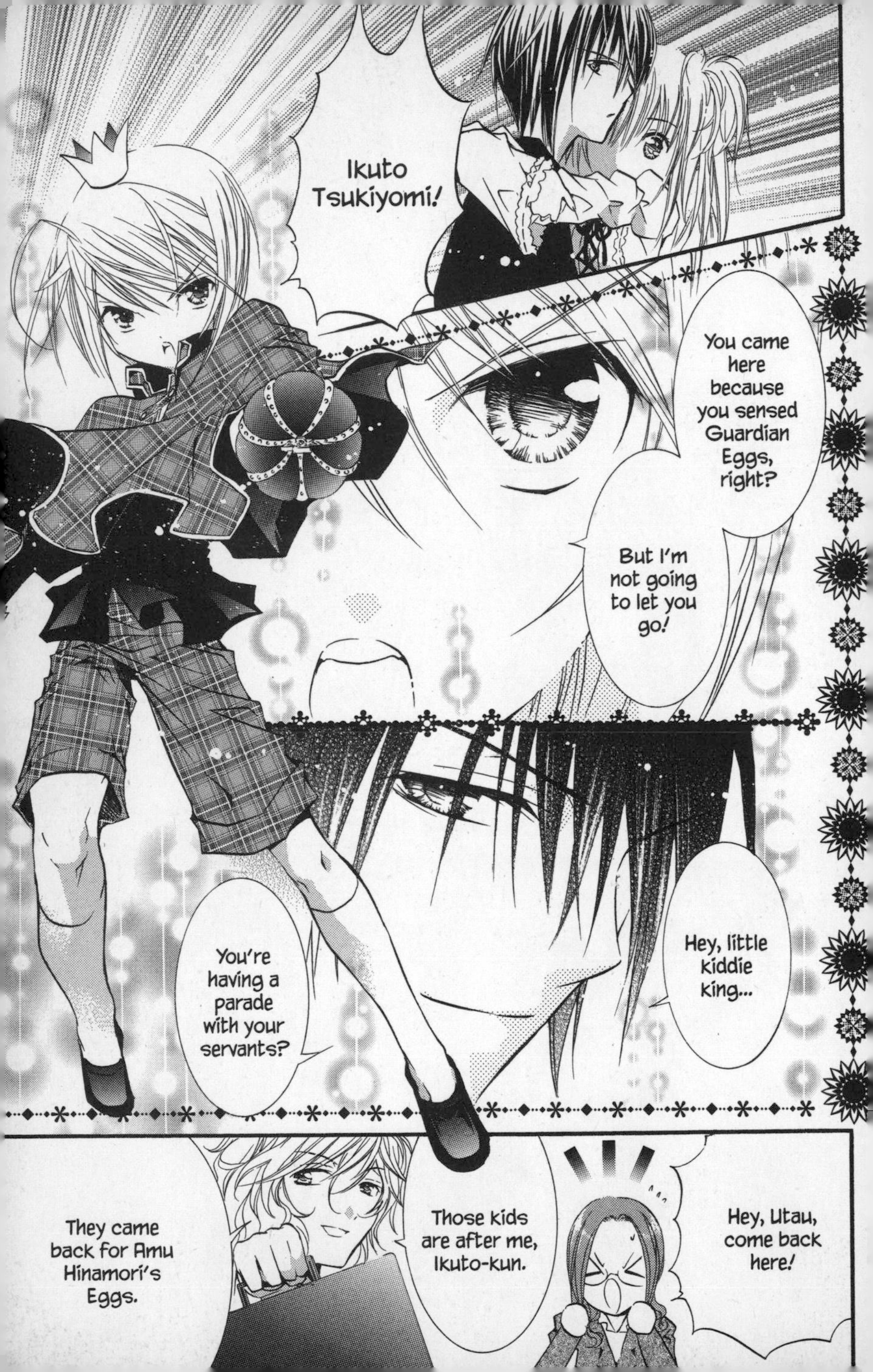
Ikuto Tsukiyomi!
You came here because you sensed Guardian Eggs, right?
But I'm not going to let you go!
Hey, little kiddie king...
You're having a parade with your servants?
Hey, Utau, come back here!
Those kids are after me, Ikuto-kun.
They came back for Amu Hinamori's Eggs.

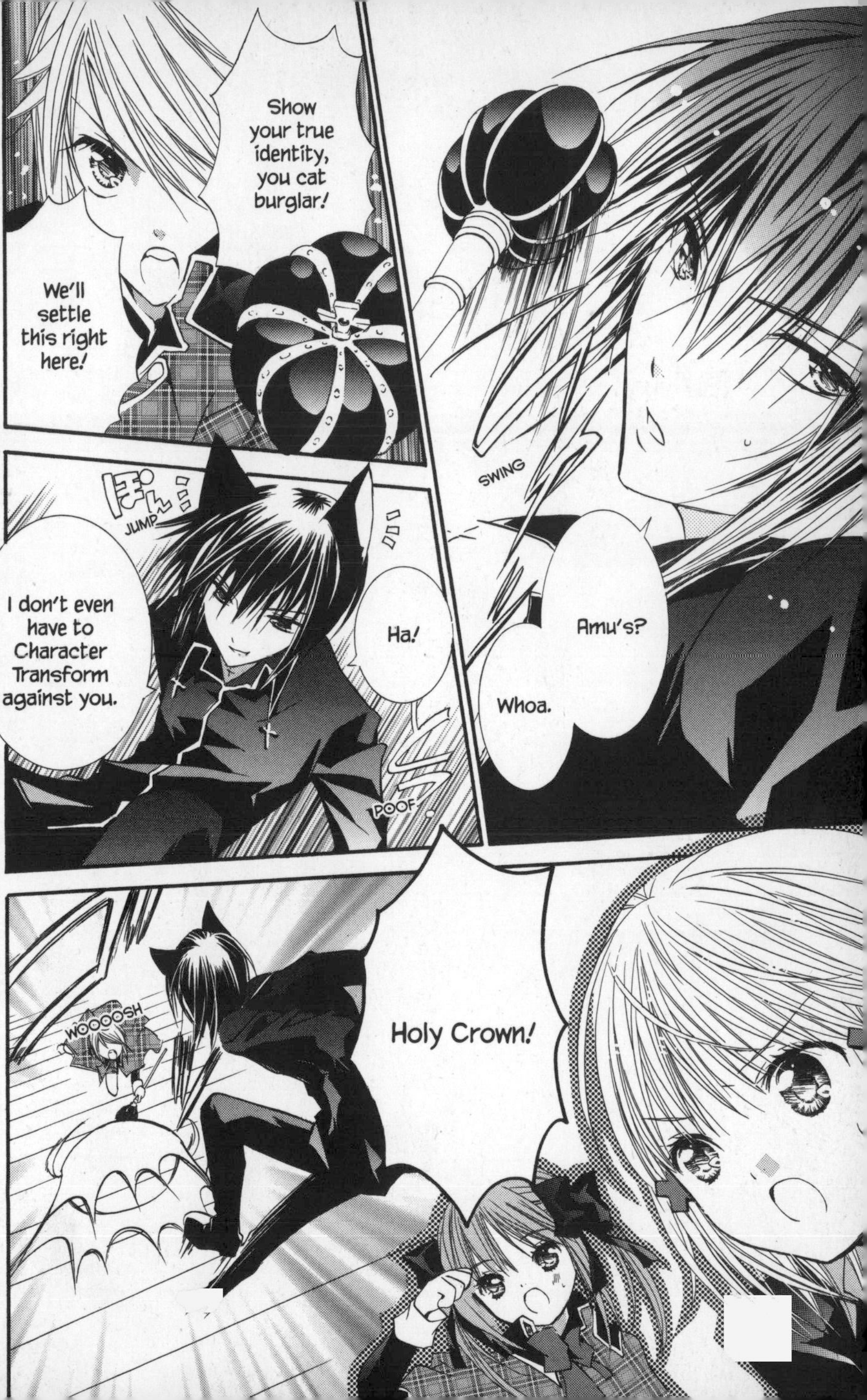
SWING
Amu's?
Whoa.
Show your true identity, you cat burglar!
We'll settle this right here!
JUMP
Ha!
I don't even have to Character Transform against you.
POOF
Holy Crown!
WOOOOSH

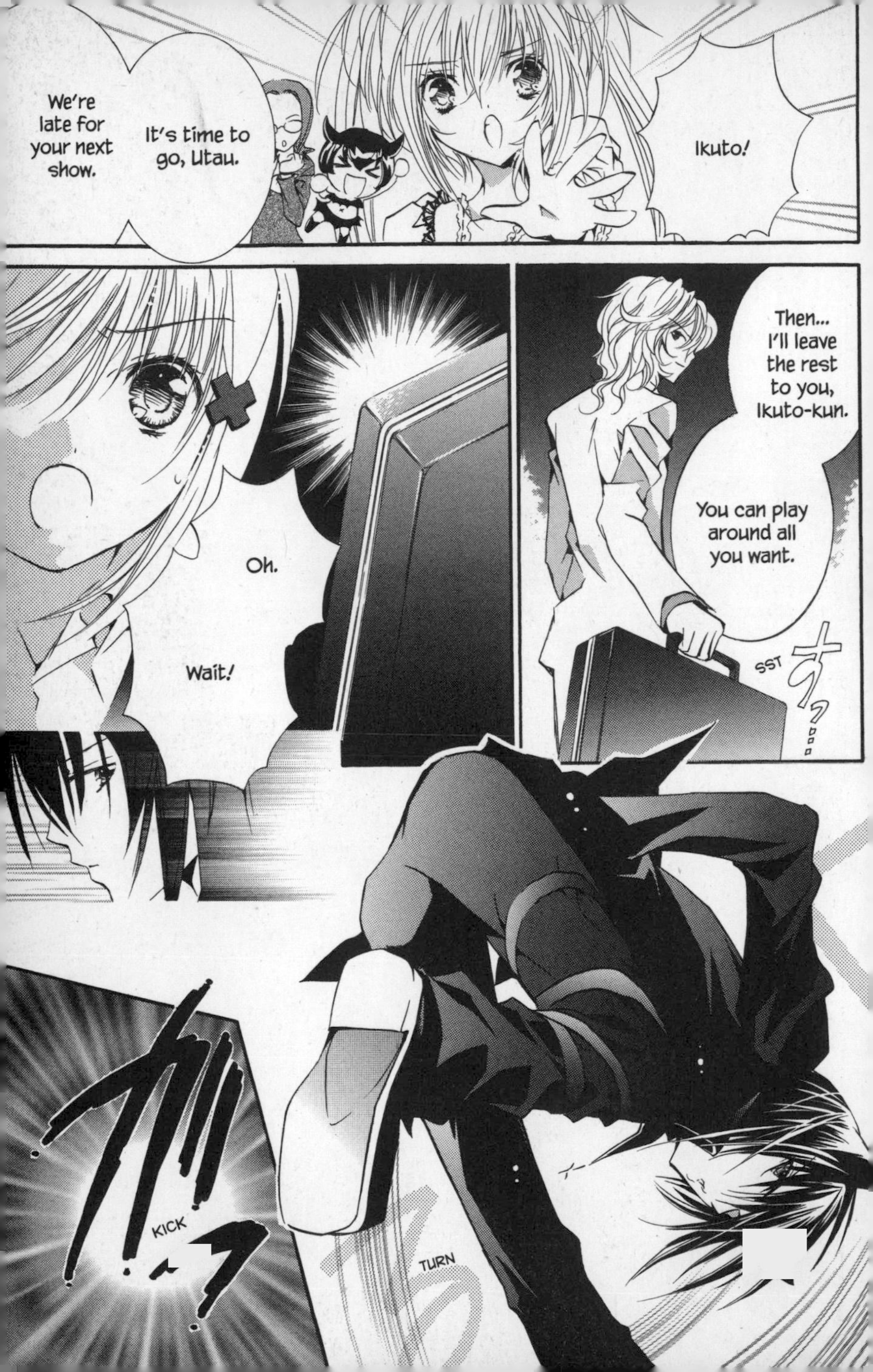
Ikuto!
It's time to go, Utau.
We're late for your next show.
Then... I'll leave the rest to you, Ikuto-kun.
You can play around all you want.
SST
Oh.
Wait!
TURN
KICK

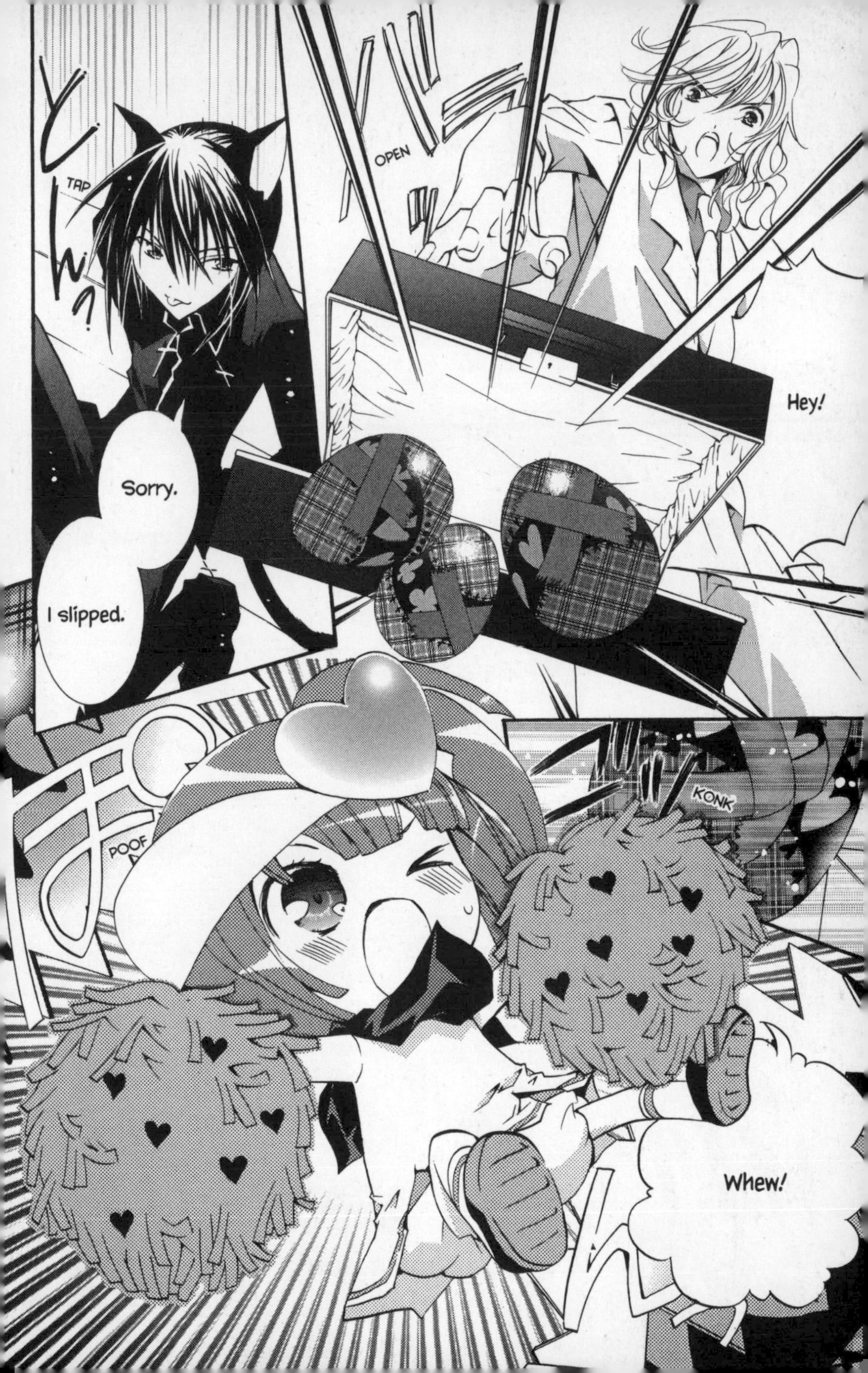

OPEN
Hey!
TAP
Sorry.
I slipped.
KONK
POOF
Whew!

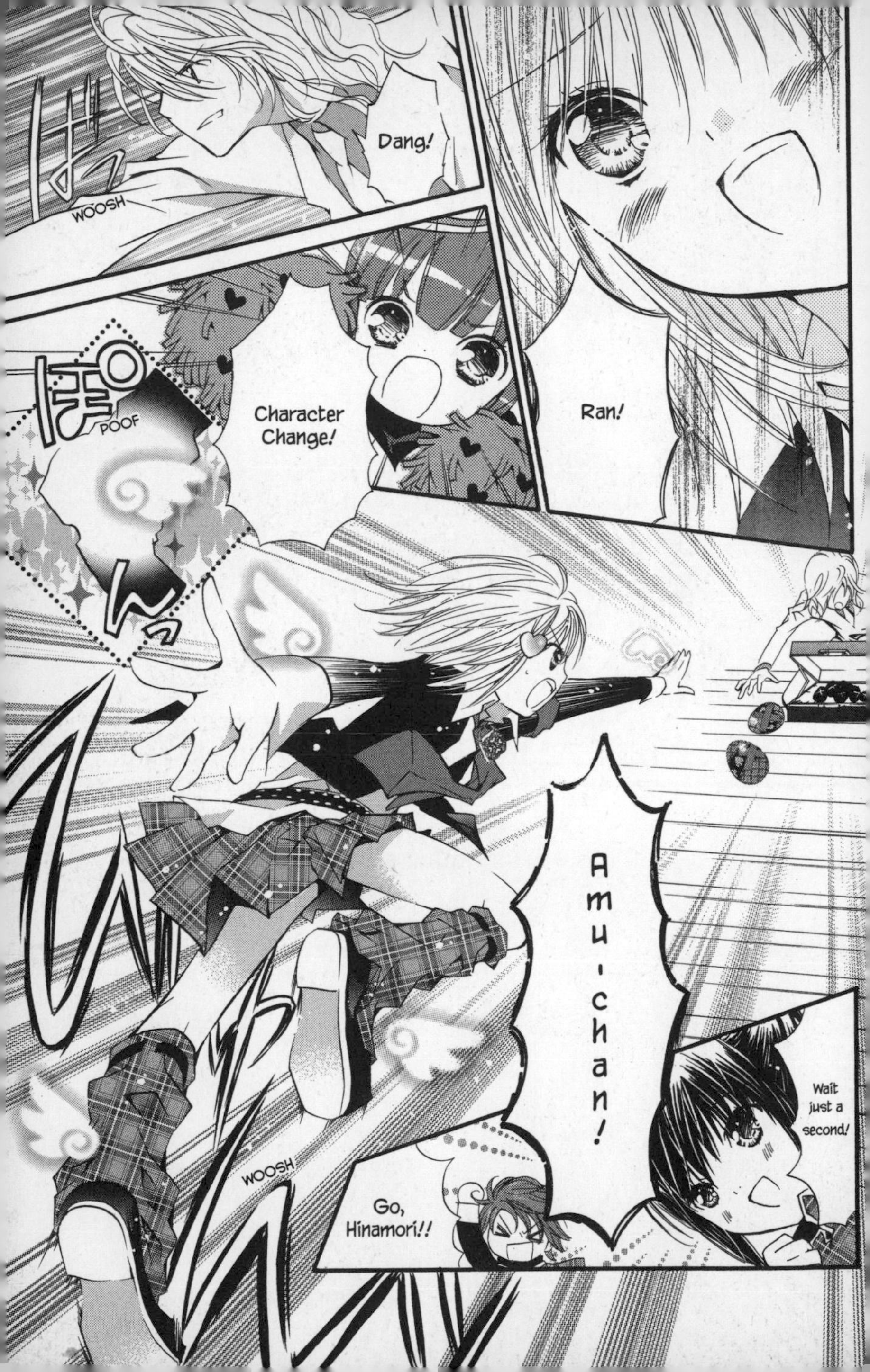

Ran!
Dang!
WOOSH
Character Change!
POOF
Amu-chan!
Wait just a second!
Go, Hinamori!!
WOOSH

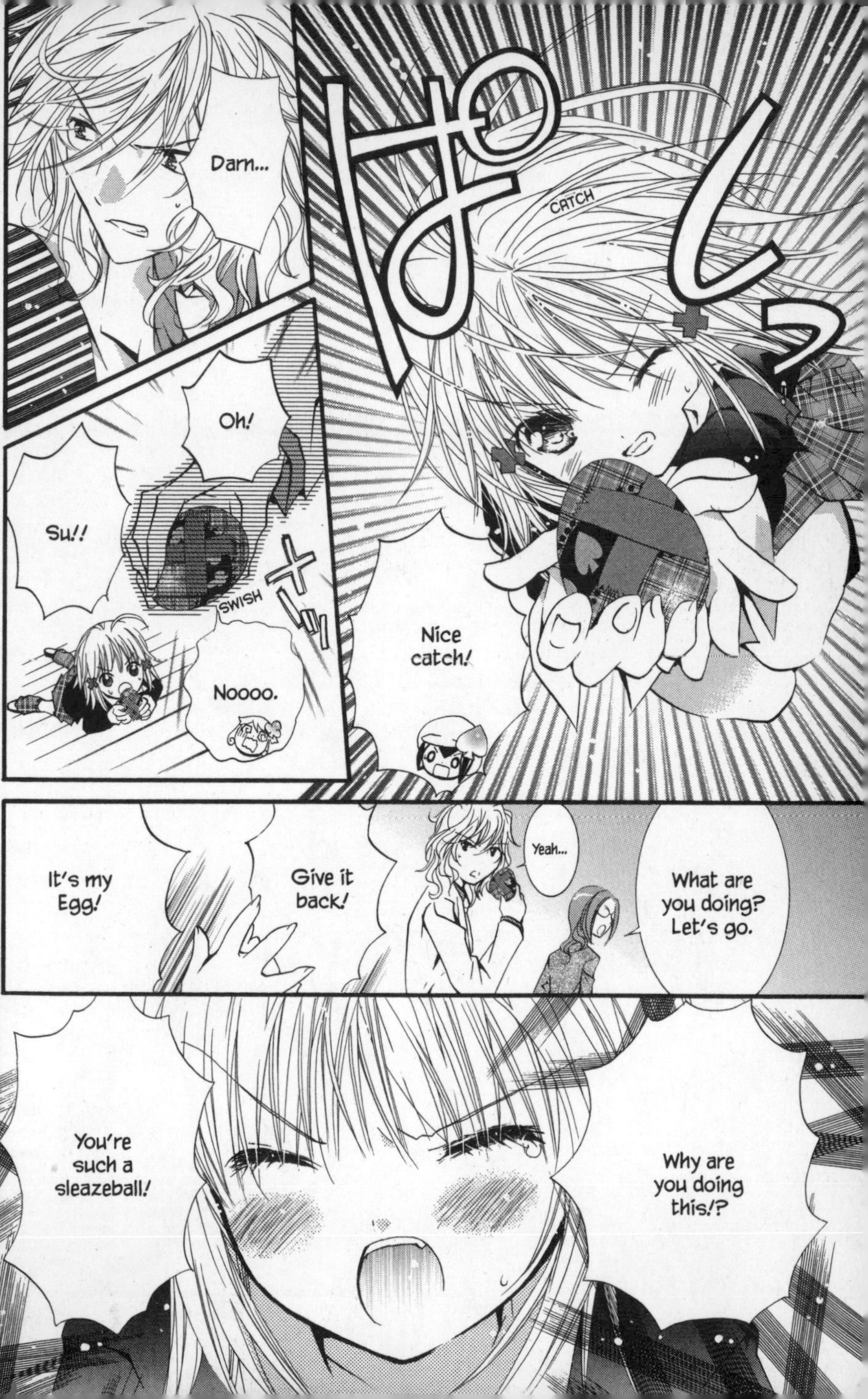
ぱしっ
CATCH
Nice catch!
Darn...
Oh!
Su!!
SWISH
Noooo.
What are you doing? Let's go.
Yeah...
Give it back!
It's my Egg!
Why are you doing this!?
You're such a sleazeball!

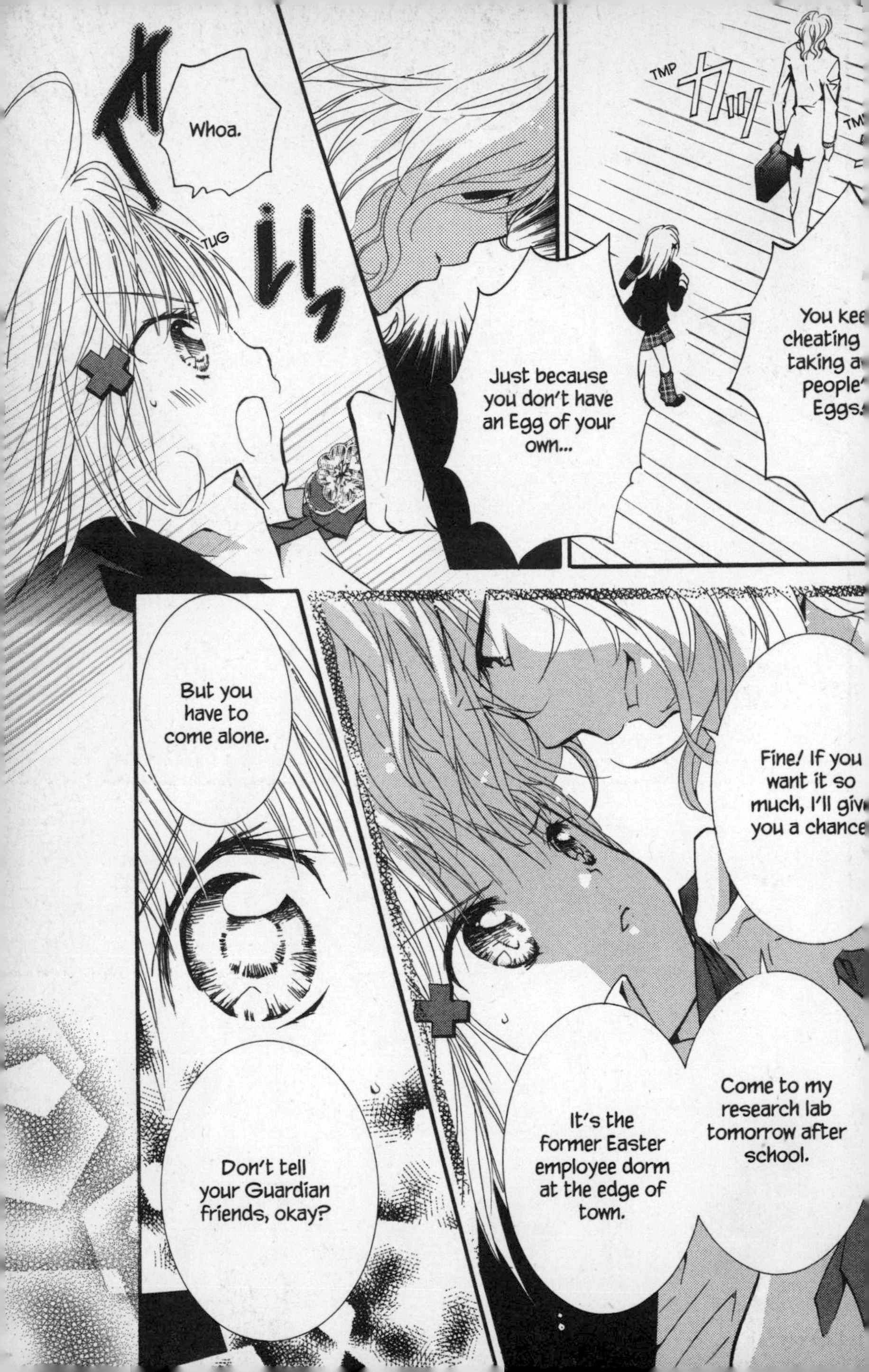
TMP
カッ
TM
You kee cheating taking a people' Eggs.
Just because you don't have an Egg of your own...
Whoa.
TUG
Fine! If you want it so much, I'll giv you a chance
Come to my research lab tomorrow after school.
It's the former Easter employee dorm at the edge of town.
But you have to come alone.
Don't tell your Guardian friends, okay?

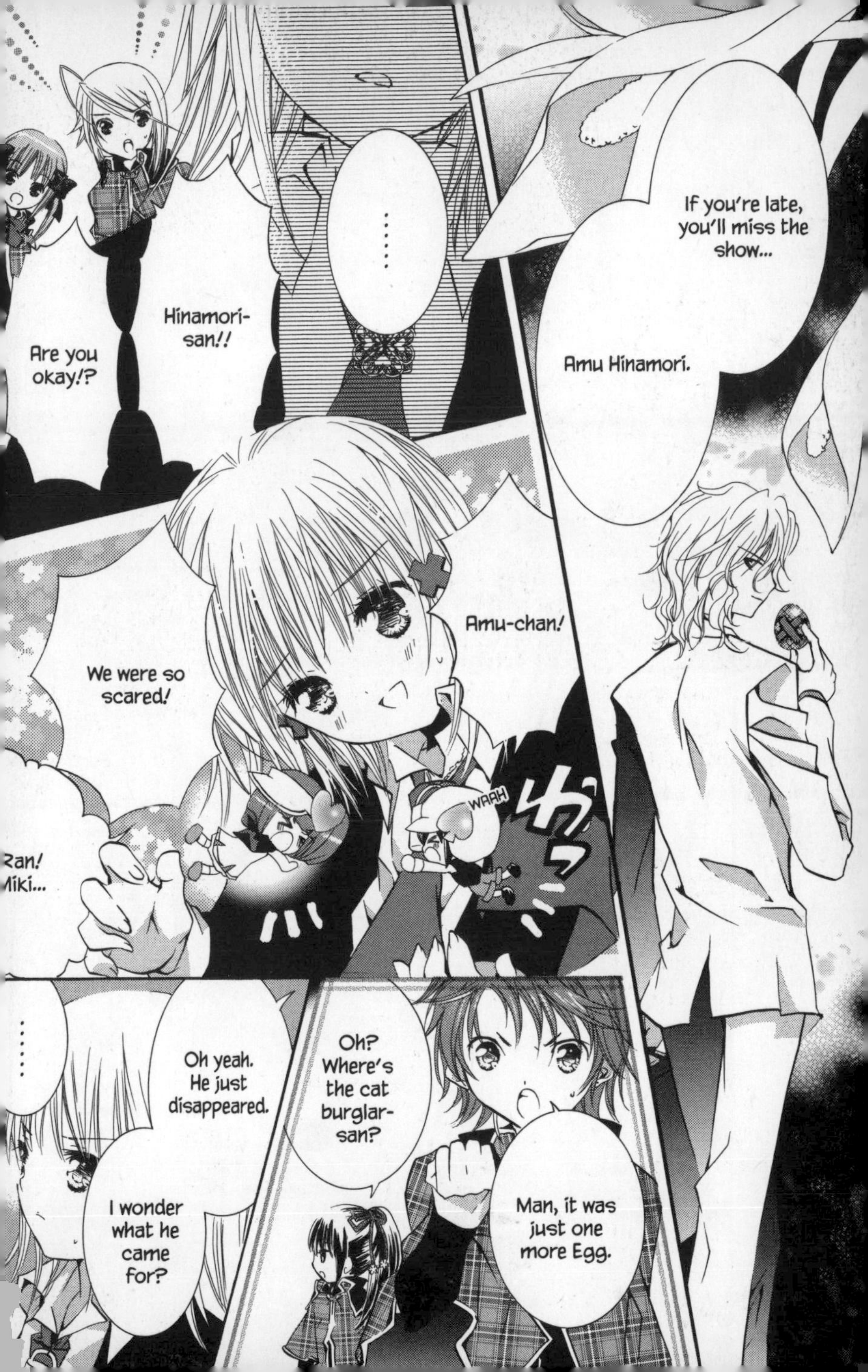

If you're late, you'll miss the show...
Amu Hinamori.
......
Hinamori-san!!
Are you okay!?
Amu-chan!
We were so scared!
WAAH
Ran! Miki...
Oh? Where's the cat burglar-san?
Man, it was just one more Egg.
Oh yeah. He just disappeared.
I wonder what he came for?
......

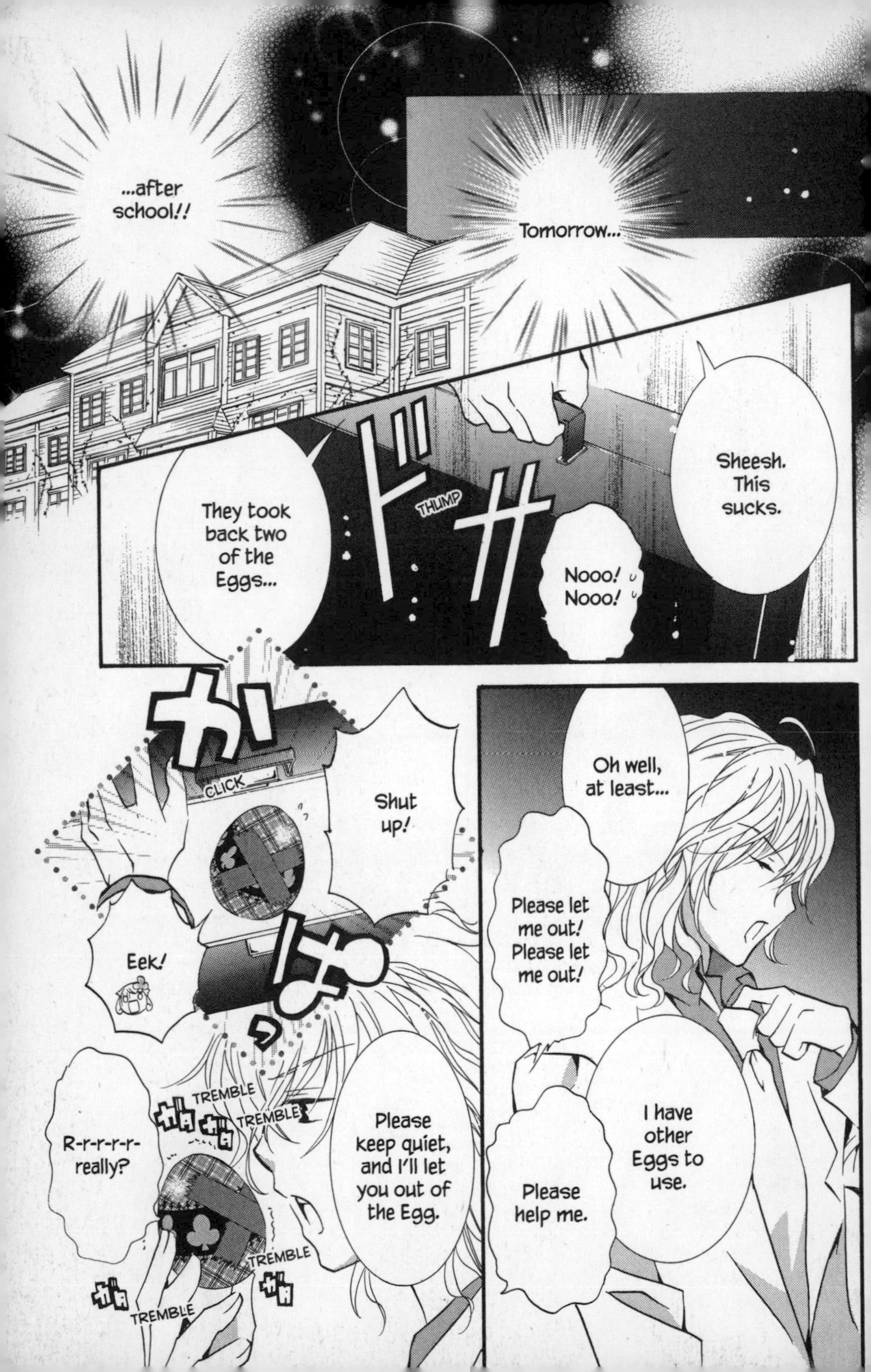
Tomorrow...
...after school!!
Sheesh. This sucks.
Nooo! Nooo!
ドサ
THUMP
They took back two of the Eggs...
Oh well, at least...
Please let me out! Please let me out!
I have other Eggs to use.
Please help me.
Shut up!
CLICK
Eek!
Please keep quiet, and I'll let you out of the Egg.
TREMBLE
TREMBLE
R-r-r-r-really?
TREMBLE
TREMBLE

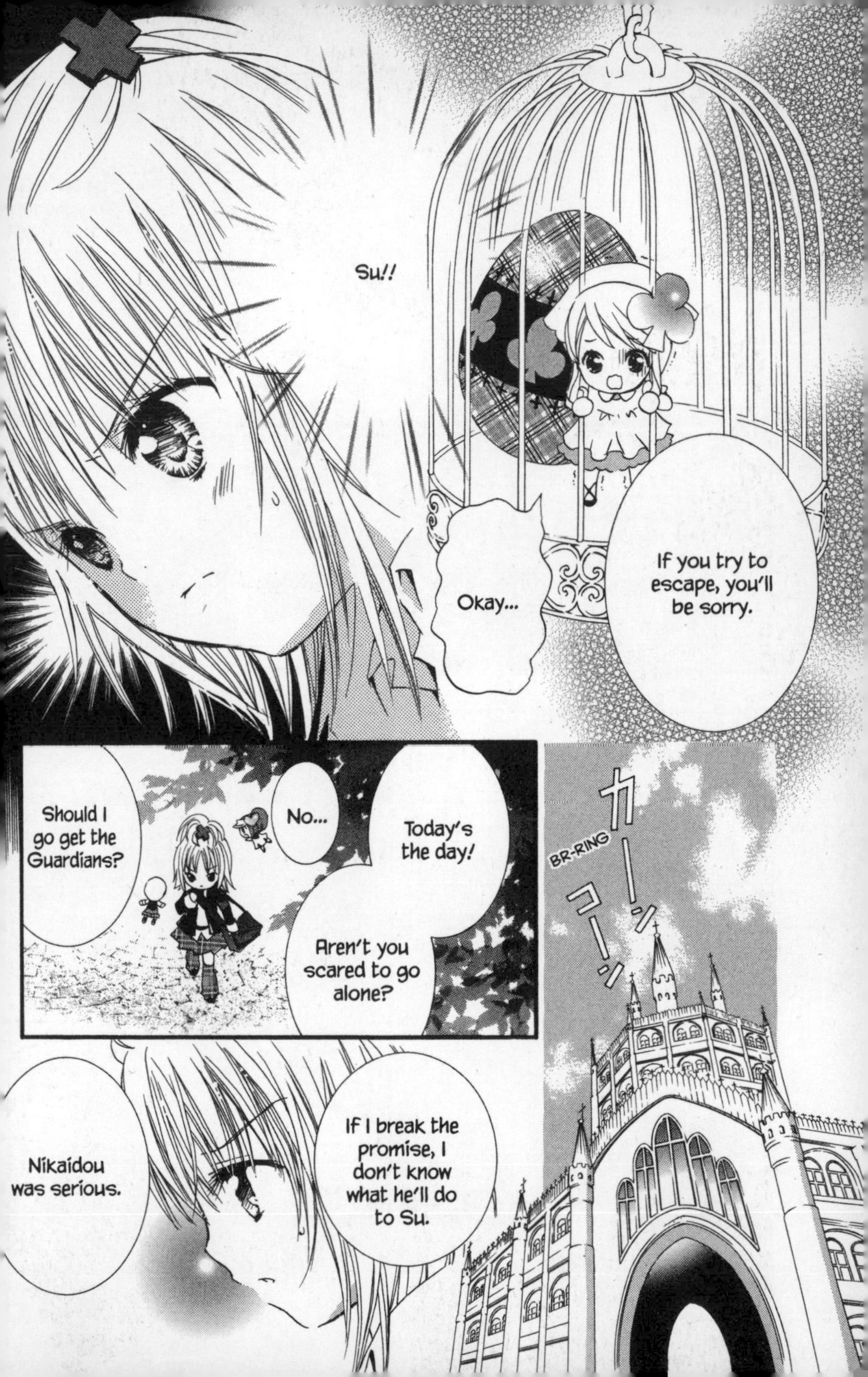
If you try to
escape, you'll
be sorry.
Okay...
Su!!
BR-RING
カーン
コーン
Today's
the day!
No...
Should I
go get the
Guardians?
Aren't you
scared to go
alone?
If I break the
promise, I
don't know
what he'll do
to Su.
Nikaidou
was serious.

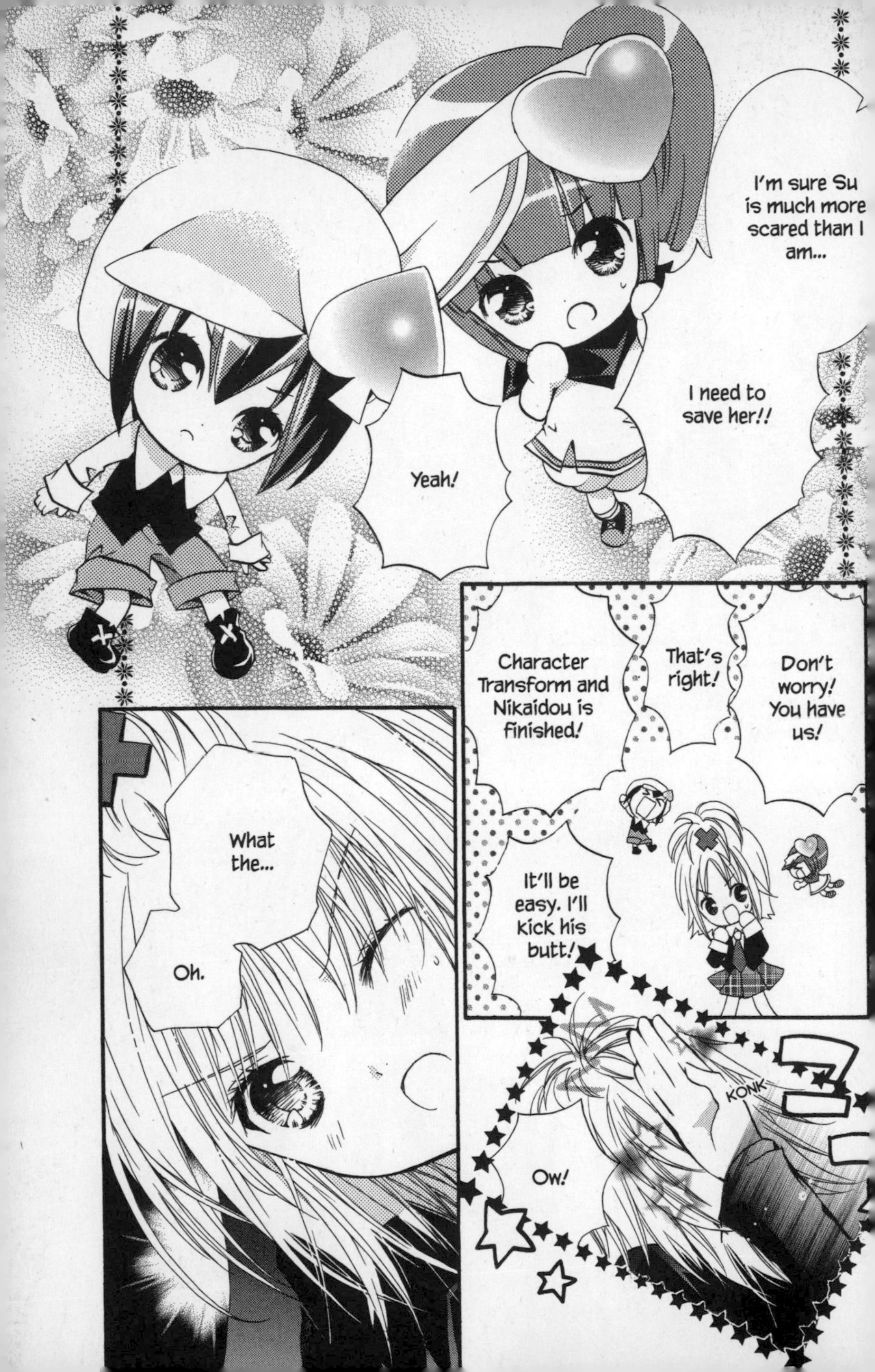
I'm sure Su is much more scared than I am...
I need to save her!!
Yeah!
Don't worry! You have us!
That's right!
Character Transform and Nikaidou is finished!
It'll be easy. I'll kick his butt!
KONK
Ow!
What the...
Oh.

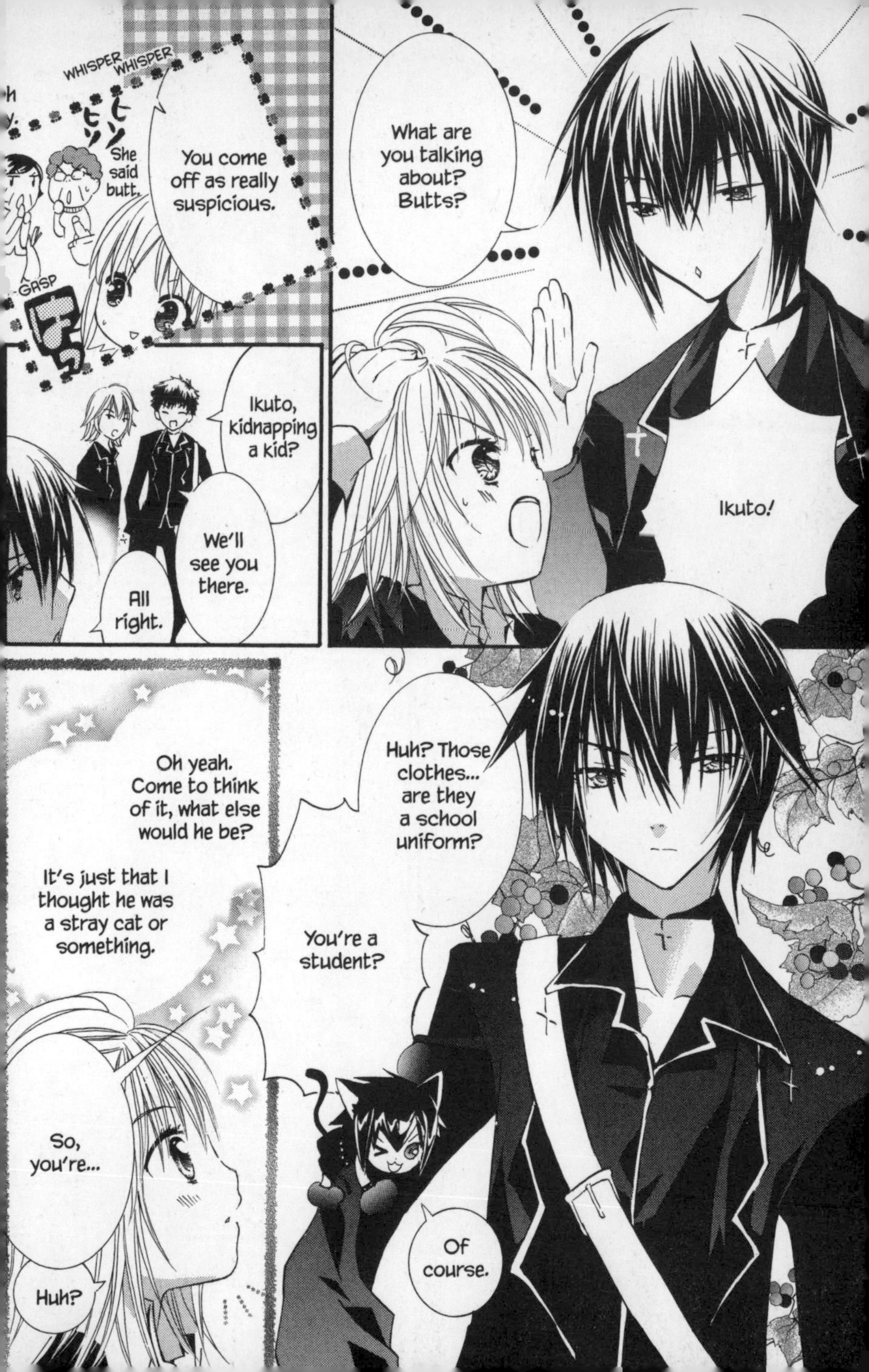
What are you talking about? Butts?
Ikuto!
You come off as really suspicious.
WHISPER WHISPER
She said butt.
GASP
Ikuto, kidnapping a kid?
We'll see you there.
All right.
Huh? Those clothes... are they a school uniform?
You're a student?
Of course.
Oh yeah. Come to think of it, what else would he be?
It's just that I thought he was a stray cat or something.
So, you're...
Huh?

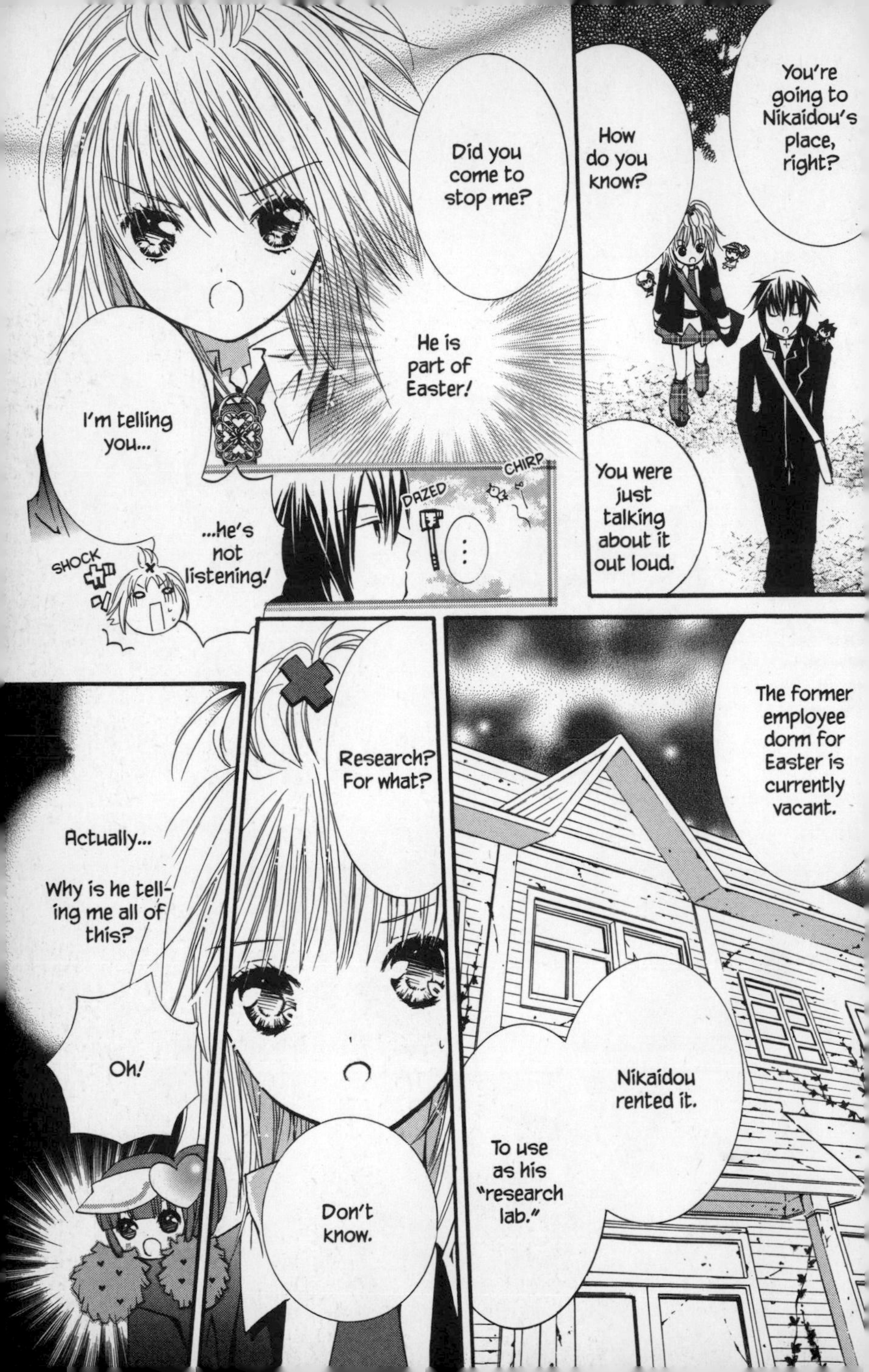
You're going to Nikaidou's place, right?
How do you know?
You were just talking about it out loud.
Did you come to stop me?
He is part of Easter!
I'm telling you...
CHIRP
DAZED
...
...he's not listening!
SHOCK
The former employee dorm for Easter is currently vacant.
Nikaidou rented it.
To use as his "research lab."
Research? For what?
Don't know.
Actually...
Why is he telling me all of this?
Oh!

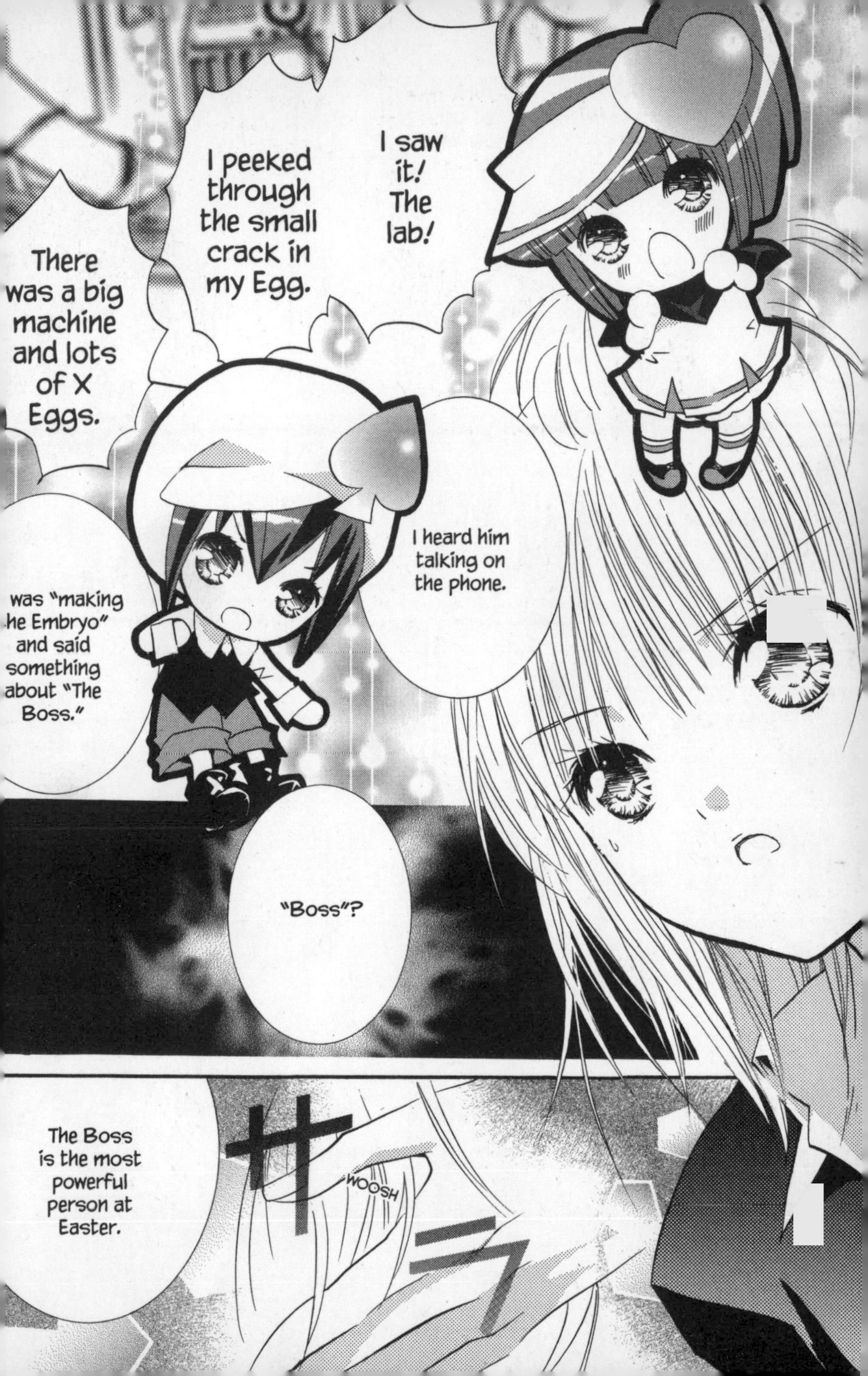
I saw it! The lab!
I peeked through the small crack in my Egg.
There was a big machine and lots of X Eggs.
I heard him talking on the phone.
was "making he Embryo" and said something about "The Boss."
"Boss"?
WOOSH
The Boss is the most powerful person at Easter.

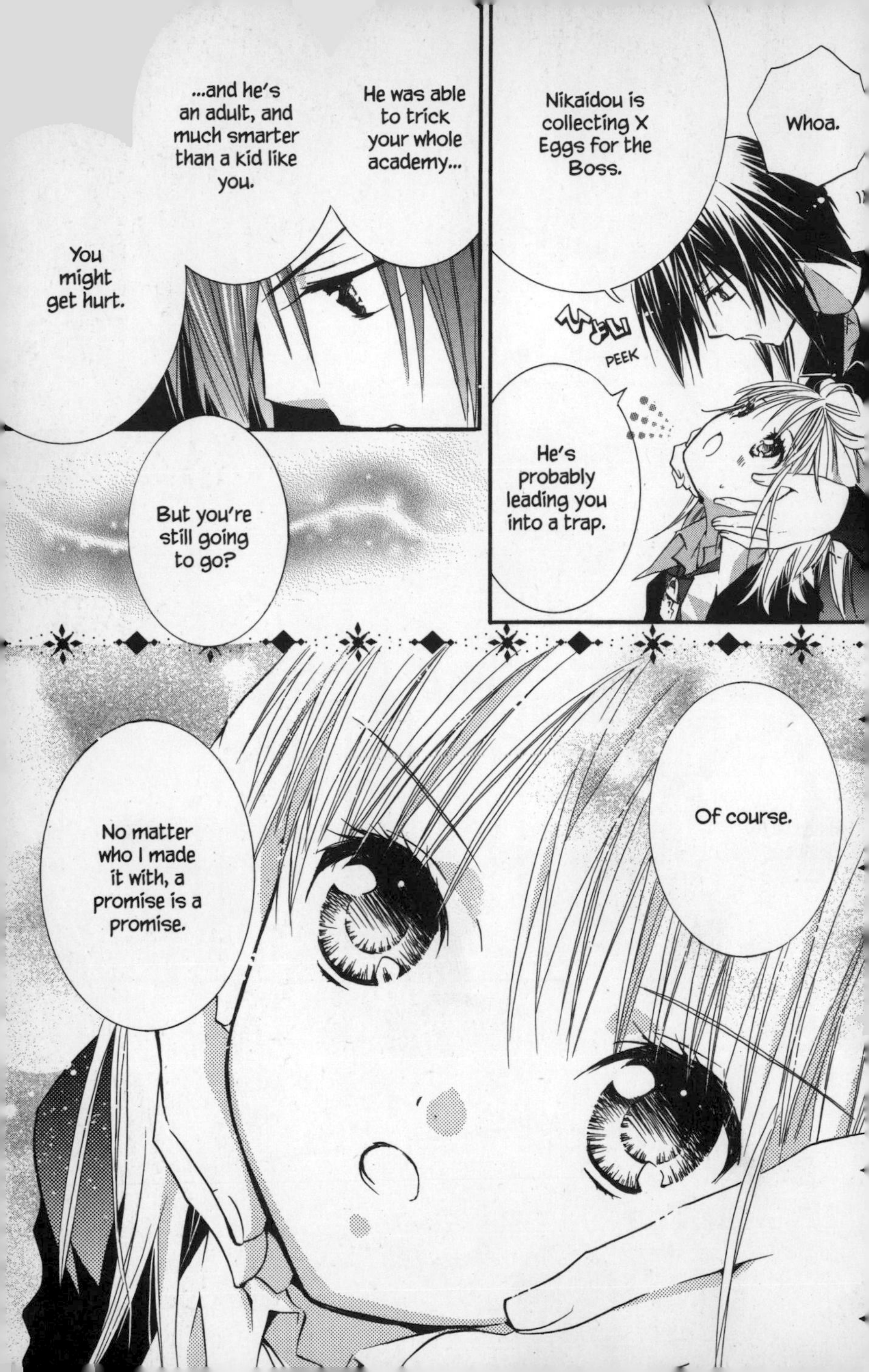
Whoa.
Nikaidou is collecting X Eggs for the Boss.
PEEK
He's probably leading you into a trap.
He was able to trick your whole academy...
...and he's an adult, and much smarter than a kid like you.
You might get hurt.
But you're still going to go?
Of course.
No matter who I made it with, a promise is a promise.

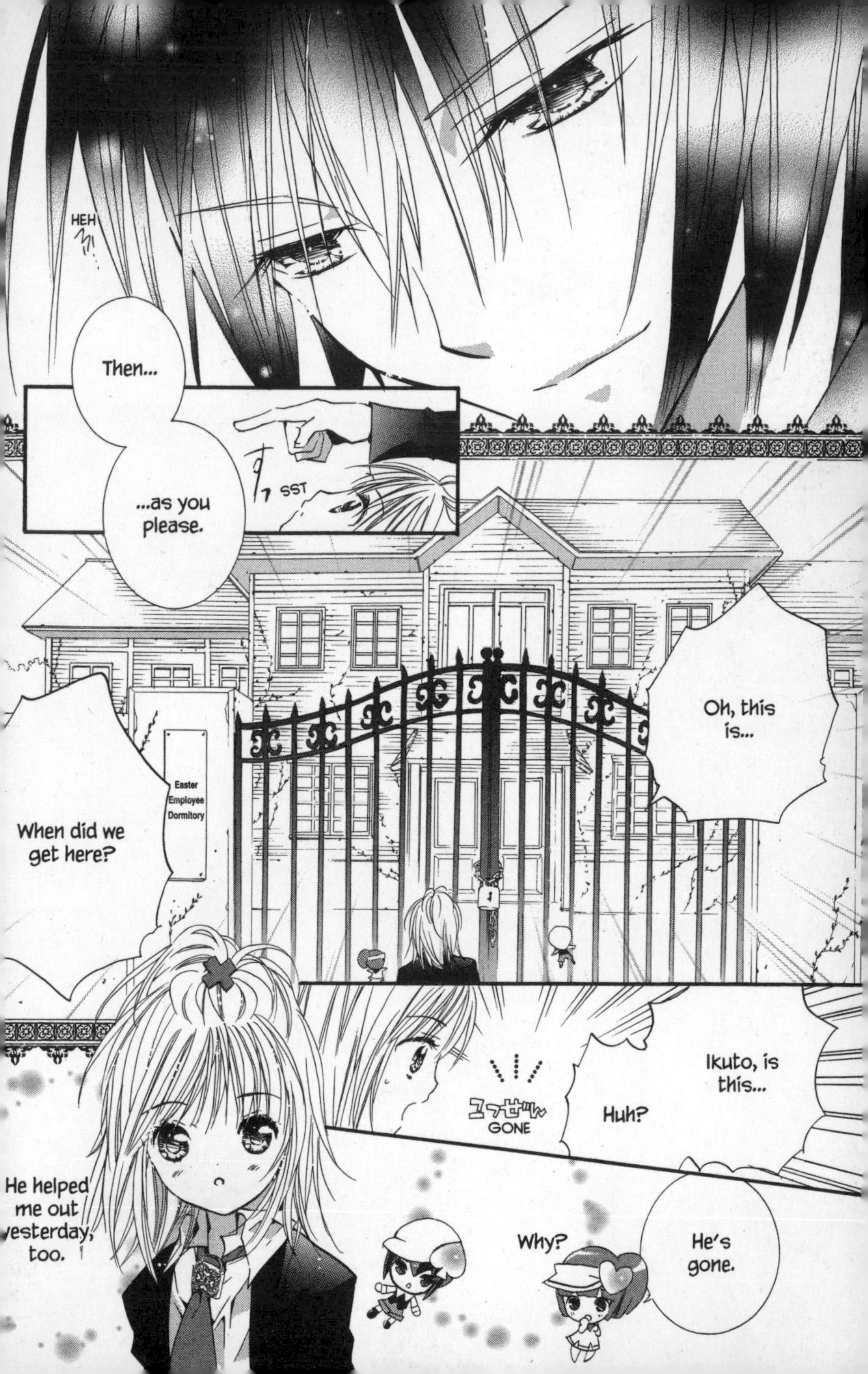
HEH
Then...
SST
...as you please.
Oh, this is...
Easter Employee Dormitory
When did we get here?
Ikuto, is this...
Huh?
GONE
He's gone.
Why?
He helped me out yesterday, too.

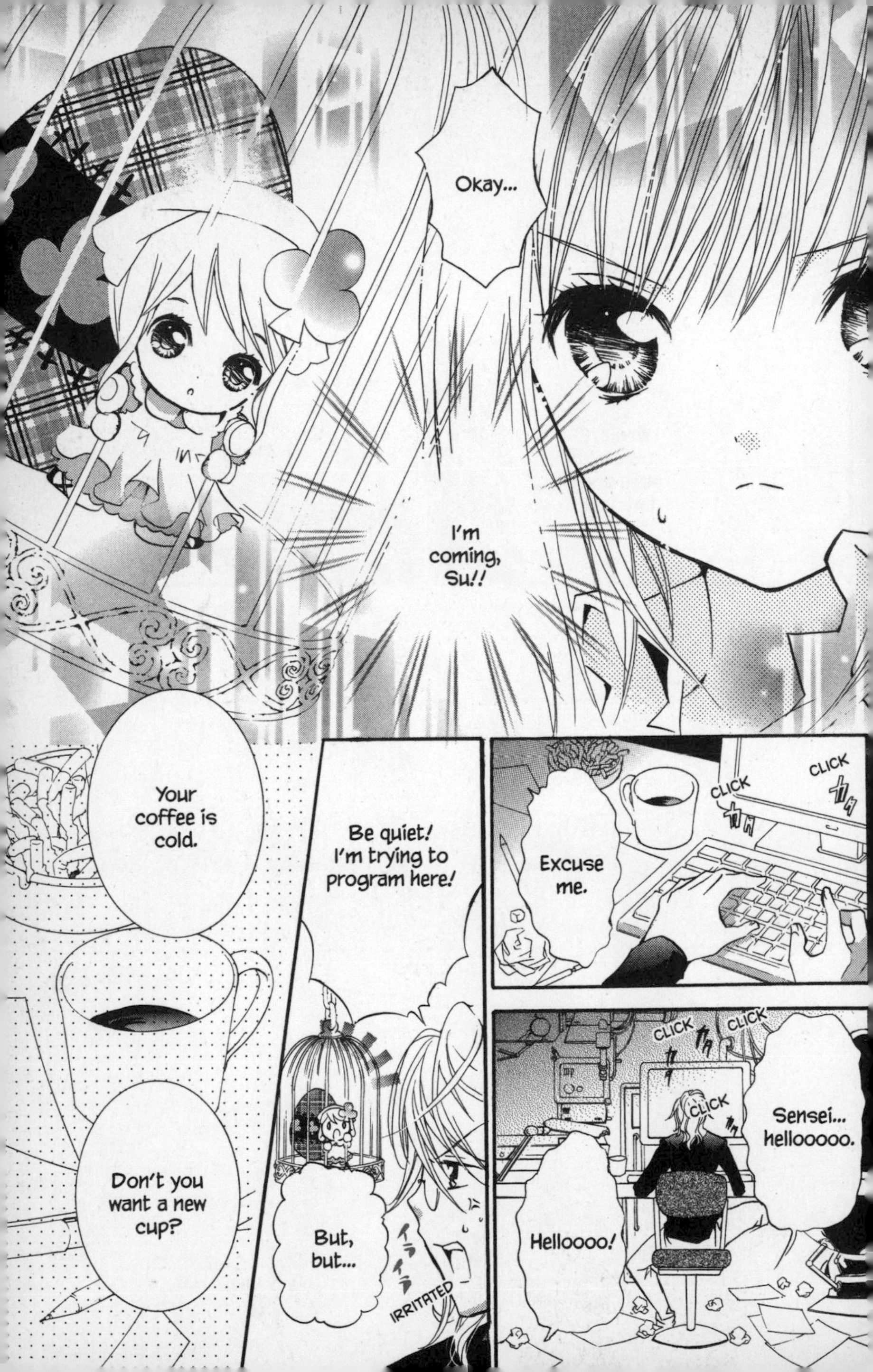
Okay...
I'm coming, Su!!
CLICK
CLICK
Excuse me.
CLICK
CLICK
Sensei... hellooooo.
CLICK
Helloooo!
Be quiet! I'm trying to program here!
But, but...
IRRITATED
Your coffee is cold.
Don't you want a new cup?

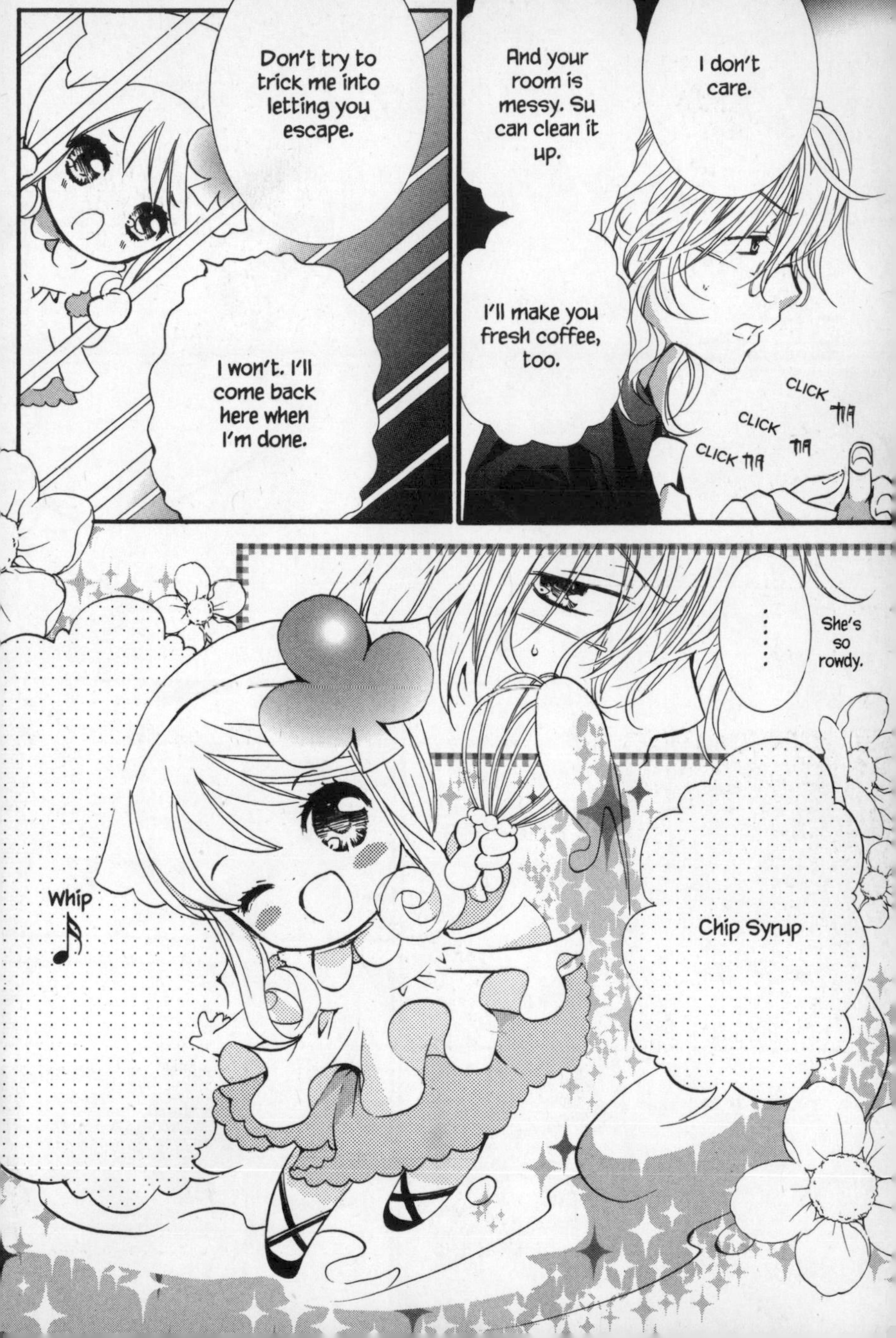
I don't care.
And your room is messy. Su can clean it up.
I'll make you fresh coffee, too.
CLICK
CLICK
CLICK
Don't try to trick me into letting you escape.
I won't. I'll come back here when I'm done.
......
She's so rowdy.
Chip Syrup
Whip

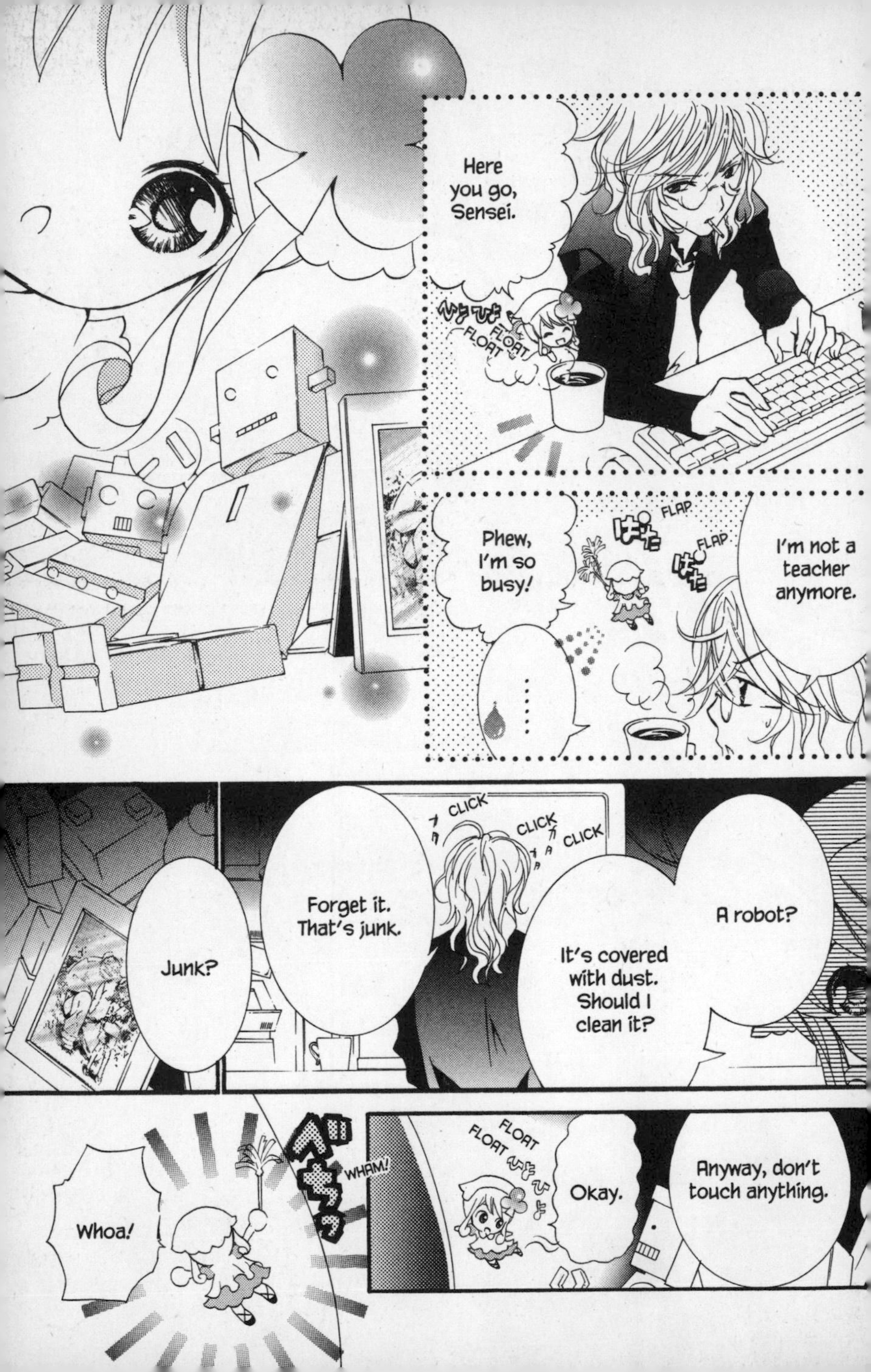

Here you go, Sensei.
FLOAT
FLOAT
I'm not a teacher anymore.
FLAP
FLAP
Phew, I'm so busy!
......
A robot?
It's covered with dust. Should I clean it?
CLICK
CLICK
CLICK
Forget it. That's junk.
Junk?
Anyway, don't touch anything.
FLOAT
FLOAT
Okay.
WHAM!
Whoa!

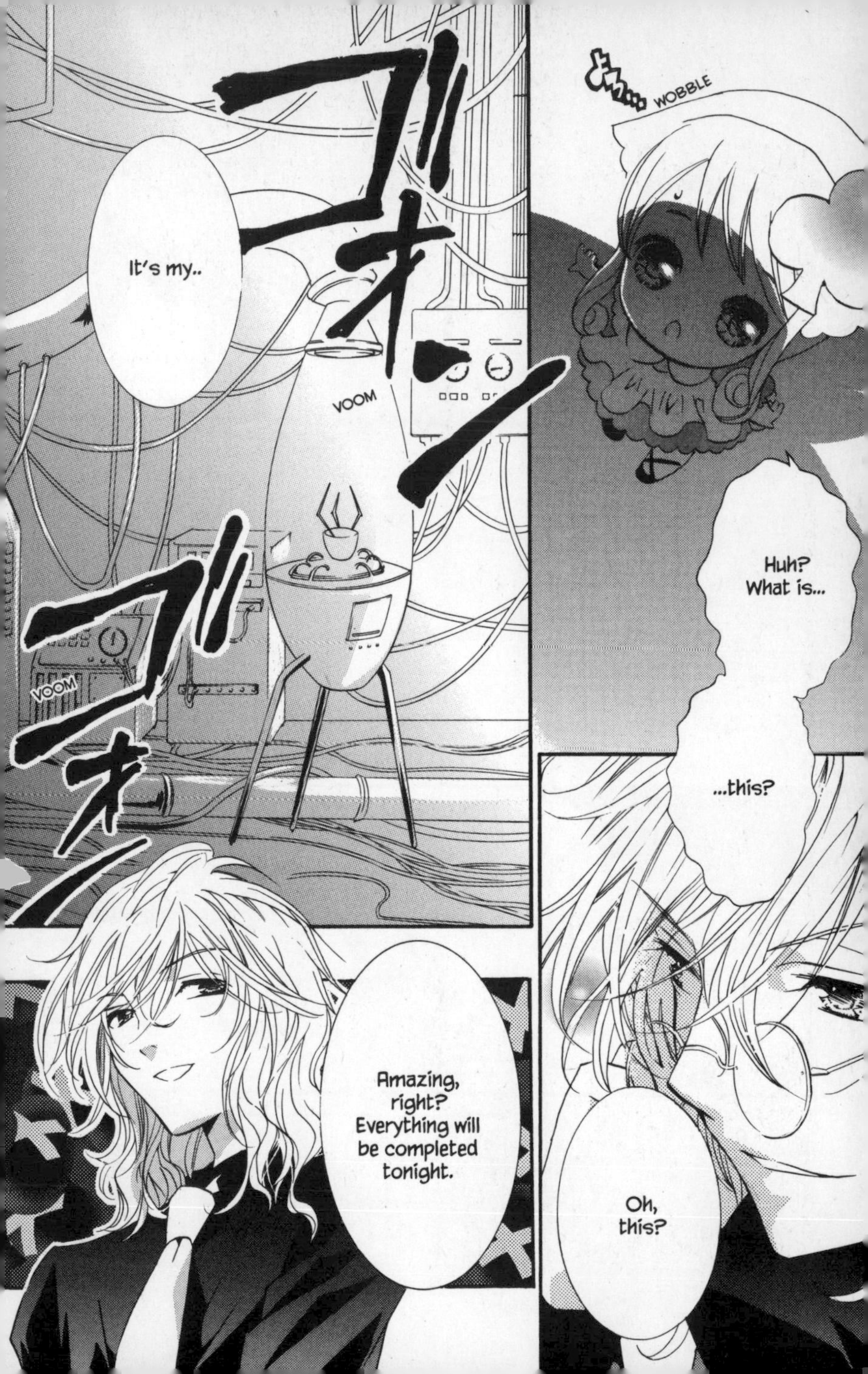
WOBBLE
Huh? What is...
...this?
Oh, this?
It's my..
VOOM
VOOM
Amazing, right? Everything will be completed tonight.

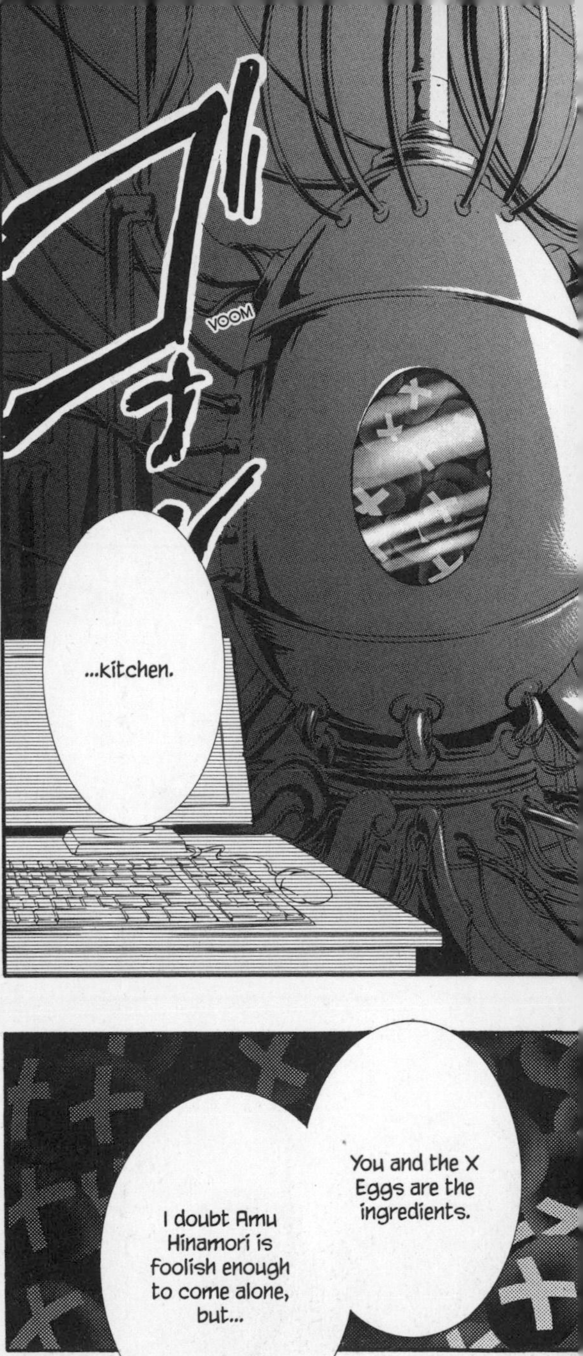
VOOM
...kitchen.
You and the X Eggs are the ingredients.
I doubt Amu Hinamori is foolish enough to come alone, but...

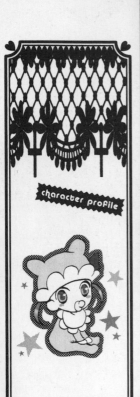

character profile

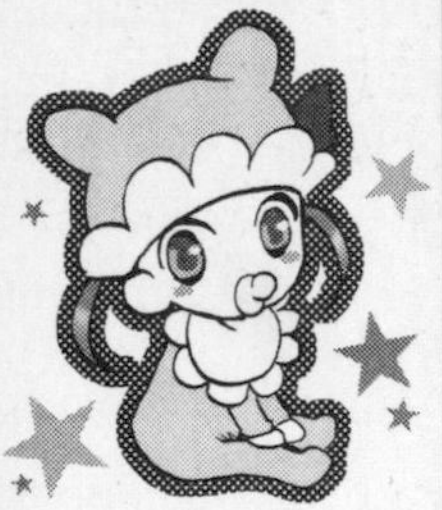

PEPE
Guardian Character of: Yaya
Special Skill: Being immature
Hates: Mad people

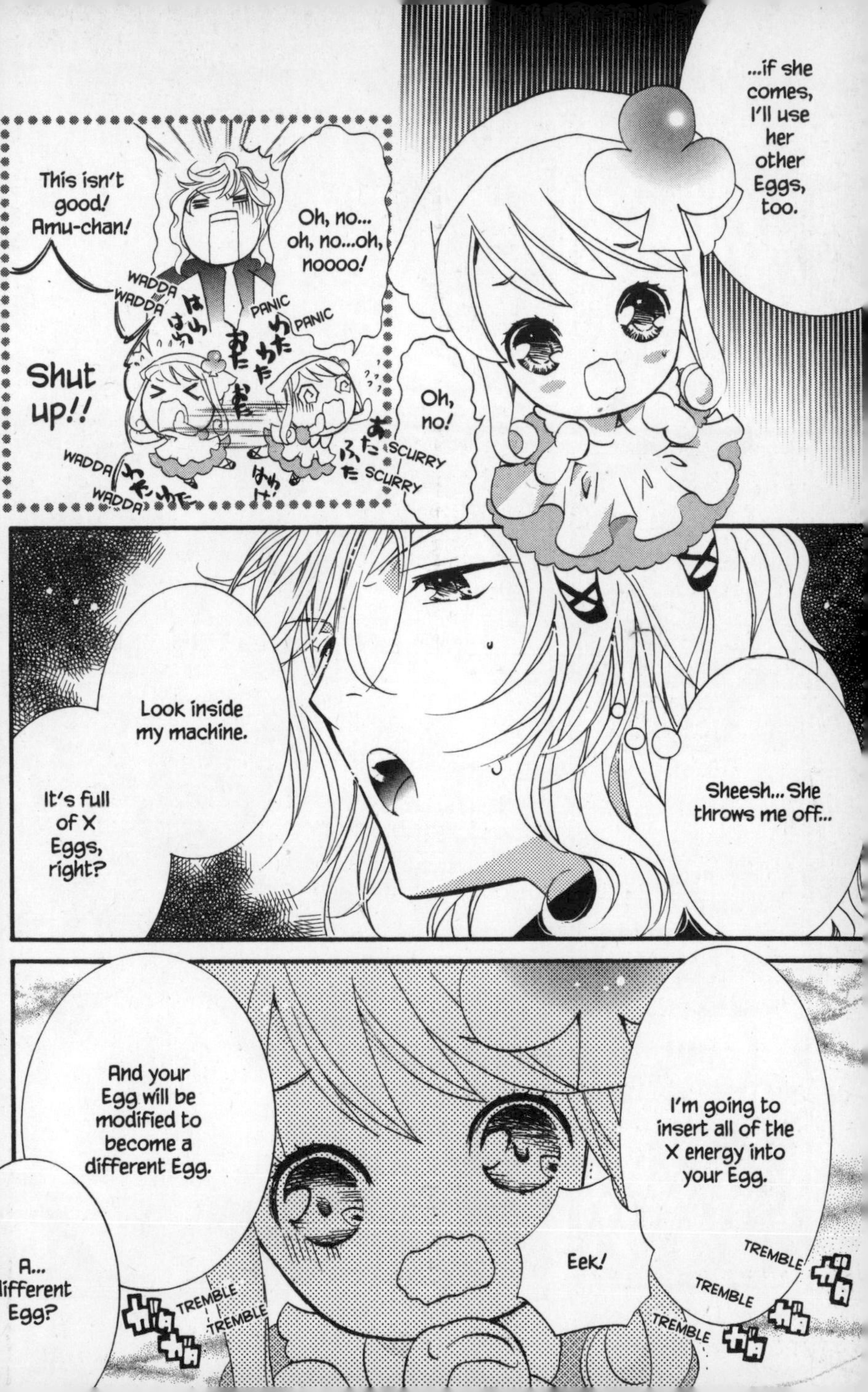
...if she comes, I'll use her other Eggs, too.
Oh, no!
Oh, no... oh, no...oh, noooo!
This isn't good! Amu-chan!
PANIC
PANIC
WADDA
WADDA
SCURRY
SCURRY
Shut up!!
WADDA
WADDA
Sheesh... She throws me off...
Look inside my machine.
It's full of X Eggs, right?
I'm going to insert all of the X energy into your Egg.
TREMBLE
TREMBLE
TREMBLE
Eek!
And your Egg will be modified to become a different Egg.
A... different Egg?
TREMBLE
TREMBLE

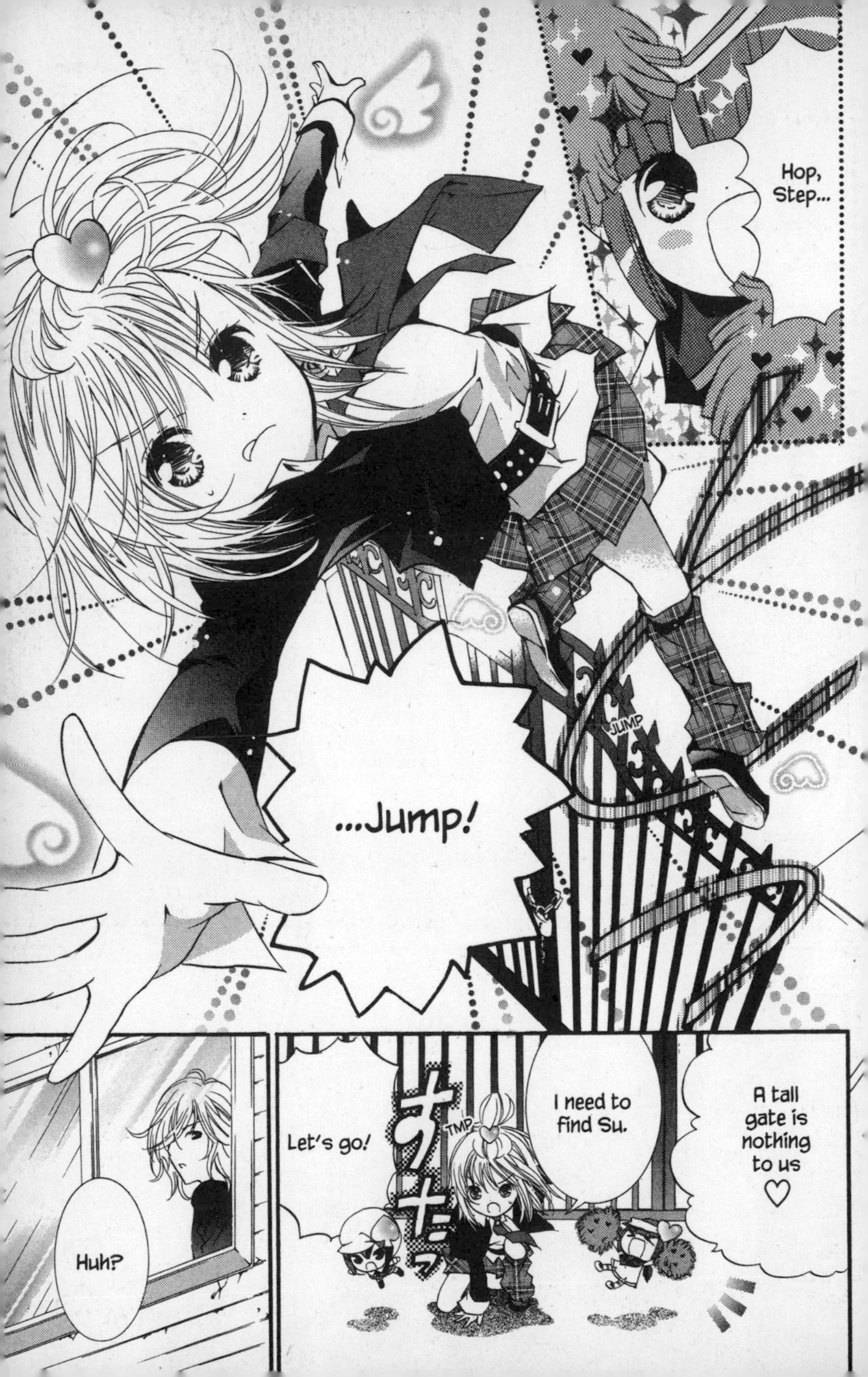
Hop, Step...
JUMP
...Jump!
A tall gate is nothing to us ♡
I need to find Su.
TMP
すたっ
Let's go!
Huh?

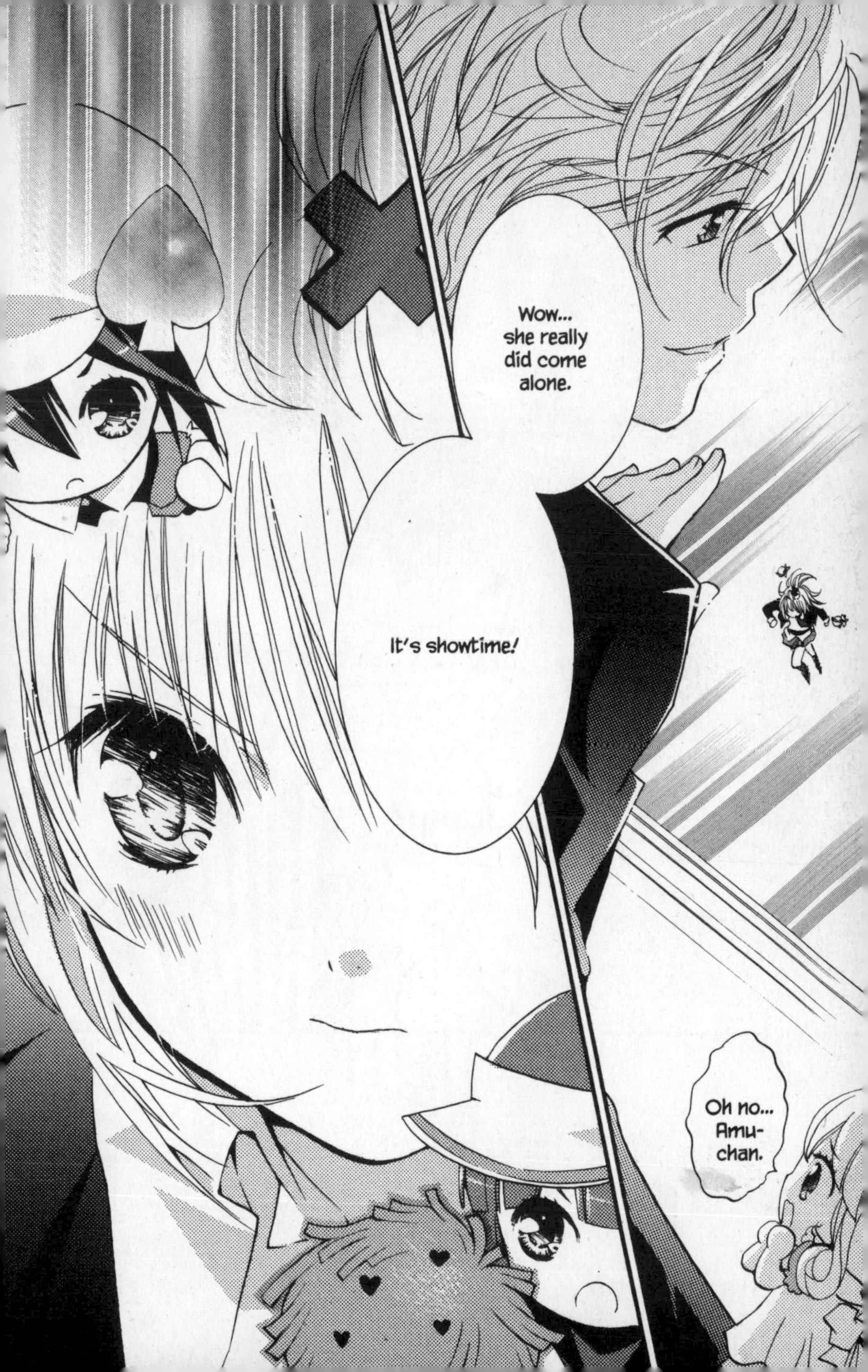
Wow... she really did come alone.
It's showtime!
Oh no... Amu-chan.

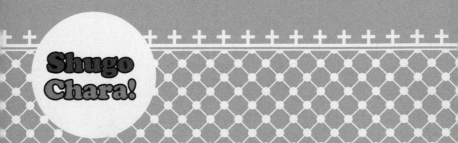

Shugo
Chara!

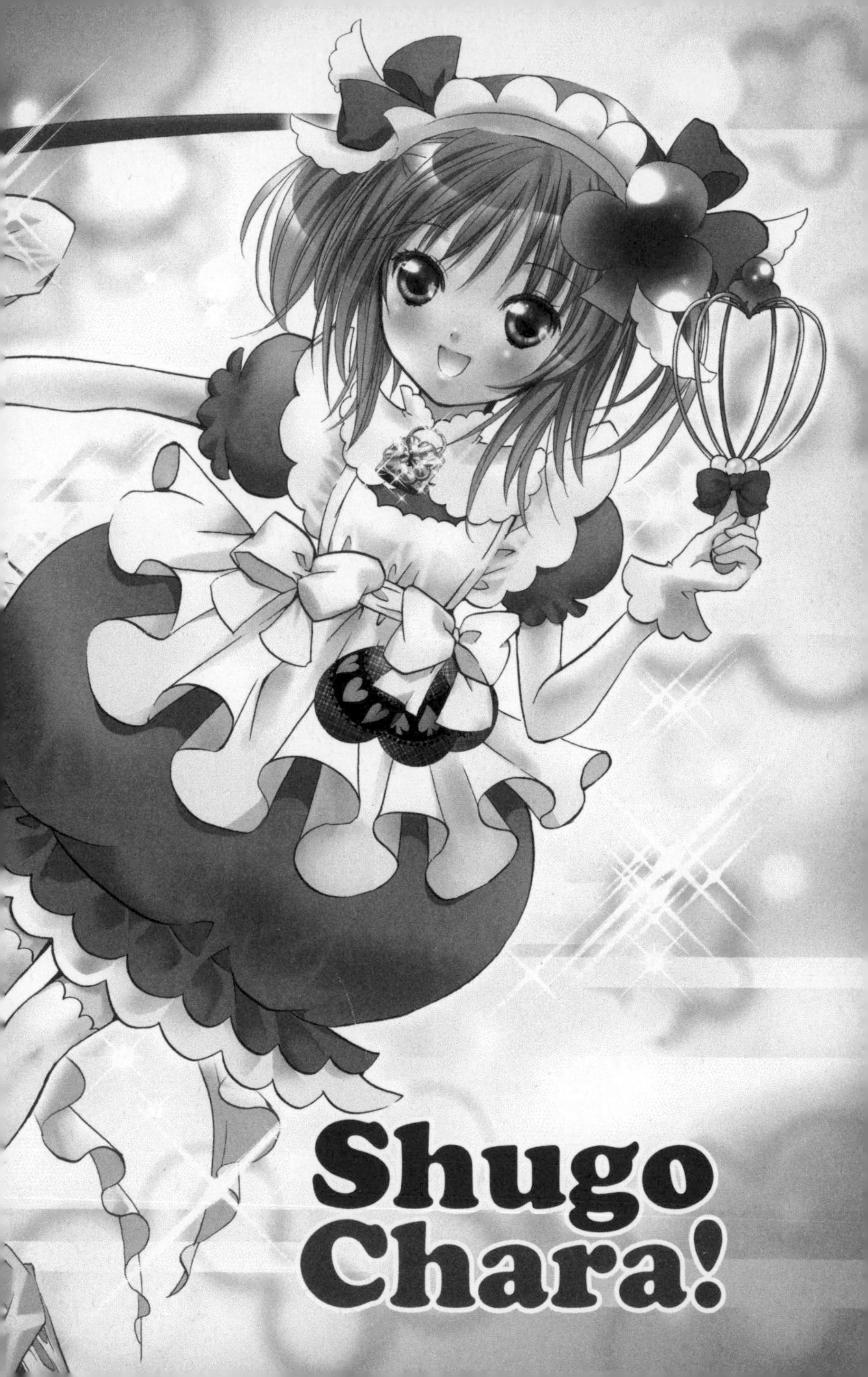
Shugo
Chara!

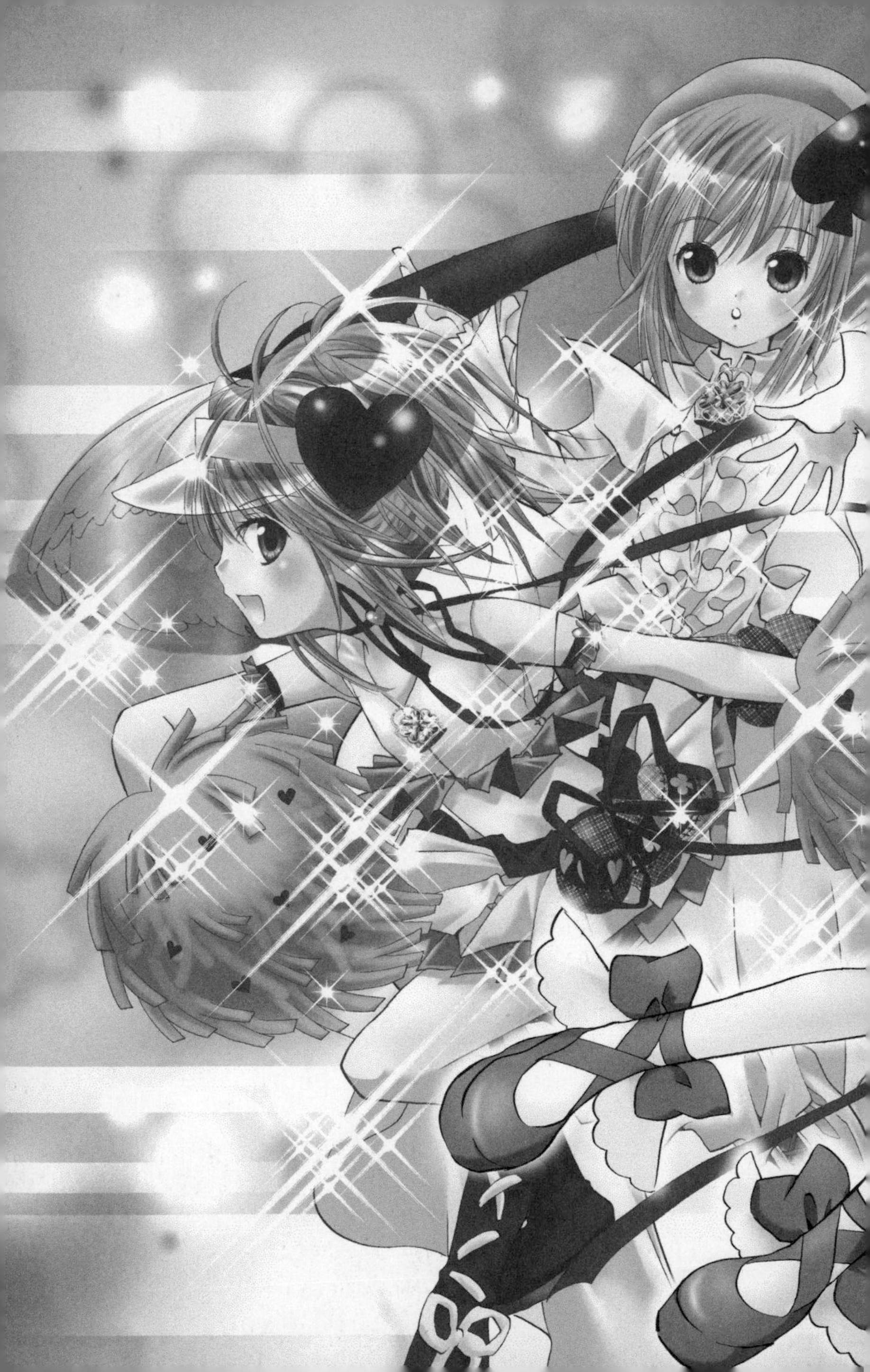

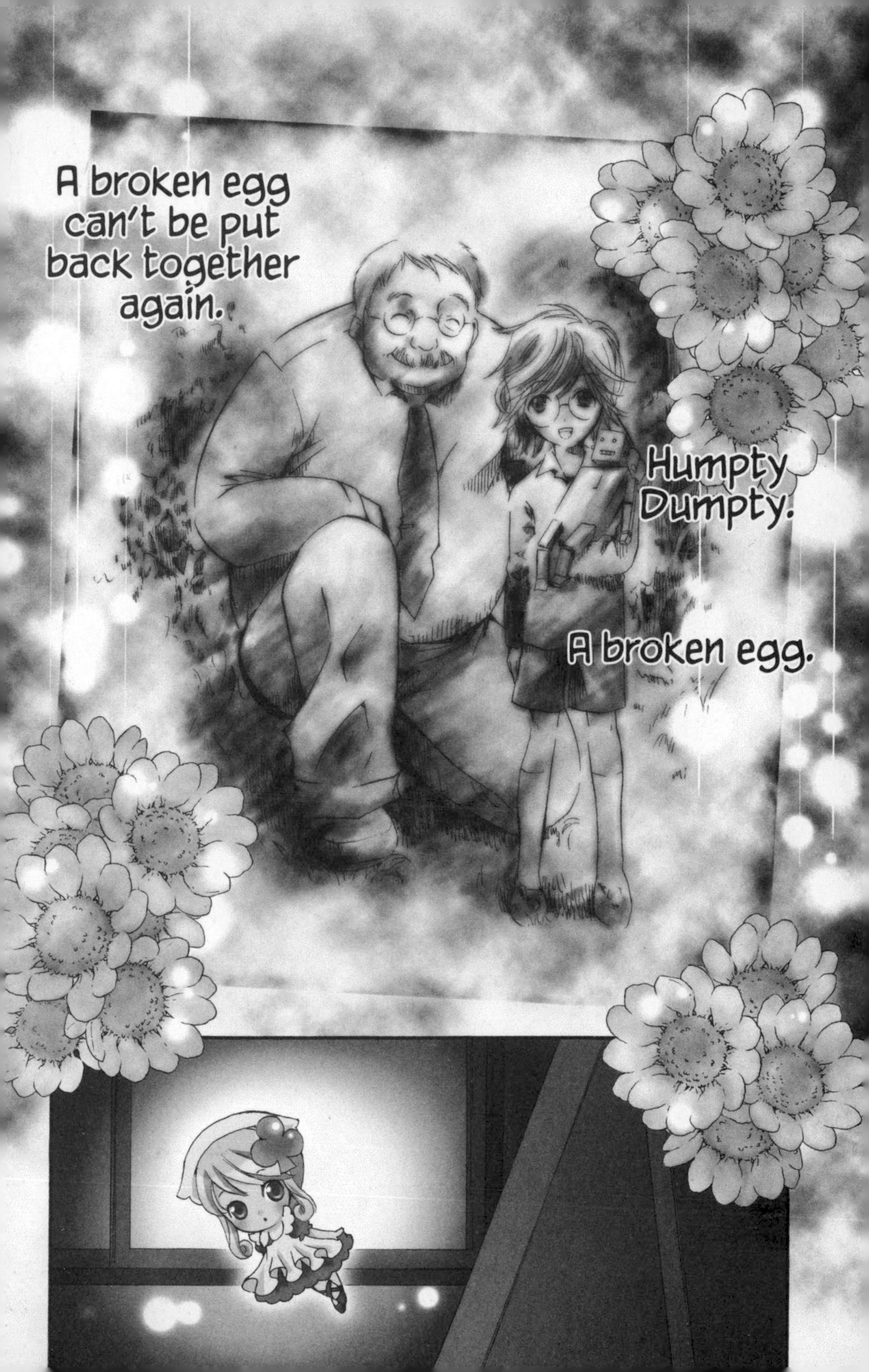
Humpty Dumpty.
A broken egg.
A broken egg can't be put back together again.

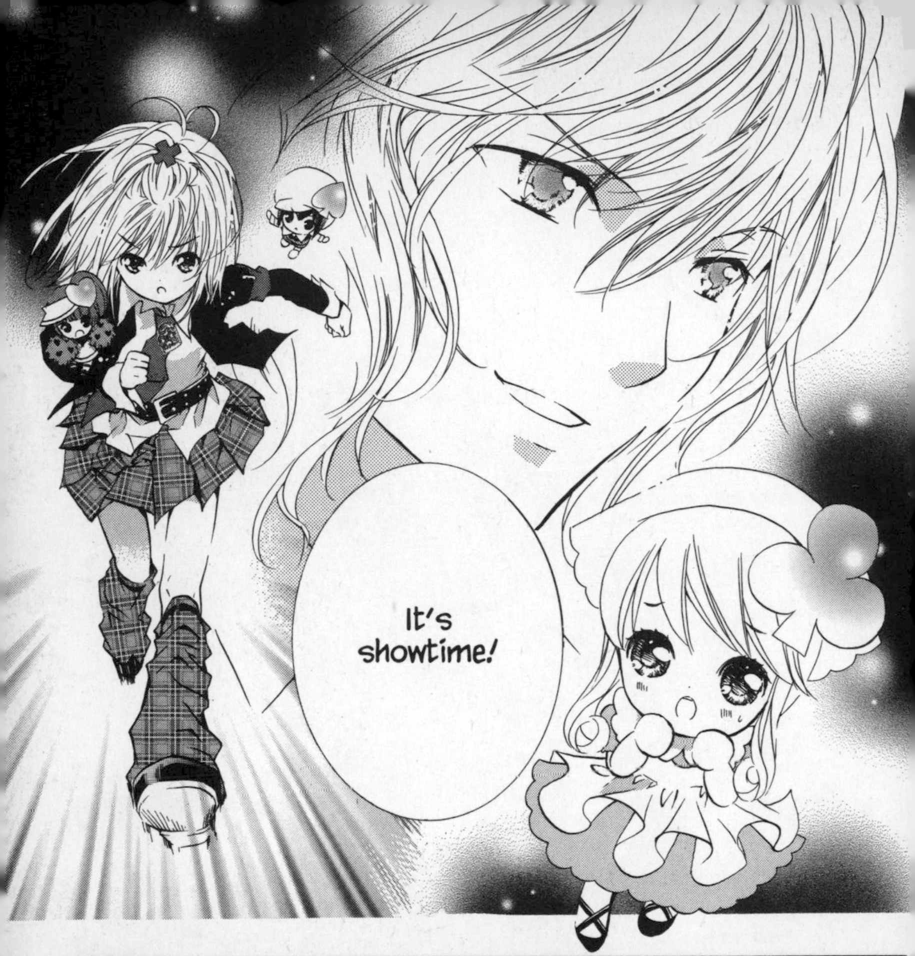
It's showtime!

Q2: What clubs were you in at school? I'm on the volleyball team!

A2: How nice and sporty! Ebara was in the Drama Club, and Sendo wasn't in anything. Both of us were bad at sports, and we were amazed by our friends who were on sports teams.

Q3: Where are you from?

A3: We're both from the Chiba prefecture.

Q4: What's ajitama?

A4: Ajitama are flavored eggs. They're a ramen topping ♡
You can try making them with your mom!

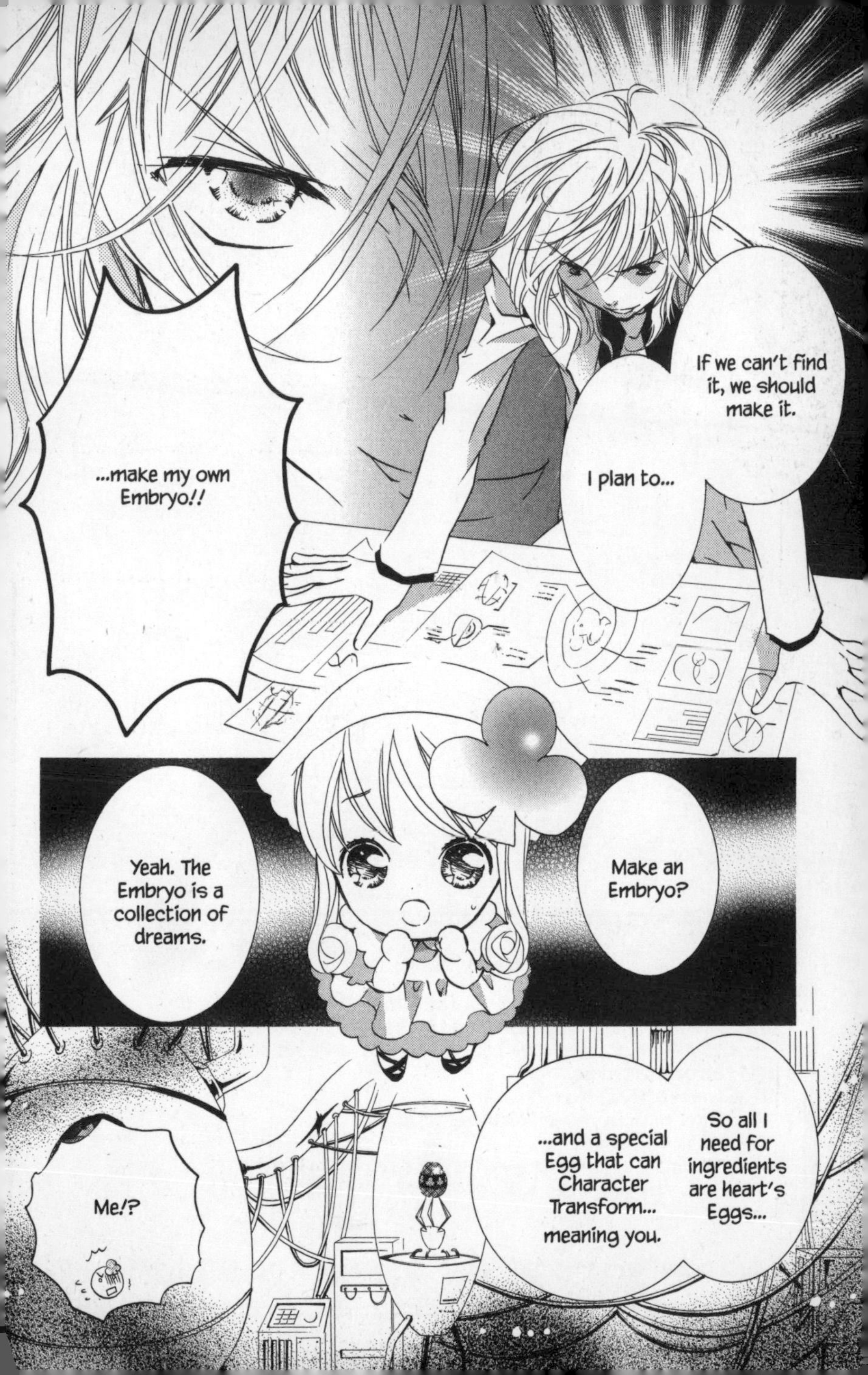
If we can't find it, we should make it.
I plan to...
...make my own Embryo!!
Make an Embryo?
Yeah. The Embryo is a collection of dreams.
So all I need for ingredients are heart's Eggs...
...and a special Egg that can Character Transform... meaning you.
Me!?

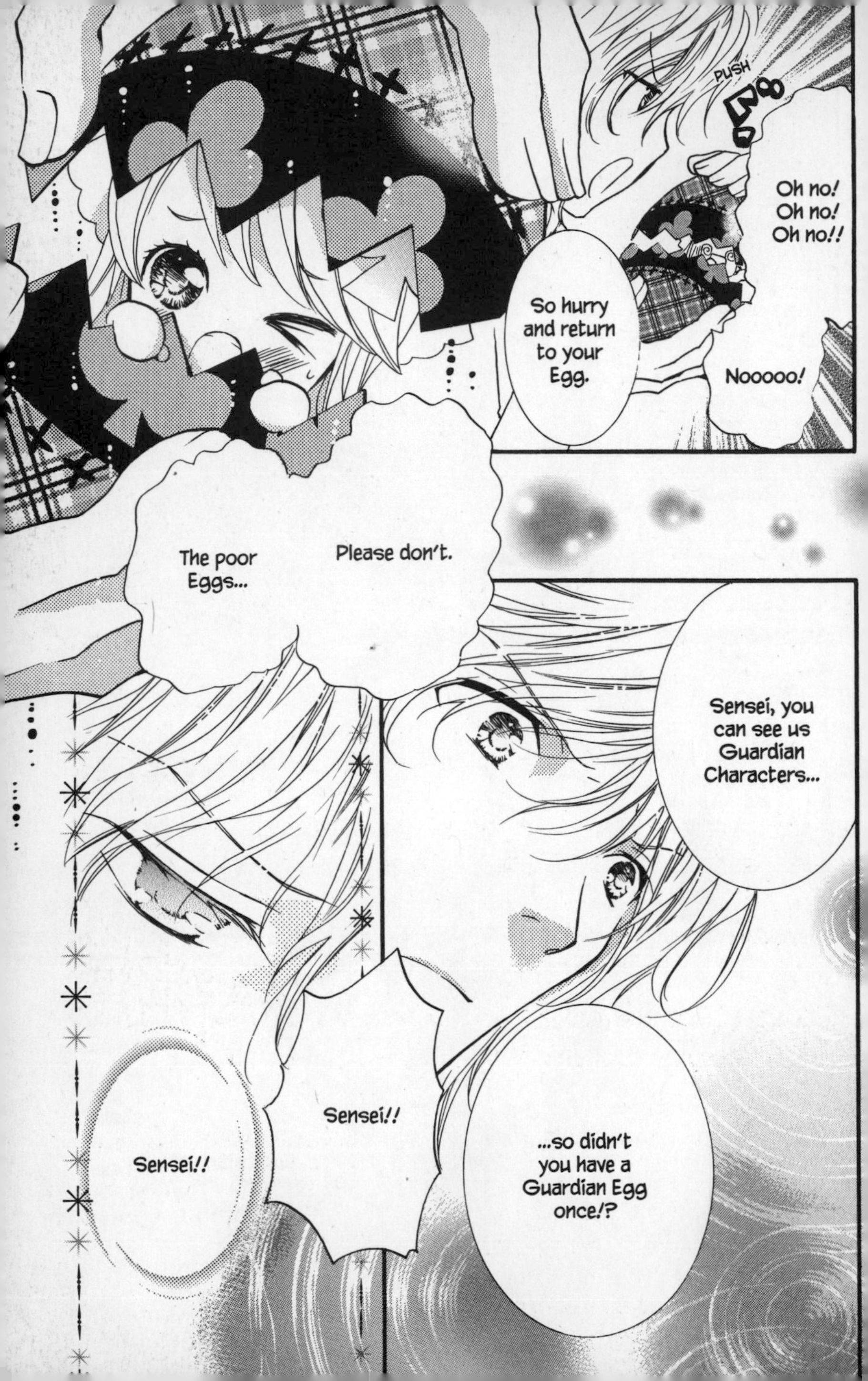
PUSH
Oh no!
Oh no!
Oh no!!
So hurry and return to your Egg.
Nooooo!
Please don't.
The poor Eggs...
Sensei, you can see us Guardian Characters...
...so didn't you have a Guardian Egg once!?
Sensei!!
Sensei!!

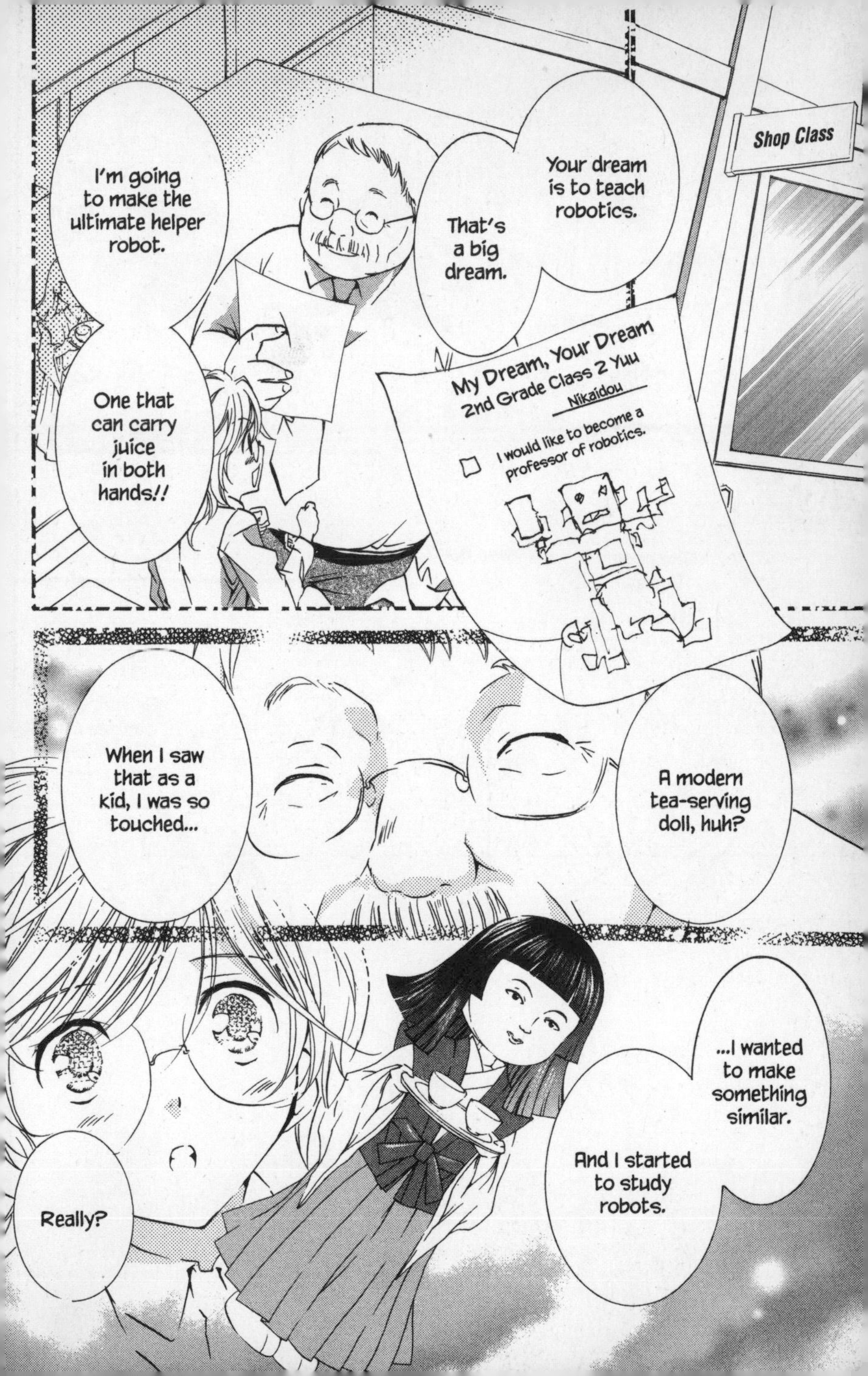
Shop Class
Your dream is to teach robotics.
That's a big dream.
My Dream, Your Dream
2nd Grade Class 2 Yuu Nikaidou
I would like to become a professor of robotics.
I'm going to make the ultimate helper robot.
One that can carry juice in both hands!!
A modern tea-serving doll, huh?
When I saw that as a kid, I was so touched...
...I wanted to make something similar.
And I started to study robots.
Really?

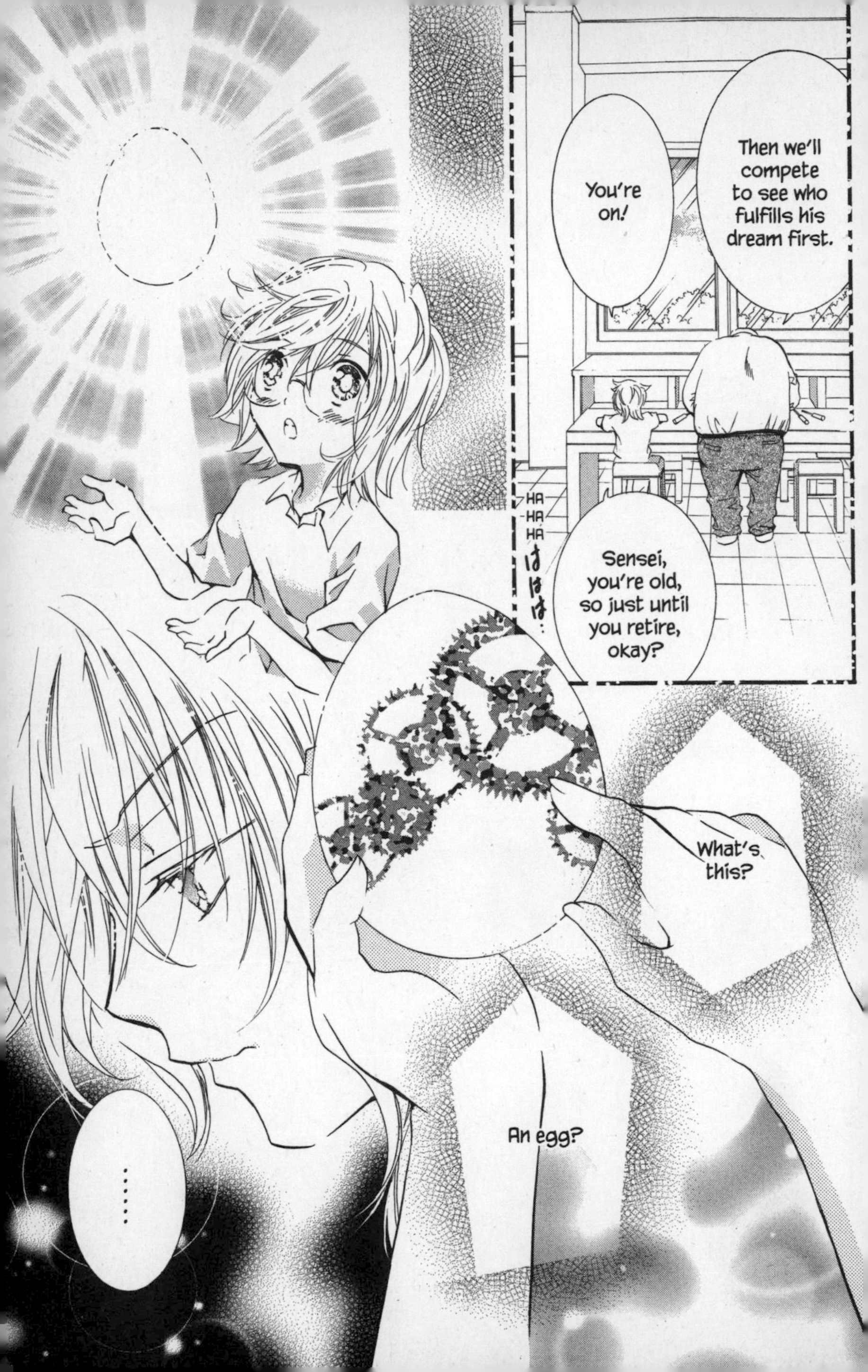
Then we'll compete to see who fulfills his dream first.
You're on!
Sensei, you're old, so just until you retire, okay?
HA-HA-HA
ははは…
What's this?
An egg?
……

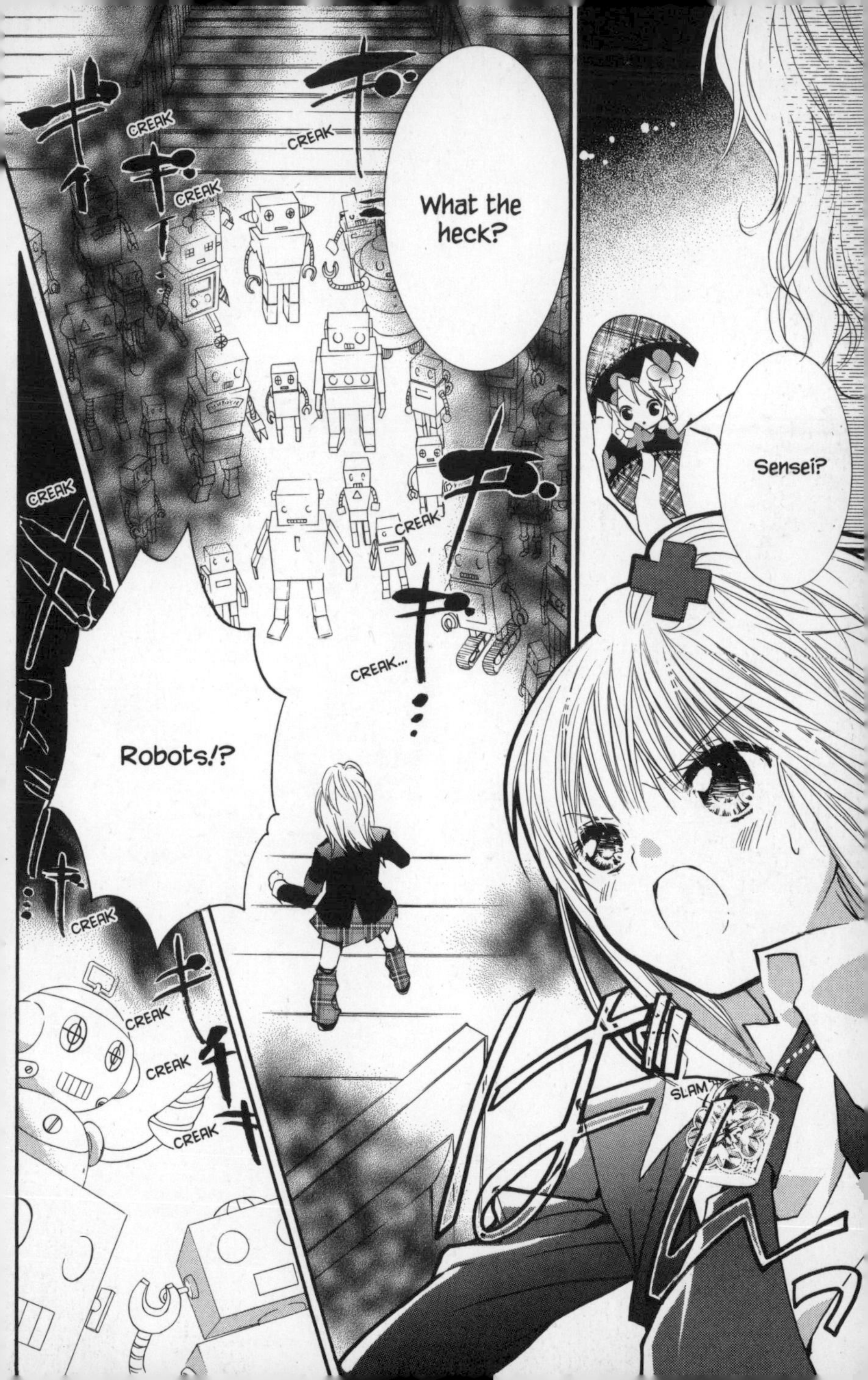
Sensei?
SLAM
What the heck?
CREAK
CREAK
CREAK
CREAK
CREAK
CREAK...
Robots!?
CREAK
CREAK
CREAK
CREAK

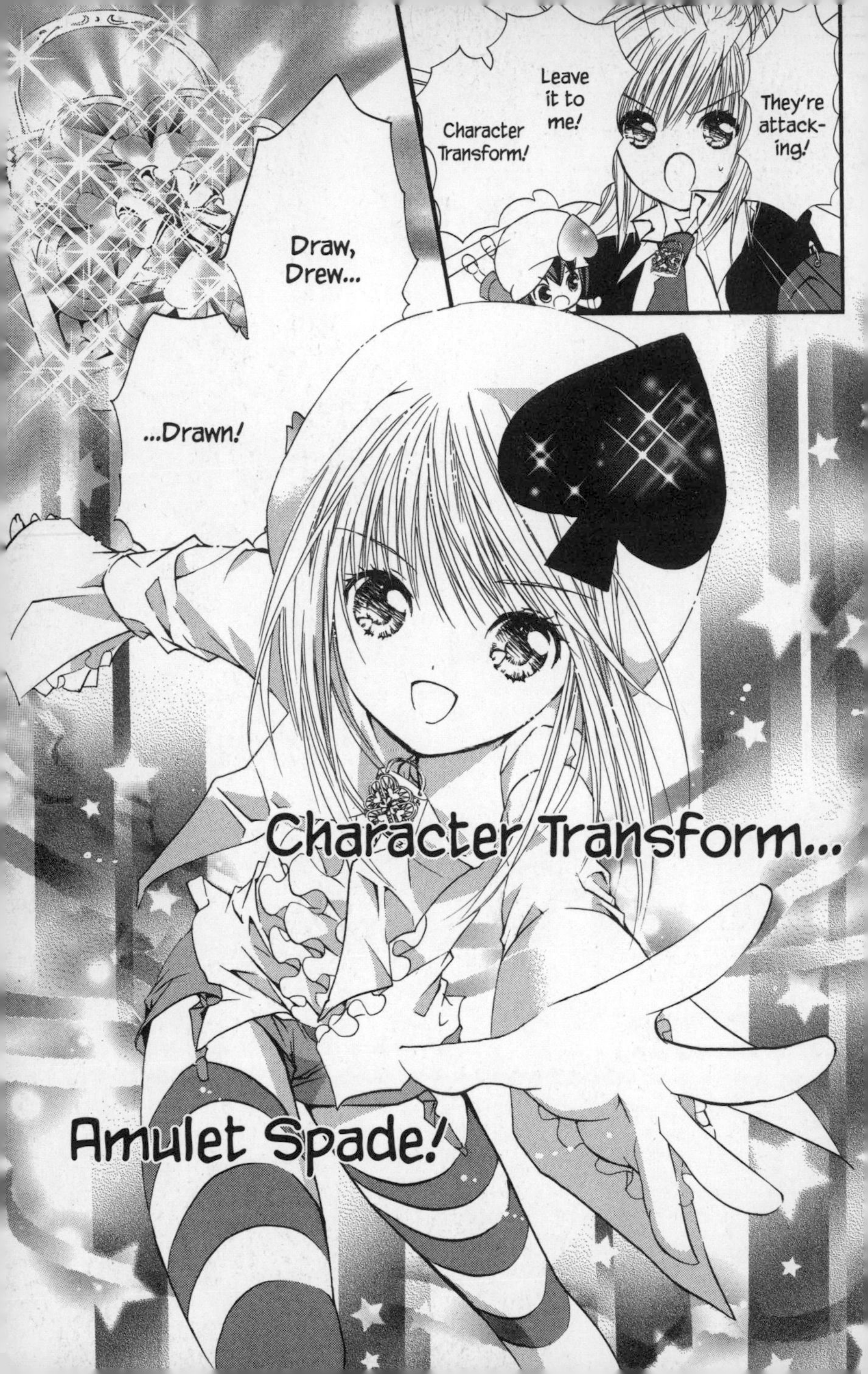
They're attack-ing!
Leave it to me!
Character Transform!
Draw, Drew...
...Drawn!
Character Transform...
Amulet Spade!

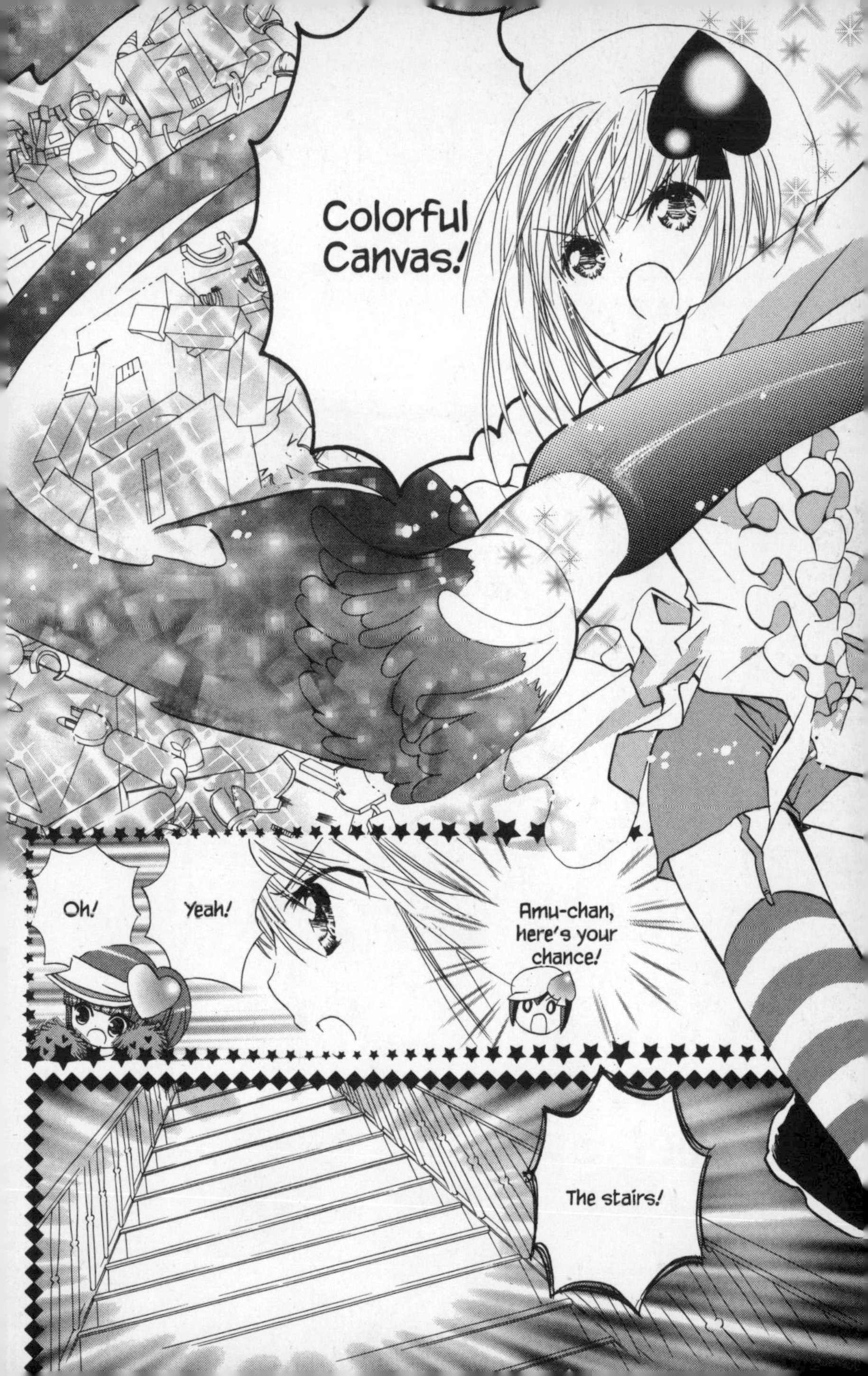
Colorful Canvas!
Amu-chan, here's your chance!
Yeah!
Oh!
The stairs!

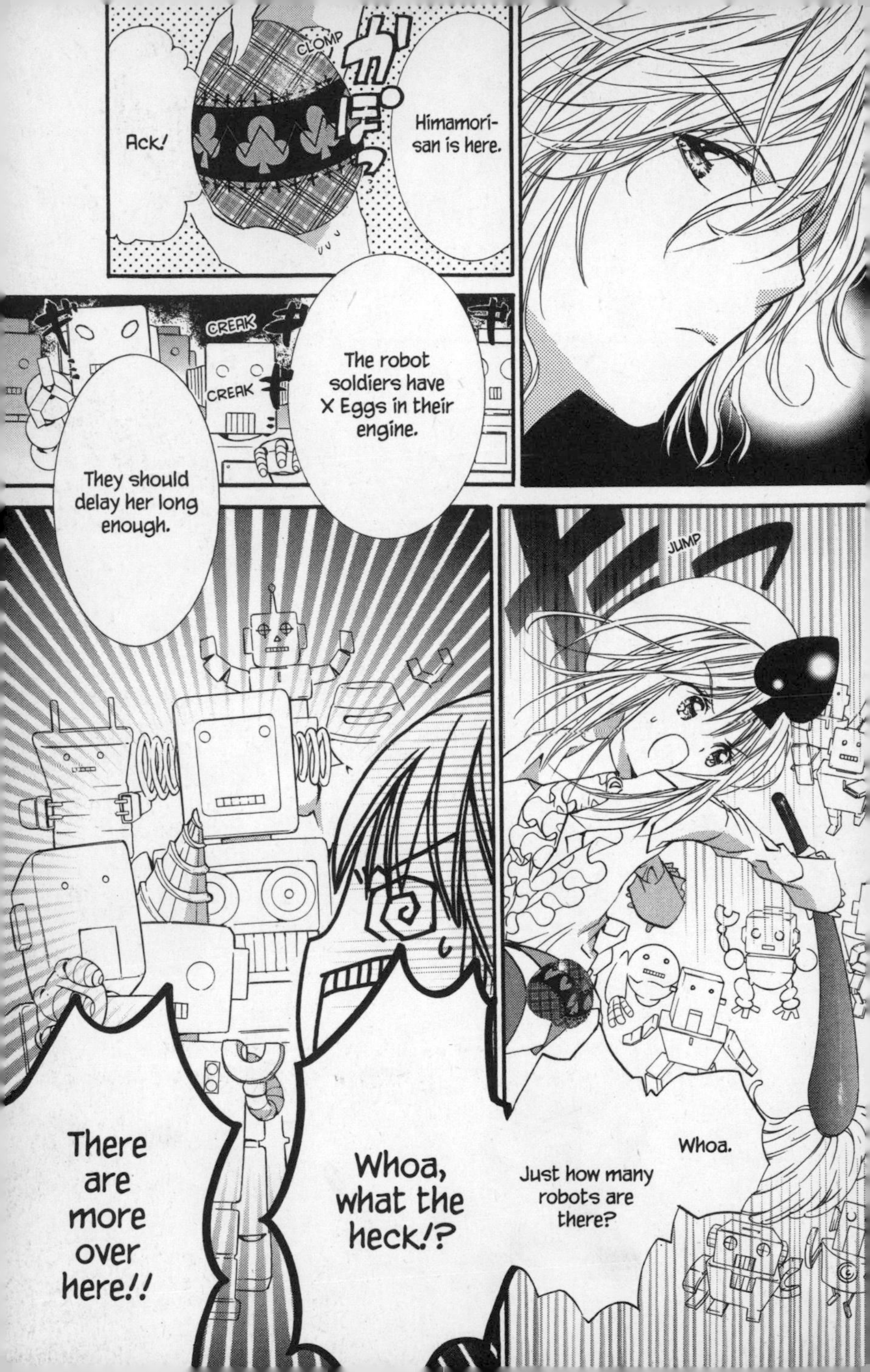
Himamori-san is here.
CLOMP
Ack!
The robot soldiers have X Eggs in their engine.
CREAK
CREAK
They should delay her long enough.
JUMP
Whoa.
Just how many robots are there?
Whoa, what the heck!?
There are more over here!!

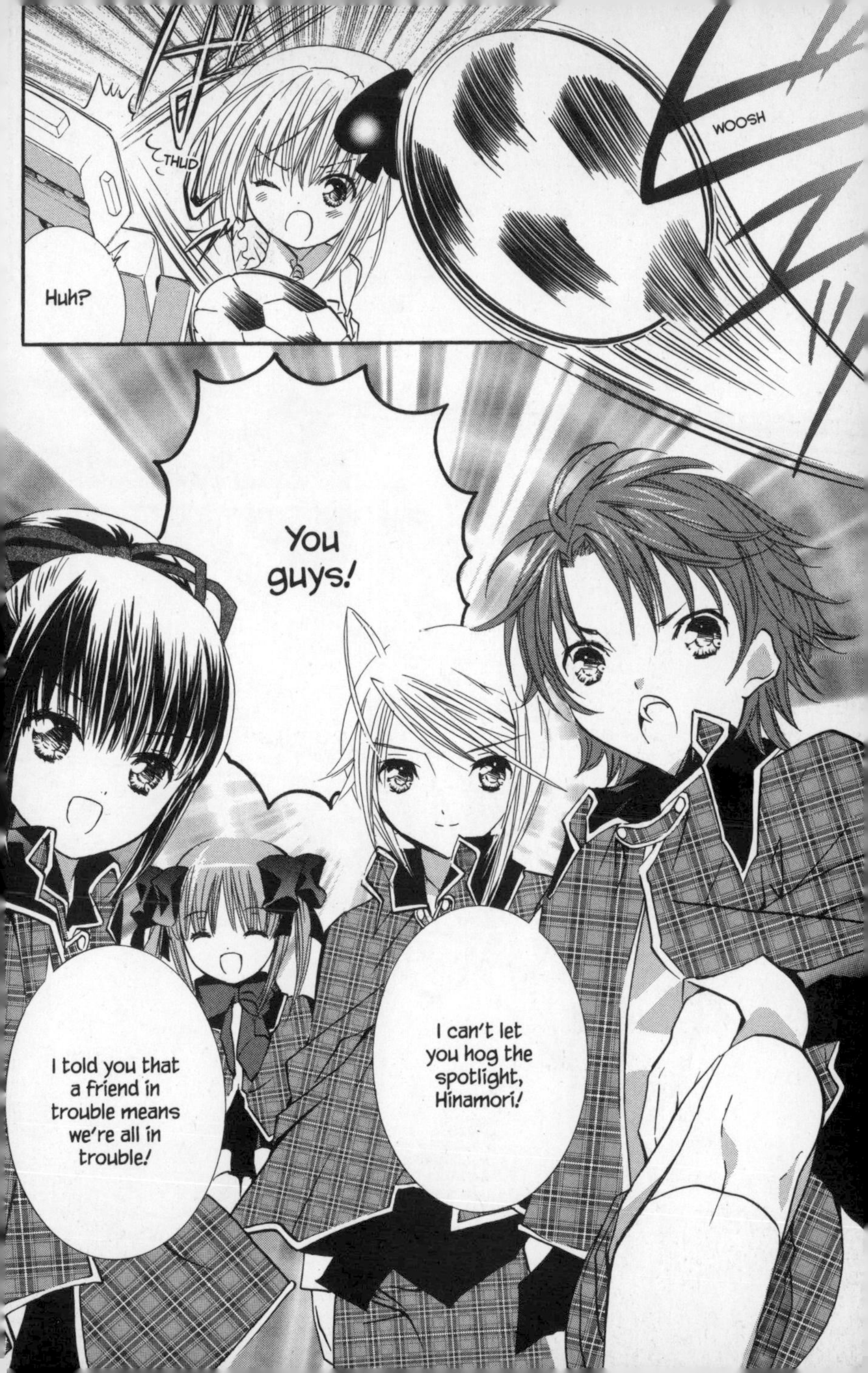
WOOSH
THUD
Huh?
You guys!
I can't let you hog the spotlight, Hinamori!
I told you that a friend in trouble means we're all in trouble!

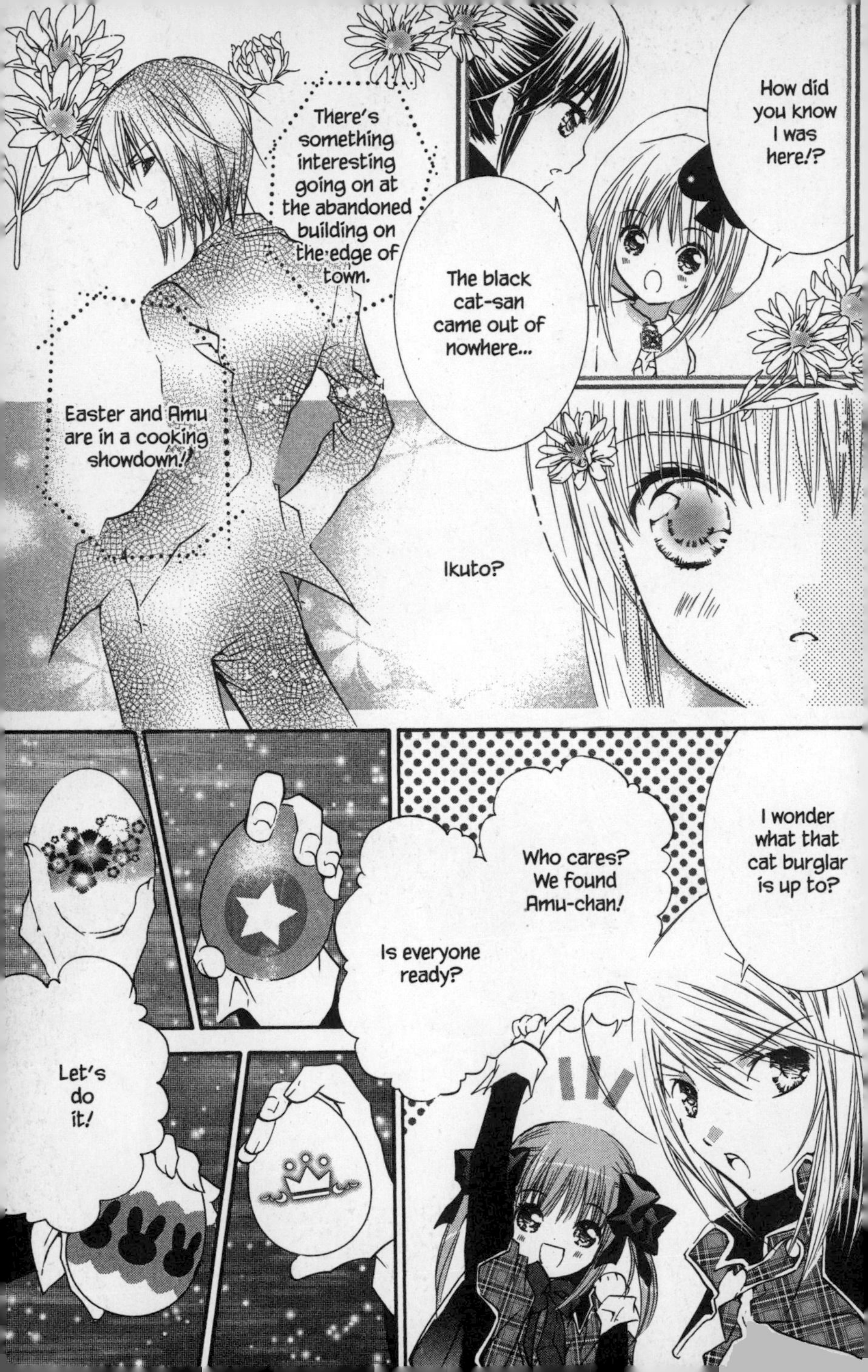
How did you know I was here!?
The black cat-san came out of nowhere...
Ikuto?
There's something interesting going on at the abandoned building on the edge of town.
Easter and Amu are in a cooking showdown!
I wonder what that cat burglar is up to?
Who cares? We found Amu-chan!
Is everyone ready?
Let's do it!

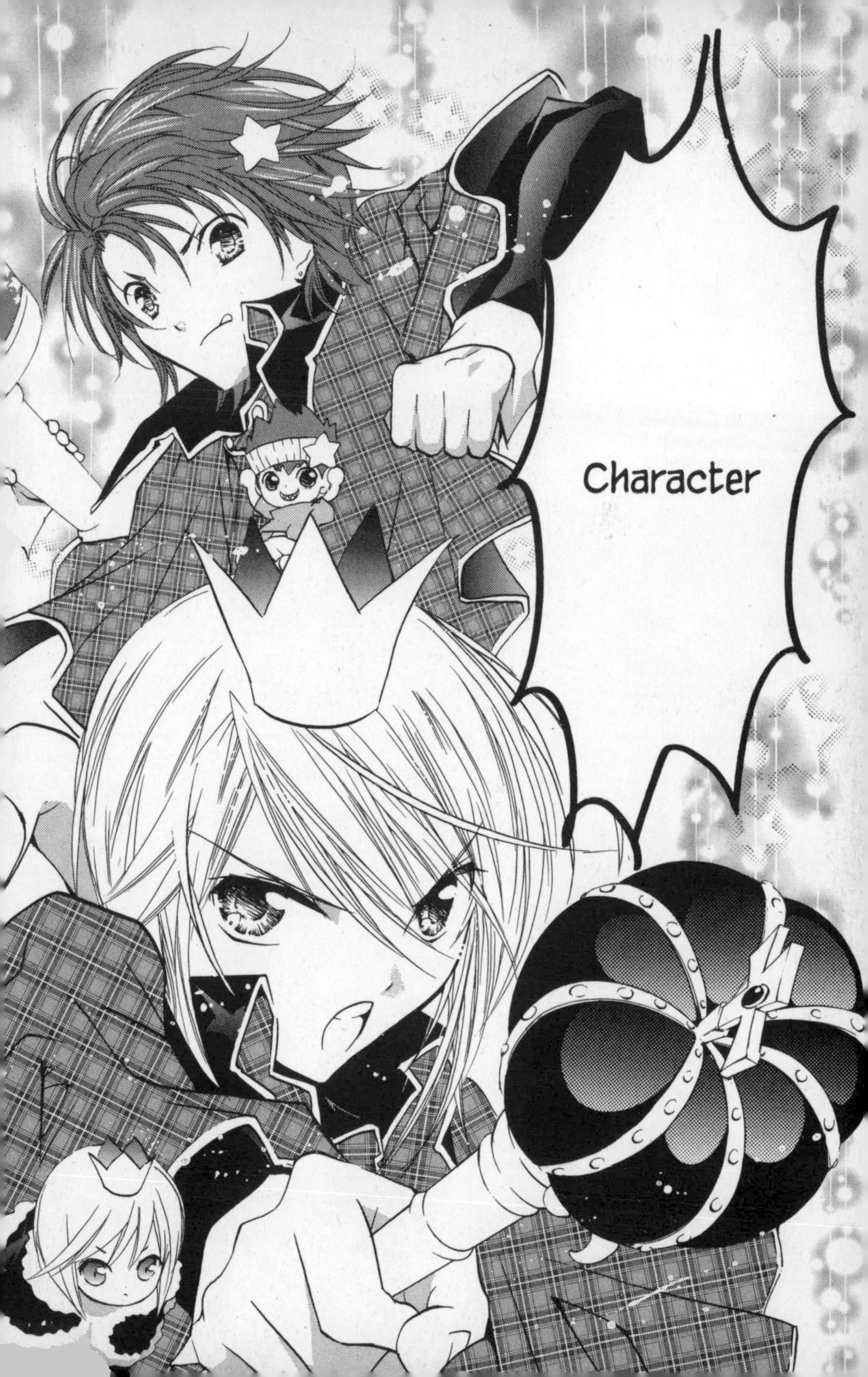
Character

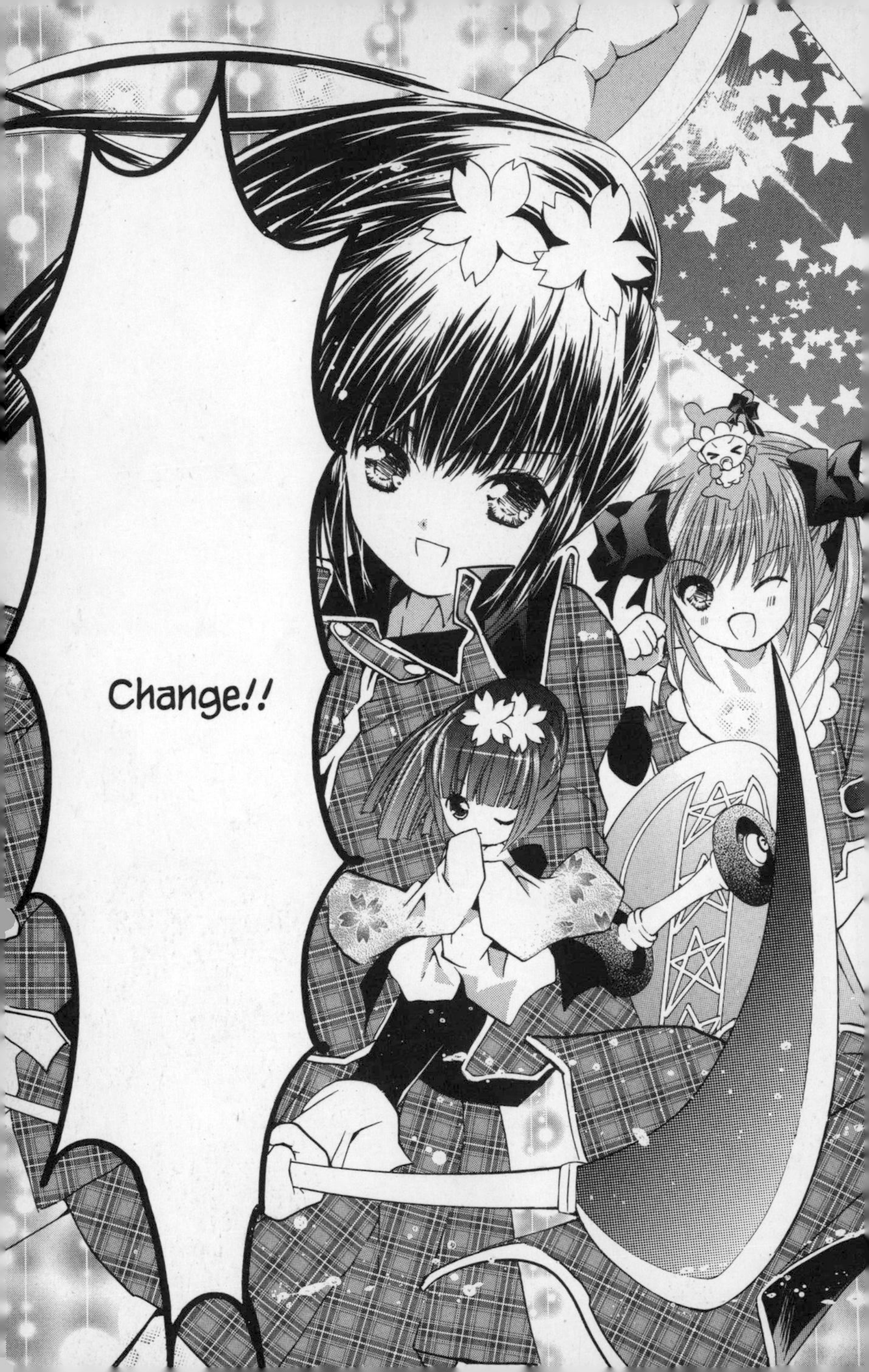
Change!!

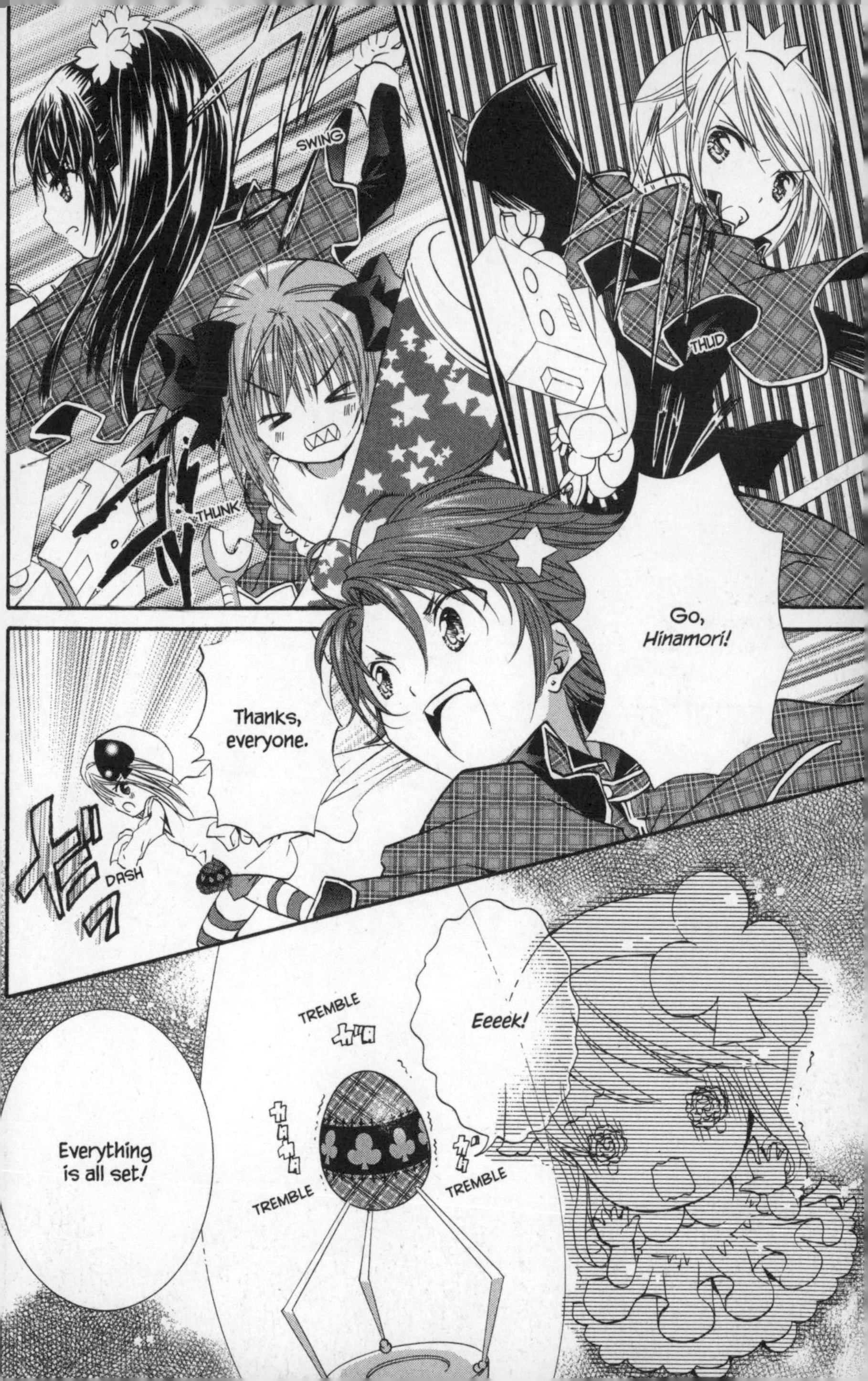
THUD
SWING
THUNK
Go, Hinamori!
Thanks, everyone.
DASH
Eeeek!
TREMBLE
TREMBLE
TREMBLE
Everything is all set!

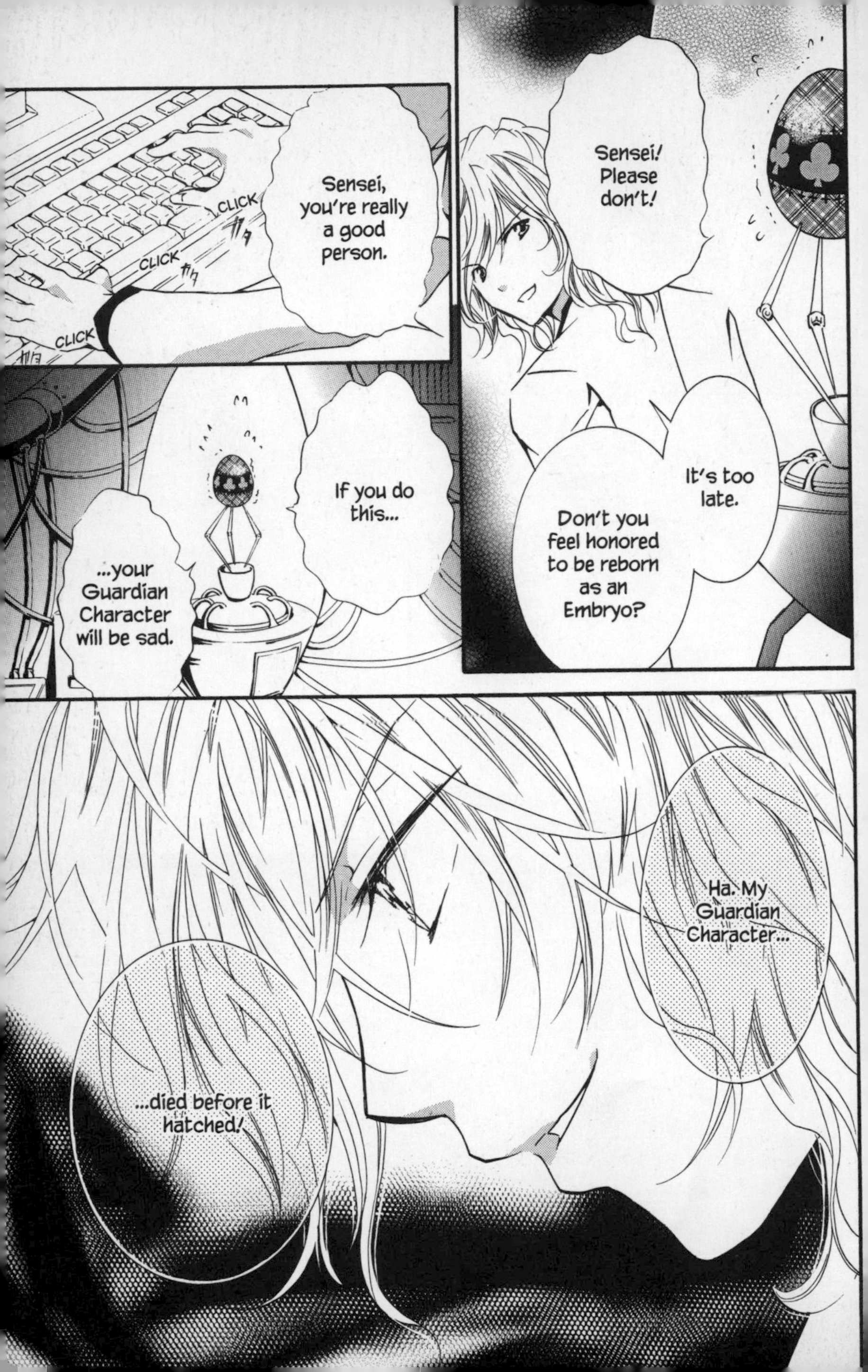
Sensei! Please don't!
It's too late.
Don't you feel honored to be reborn as an Embryo?
Sensei, you're really a good person.
CLICK
CLICK
CLICK
If you do this...
...your Guardian Character will be sad.
Ha. My Guardian Character...
...died before it hatched!

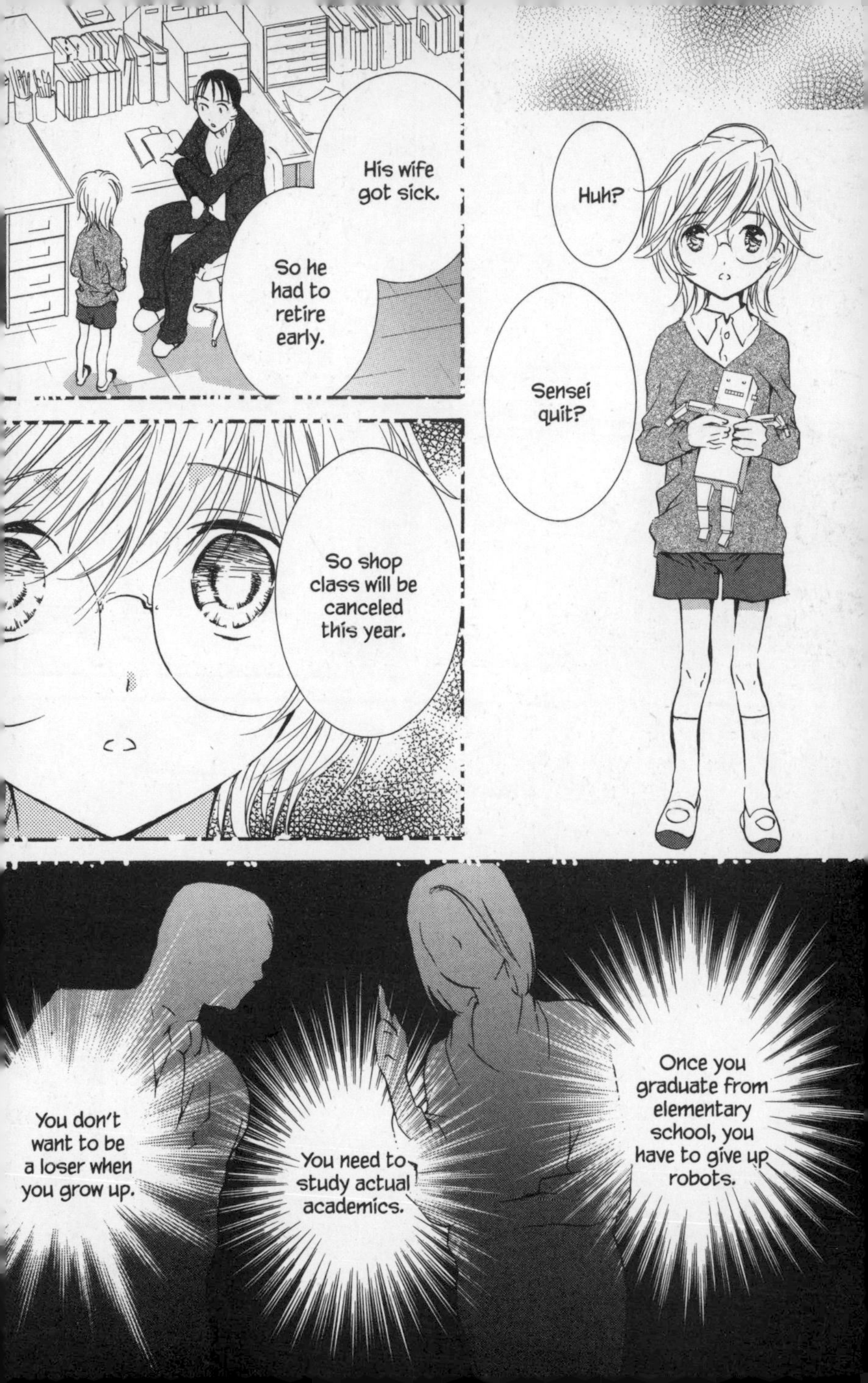
Huh?
Sensei quit?
His wife got sick.
So he had to retire early.
So shop class will be canceled this year.
Once you graduate from elementary school, you have to give up robots.
You need to study actual academics.
You don't want to be a loser when you grow up.

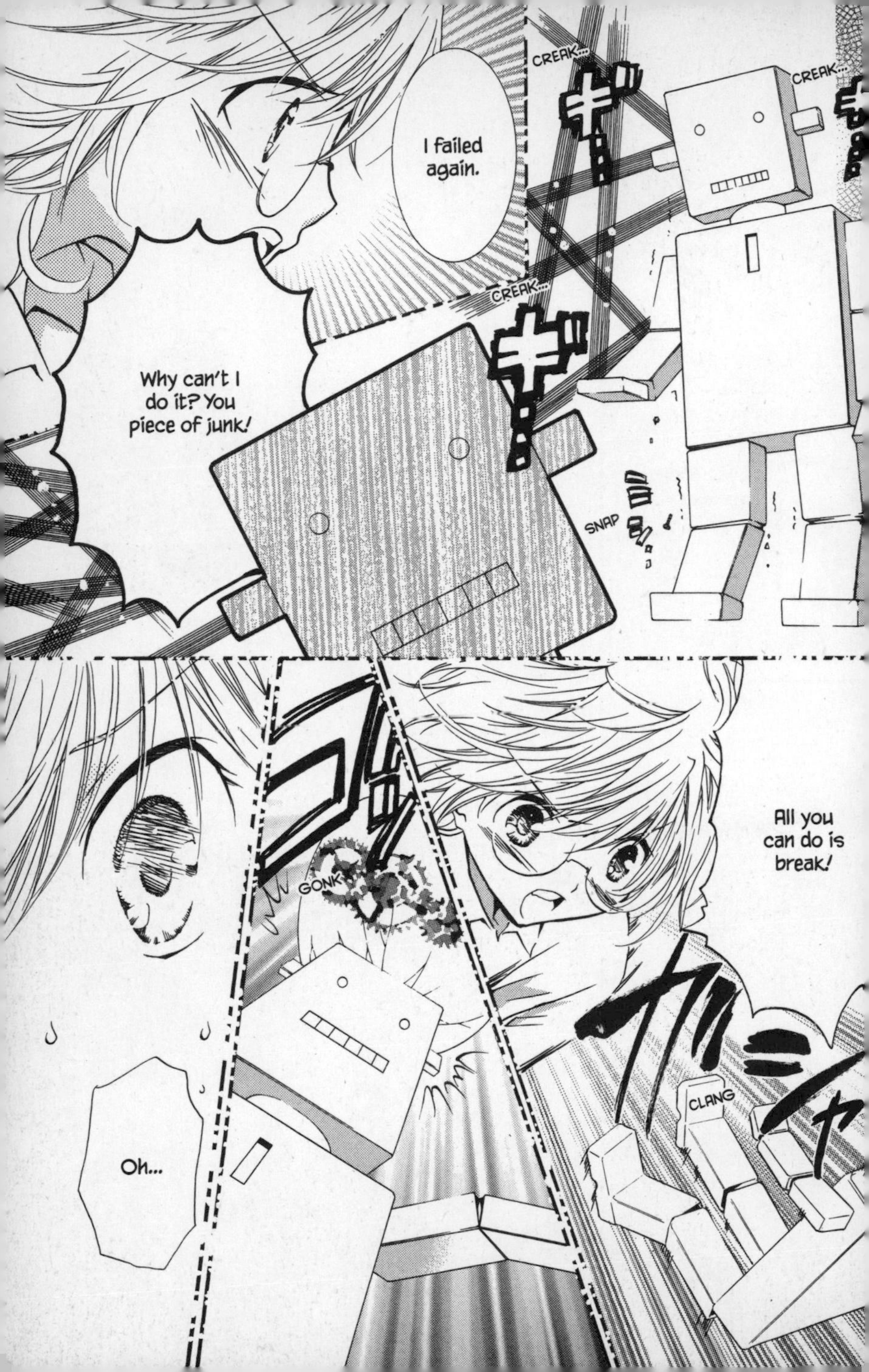
CREAK...
CREAK...
CREAK...
SNAP
I failed again.
Why can't I do it? You piece of junk!
All you can do is break!
CLANG
GONK
Oh...

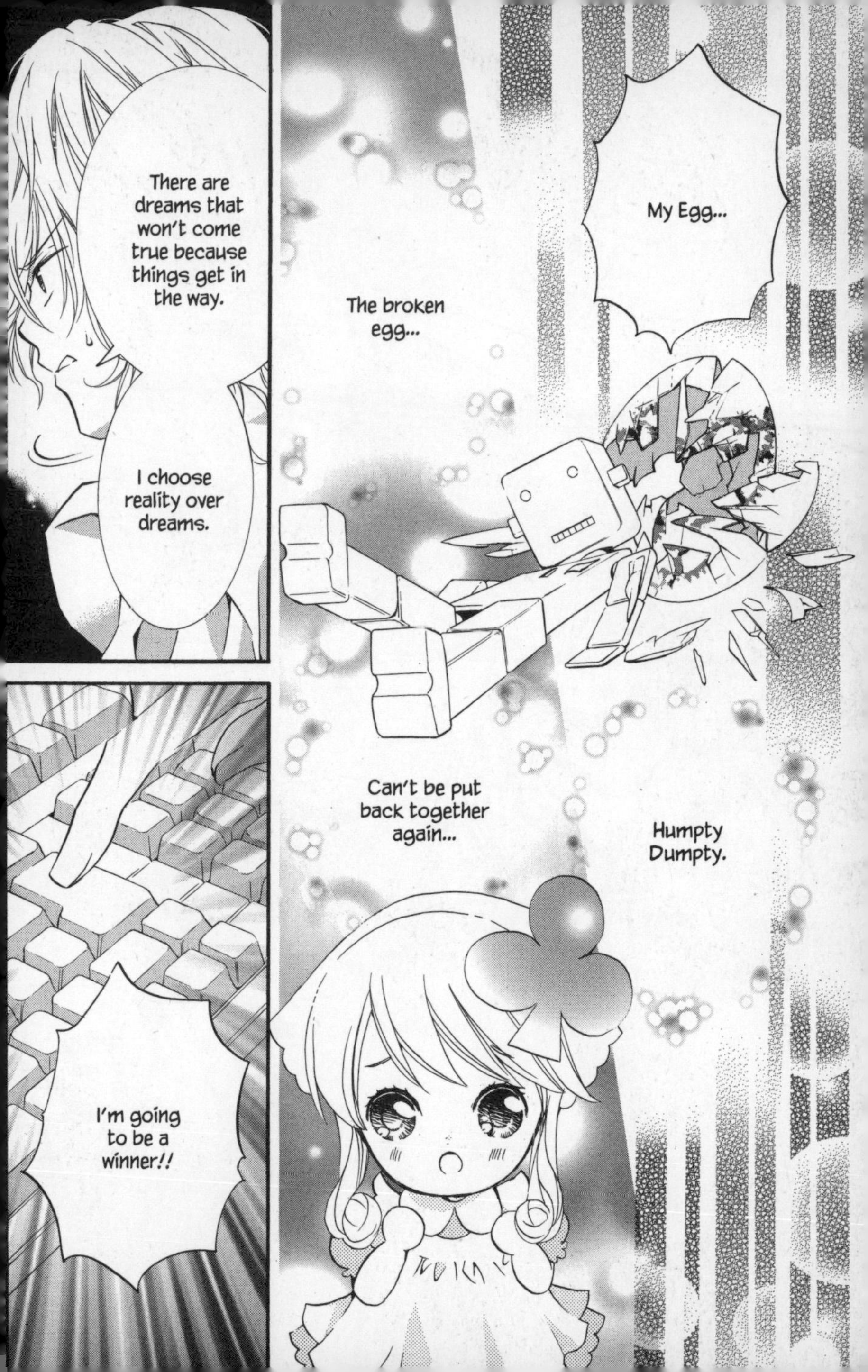
My Egg...
The broken egg...
Humpty Dumpty.
Can't be put back together again...
There are dreams that won't come true because things get in the way.
I choose reality over dreams.
I'm going to be a winner!!

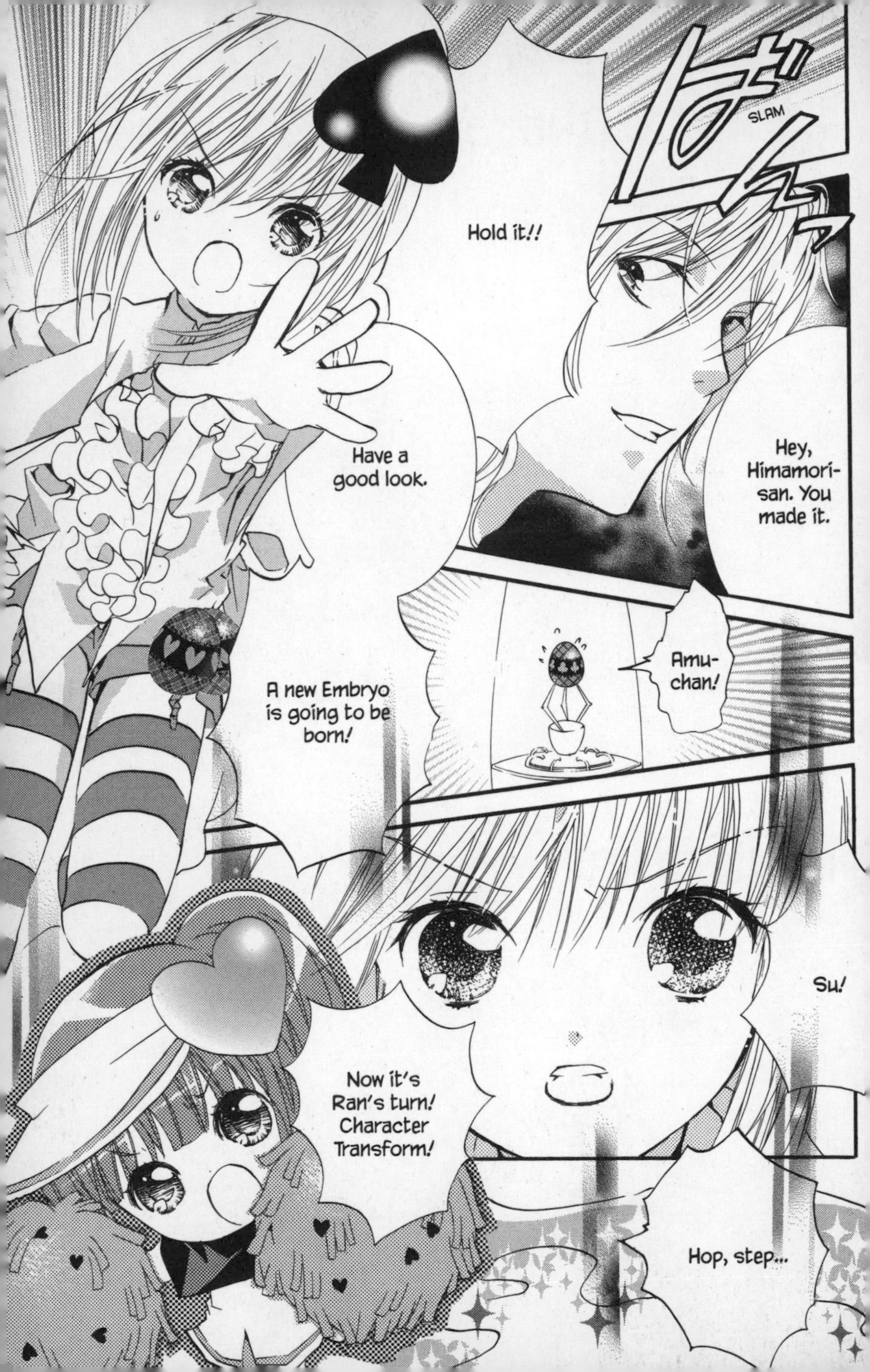
SLAM
Hold it!!
Hey, Himamori-san. You made it.
Have a good look.
A new Embryo is going to be born!
Amu-chan!
Su!
Now it's Ran's turn! Character Transform!
Hop, step...

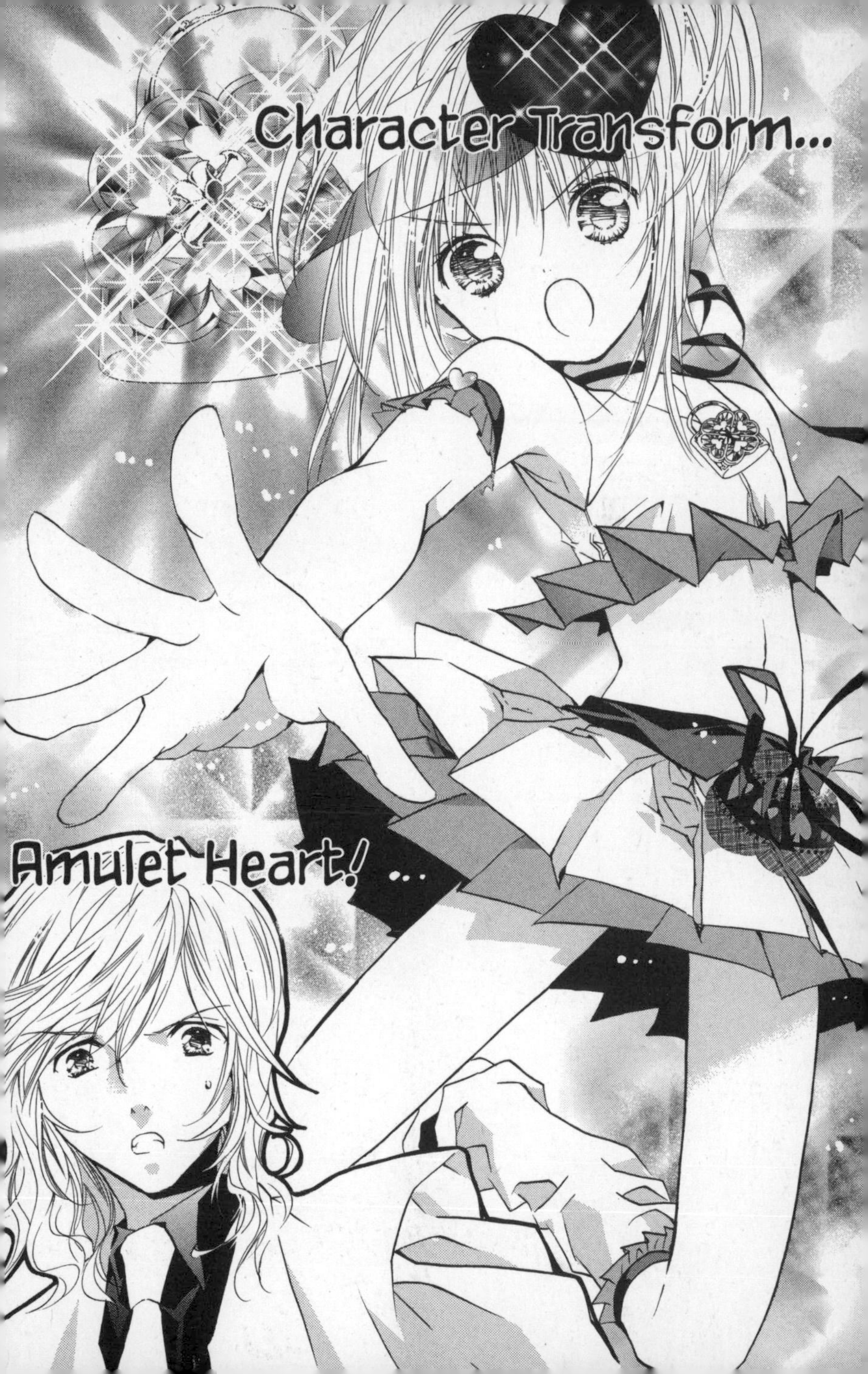
Character Transform...
Amulet Heart!
...

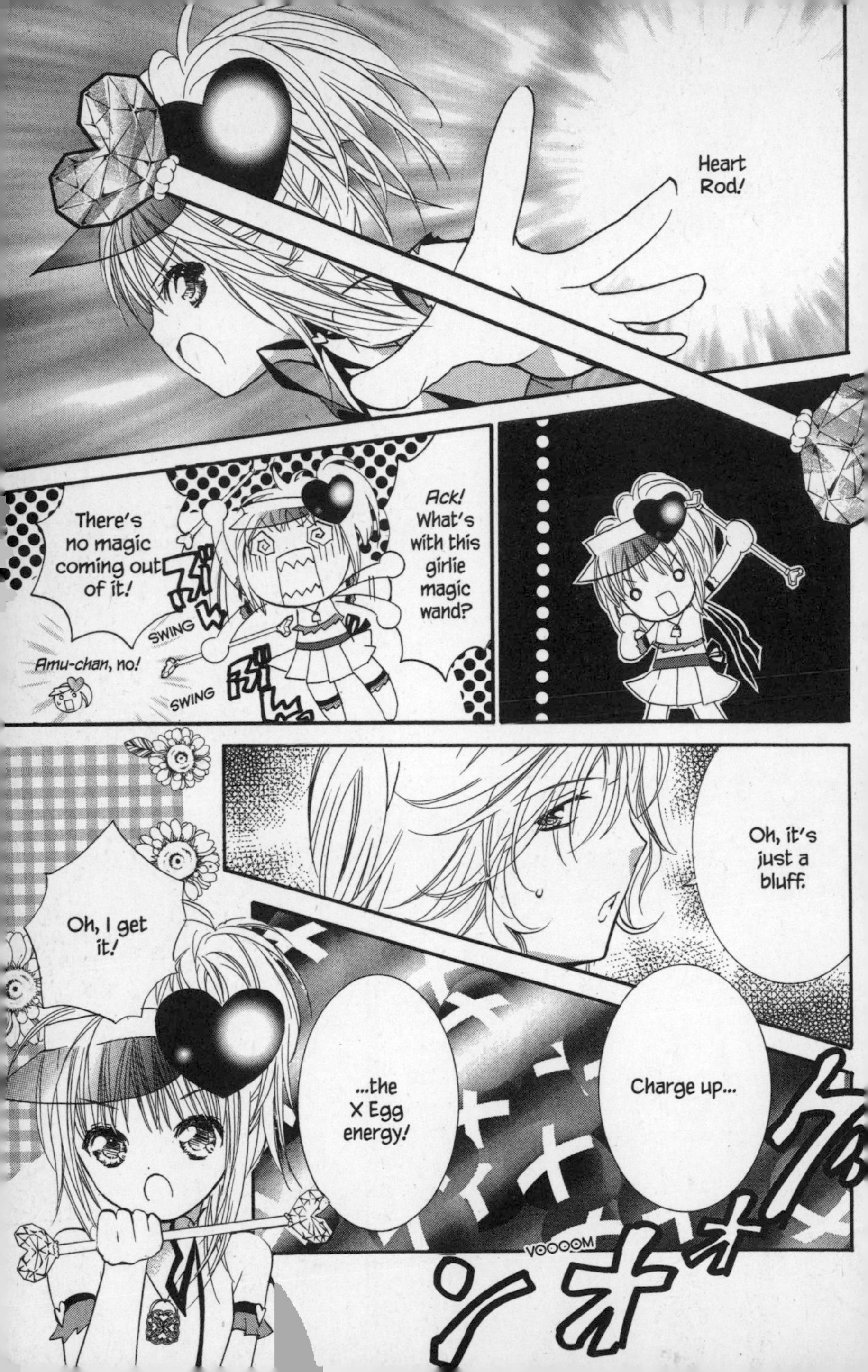
Heart Rod!
Ack! What's with this girlie magic wand?
There's no magic coming out of it!
SWING
SWING
Amu-chan, no!
Oh, it's just a bluff.
Oh, I get it!
Charge up...
...the X Egg energy!
VOOOOM

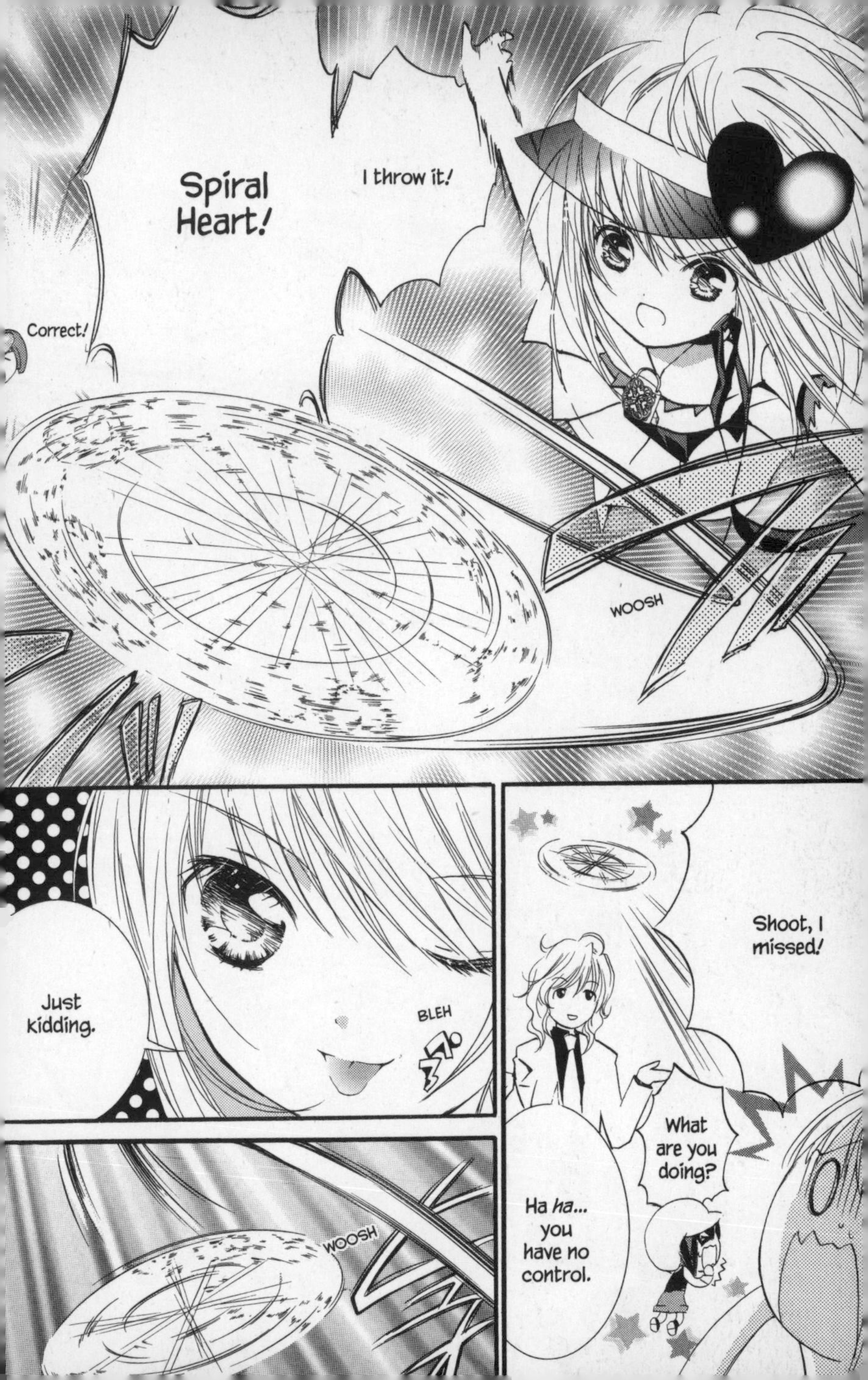
I throw it!
Spiral Heart!
Correct!
WOOSH
Shoot, I missed!
What are you doing?
Ha *ha*... you have no control.
Just kidding.
BLEH
WOOSH

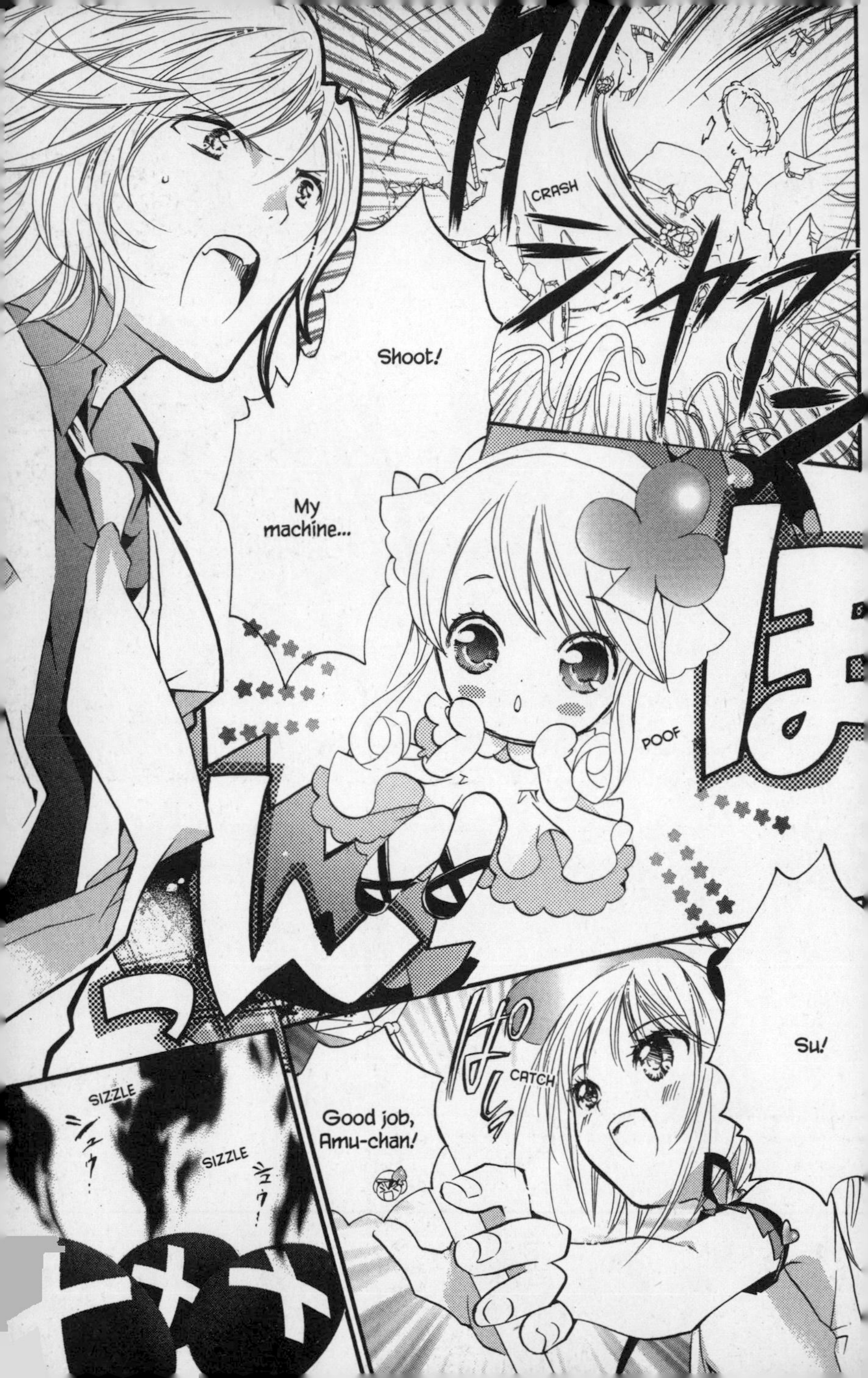
CRASH
Shoot!
POOF
My machine...
Su!
CATCH
Good job, Amu-chan!
SIZZLE
SIZZLE

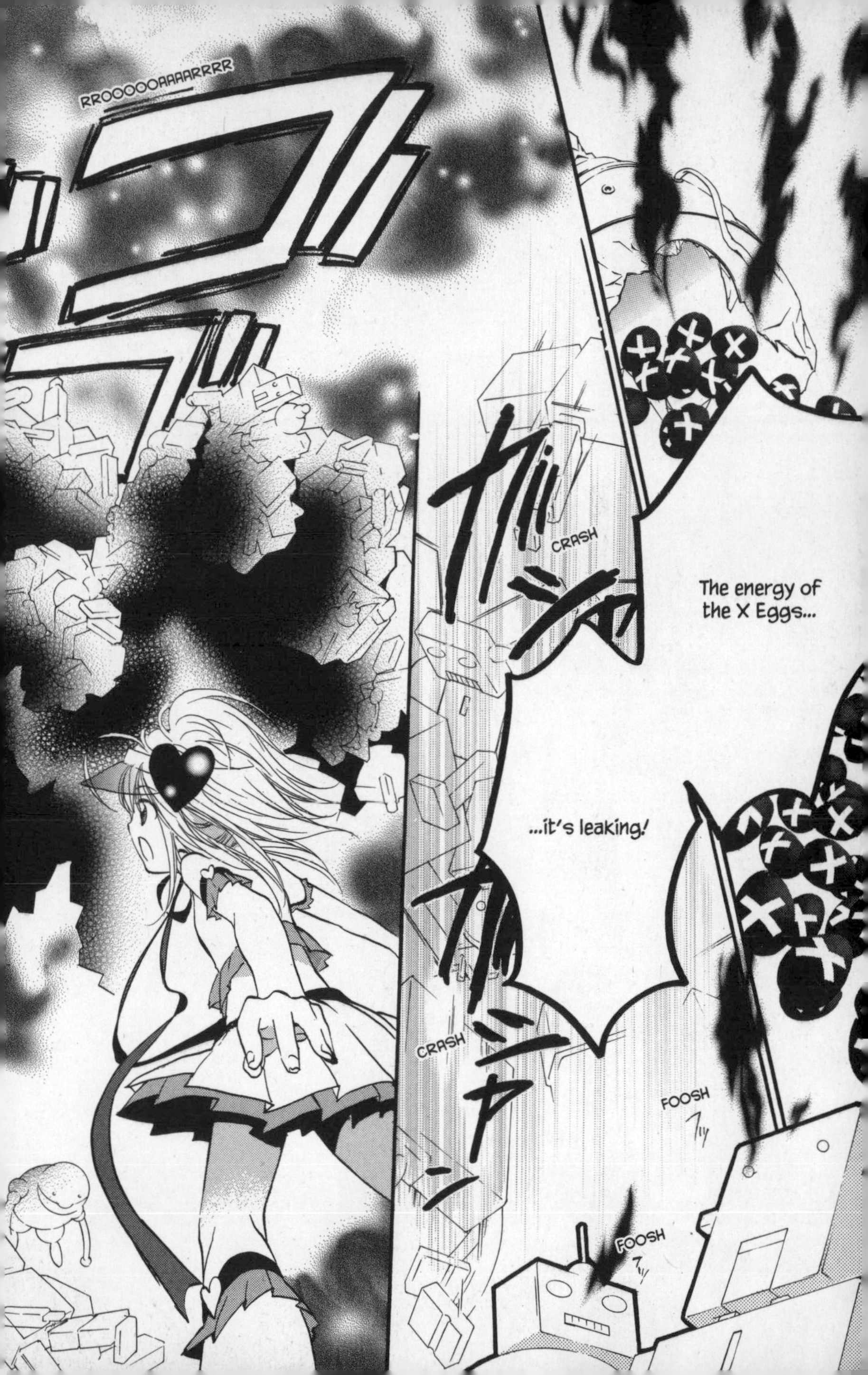
The energy of the X Eggs...
CRASH
...it's leaking!
CRASH
FOOSH
FOOSH
RROOOOOAAAARRRR

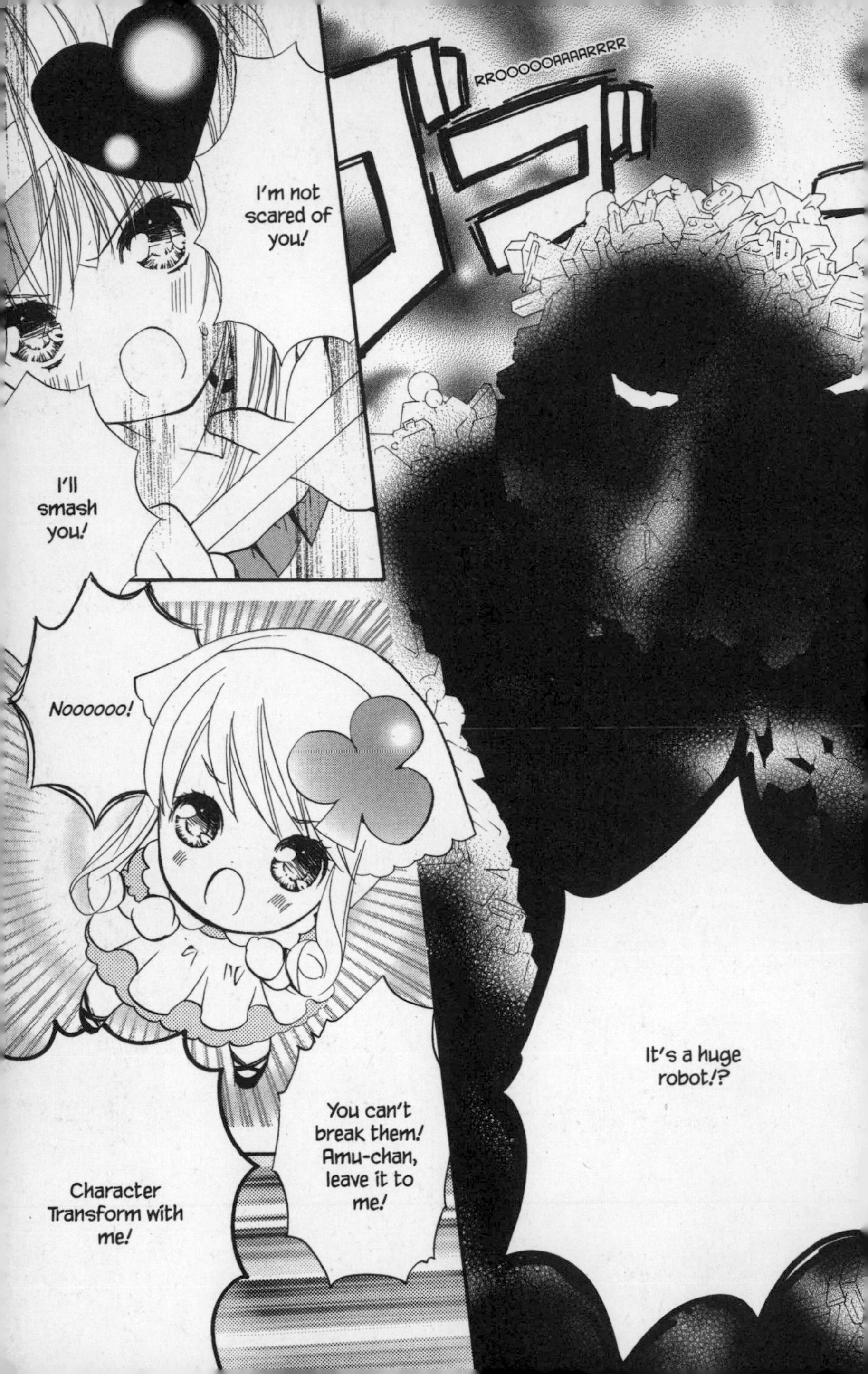
RROOOOOOAAAARRRR
It's a huge robot!?
I'm not scared of you!
I'll smash you!
Noooooo!
You can't break them! Amu-chan, leave it to me!
Character Transform with me!

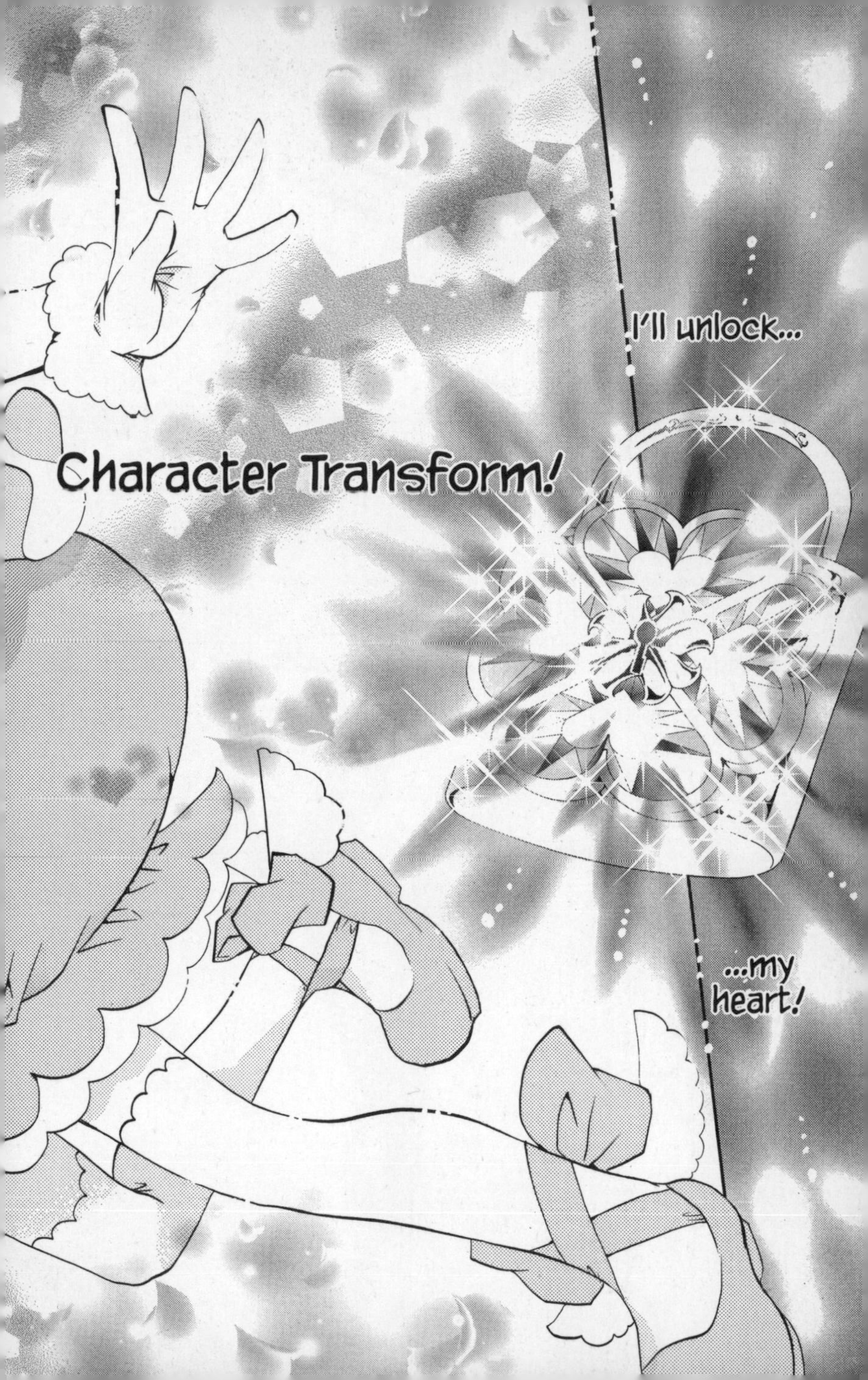
I'll unlock...
...my heart!
Character Transform!

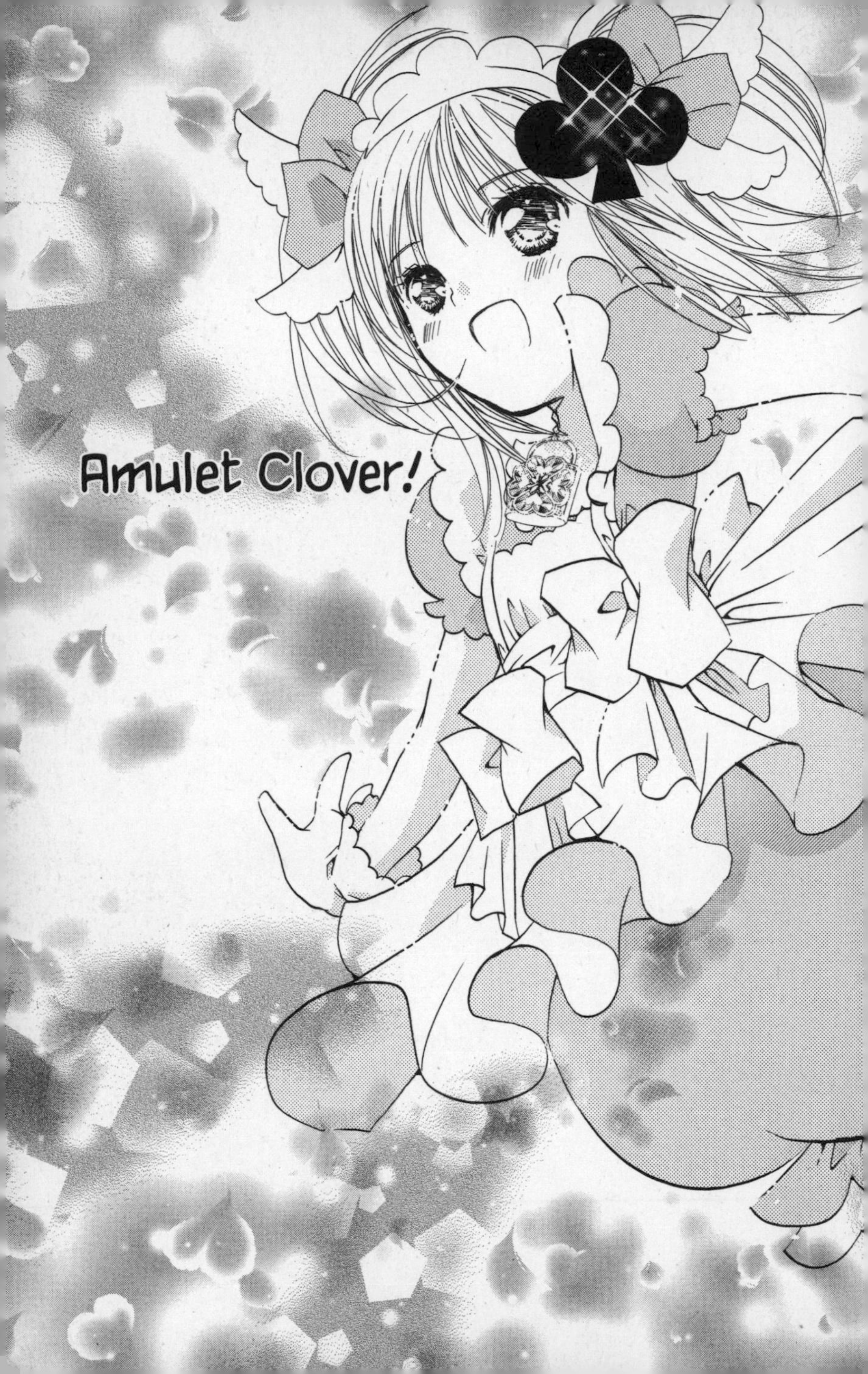
Amulet Clover!

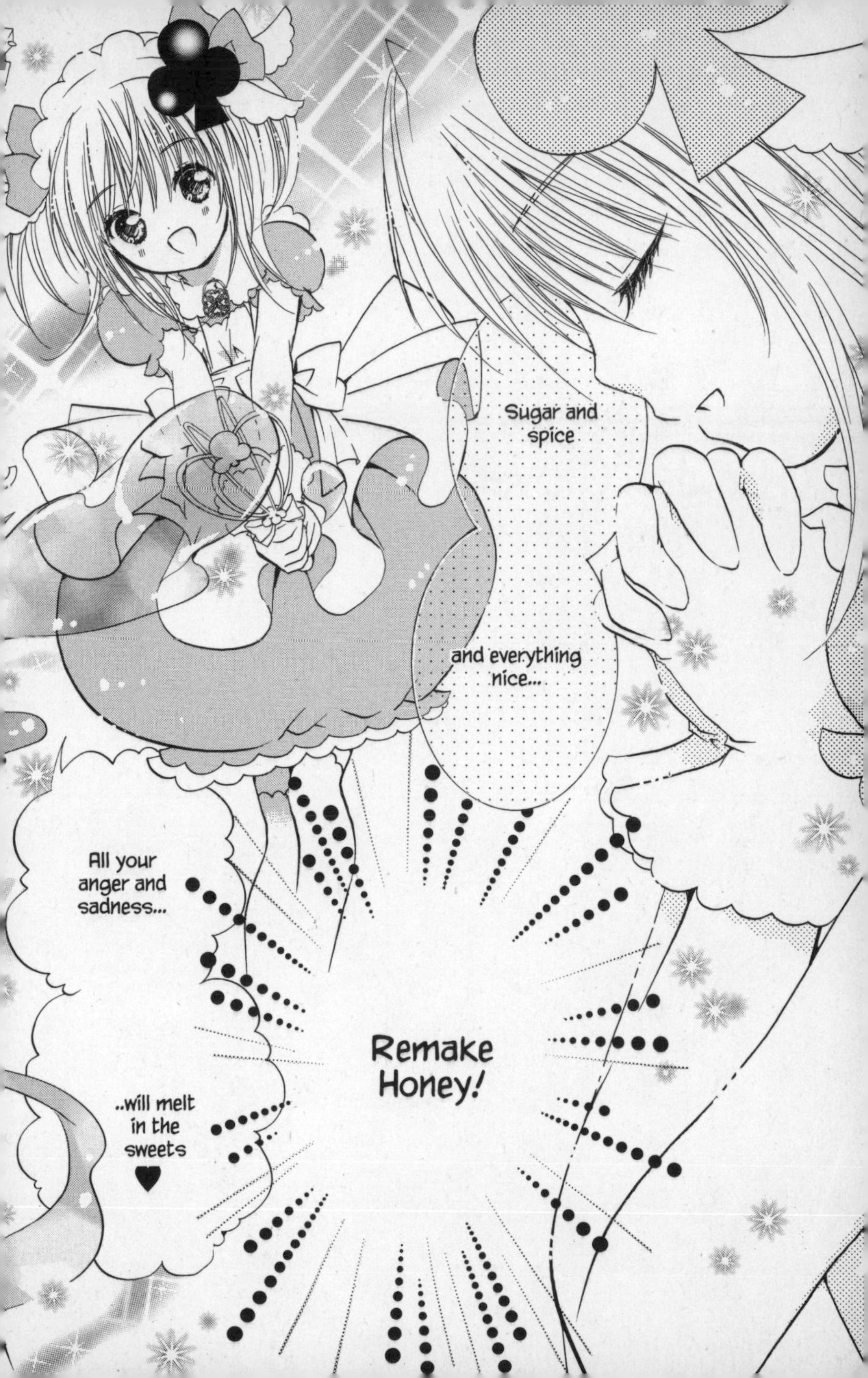
Sugar and spice
and everything nice...
All your anger and sadness...
..will melt in the sweets ♥
Remake Honey!

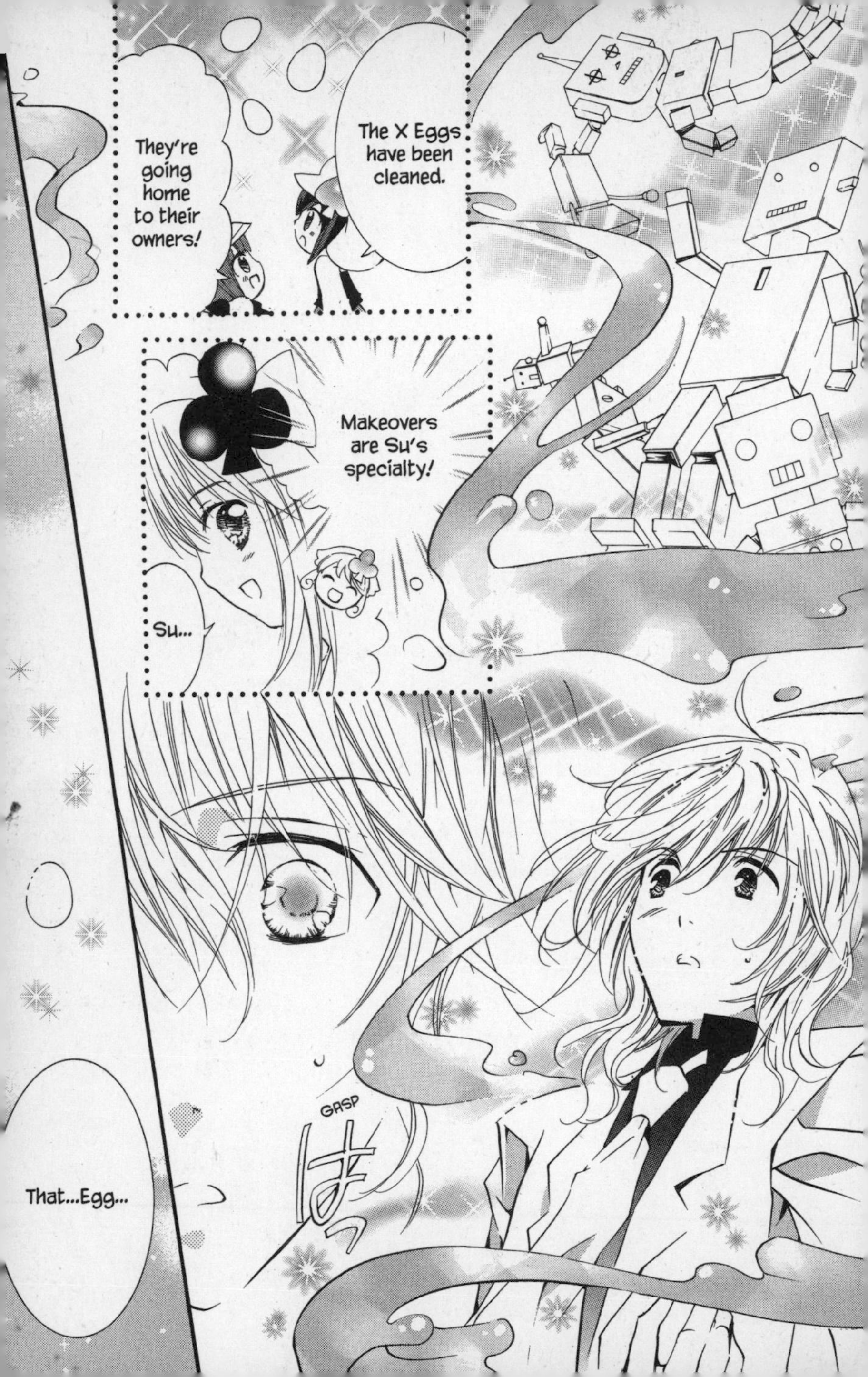
The X Eggs have been cleaned.
They're going home to their owners!
Makeovers are Su's specialty!
Su...
GASP
That...Egg...

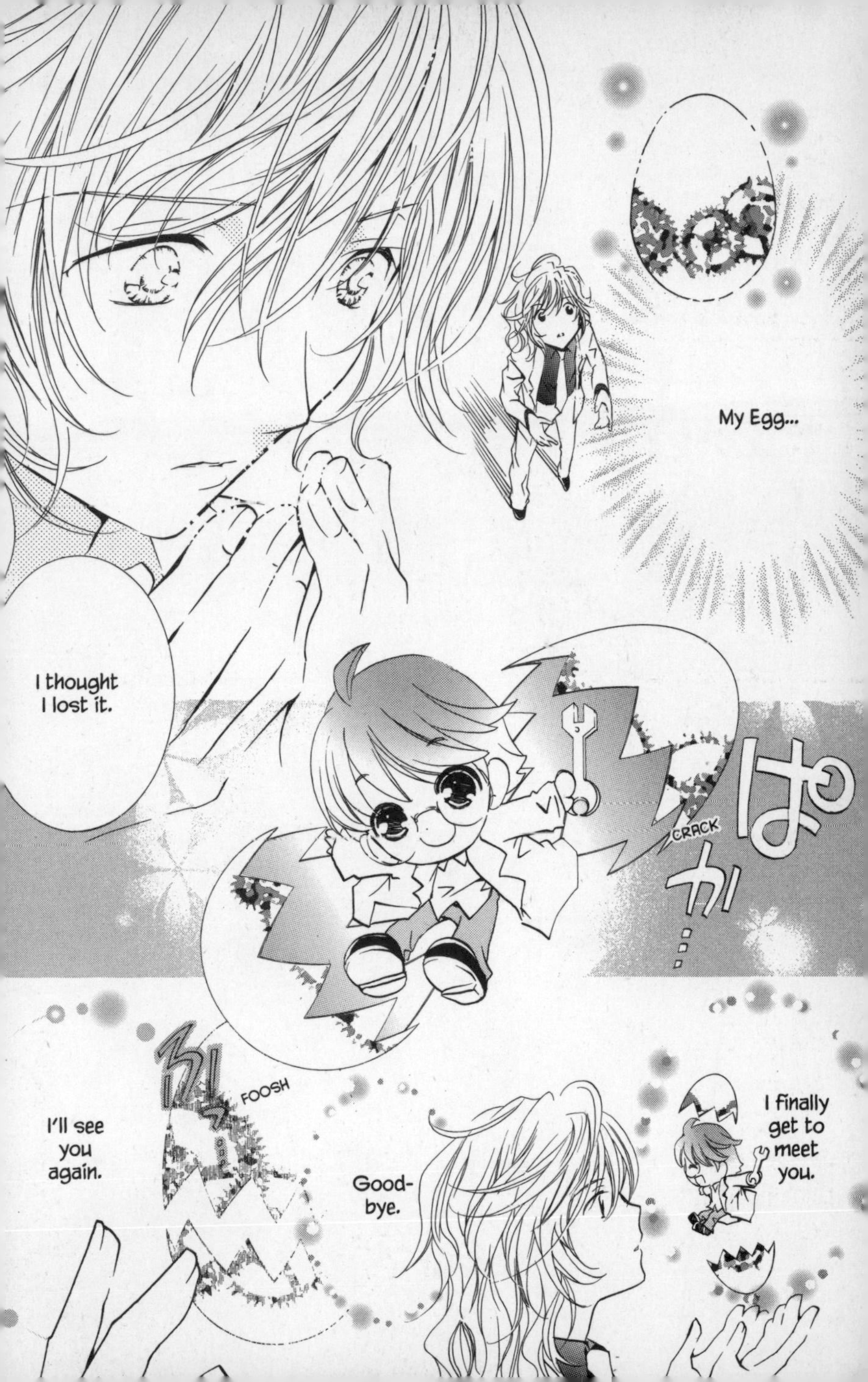
My Egg...
I thought I lost it.
ぱか…
CRACK
I finally get to meet you.
Good-bye.
FOOSH
I'll see you again.

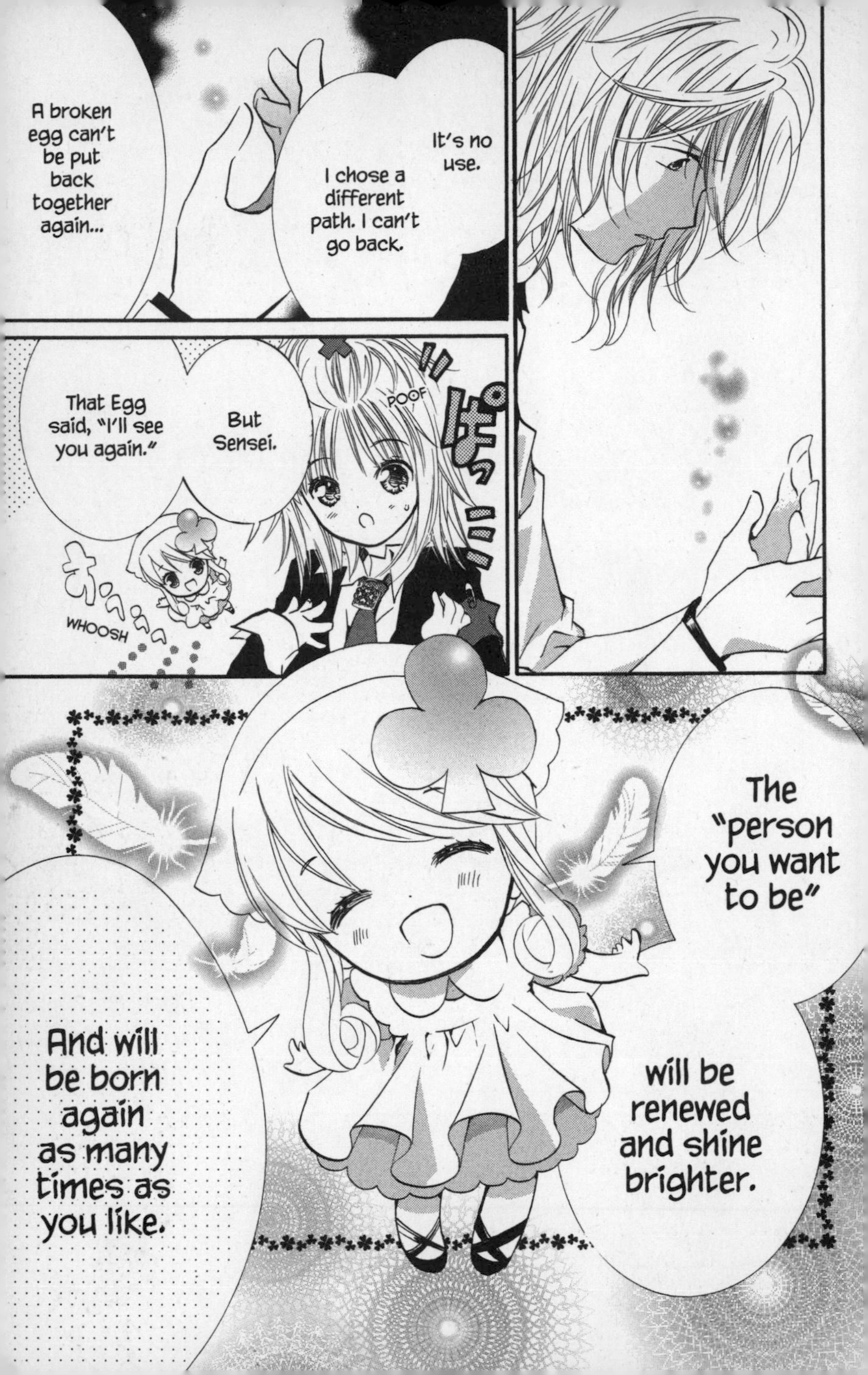

It's no use.
I chose a different path. I can't go back.
A broken egg can't be put back together again...
POOF
But Sensei.
That Egg said, "I'll see you again."
WHOOSH
The "person you want to be"
will be renewed and shine brighter.
And will be born again as many times as you like.

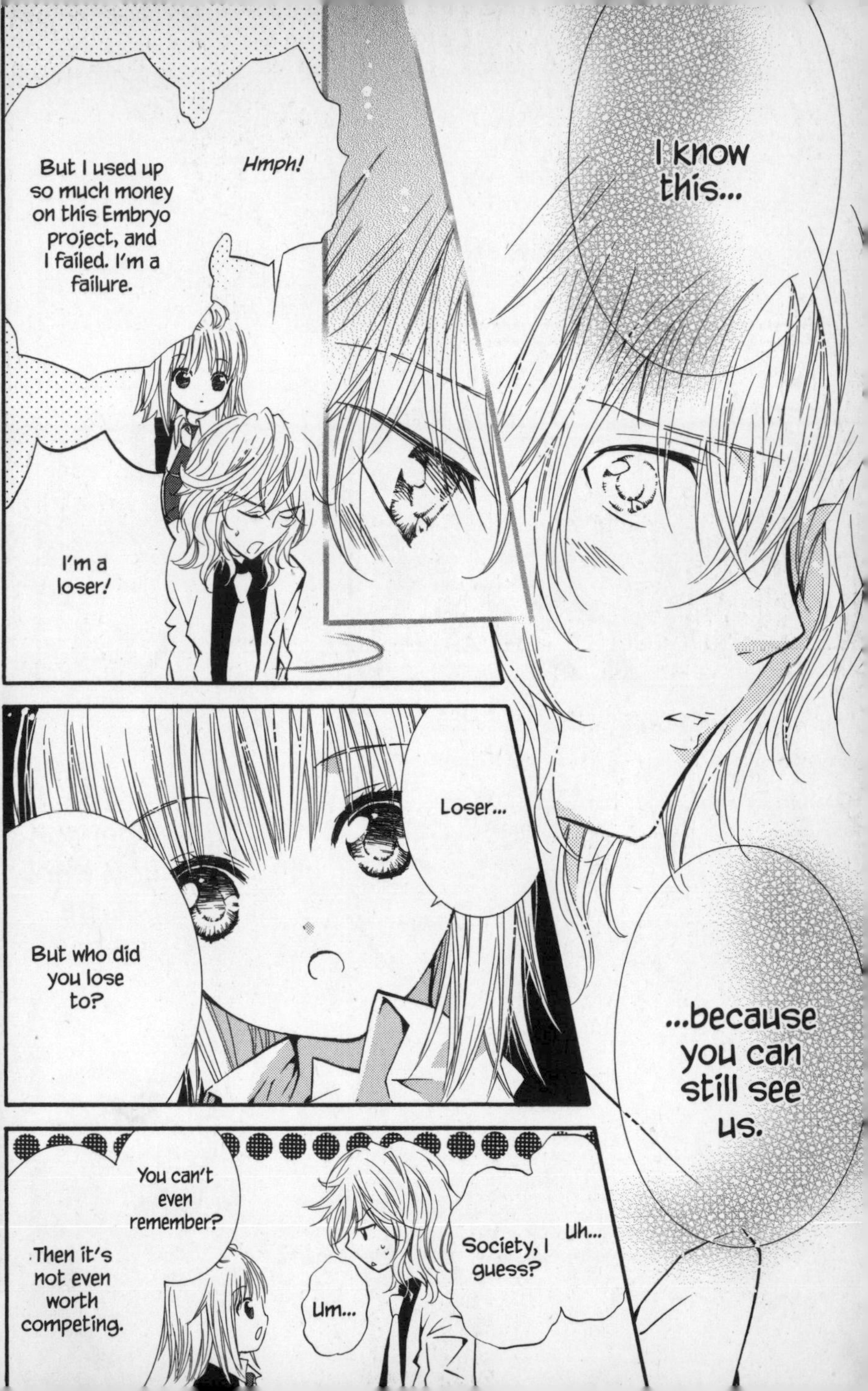
I know this...
...because you can still see us.
Hmph!
But I used up so much money on this Embryo project, and I failed. I'm a failure.
I'm a loser!
Loser...
But who did you lose to?
Uh...
Society, I guess?
Um...
You can't even remember?
Then it's not even worth competing.

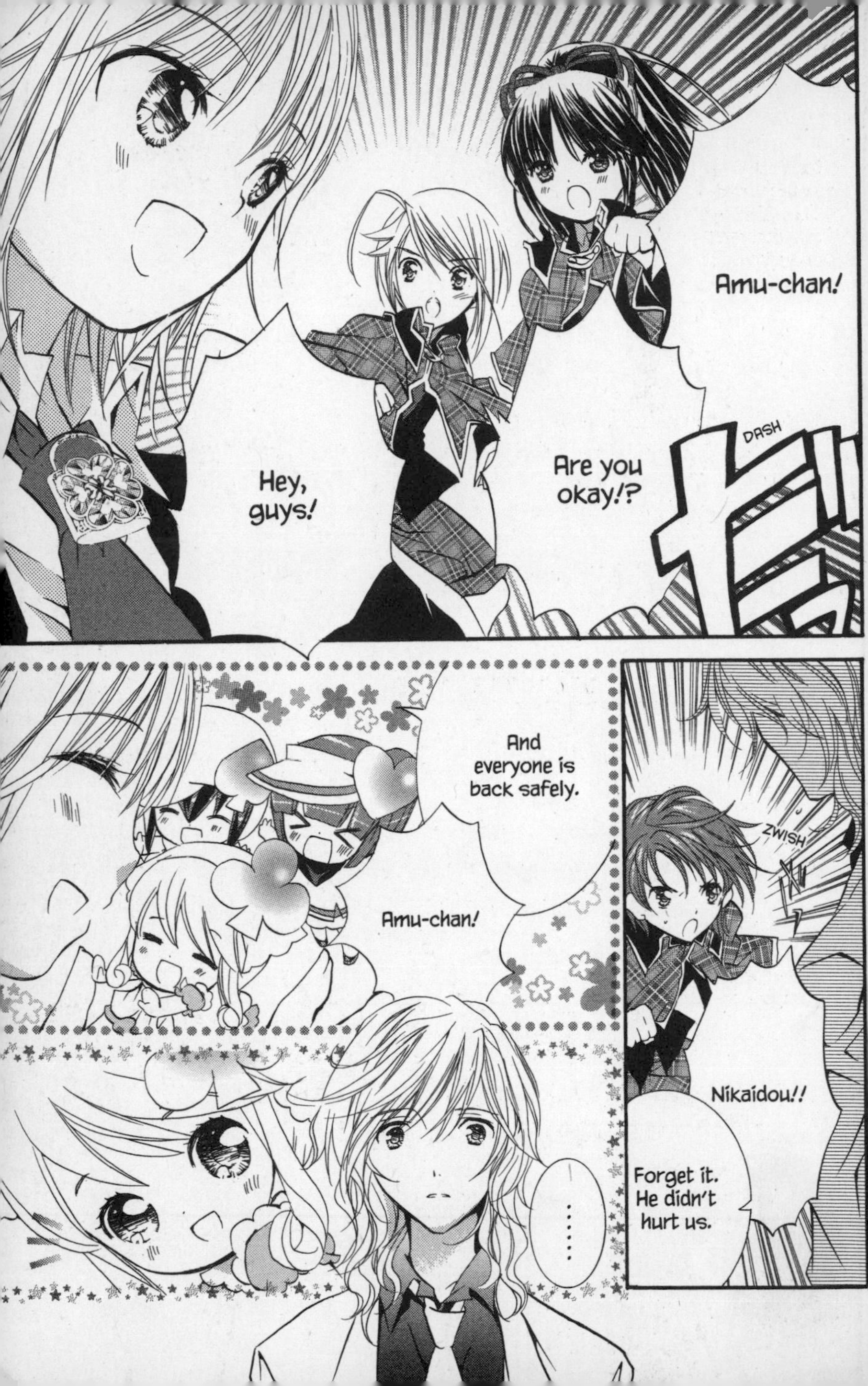
Amu-chan!
DASH
Are you okay!?
Hey, guys!
ZWISH
Nikaidou!!
Forget it. He didn't hurt us.
And everyone is back safely.
Amu-chan!
!
......

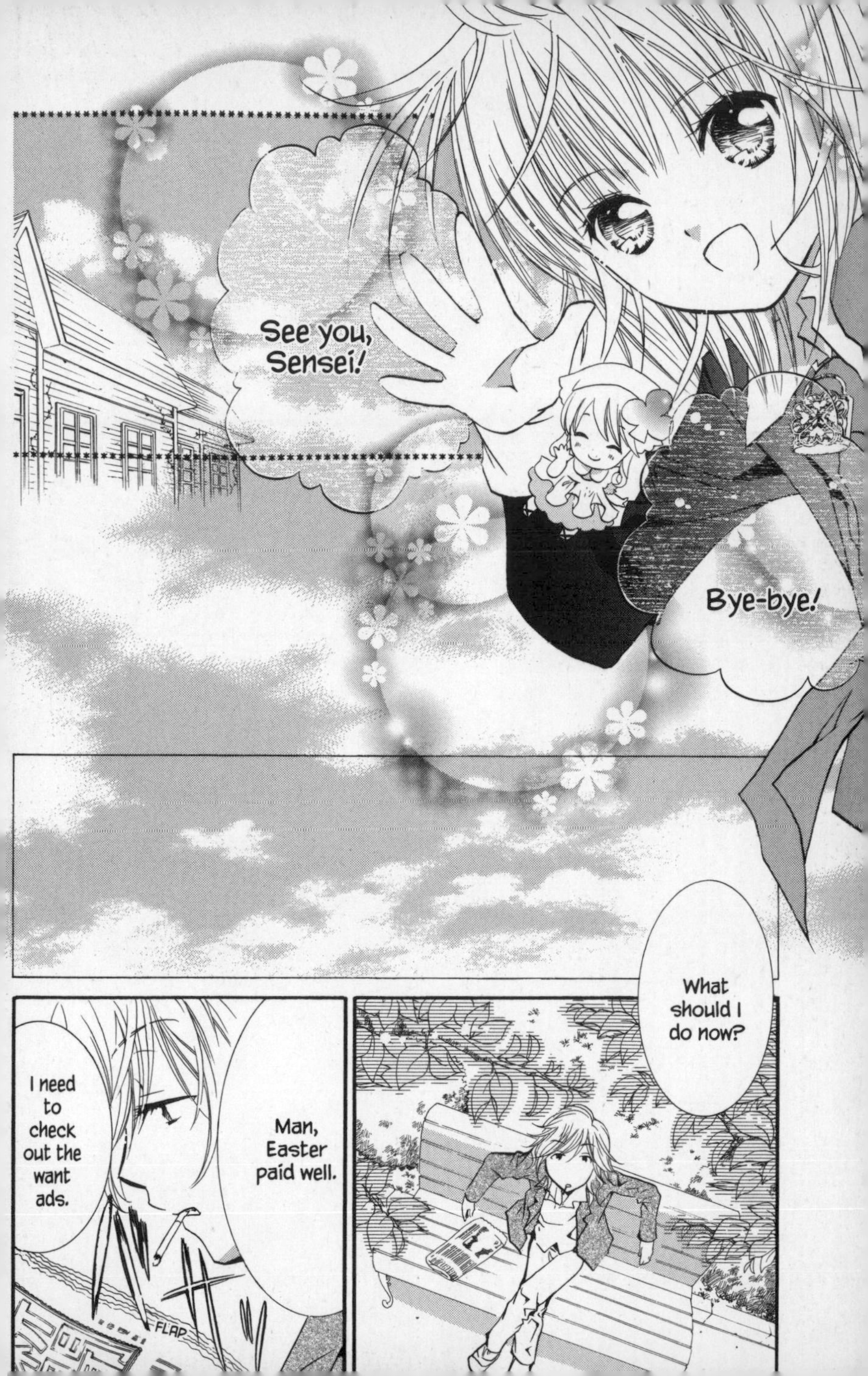
See you, Sensei!
Bye-bye!
What should I do now?
Man, Easter paid well.
I need to check out the want ads.
FLAP

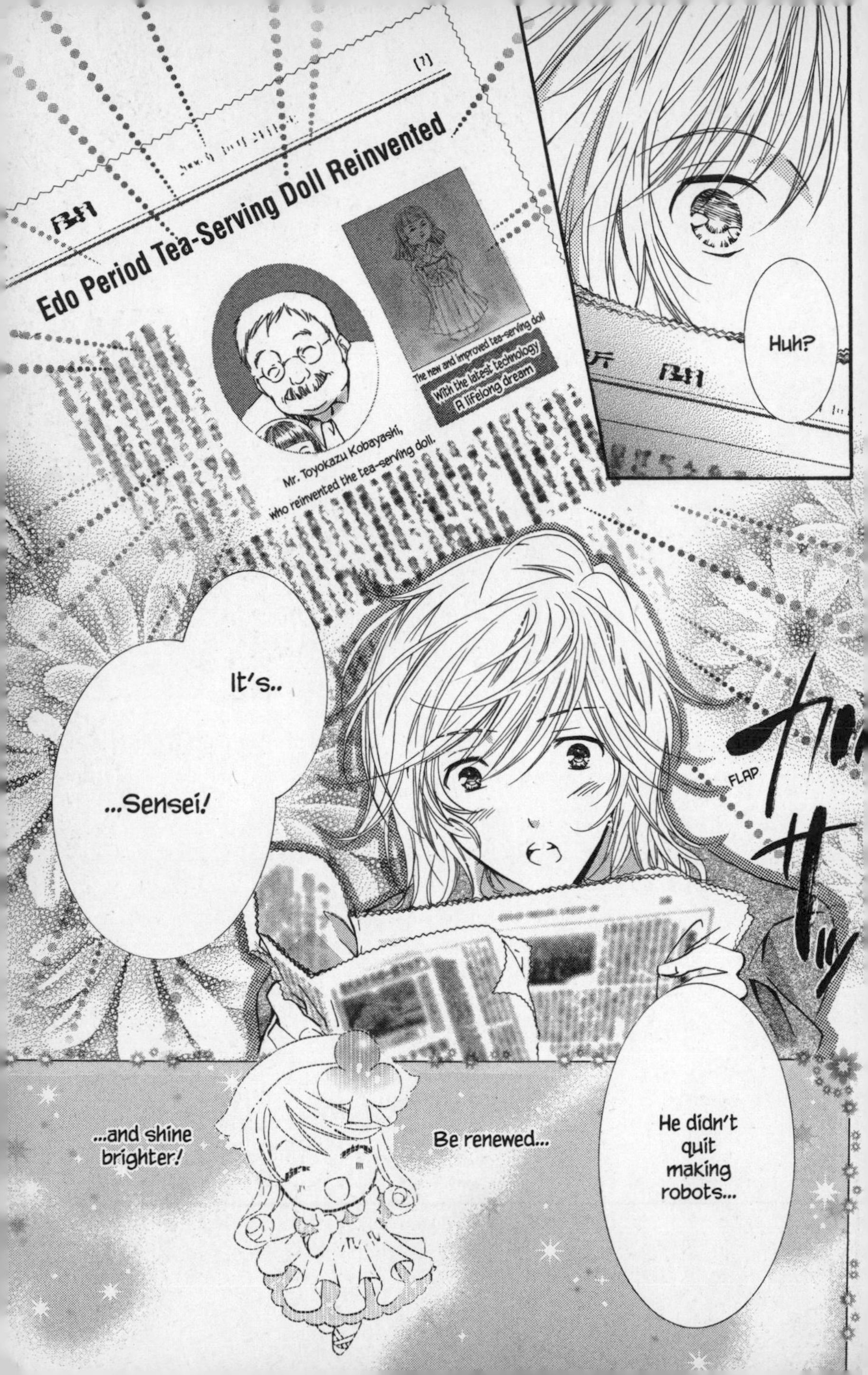
Huh?
Edo Period Tea-Serving Doll Reinvented
The new and improved tea-serving doll
With the latest technology
A lifelong dream
Mr. Toyokazu Kobayashi, who reinvented the tea-serving doll.
FLAP
It's..
...Sensei!
He didn't quit making robots...
Be renewed...
...and shine brighter!

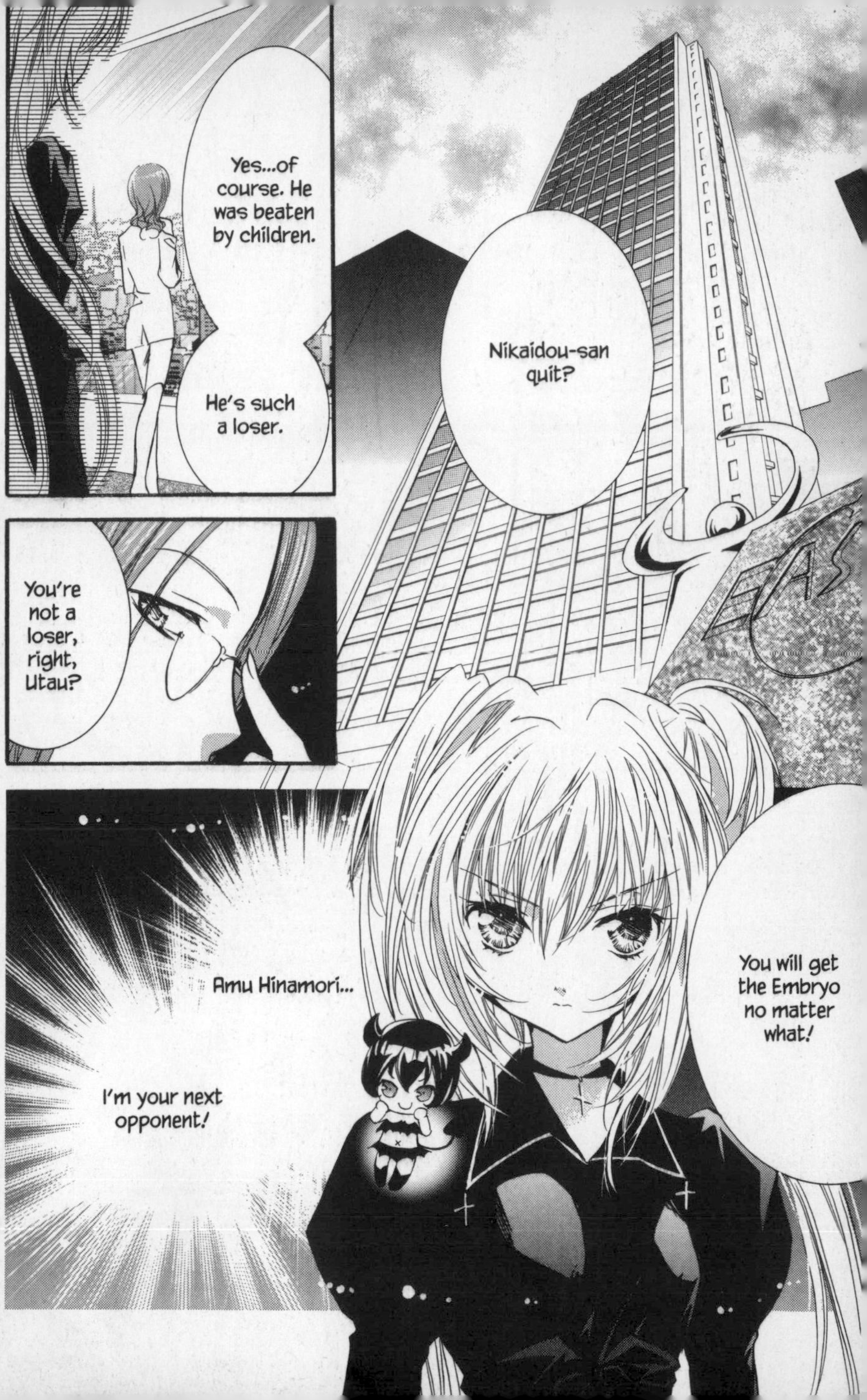
Nikaidou-san quit?
Yes...of course. He was beaten by children.
He's such a loser.
You're not a loser, right, Utau?
You will get the Embryo no matter what!
Amu Hinamori...
I'm your next opponent!

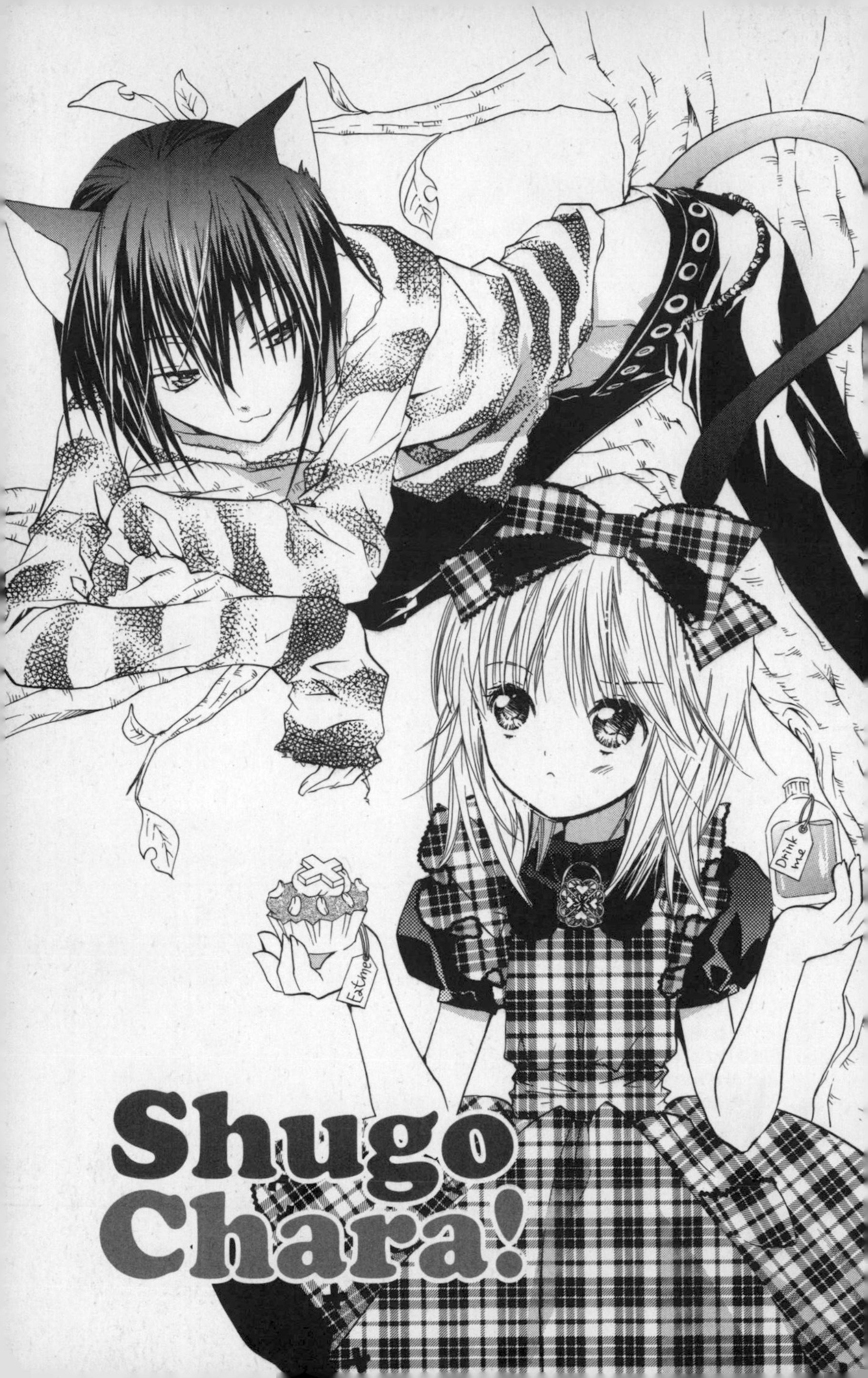
Eat me
Drink me
Shugo Chara!

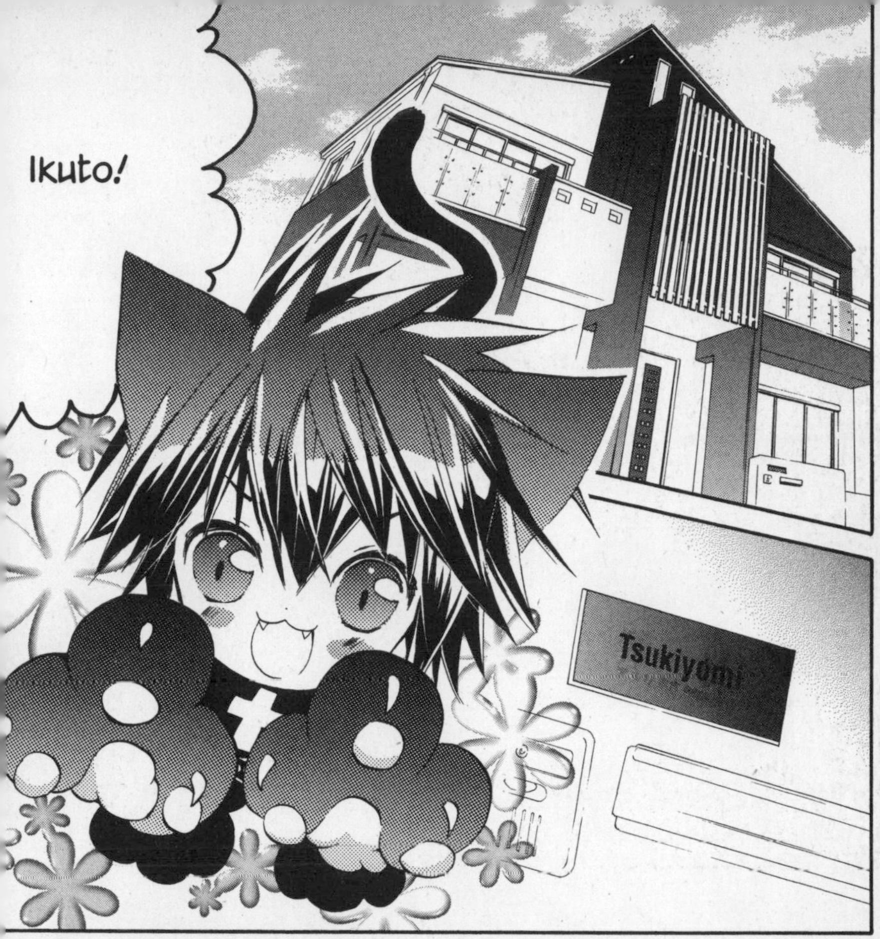
Tsukiyomi
Ikuto!

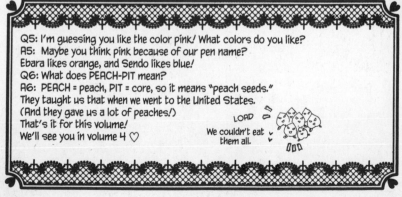

Q5: I'm guessing you like the color pink! What colors do you like?
A5: Maybe you think pink because of our pen name?
Ebara likes orange, and Sendo likes blue!
Q6: What does PEACH-PIT mean?
A6: PEACH = peach, PIT = core, so it means "peach seeds."
They taught us that when we went to the United States.
(And they gave us a lot of peaches!)
That's it for this volume!
We'll see you in volume 4 ♡

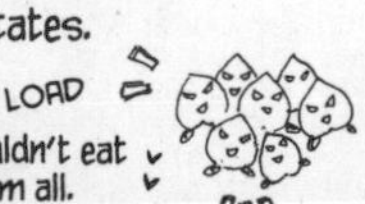
LOAD
We couldn't eat them all.

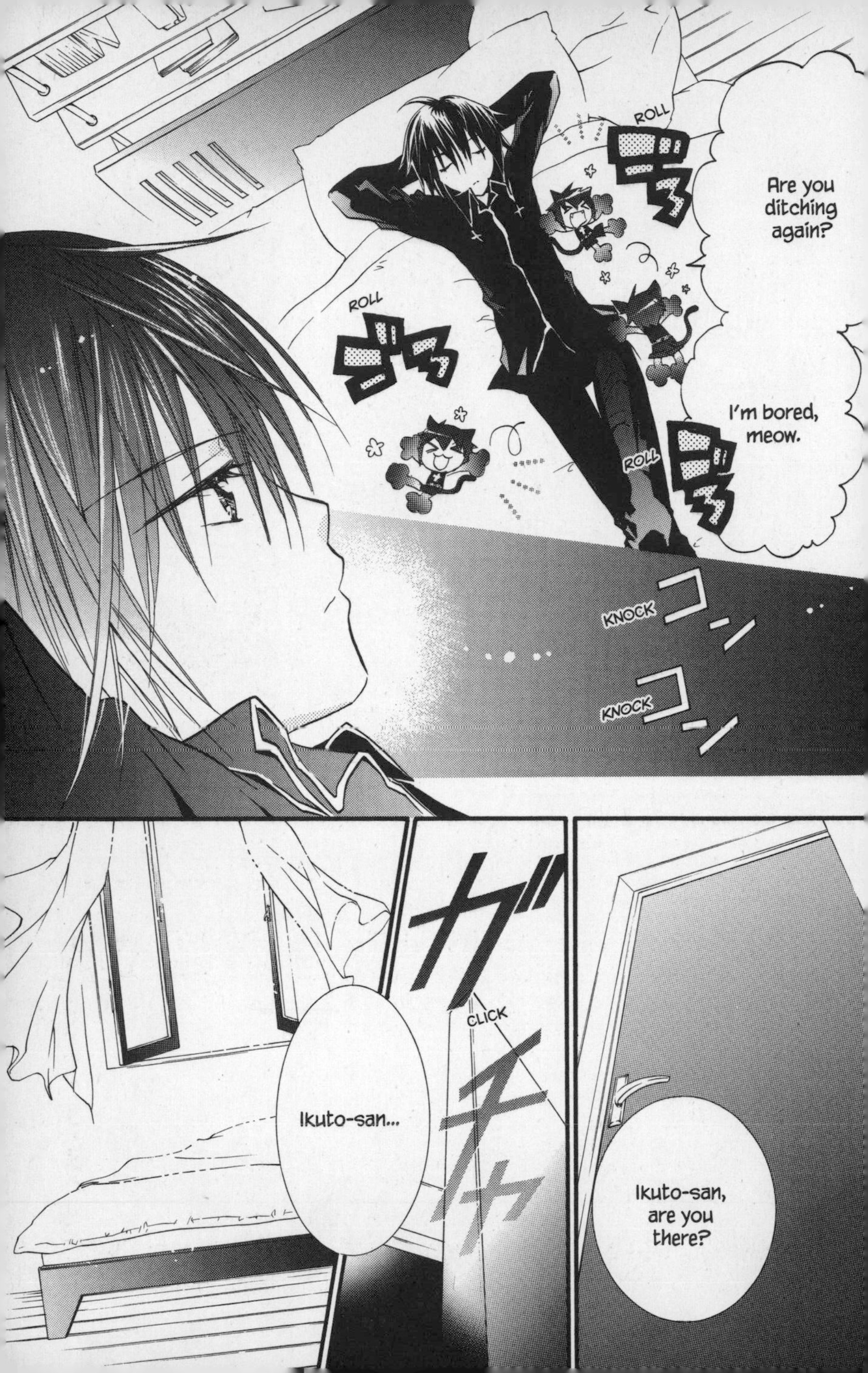
ROLL
Are you ditching again?
I'm bored, meow.
ROLL
ROLL
KNOCK
KNOCK
Ikuto-san, are you there?
CLICK
Ikuto-san...

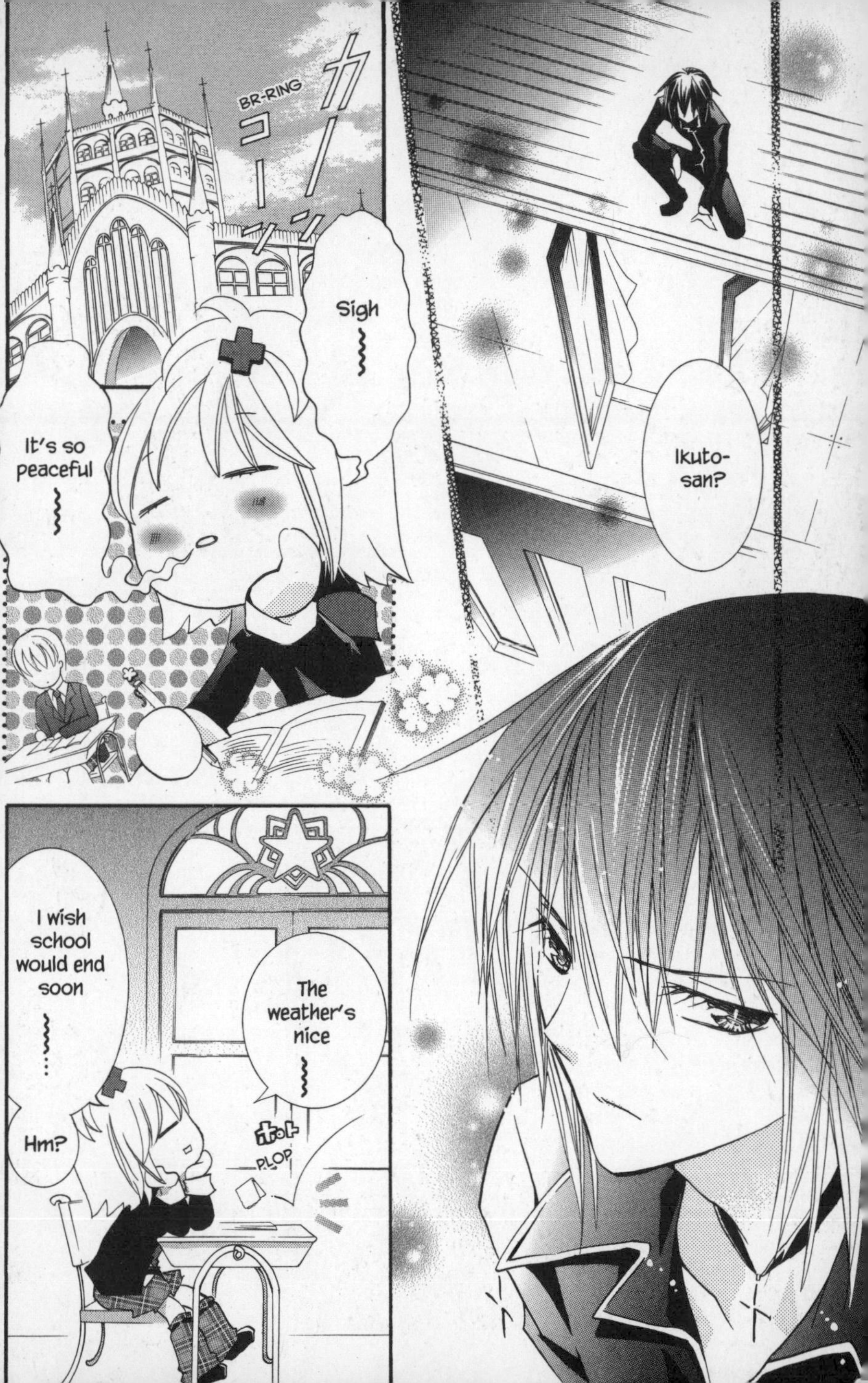
Ikuto-san?
BR-RING
Sigh ...
It's so peaceful ...
I wish school would end soon ......
The weather's nice ...
Hm?
PLOP

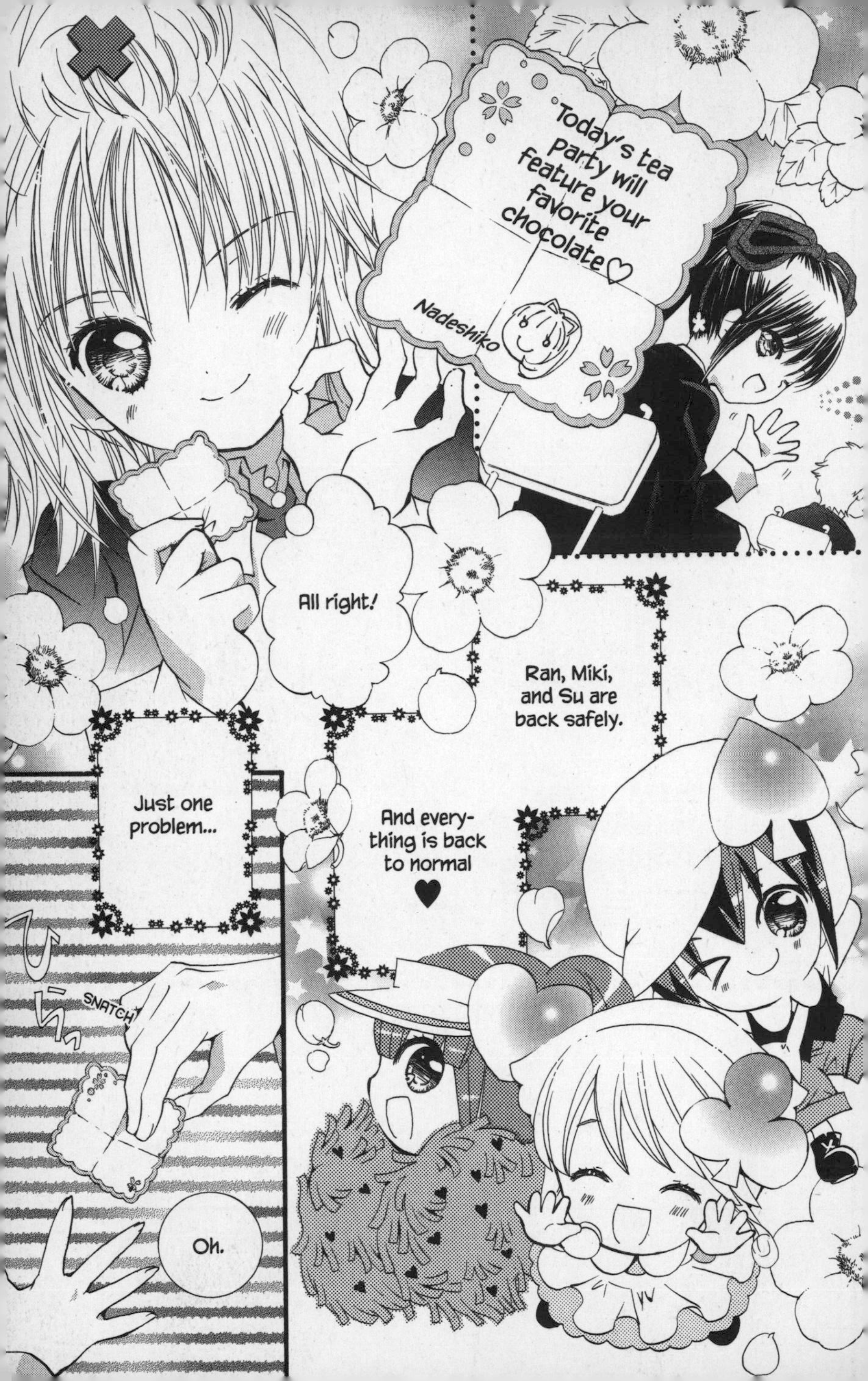
Today's tea party will feature your favorite chocolate♡
Nadeshiko
All right!
Ran, Miki, and Su are back safely.
And every-thing is back to normal ♥
Just one problem...
SNATCH
Oh.

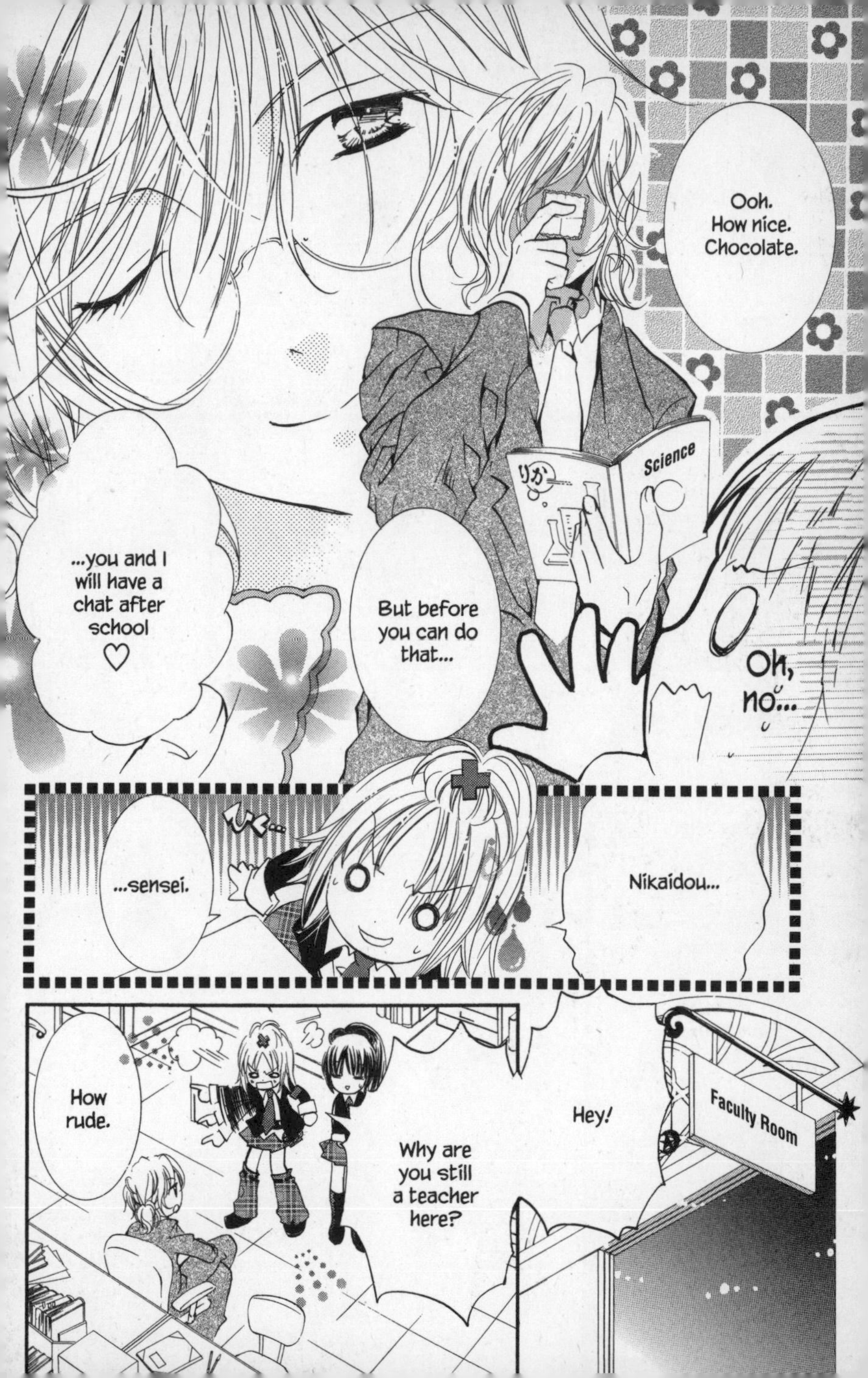
Ooh. How nice. Chocolate.
りか
Science
Oh, no...
But before you can do that...
...you and I will have a chat after school ♡
Nikaidou...
...sensei.
Faculty Room
Hey!
Why are you still a teacher here?
How rude.

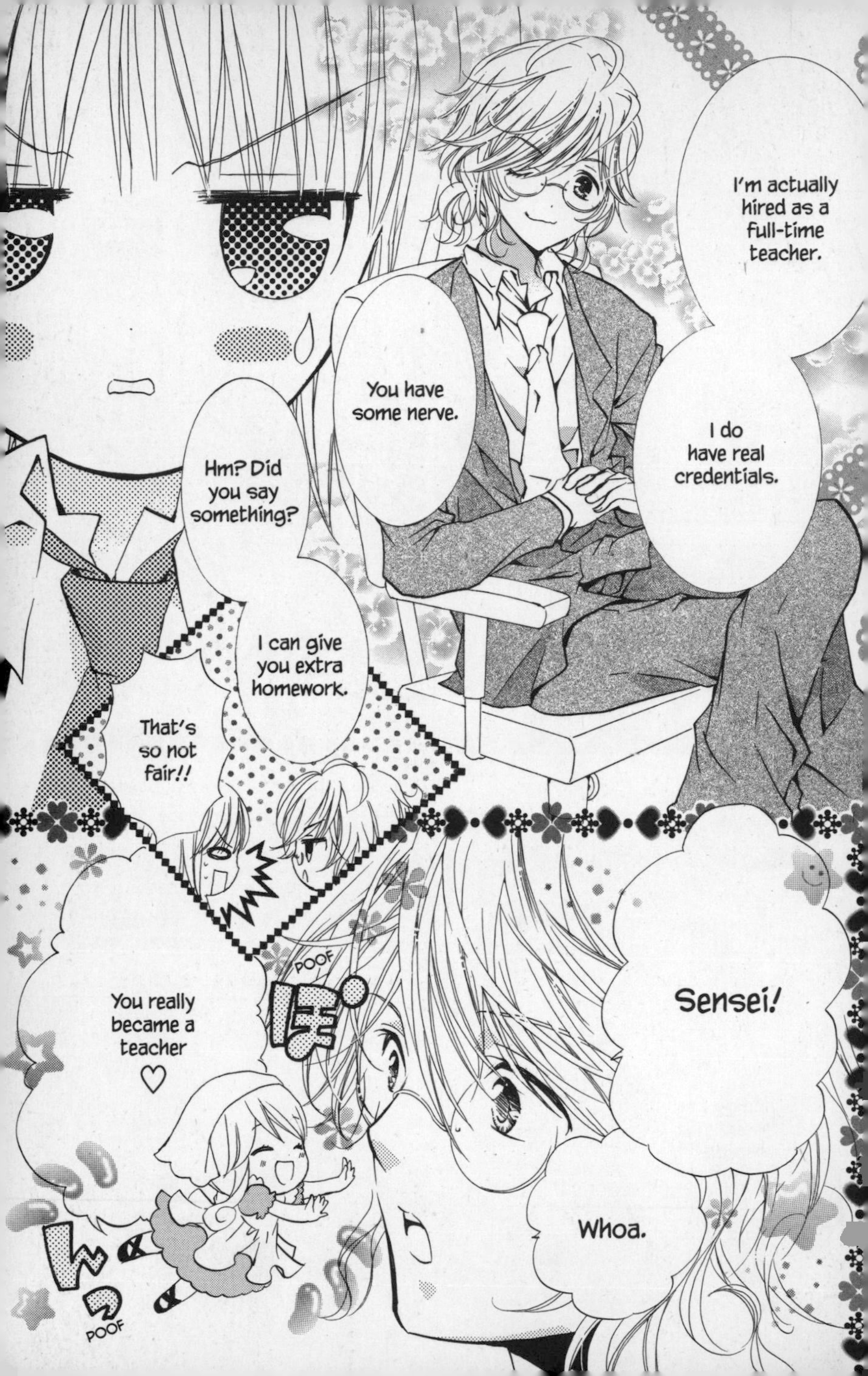
I'm actually hired as a full-time teacher.
I do have real credentials.
You have some nerve.
Hm? Did you say something?
I can give you extra homework.
That's so not fair!!
Sensei!
Whoa.
POOF
You really became a teacher ♡
POOF

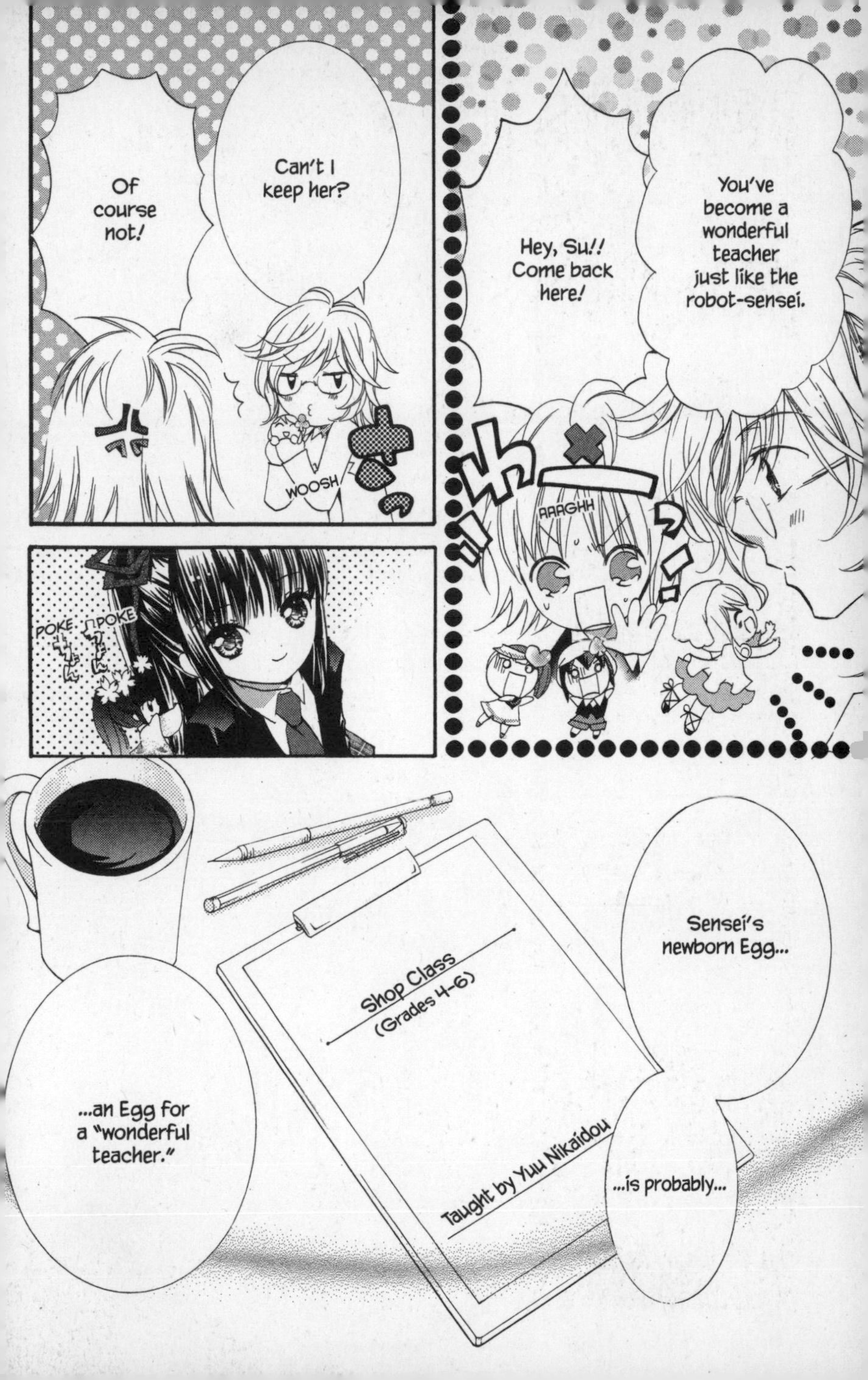
You've become a wonderful teacher just like the robot-sensei.
Hey, Su!! Come back here!
RAAGHH
Can't I keep her?
Of course not!
WOOSH
POKE
POKE
Sensei's newborn Egg...
...is probably...
...an Egg for a "wonderful teacher."
Shop Class
(Grades 4-6)
Taught by Yuu Nikaidou

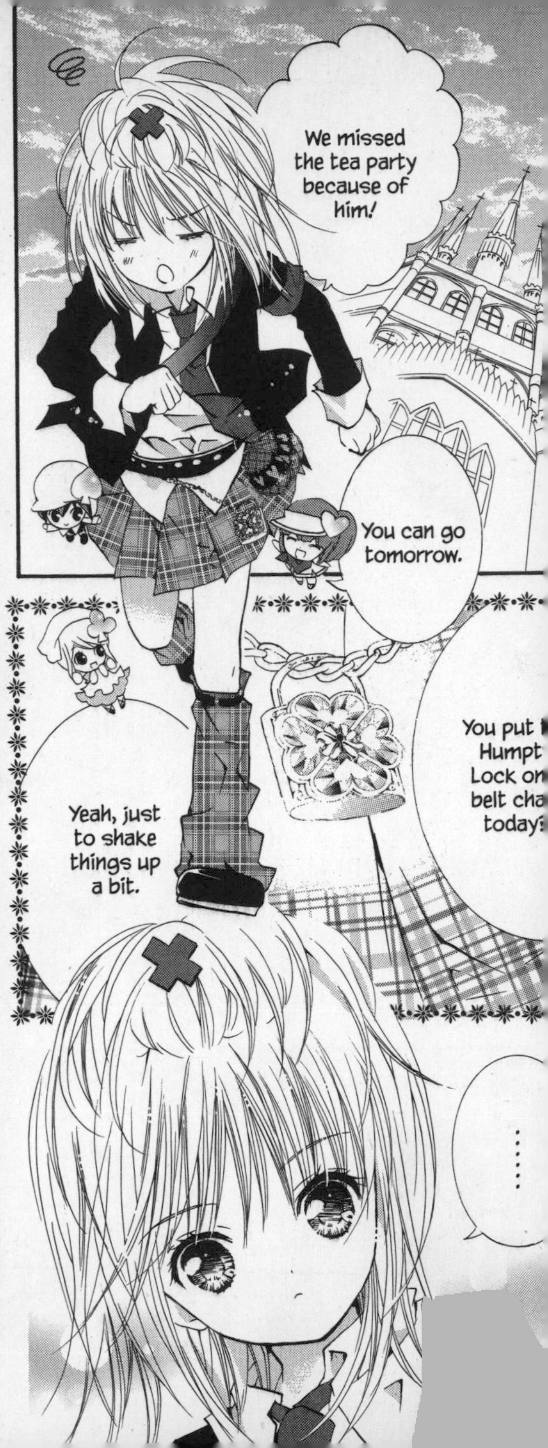
We missed the tea party because of him!
You can go tomorrow.
You put t Humpt Lock on belt cha today?
Yeah, just to shake things up a bit.
......

character profile

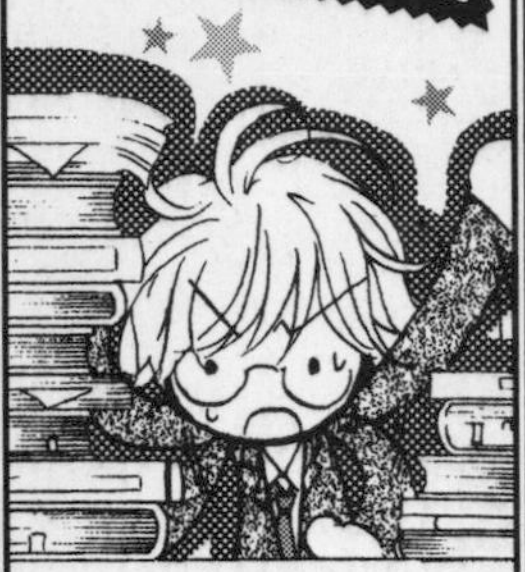

Yuu Nikaidou

Birthday: 9/18
Blood Type: A
Sign: Virgo

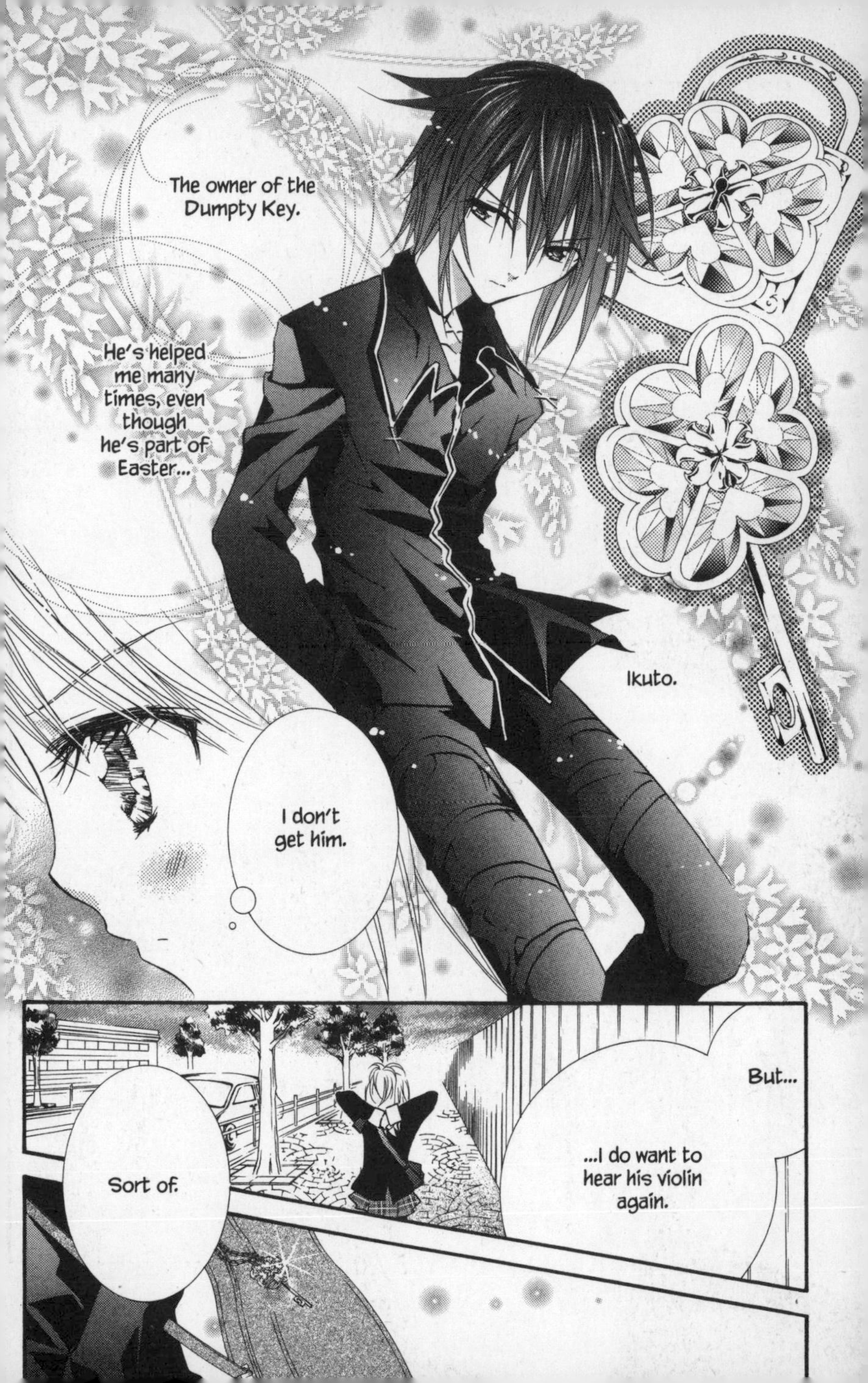
The owner of the Dumpty Key.
He's helped me many times, even though he's part of Easter...
Ikuto.
I don't get him.
But...
...I do want to hear his violin again.
Sort of.

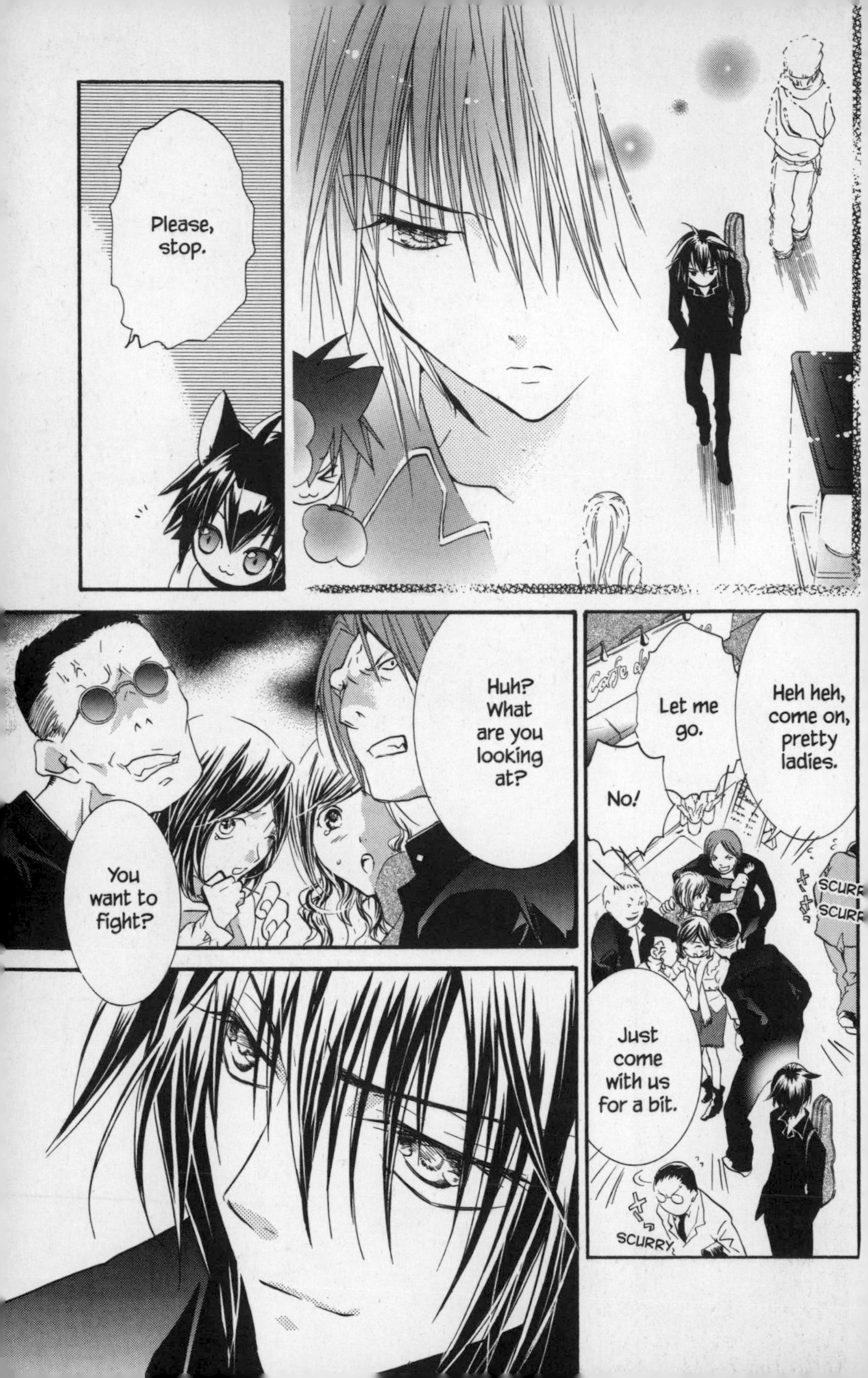
Please, stop.
Heh heh, come on, pretty ladies.
Let me go.
No!
SCURR
SCURR
Just come with us for a bit.
SCURRY
Huh? What are you looking at?
You want to fight?

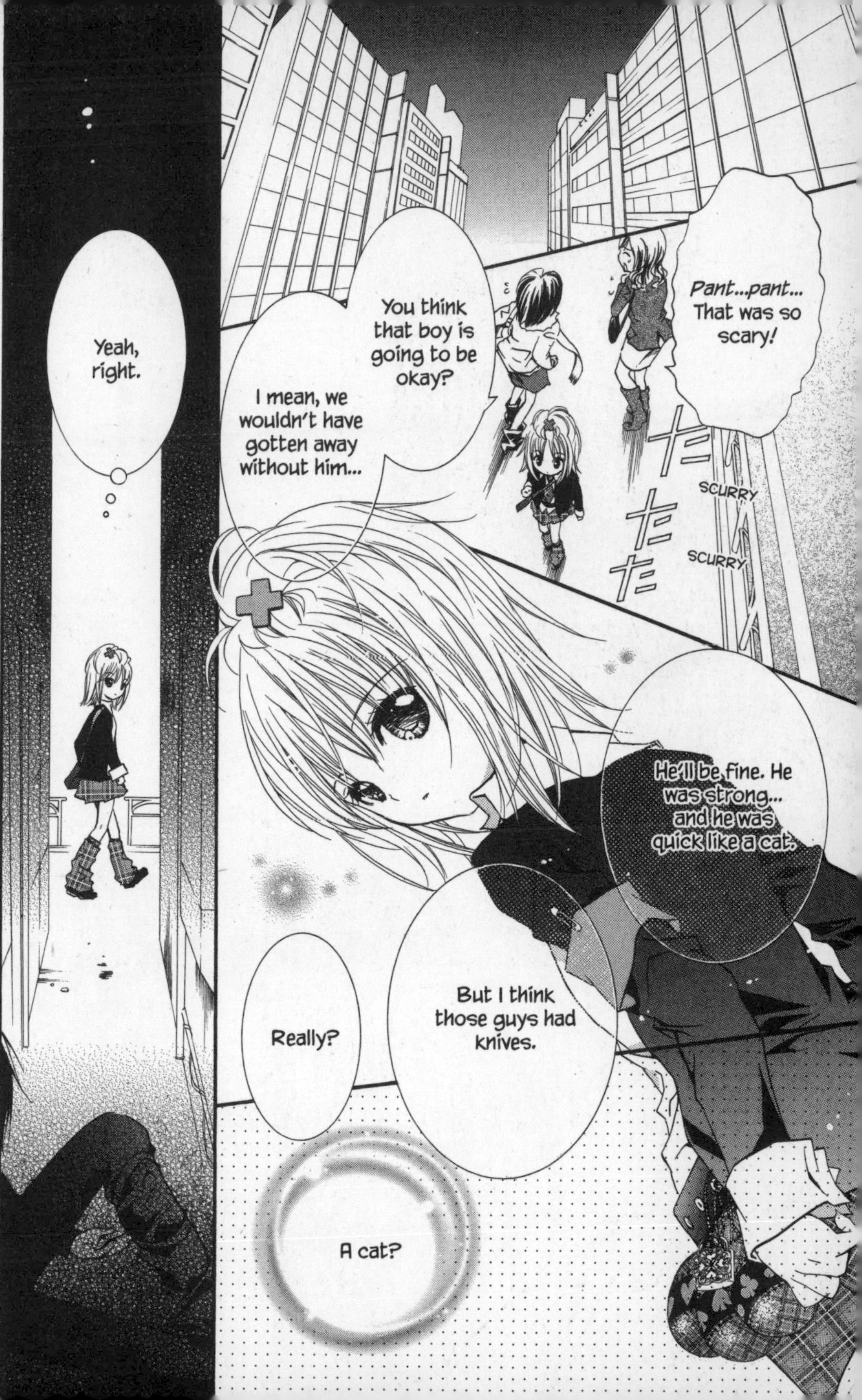

Pant...pant... That was so scary!
You think that boy is going to be okay?
I mean, we wouldn't have gotten away without him...
SCURRY
SCURRY
He'll be fine. He was strong... and he was quick like a cat.
But I think those guys had knives.
Really?
A cat?
Yeah, right.

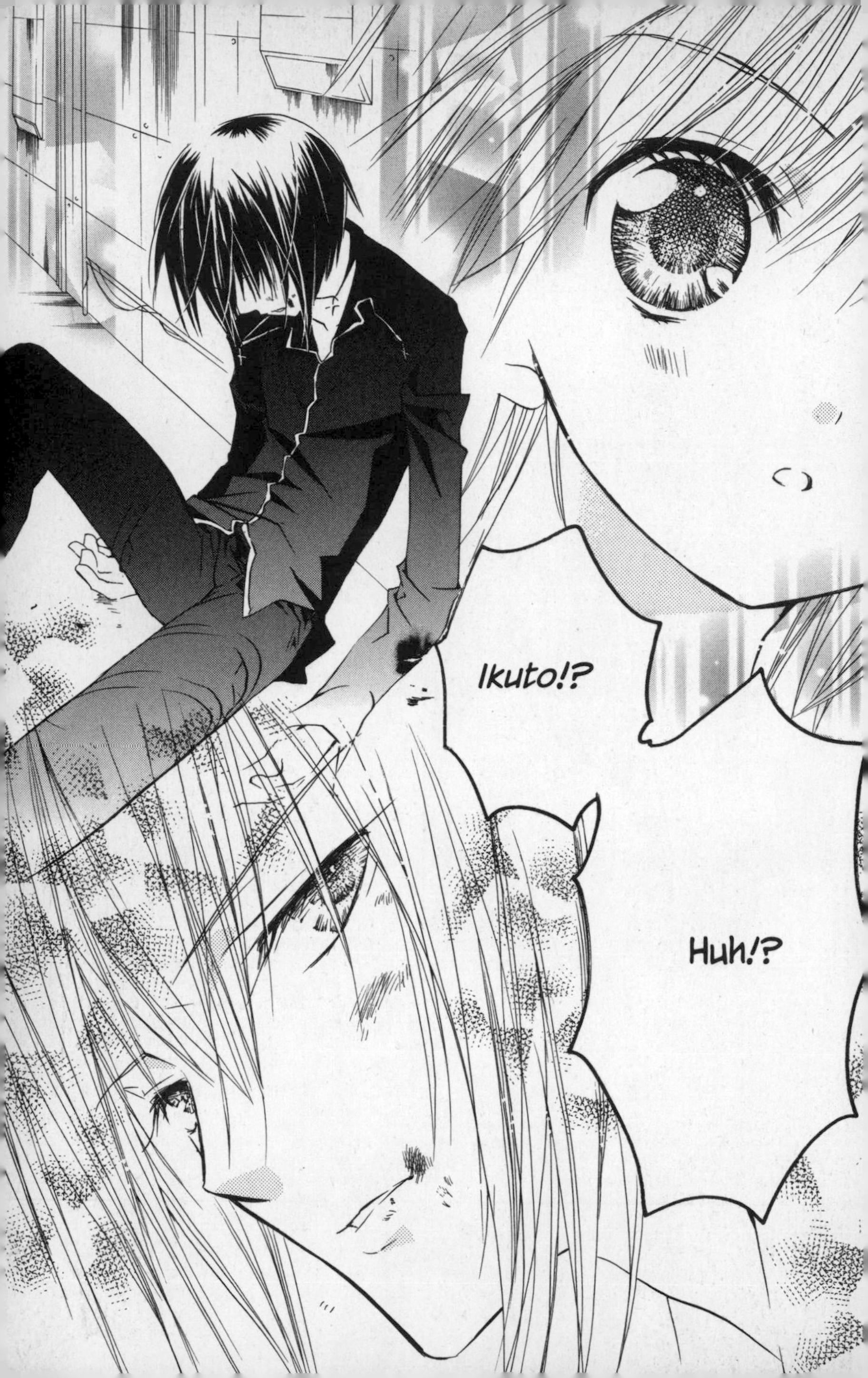
Ikuto!?
Huh!?

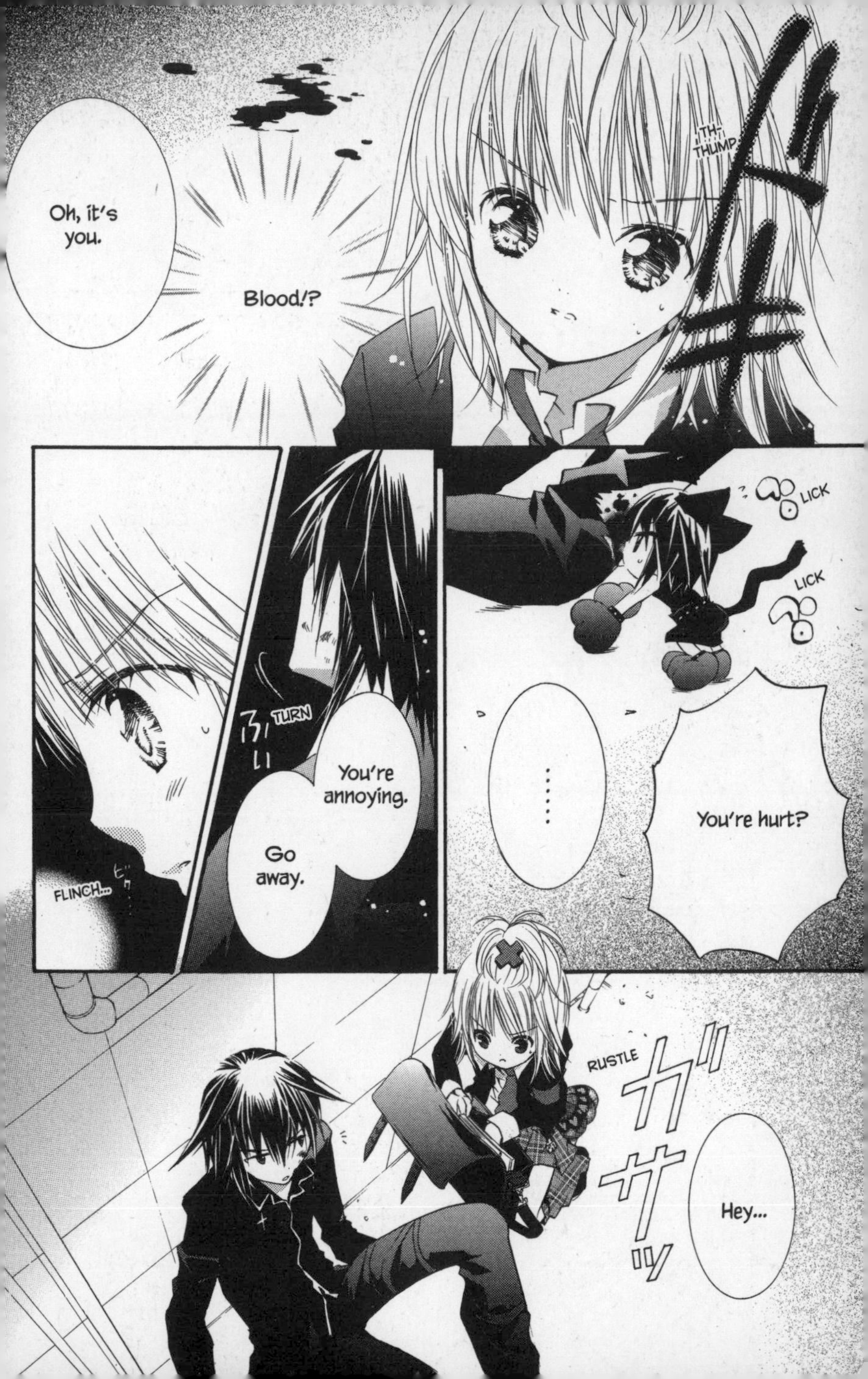
TH-THUMP
Blood!?
Oh, it's you.
LICK
LICK
You're hurt?
......
TURN
You're annoying.
Go away.
FLINCH...
RUSTLE
Hey...

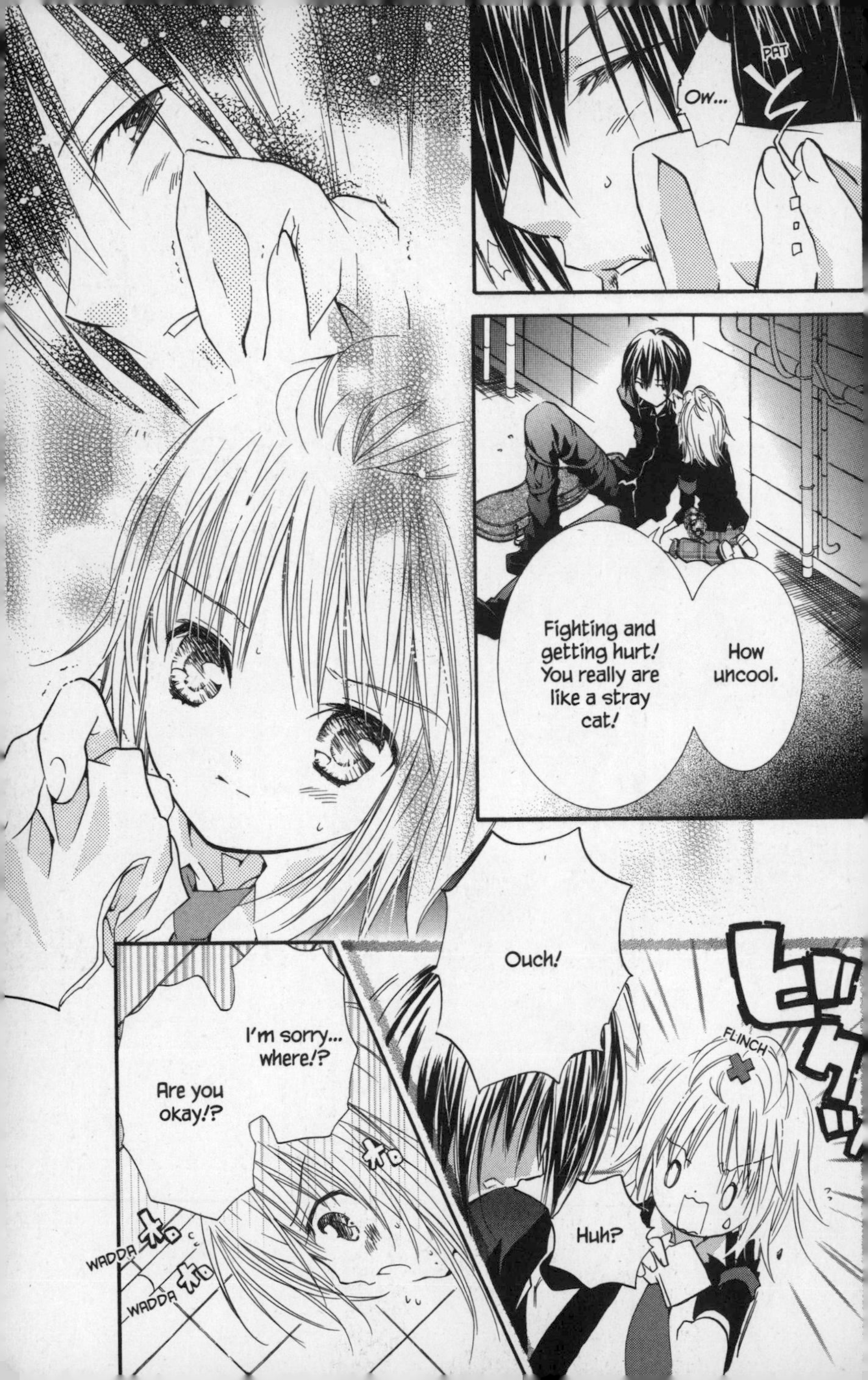
PAT
Ow...
How uncool.
Fighting and getting hurt! You really are like a stray cat!
Ouch!
ビクッ
FLINCH
Huh?
I'm sorry... where!?
Are you okay!?
WADDA
WADDA

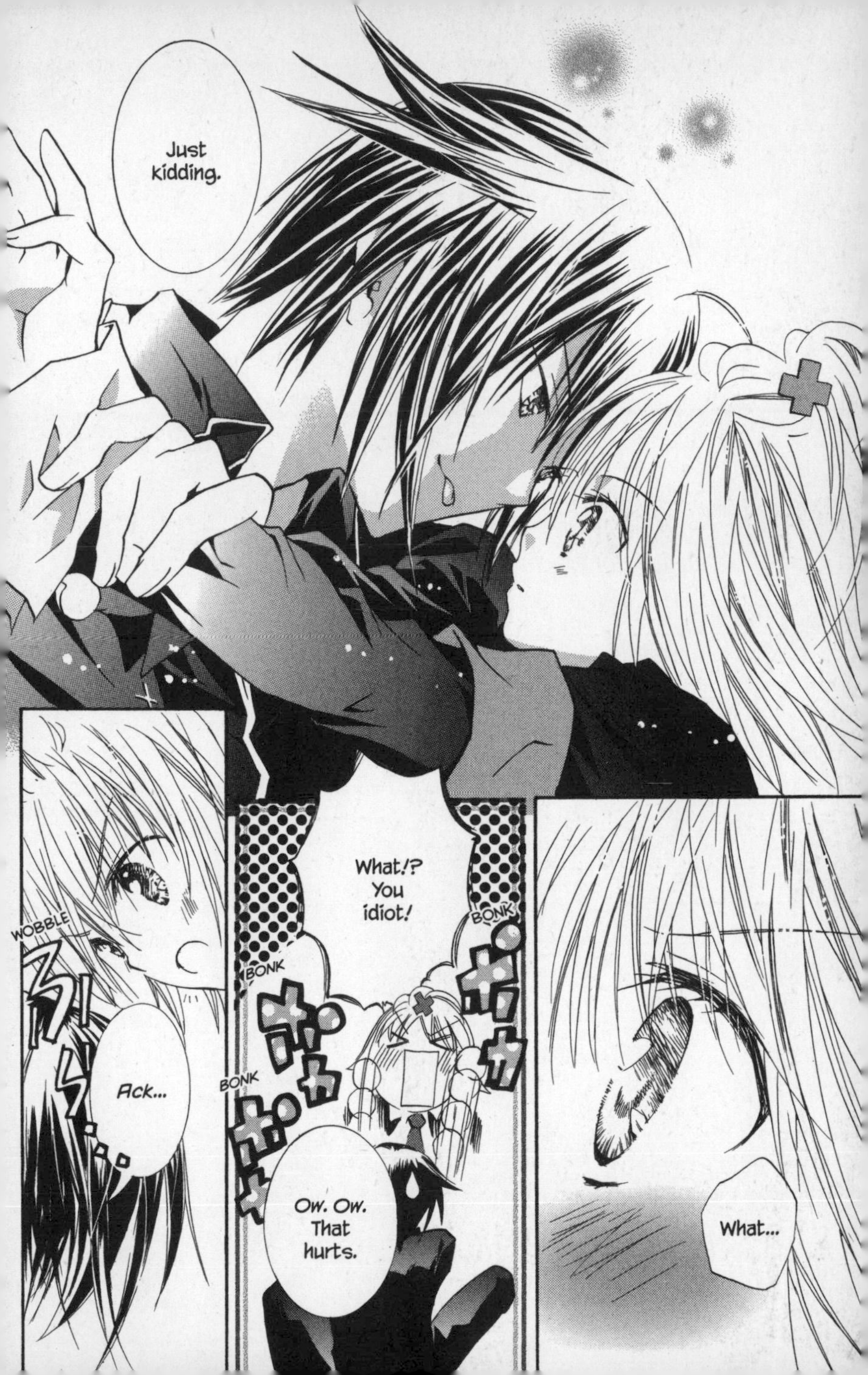

Just kidding.
What...
What!? You idiot!
BONK
BONK
BONK
Ow. Ow. That hurts.
WOBBLE
Ack...

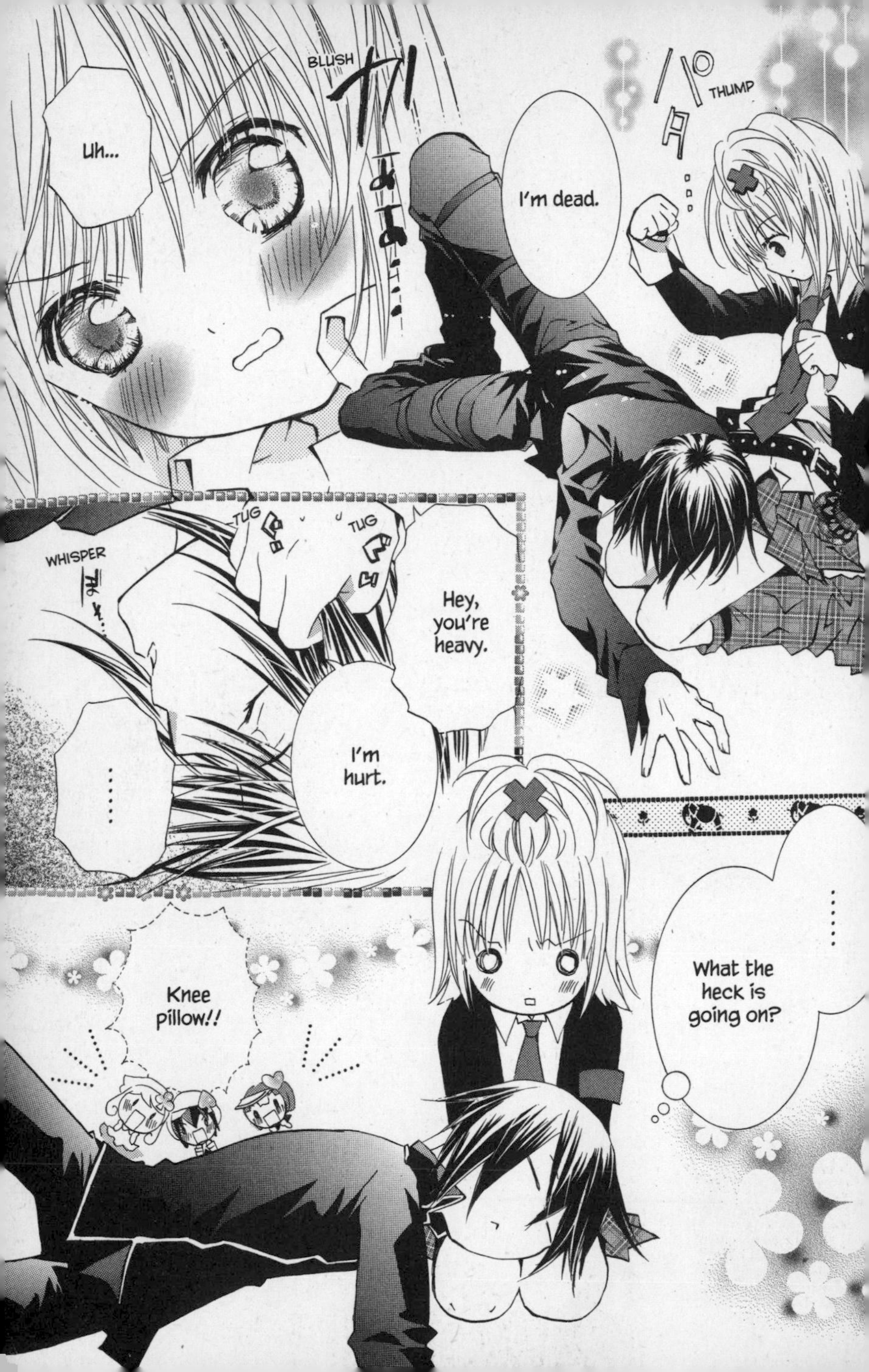
THUMP
I'm dead.
BLUSH
Uh...
TUG
TUG
Hey, you're heavy.
I'm hurt.
WHISPER
......
......
What the heck is going on?
Knee pillow!!

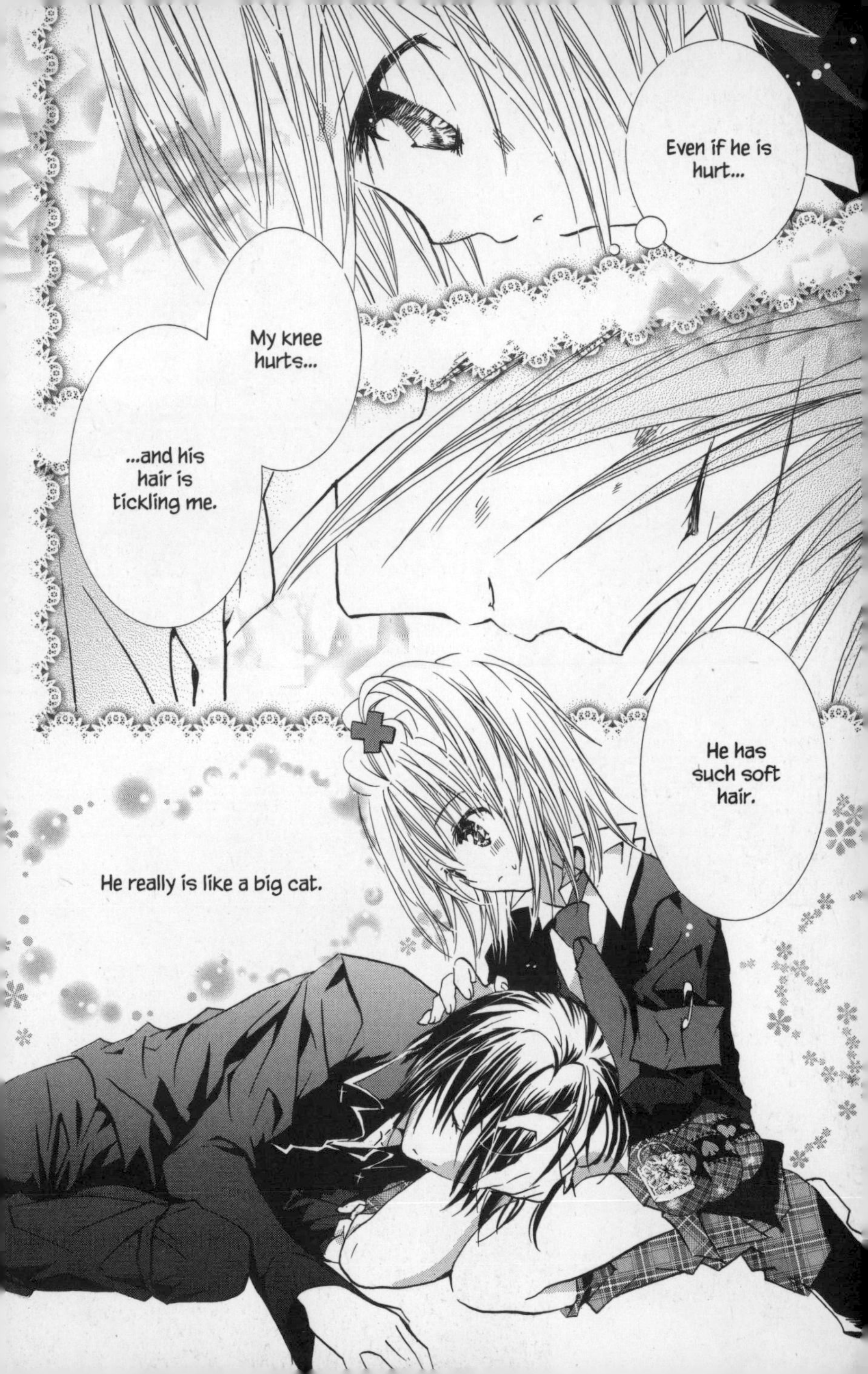
Even if he is hurt...
My knee hurts...
...and his hair is tickling me.
He has such soft hair.
He really is like a big cat.

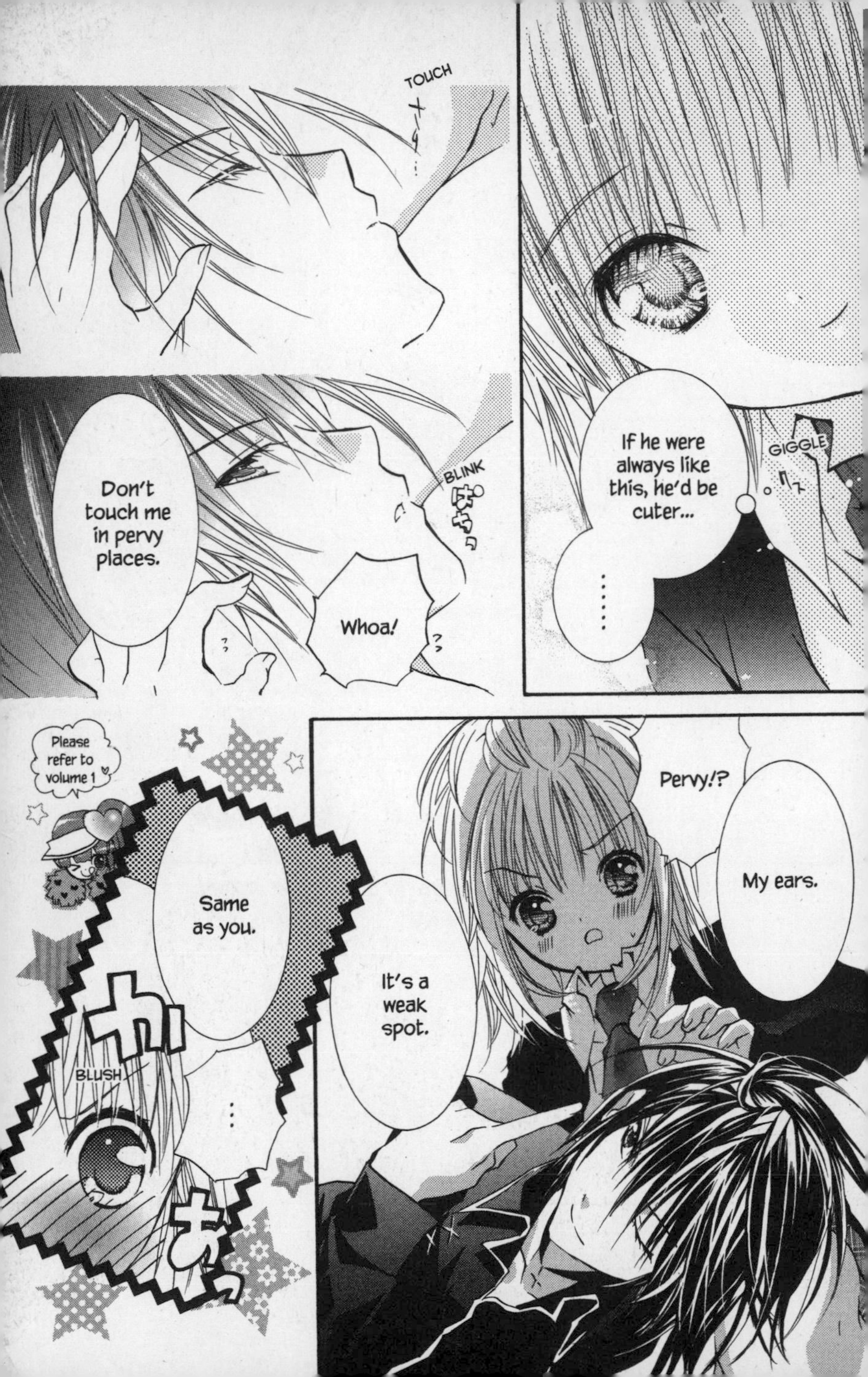

If he were always like this, he'd be cuter...
......
GIGGLE
TOUCH
BLINK
Whoa!
Don't touch me in pervy places.
Pervy!?
My ears.
It's a weak spot.
Please refer to volume 1
Same as you.
...
BLUSH

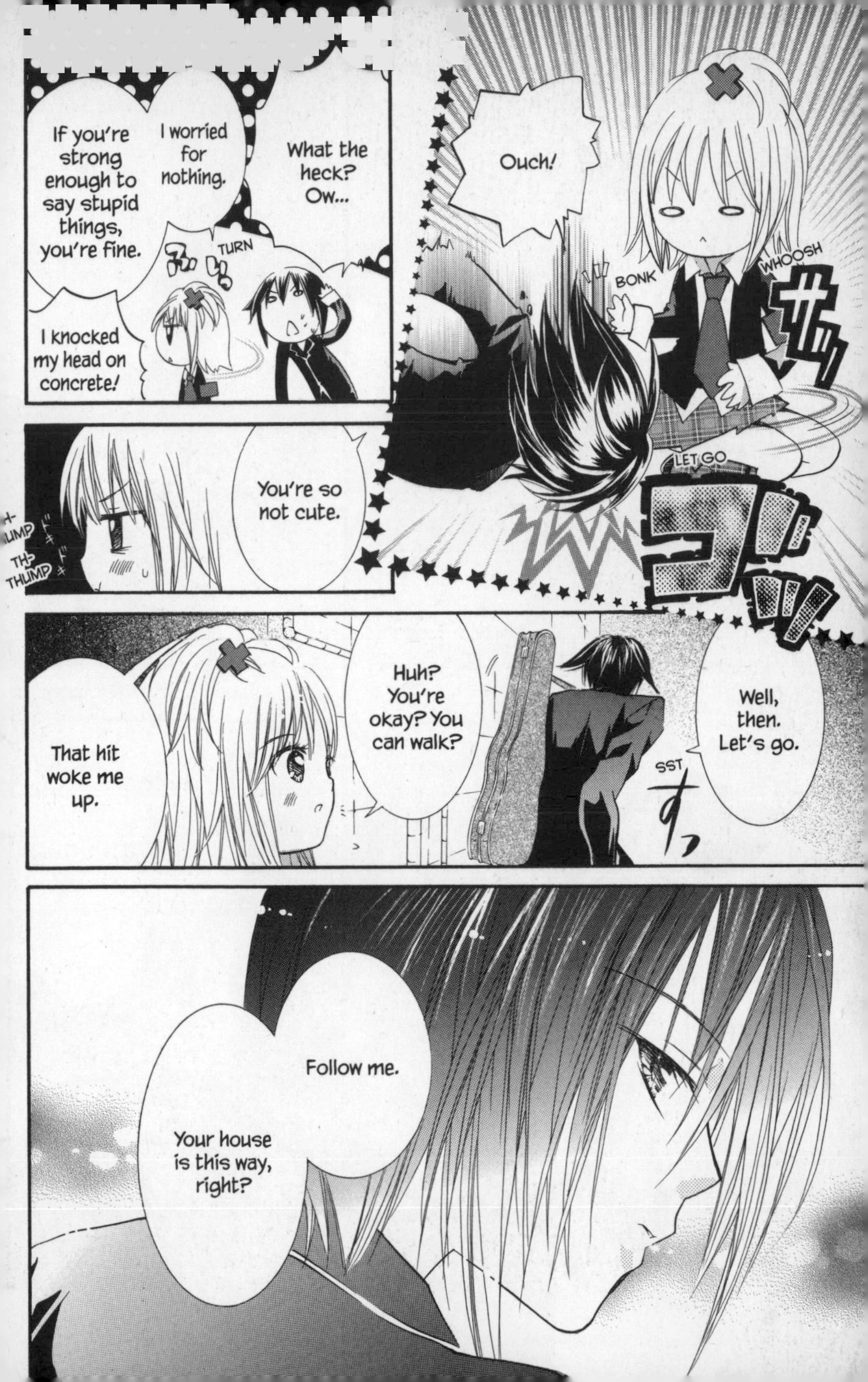
Ouch!
WHOOSH
BONK
LET GO
What the heck? Ow...
I worried for nothing.
If you're strong enough to say stupid things, you're fine.
TURN
I knocked my head on concrete!
You're so not cute.
TH-THUMP
TH-THUMP
Well, then. Let's go.
SST
Huh? You're okay? You can walk?
That hit woke me up.
Follow me.
Your house is this way, right?

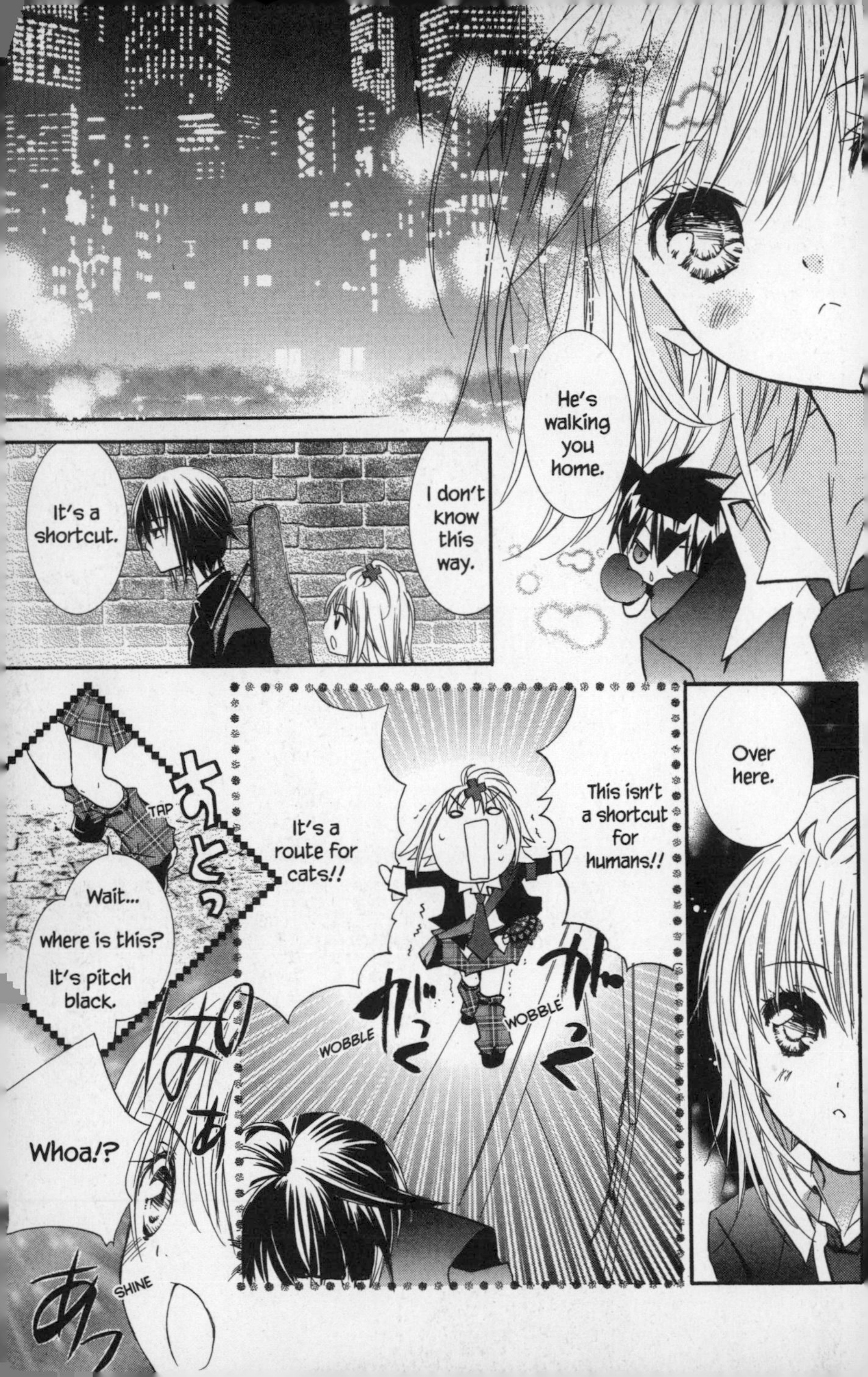
He's walking you home.
I don't know this way.
It's a shortcut.
Over here.
This isn't a shortcut for humans!!
It's a route for cats!!
WOBBLE
WOBBLE
TAP
Wait... where is this? It's pitch black.
Whoa!?
SHINE

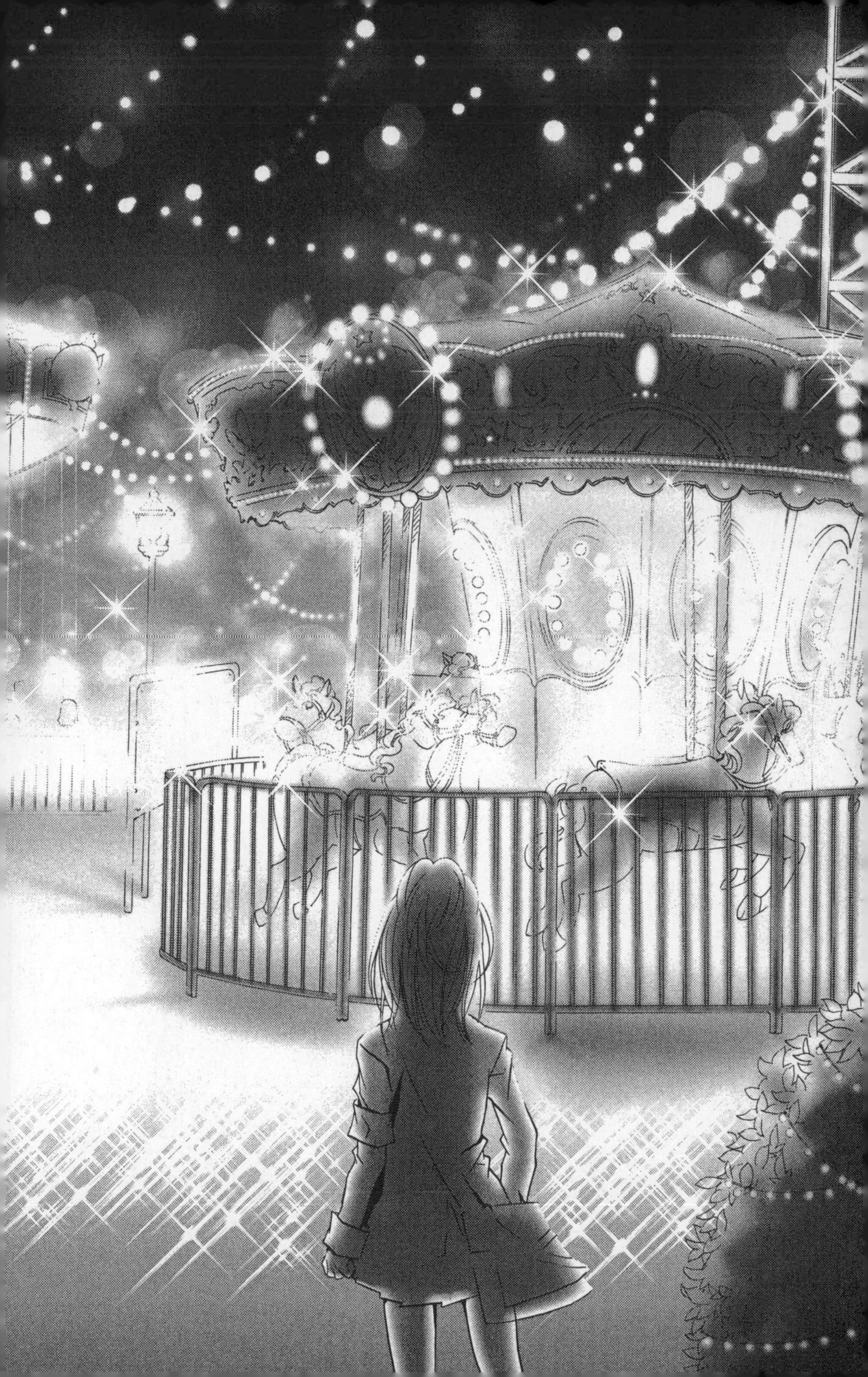

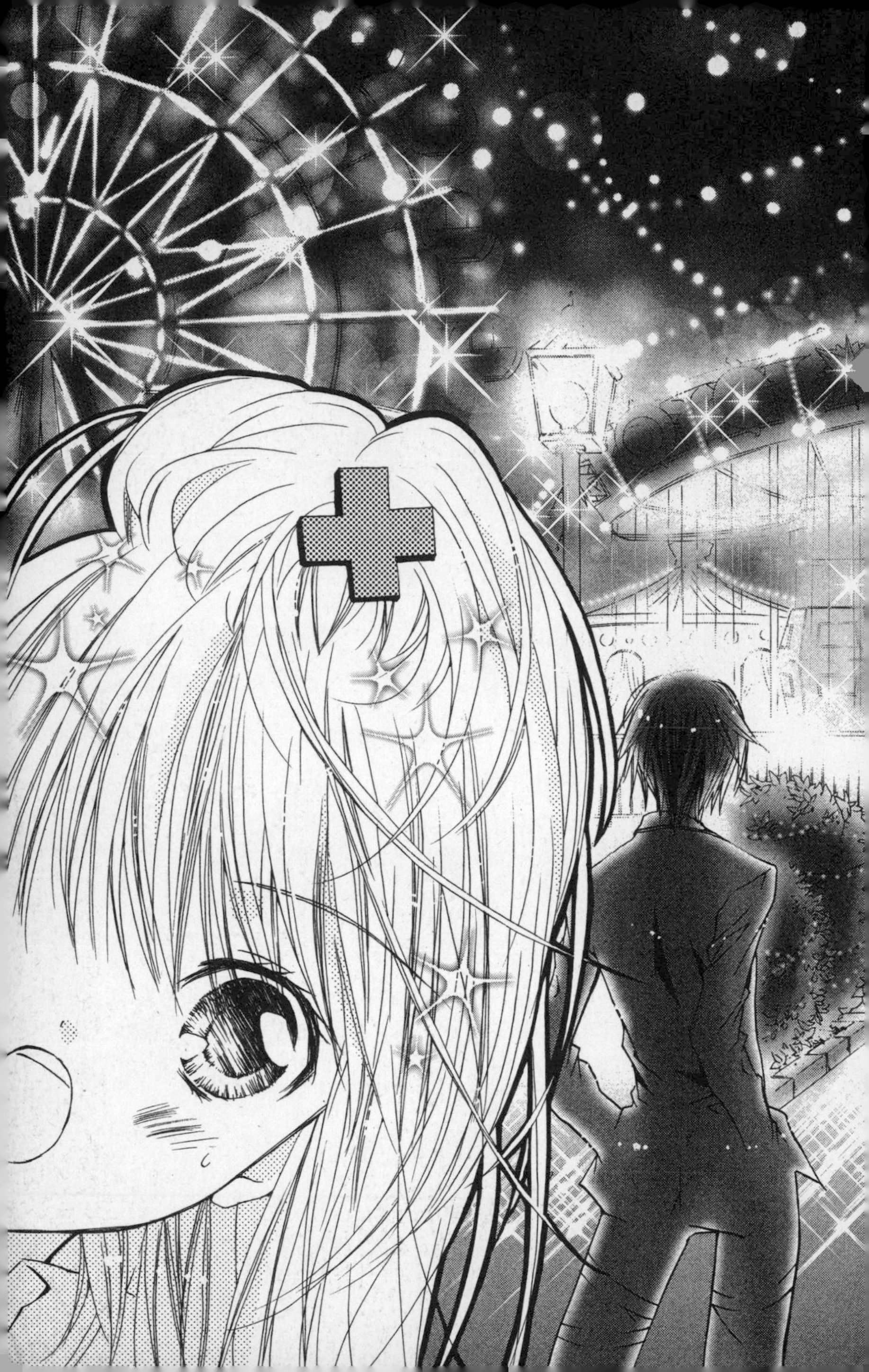

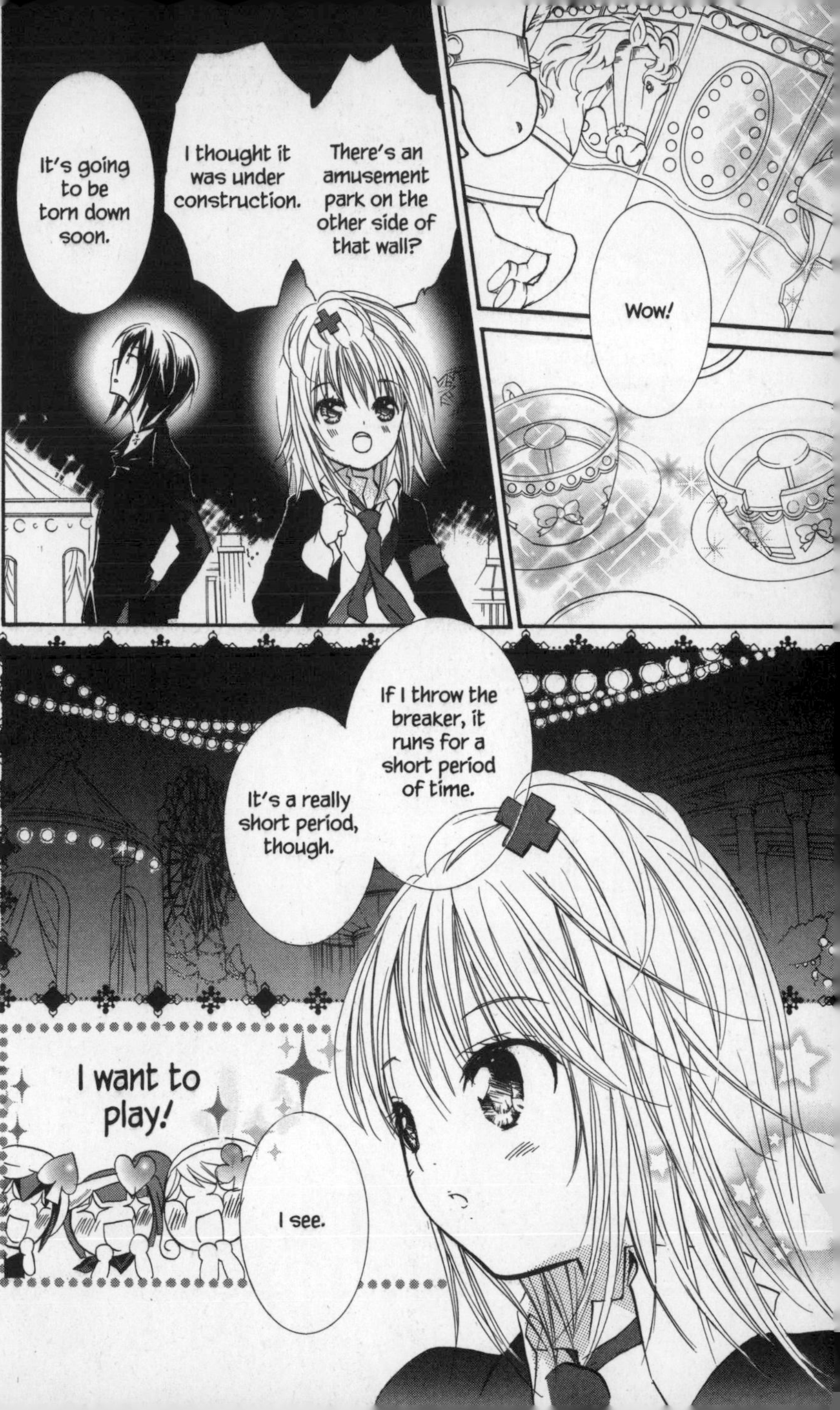
Wow!
There's an amusement park on the other side of that wall?
I thought it was under construction.
It's going to be torn down soon.
If I throw the breaker, it runs for a short period of time.
It's a really short period, though.
I see.
I want to play!

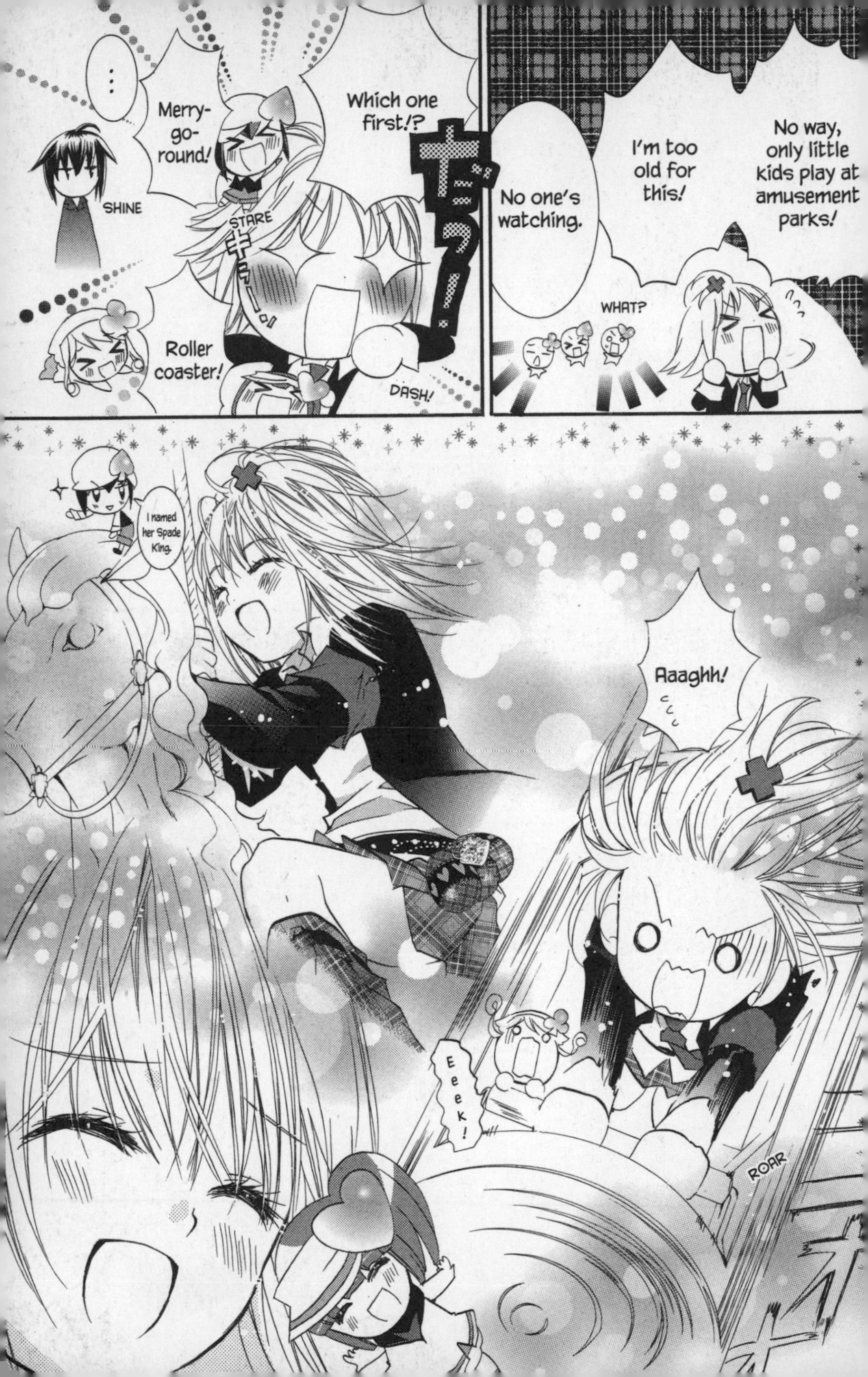
No way, only little kids play at amusement parks!
I'm too old for this!
No one's watching.
WHAT?
Which one first!?
DASH!
Merry-go-round!
STARE
...
SHINE
Roller coaster!
Aaaghh!
I named her Spade King.
ROAR
Eeek!

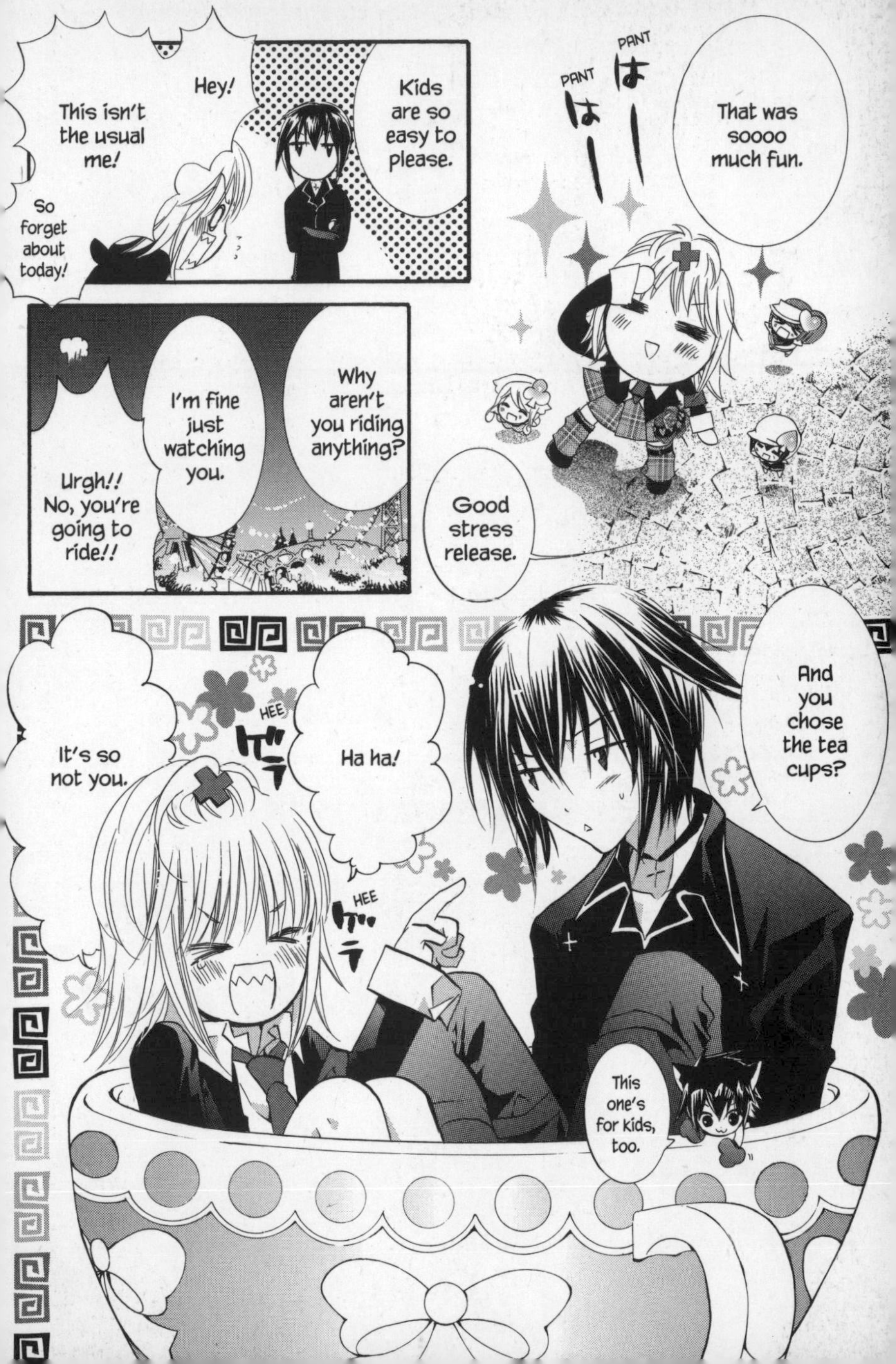
PANT
はー
PANT
はー
That was soooo much fun.
Good stress release.
Kids are so easy to please.
Hey!
This isn't the usual me!
So forget about today!
Why aren't you riding anything?
I'm fine just watching you.
Urgh!! No, you're going to ride!!
And you chose the tea cups?
HEE
Ha ha!
It's so not you.
HEE
This one's for kids, too.

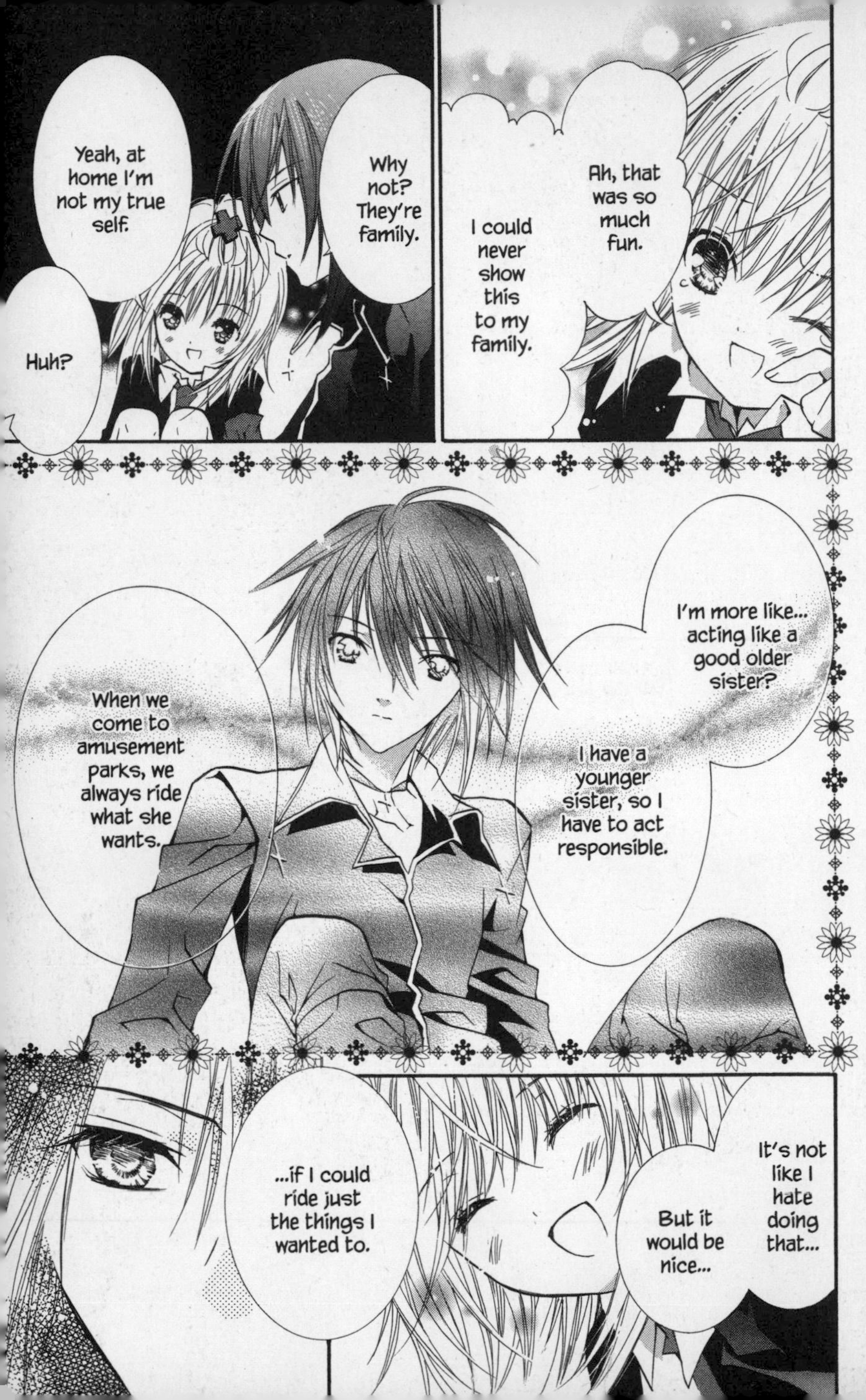
Ah, that was so much fun.
I could never show this to my family.
Why not? They're family.
Yeah, at home I'm not my true self.
Huh?
I'm more like... acting like a good older sister?
I have a younger sister, so I have to act responsible.
When we come to amusement parks, we always ride what she wants.
It's not like I hate doing that...
But it would be nice...
...if I could ride just the things I wanted to.

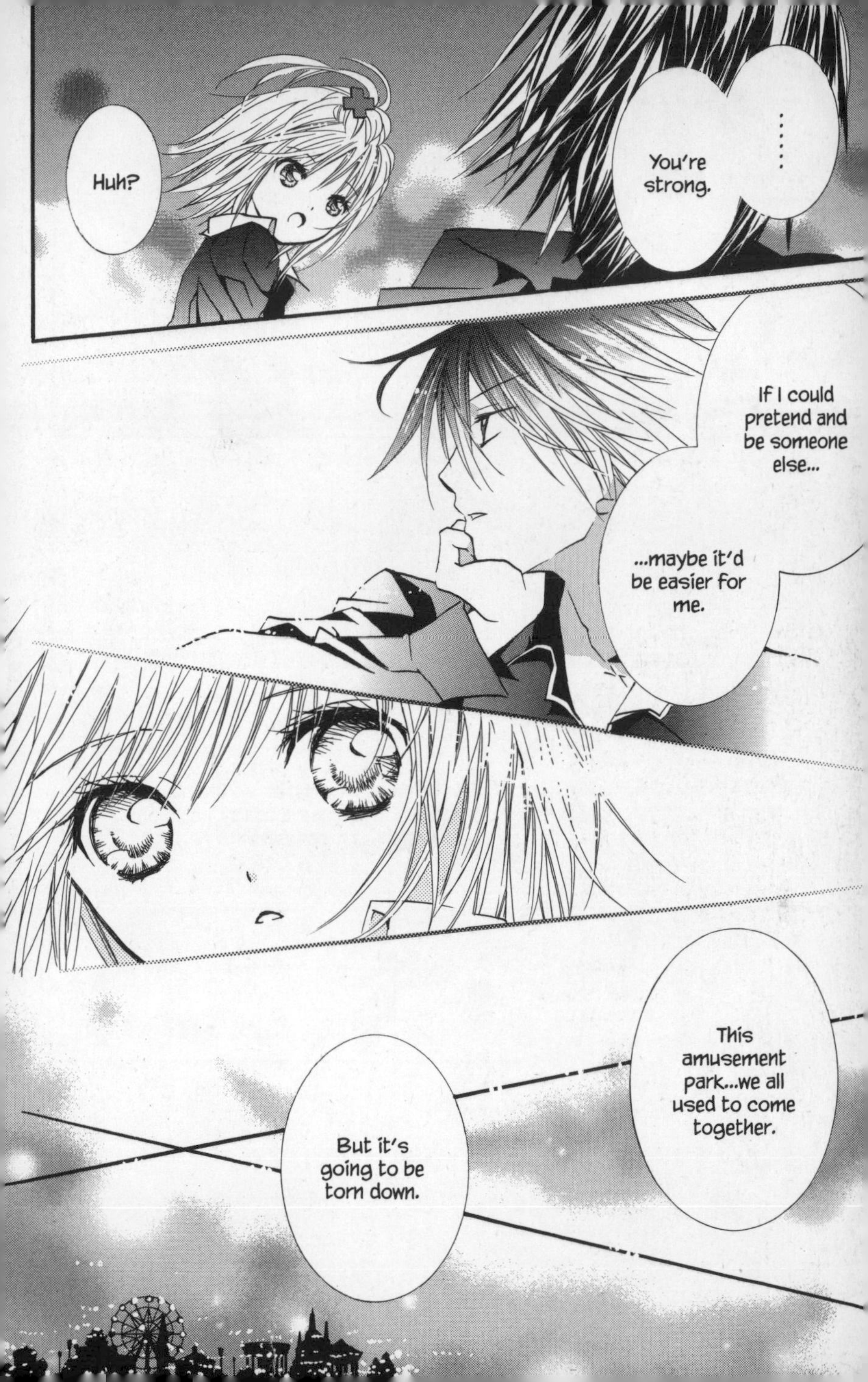
......
You're strong.
Huh?
If I could pretend and be someone else...
...maybe it'd be easier for me.
This amusement park...we all used to come together.
But it's going to be torn down.

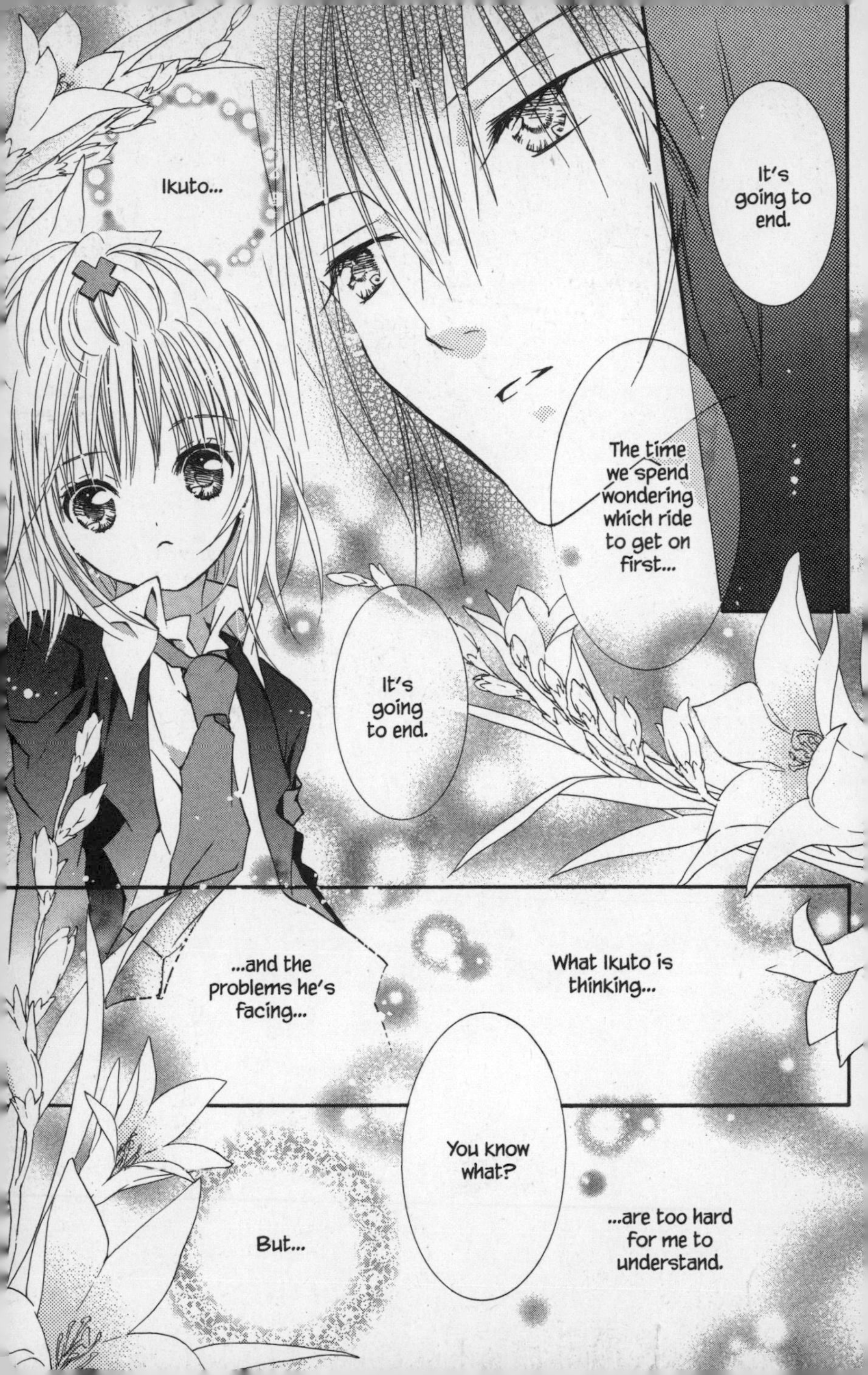
It's going to end.
Ikuto...
The time we spend wondering which ride to get on first...
It's going to end.
What Ikuto is thinking...
...and the problems he's facing...
...are too hard for me to understand.
You know what?
But...

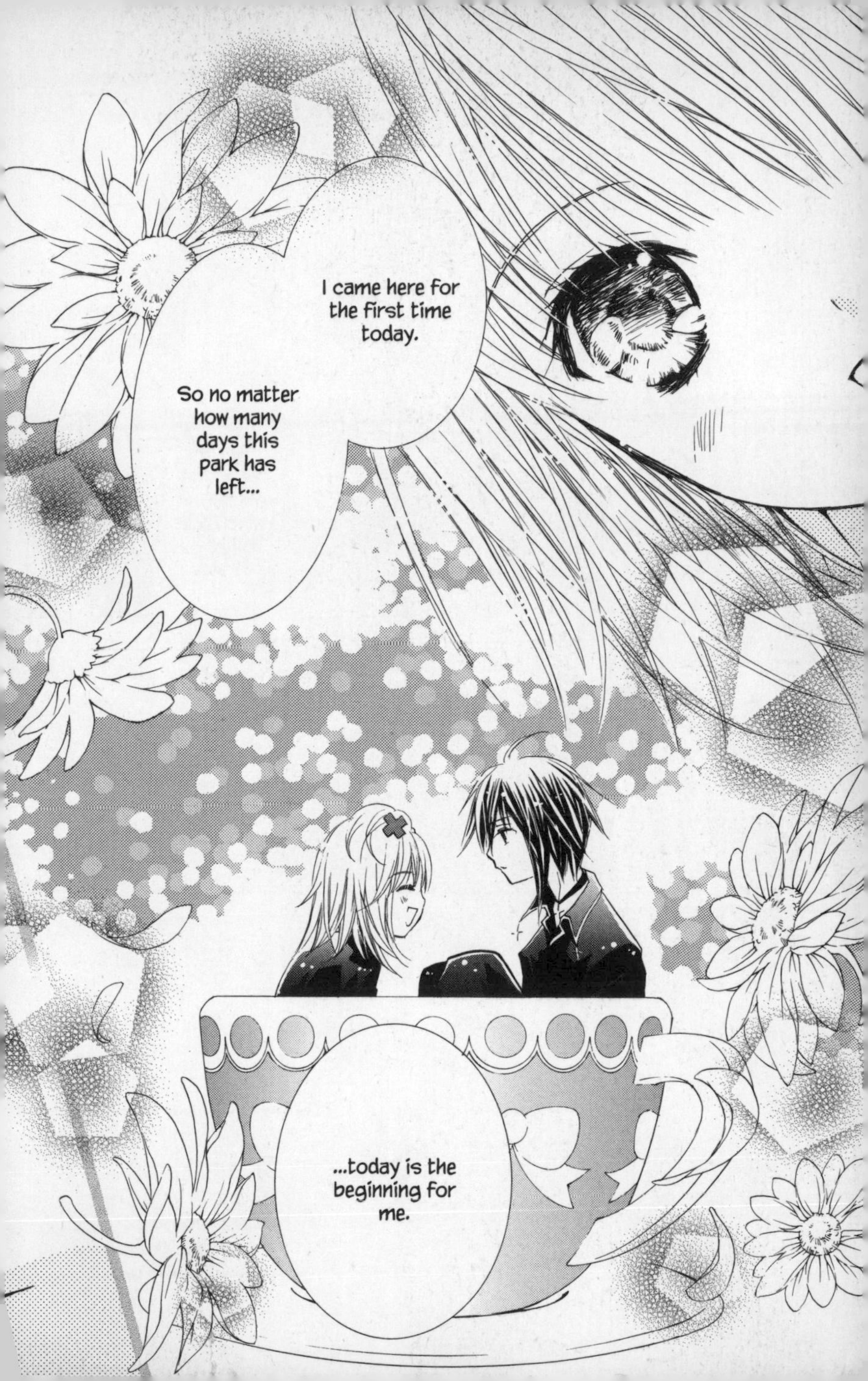
I came here for the first time today.
So no matter how many days this park has left...
...today is the beginning for me.

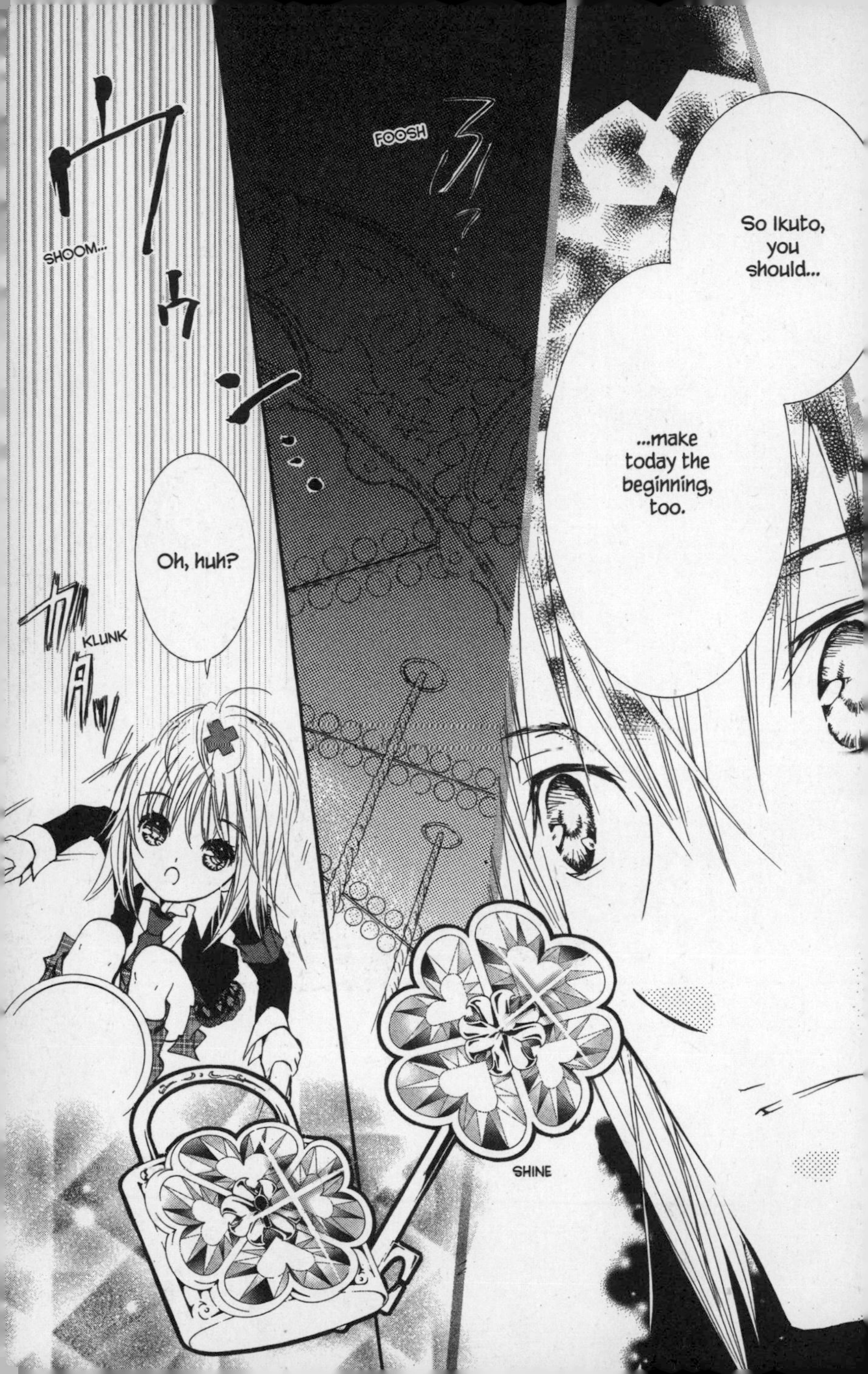
So Ikuto, you should...
...make today the beginning, too.
FOOSH
SHOOM...
Oh, huh?
KLUNK
SHINE

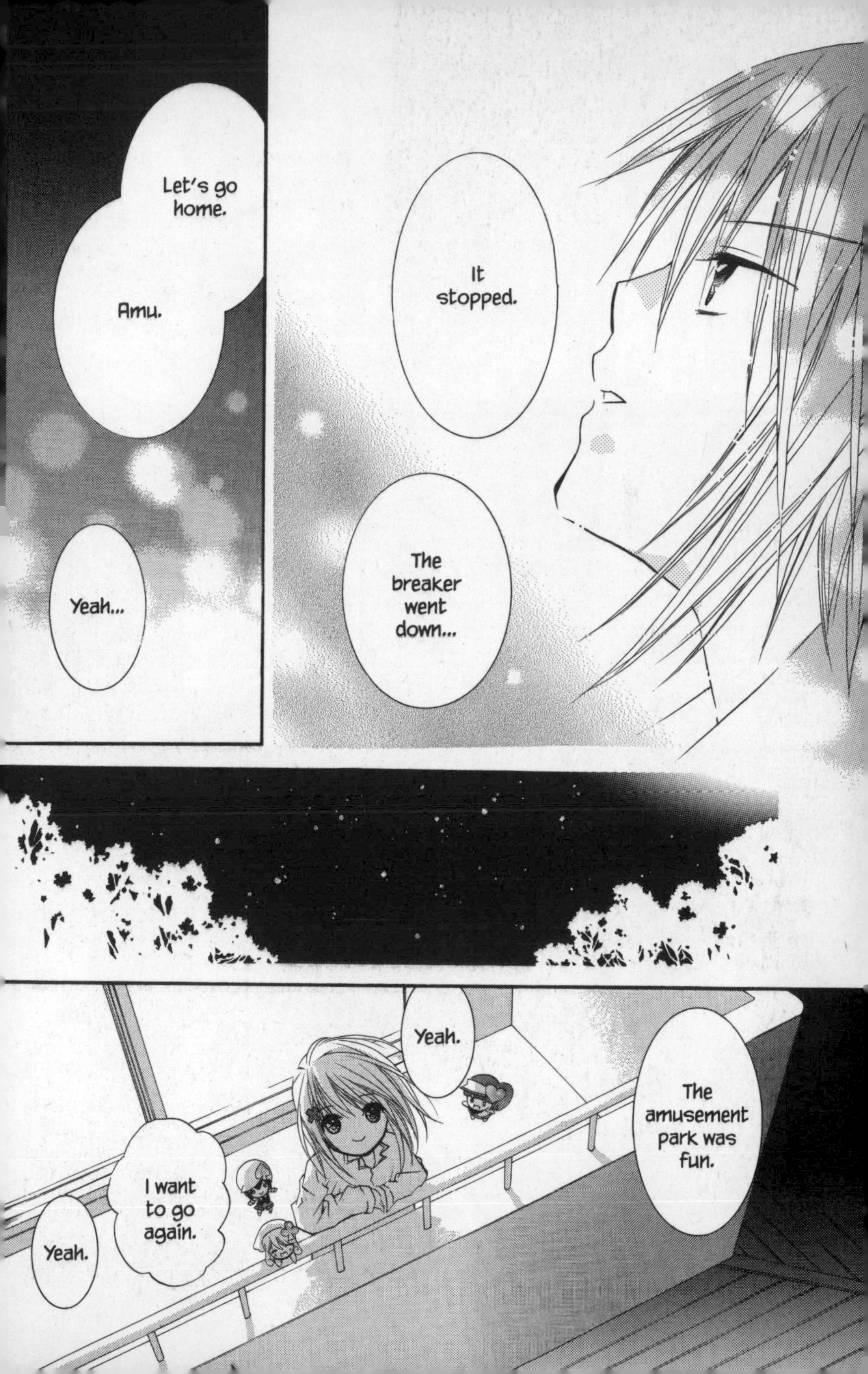
It stopped.
The breaker went down...
Let's go home.
Amu.
Yeah...
The amusement park was fun.
Yeah.
I want to go again.
Yeah.

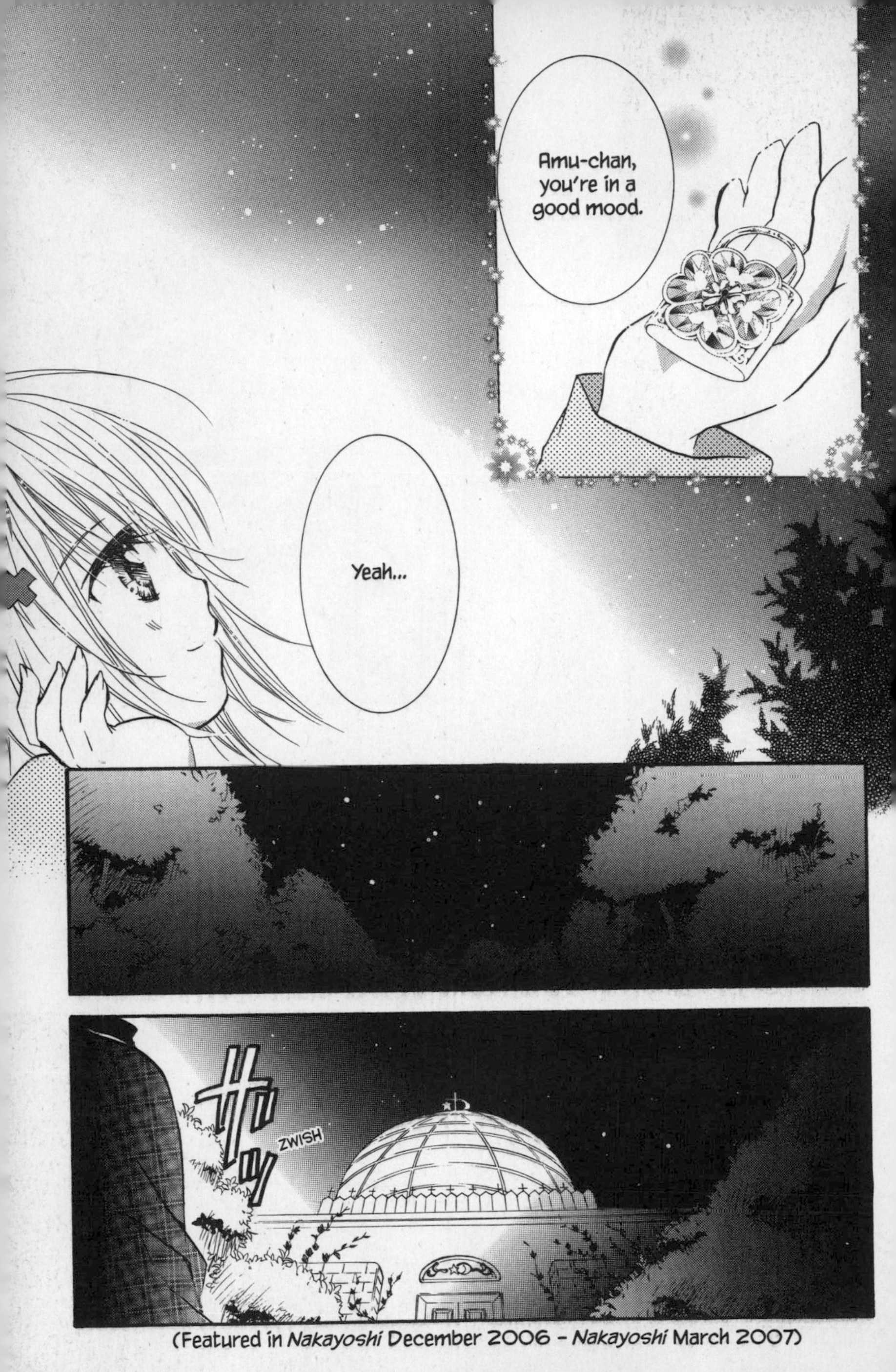
Amu-chan, you're in a good mood.
Yeah...
ZWISH

(Featured in *Nakayoshi* December 2006 - *Nakayoshi* March 2007)

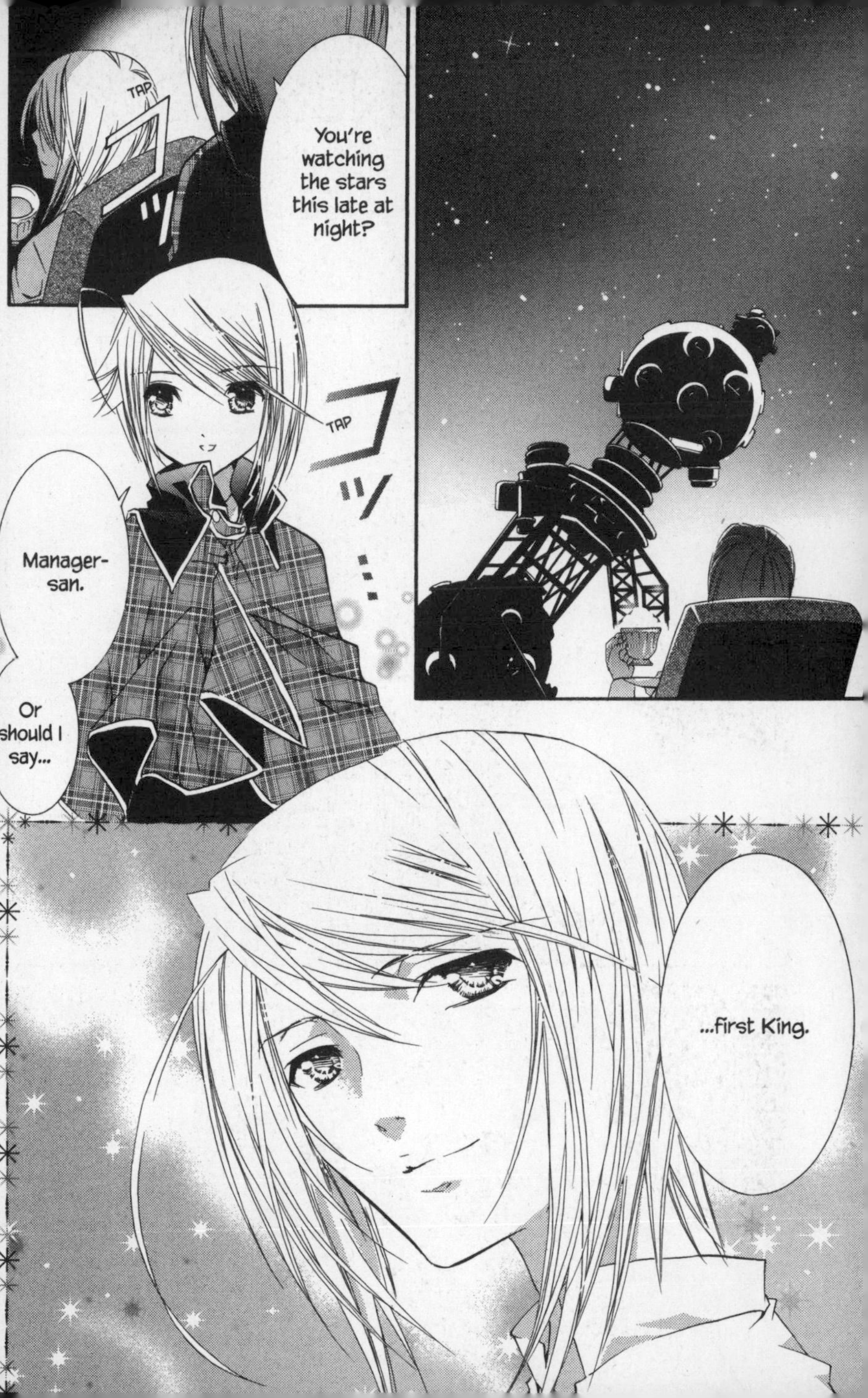
TAP
You're watching the stars this late at night?
TAP
Manager-san.
Or should I say...
...first King.

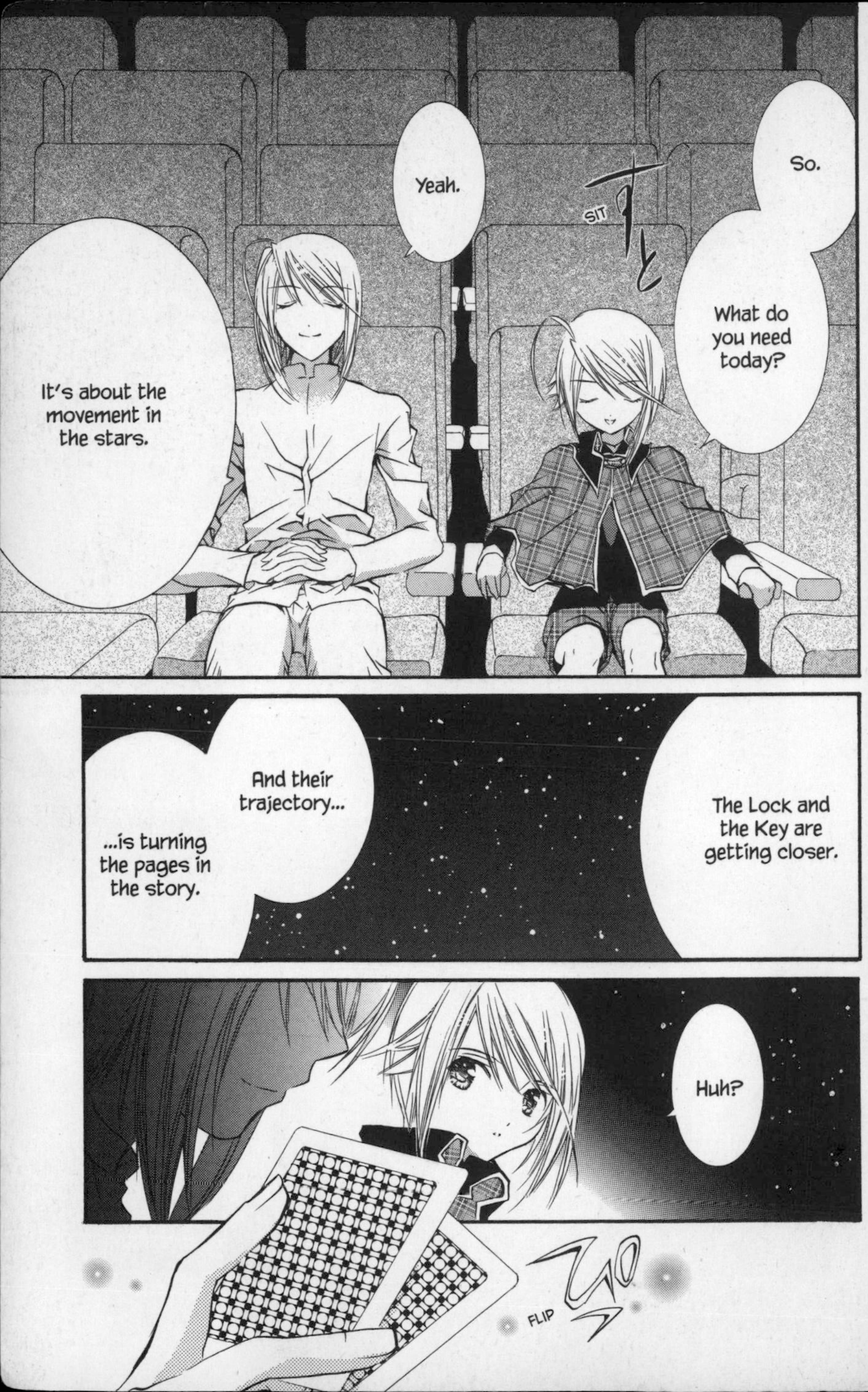
So.
What do you need today?
SIT
Yeah.
It's about the movement in the stars.
The Lock and the Key are getting closer.
And their trajectory...
...is turning the pages in the story.
Huh?
FLIP

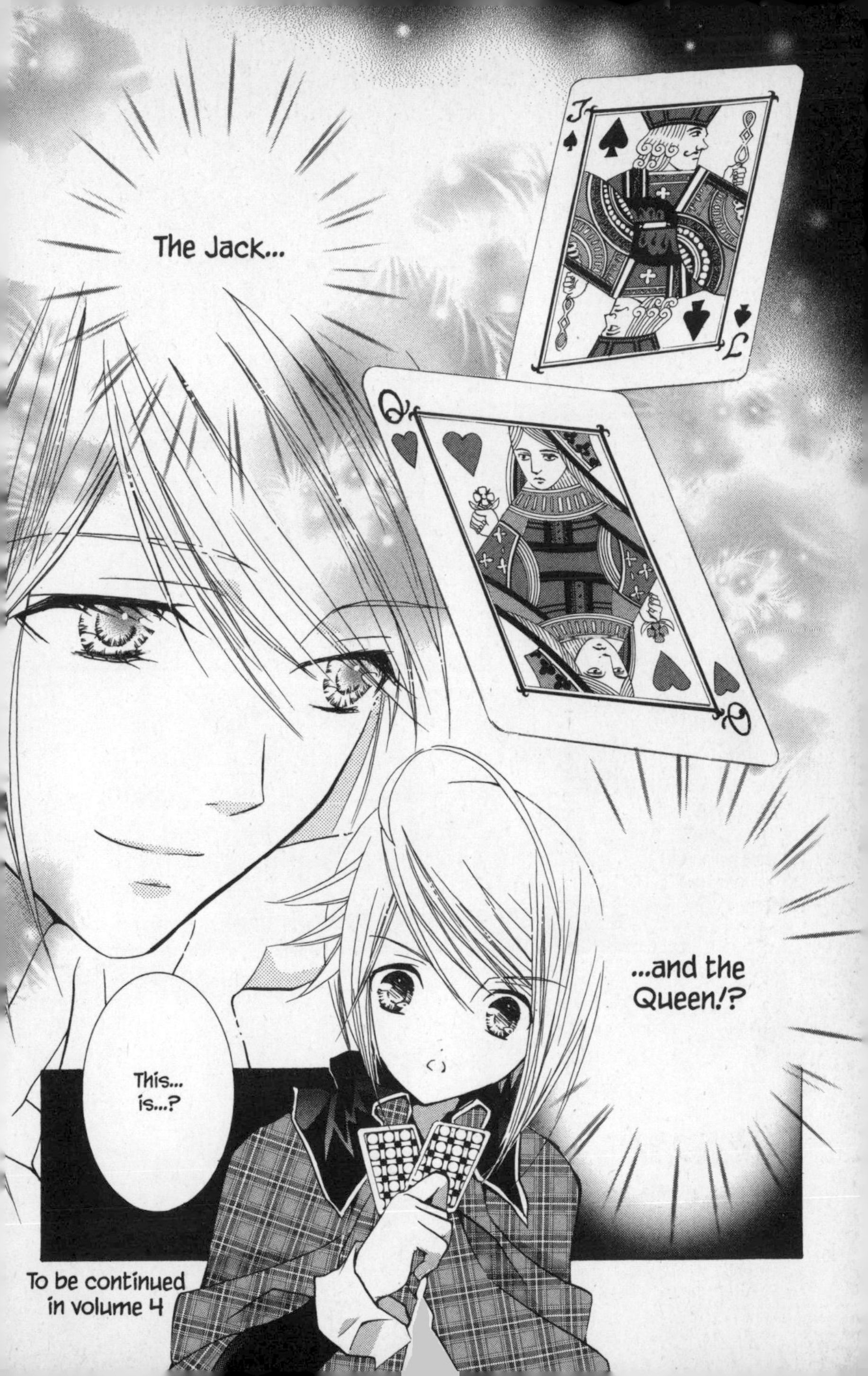
The Jack...
...and the Queen!?
This... is...?

To be continued in volume 4

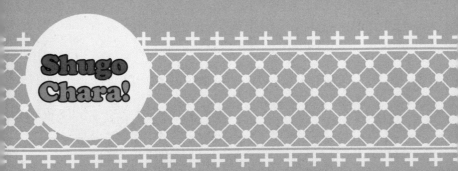
Shugo Chara!

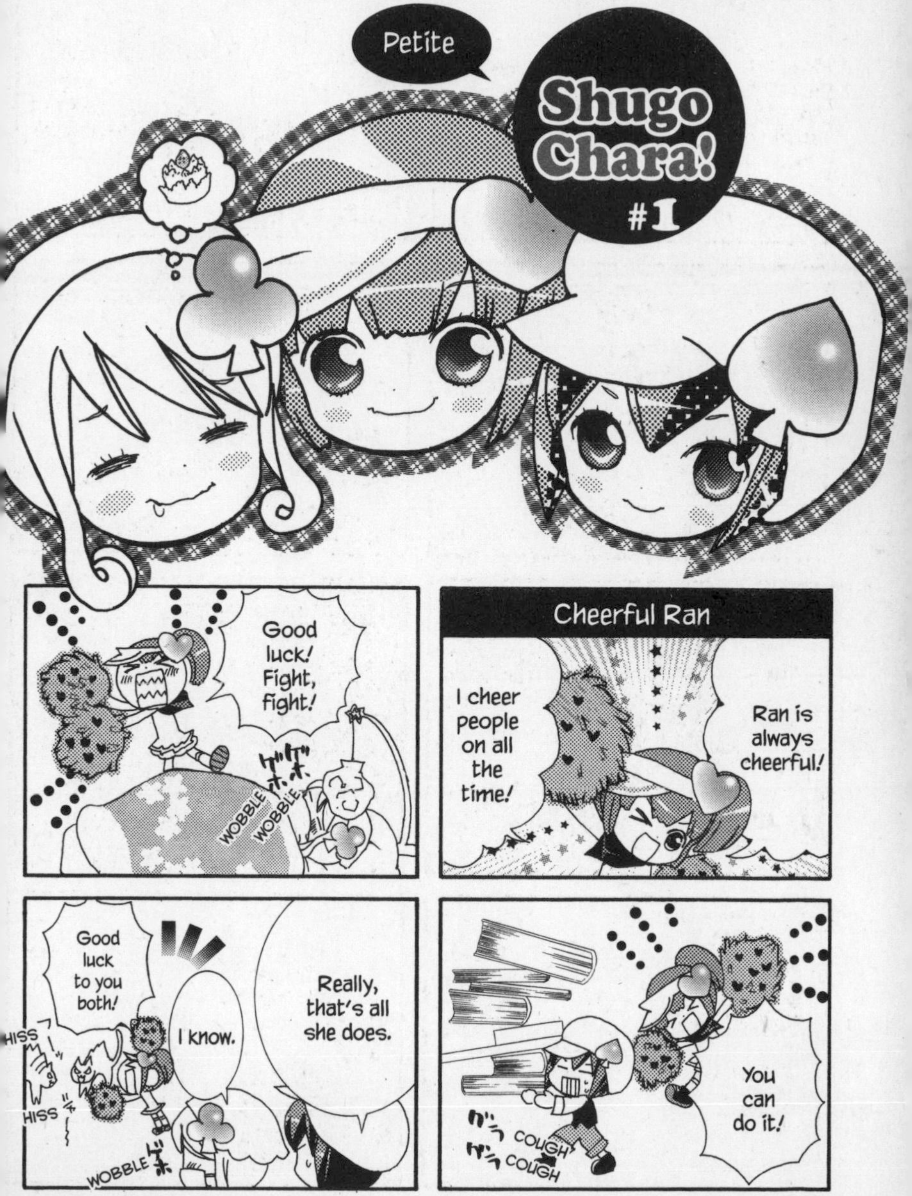

Petite
Shugo Chara!
#1
Cheerful Ran
Ran is always cheerful!
I cheer people on all the time!
Good luck! Fight, fight!
WOBBLE
WOBBLE
You can do it!
COUGH
COUGH
Really, that's all she does.
I know.
Good luck to you both!
HISS
HISS
WOBBLE

Charismatic Miki

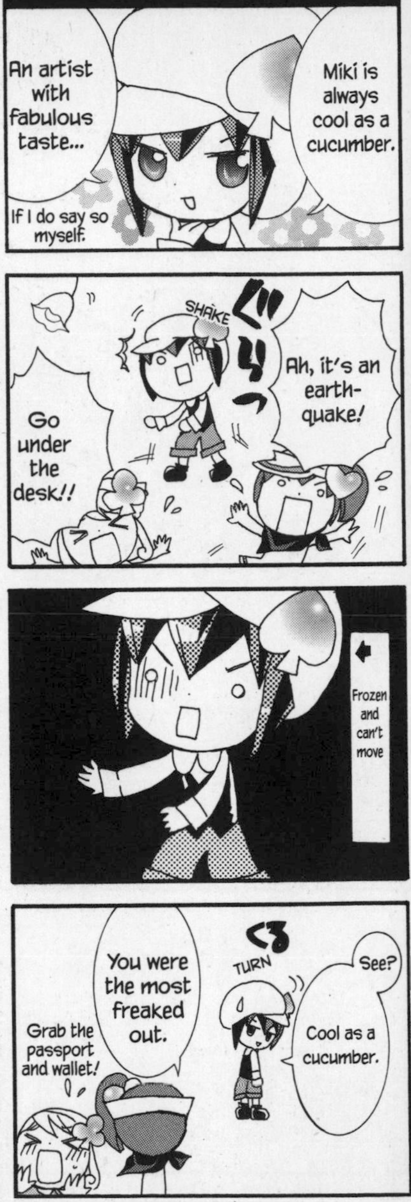
Miki is always cool as a cucumber.
An artist with fabulous taste...
If I do say so myself.
SHAKE
Ah, it's an earthquake!
Go under the desk!!
Frozen and can't move
See?
Cool as a cucumber.
TURN
You were the most freaked out.
Grab the passport and wallet!

Lovely Su

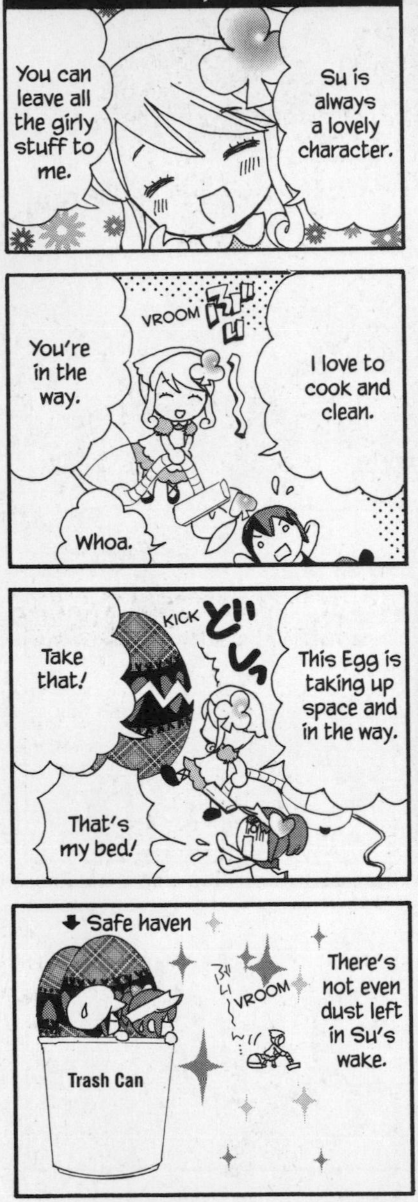
Su is always a lovely character.
You can leave all the girly stuff to me.
I love to cook and clean.
VROOM
You're in the way.
Whoa.
This Egg is taking up space and in the way.
KICK
Take that!
That's my bed!
There's not even dust left in Su's wake.
VROOM
Safe haven
Trash Can

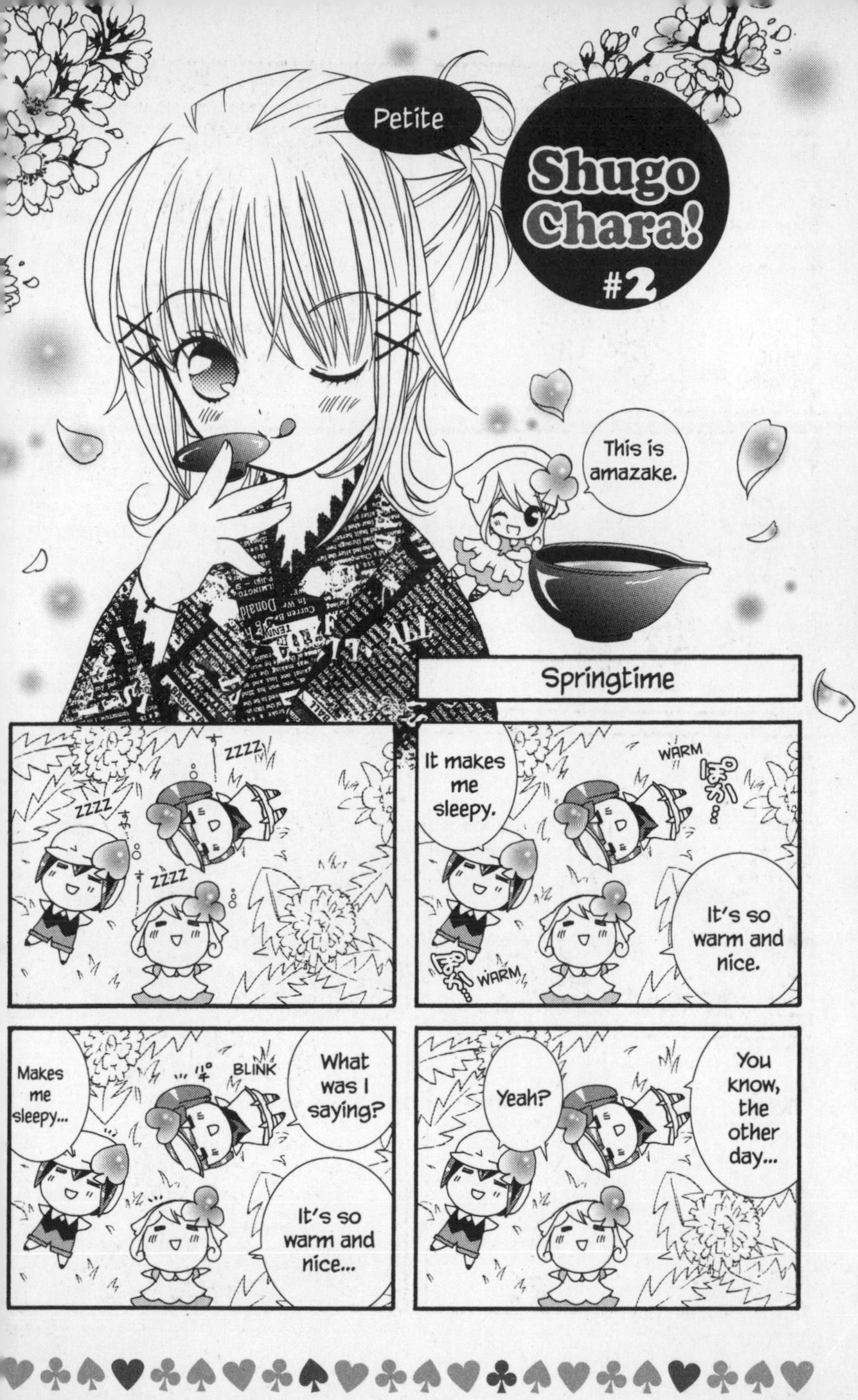
Petite
Shugo Chara!
#2
This is amazake.
Springtime
WARM
It makes me sleepy.
It's so warm and nice.
WARM
ZZZZ
ZZZZ
ZZZZ
You know, the other day...
Yeah?
What was I saying?
BLINK
Makes me sleepy...
It's so warm and nice...

Spring is About...?

Looking at flowers.
GLOOM
Changing classes...
Entering school!
Being in heat.
Can he say that in this manga?
Because we're cats.

A King's Problem

Spring...
It's a season most unsuitable for world domination.
The peasants become lightheaded and...
...their sense of urgency is gone.
Further-more...
DRIP
Tadase!! I told you not to open the window!!
BLOW
Sorry...
They both have hay fever.

Shugo Chara!

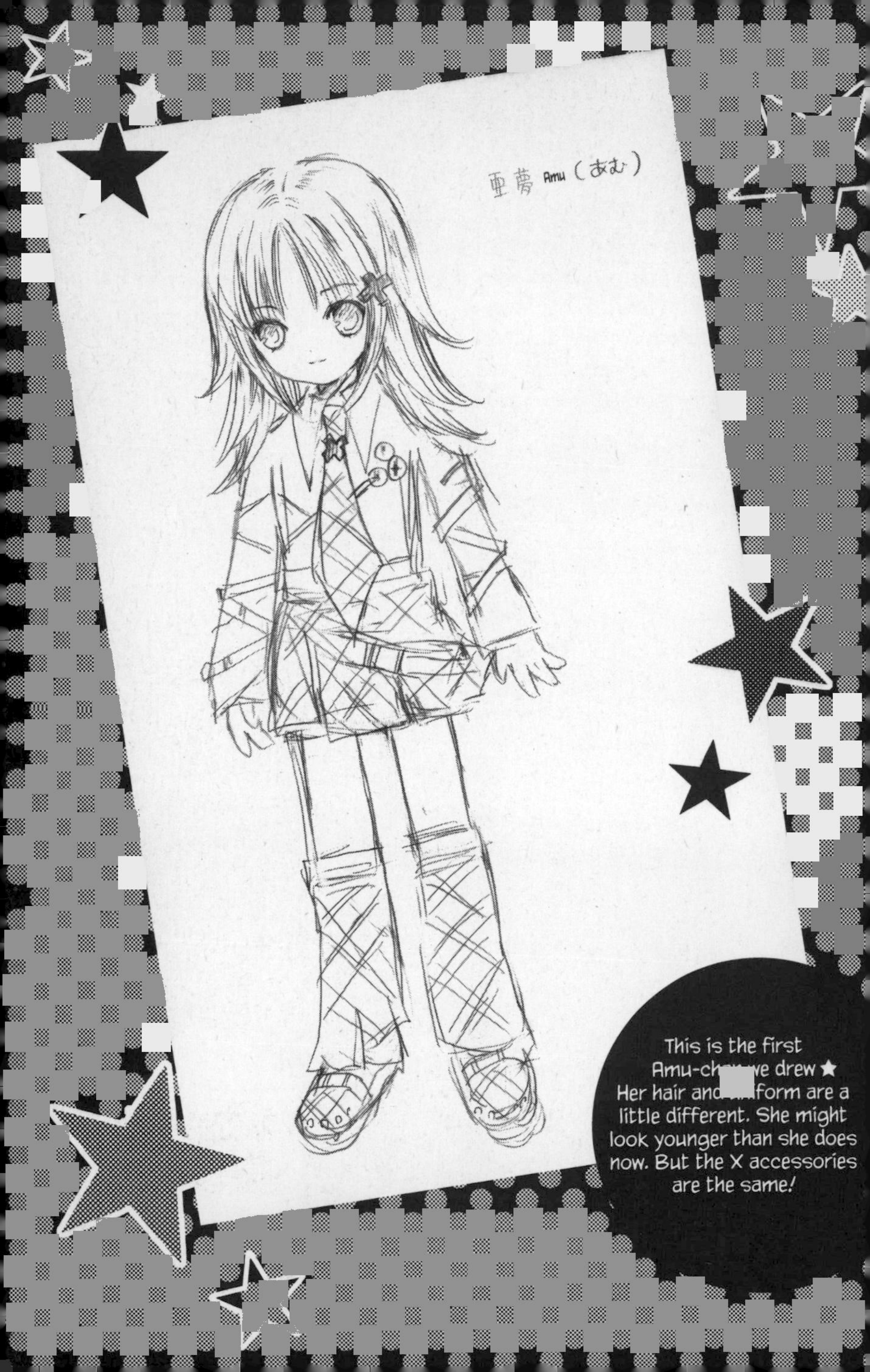
亜夢 Amu (あむ)
This is the first Amu-chan we drew ★ Her hair and uniform are a little different. She might look younger than she does now. But the X accessories are the same!

About the Creators

PEACH-PIT:

Banri Sendo was born on June 7th. Shibuko Ebara was born on June 21st. They are a pair of Gemini manga artists who work together. Sendo likes to eat sweets, and Ebara likes to eat spicy stuff. Here's something that happened recently: We almost flushed our cell phones down the toilet…twice.

Translation Notes

Japanese is a tricky language for most Westerners, and translation is often more art than science. For your edification and reading pleasure, here are notes on some of the places where we could have gone in a different direction in our translation of the work, or where a Japanese cultural reference is used.

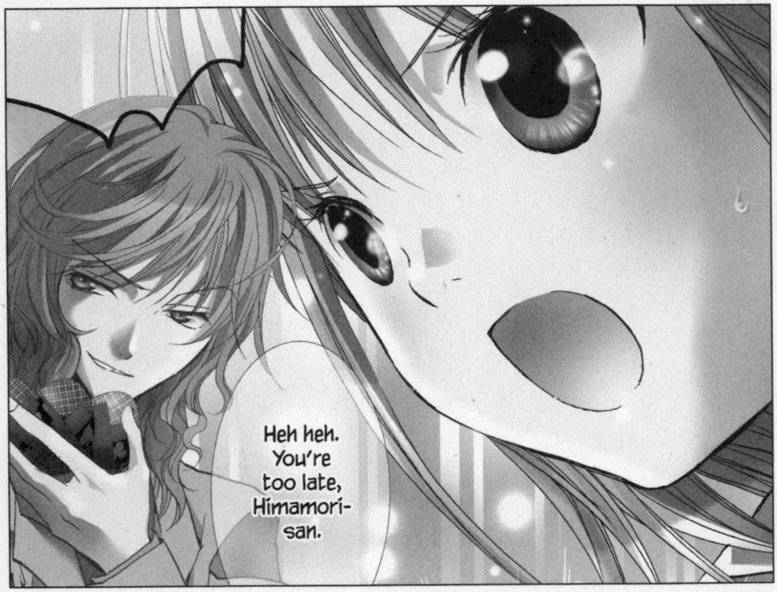
Heh heh. You're too late, Himamori-san.

Hima, page 6

This is a pun. *Hima* means "having spare time." *Hima* sounds like "Hina," and Yuu replaces it when he calls Amu by her last name. He started doing this in a previous volume and will continue to call her "Himamori-san" to belittle her. On page 66, he finally calls her by her real name.

Okinawa, page 7

Okinawa is located in the southernmost part of Japan and consists of hundreds of small islands.

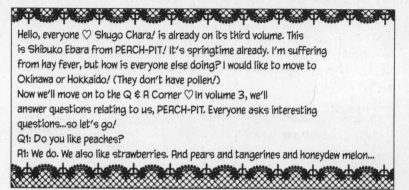

Hello, everyone ♡ Shugo Chara! is already on its third volume. This is Shibuko Ebara from PEACH-PIT! It's springtime already. I'm suffering from hay fever, but how is everyone else doing? I would like to move to Okinawa or Hokkaido! (They don't have pollen!)

Now we'll move on to the Q & A Corner ♡ In volume 3, we'll answer questions relating to us, PEACH-PIT. Everyone asks interesting questions...so let's go!

Q1: Do you like peaches?

A1: We do. We also like strawberries. And pears and tangerines and honeydew melon...

Hokkaido, page 7

Hokkaido is located in the northern part of Japan. It is the second largest island and the biggest prefecture.

TEMARI

Guardian Character of:
Nadeshiko
Special Skill: Naginata
Hates: Mud

Naginata, page 15

A *naginata* is a long-handled sword. It looks like a spear with a short sword at the tip of it. In modern Japan, it is used in women's martial arts.

Q4: What's ajitama?
A4: Ajitama are flavored eggs. They're a ramen topping ♡
You can try making them with your mom!

Ajitama, page 87

Ajitama can be translated as "flavored eggs," which are boiled eggs soaked in a sauce to add flavor. Usually the sauce is made out of soy sauce, rice wine, and water.

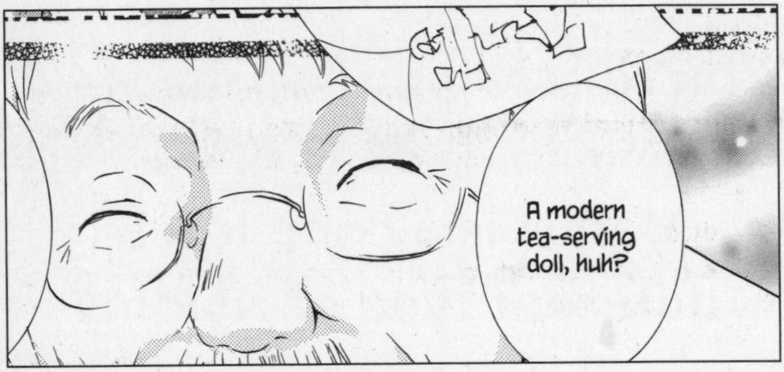
A modern tea-serving doll, huh?

Tea-serving doll, page 90

The tea-serving doll existed in the Edo period (1603–1868) and was a mechanical doll that moved on a spiral spring. It moved across the hall with the tea, lifted the tea, and then stopped. Once you drank the tea and returned it to the doll, it turned around and left the room..

Amazake, page 162

Amazake is translated as "sweet alcohol," but it's actually very low in alcohol content and can be served to children in Japan. It's sweet, made from fermented rice, and can also be served as dessert.

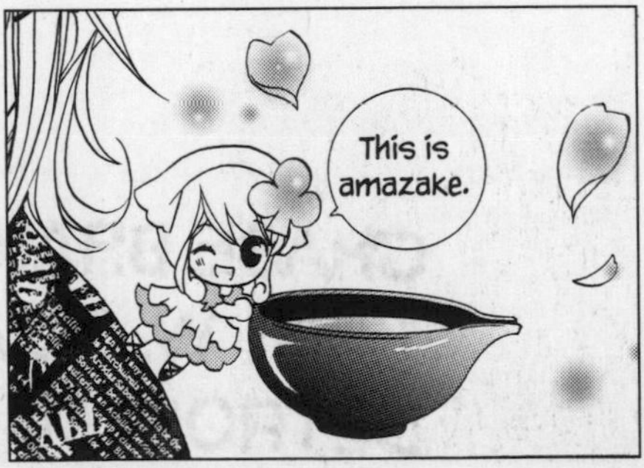
This is amazake.

TOMARE!

[STOP!]

You're going the wrong way!

Manga is a completely
different type of reading
experience.

To start at the *beginning,*
go to the *end!*

That's right! Authentic manga is read the traditional Japanese
way—from right to left. Exactly the *opposite* of how American
books are read. It's easy to follow: Just go to the other end of the
book, and read each page—and each panel—from right side to left
side, starting at the top right. Now you're experiencing manga as it
was meant to be!